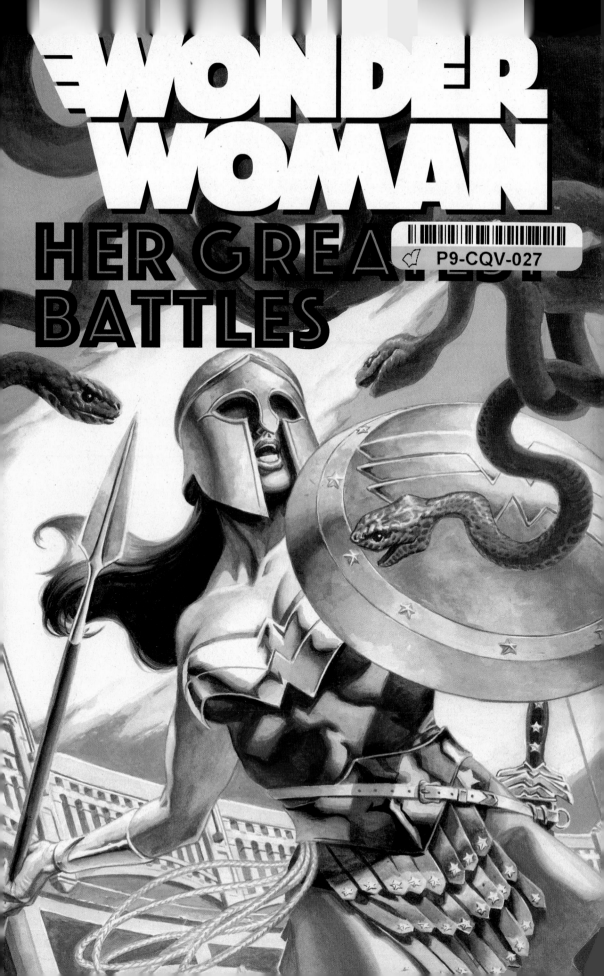

WONDER WOMAN™

HER GREATEST BATTLES

WONDER WOMAN: HER GREATEST BATTLES

DC Comics, 2900 West Alameda Ave, Burbank, CA 91505
Printed by Solisco Printers, Scott, QC, Canada. 1/6/17. First Printing.
ISBN: 978-1-4012-6897-8

Library of Congress Cataloging-in-Publication Data is available.

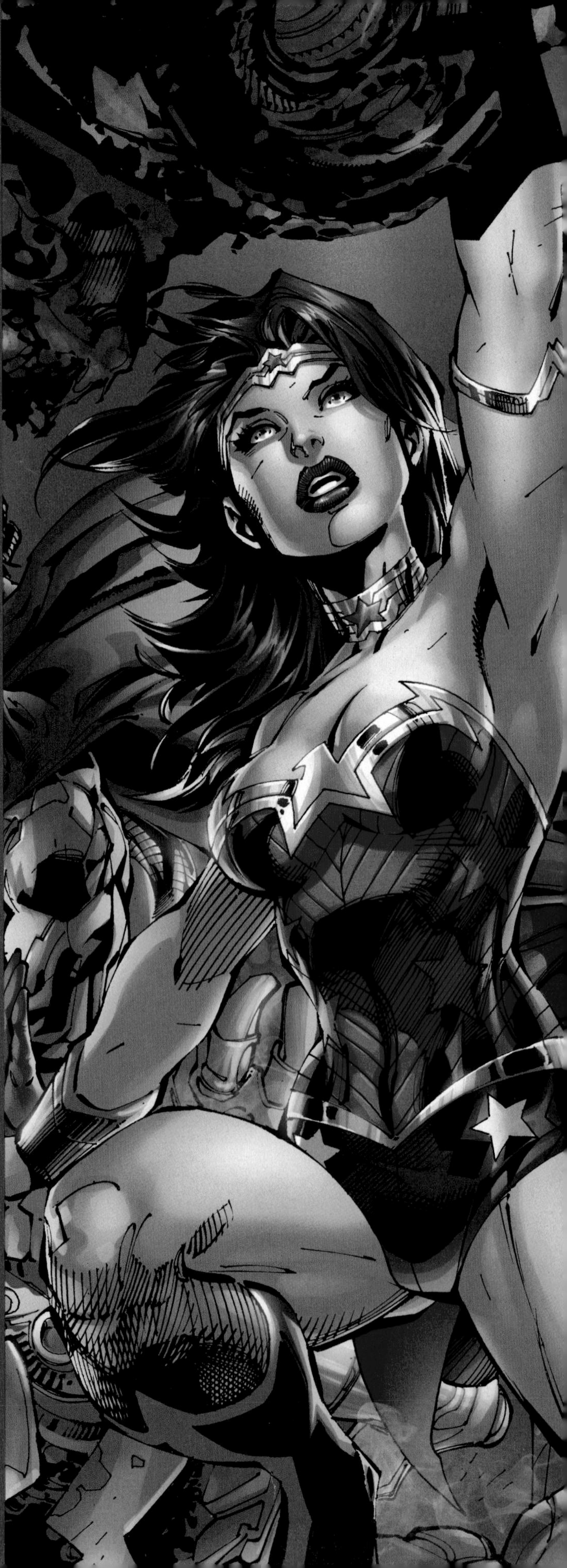

WONDER WOMAN™

HER GREATEST BATTLES

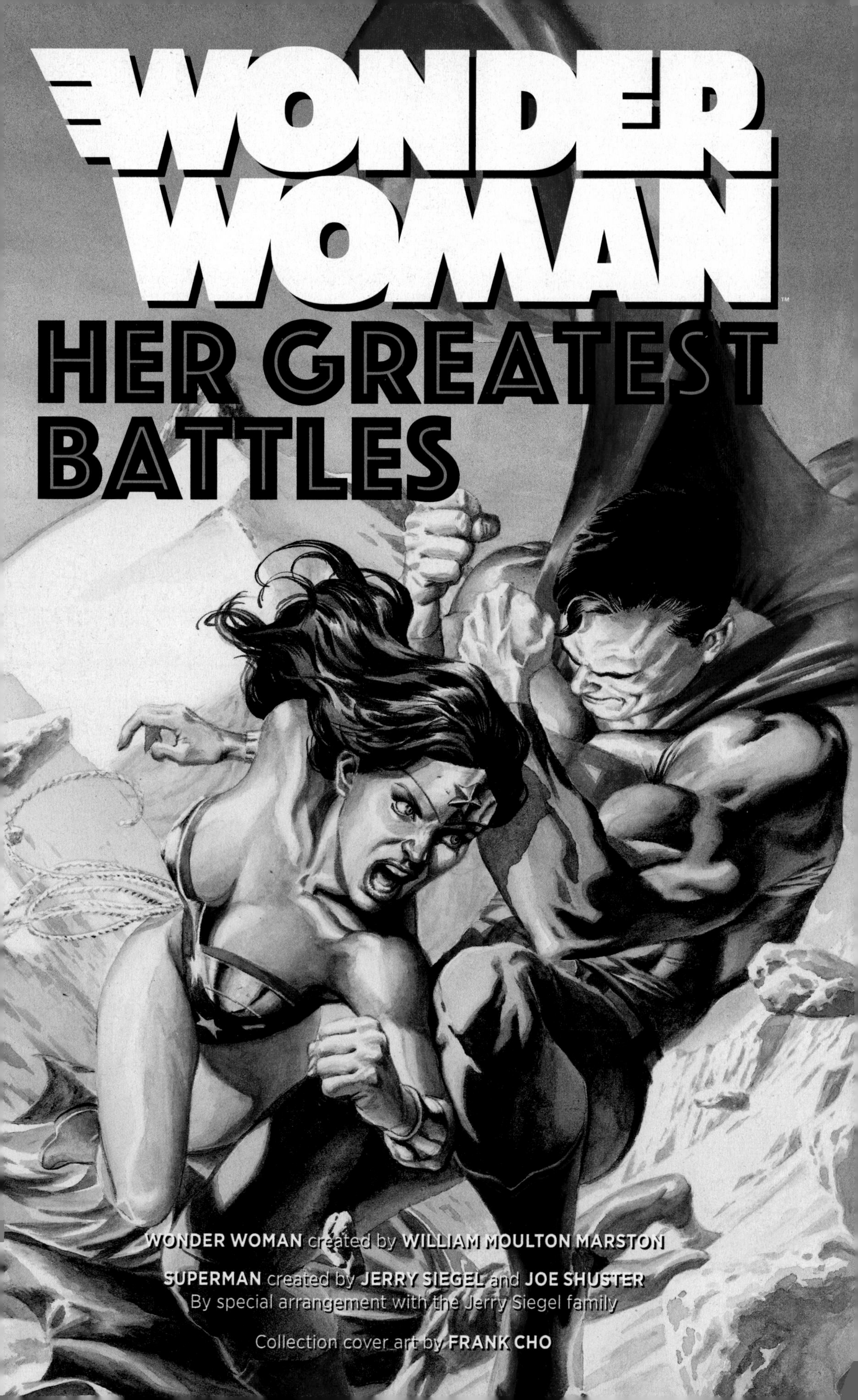

WONDER WOMAN created by **WILLIAM MOULTON MARSTON**

SUPERMAN created by **JERRY SIEGEL** and **JOE SHUSTER**
By special arrangement with the Jerry Siegel family

Collection cover art by **FRANK CHO**

TABLE OF CONTENTS

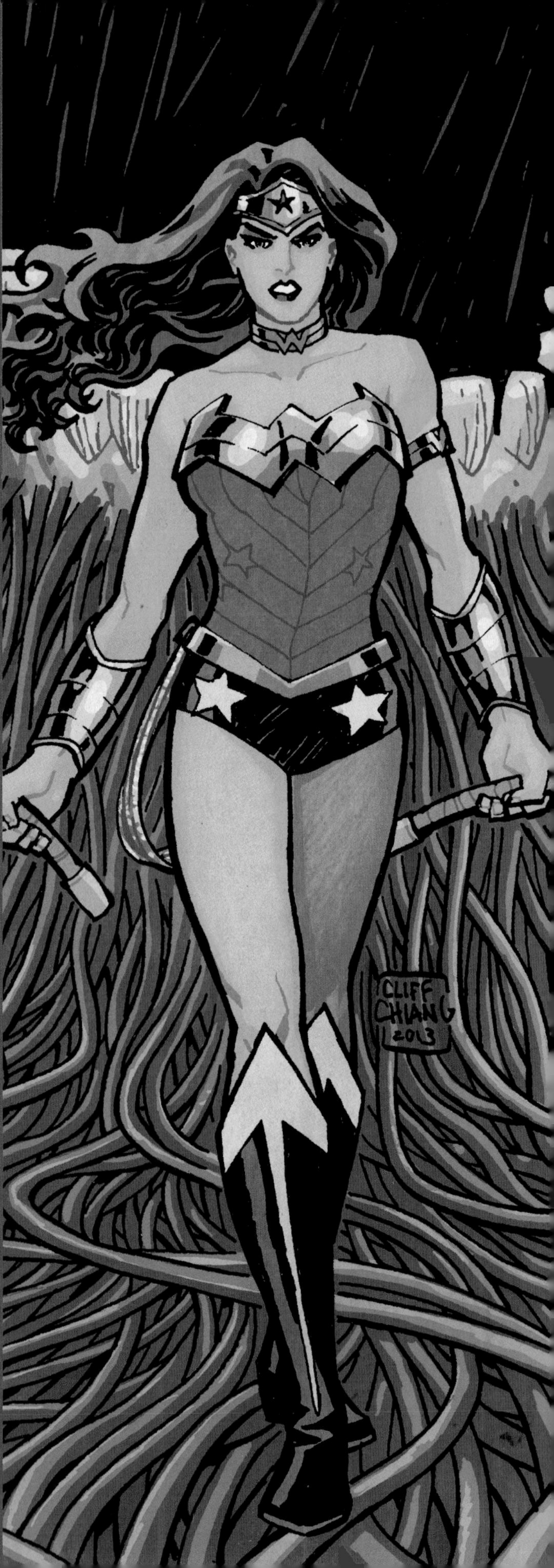

CLIFF CHIANG 2013

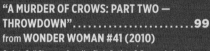

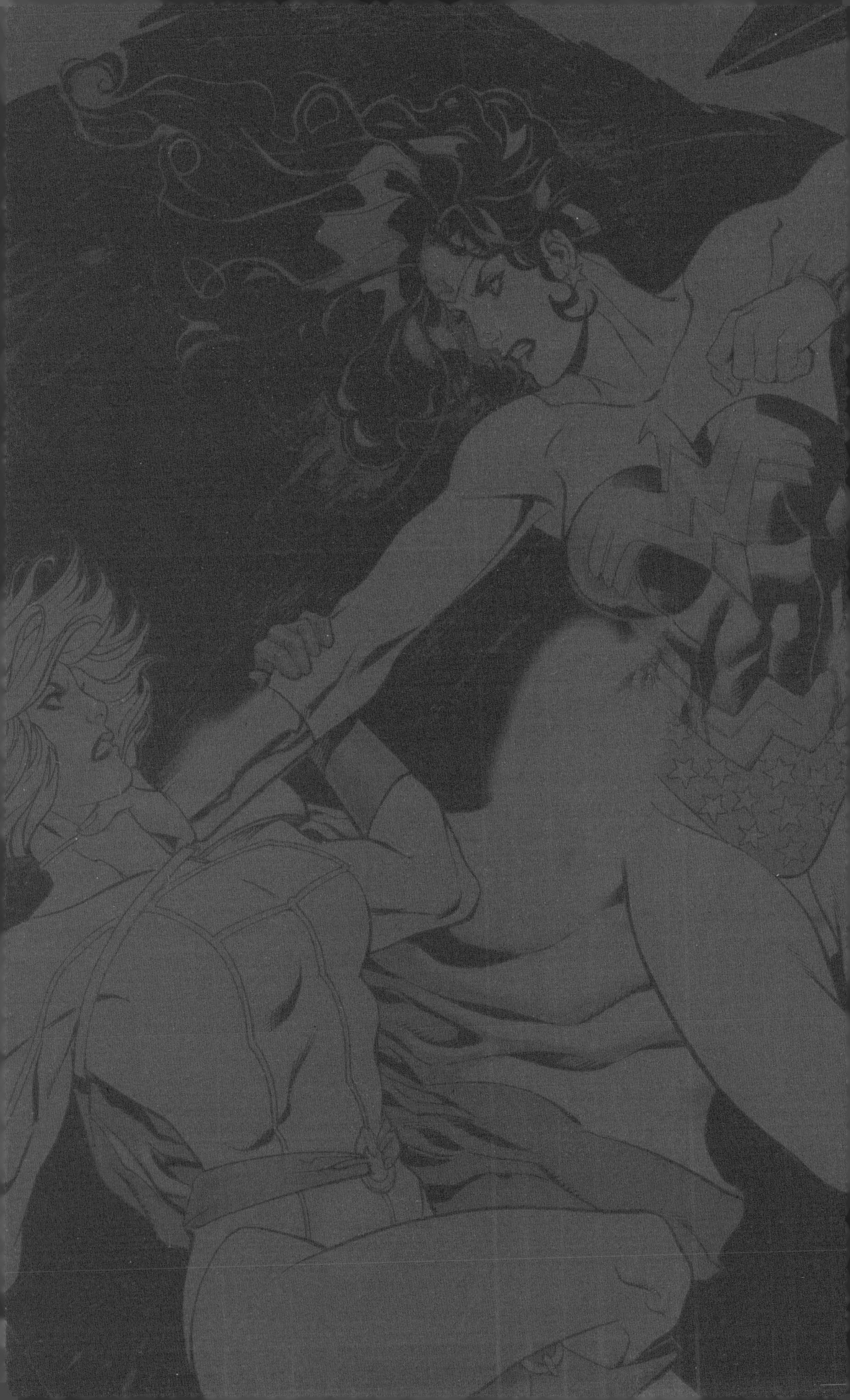

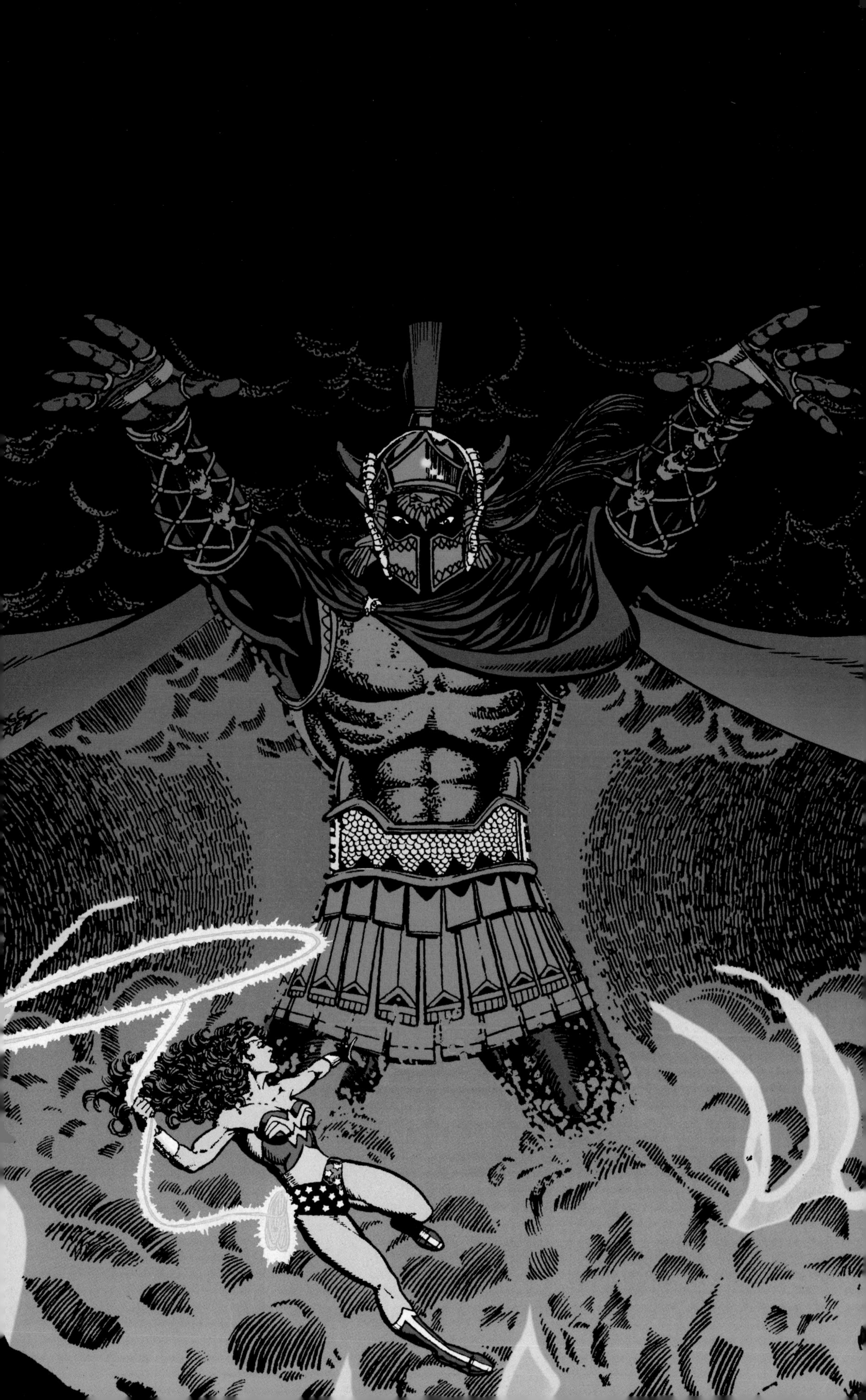

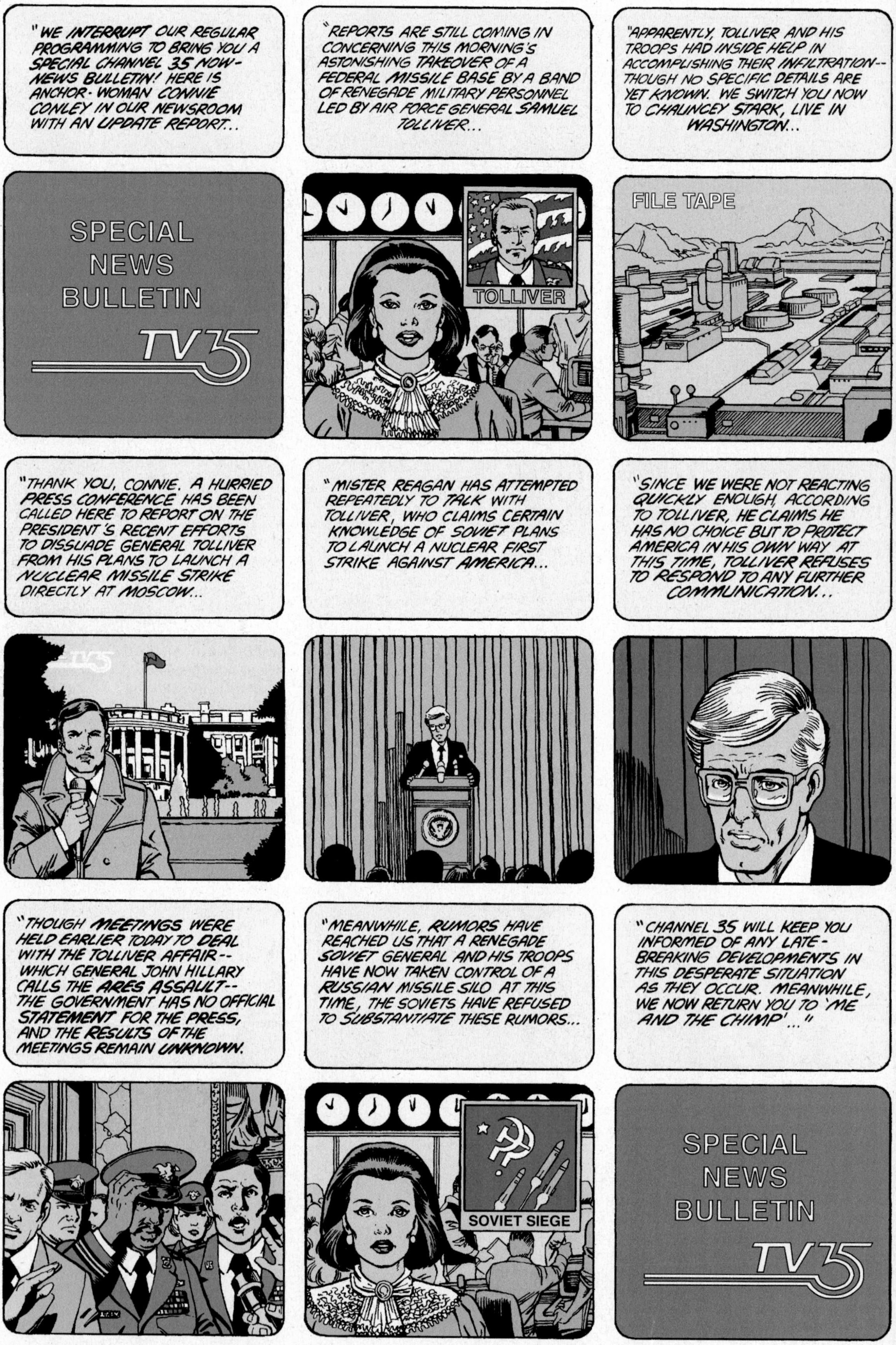
"WE INTERRUPT OUR REGULAR PROGRAMMING TO BRING YOU A SPECIAL CHANNEL 35 NOW-NEWS BULLETIN! HERE IS ANCHOR-WOMAN CONNIE CONLEY IN OUR NEWSROOM WITH AN UPDATE REPORT...
"REPORTS ARE STILL COMING IN CONCERNING THIS MORNING'S ASTONISHING TAKEOVER OF A FEDERAL MISSILE BASE BY A BAND OF RENEGADE MILITARY PERSONNEL LED BY AIR FORCE GENERAL SAMUEL TOLLIVER...
"APPARENTLY, TOLLIVER AND HIS TROOPS HAD INSIDE HELP IN ACCOMPLISHING THEIR INFILTRATION-- THOUGH NO SPECIFIC DETAILS ARE YET KNOWN. WE SWITCH YOU NOW TO CHAUNCEY STARK, LIVE IN WASHINGTON...
SPECIAL NEWS BULLETIN
TV35
TOLLIVER
FILE TAPE
"THANK YOU, CONNIE. A HURRIED PRESS CONFERENCE HAS BEEN CALLED HERE TO REPORT ON THE PRESIDENT'S RECENT EFFORTS TO DISSUADE GENERAL TOLLIVER FROM HIS PLANS TO LAUNCH A NUCLEAR MISSILE STRIKE DIRECTLY AT MOSCOW...
"MISTER REAGAN HAS ATTEMPTED REPEATEDLY TO TALK WITH TOLLIVER, WHO CLAIMS CERTAIN KNOWLEDGE OF SOVIET PLANS TO LAUNCH A NUCLEAR FIRST STRIKE AGAINST AMERICA...
"SINCE WE WERE NOT REACTING QUICKLY ENOUGH, ACCORDING TO TOLLIVER, HE CLAIMS HE HAS NO CHOICE BUT TO PROTECT AMERICA IN HIS OWN WAY. AT THIS TIME, TOLLIVER REFUSES TO RESPOND TO ANY FURTHER COMMUNICATION...
TV35
"THOUGH MEETINGS WERE HELD EARLIER TODAY TO DEAL WITH THE TOLLIVER AFFAIR-- WHICH GENERAL JOHN HILLARY CALLS THE ARES ASSAULT-- THE GOVERNMENT HAS NO OFFICIAL STATEMENT FOR THE PRESS, AND THE RESULTS OF THE MEETINGS REMAIN UNKNOWN.
"MEANWHILE, RUMORS HAVE REACHED US THAT A RENEGADE SOVIET GENERAL AND HIS TROOPS HAVE NOW TAKEN CONTROL OF A RUSSIAN MISSILE SILO. AT THIS TIME, THE SOVIETS HAVE REFUSED TO SUBSTANTIATE THESE RUMORS...
"CHANNEL 35 WILL KEEP YOU INFORMED OF ANY LATE-BREAKING DEVELOPMENTS IN THIS DESPERATE SITUATION AS THEY OCCUR. MEANWHILE, WE NOW RETURN YOU TO 'ME AND THE CHIMP'..."
SOVIET SIEGE
SPECIAL NEWS BULLETIN
TV35

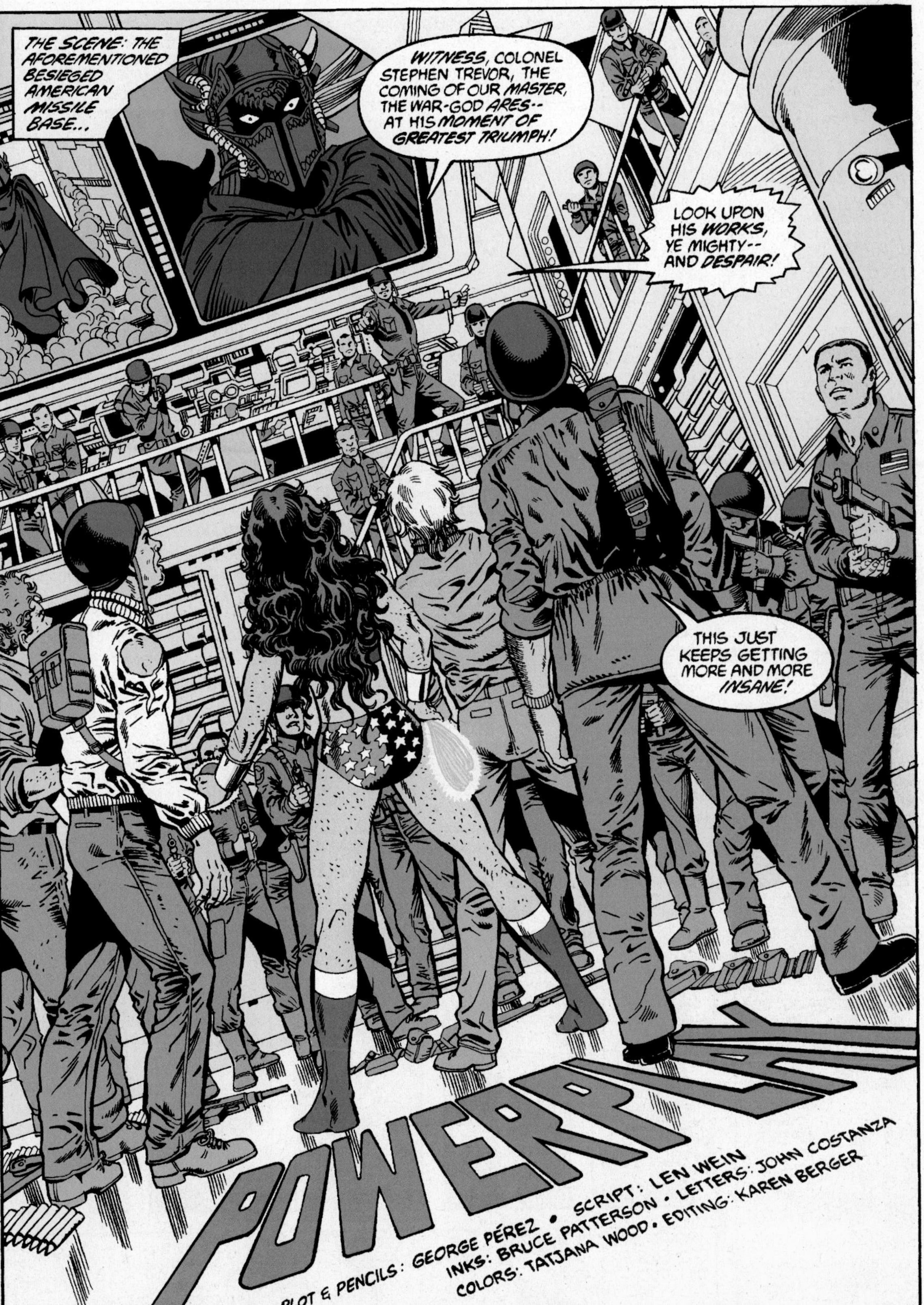
THE SCENE: THE AFOREMENTIONED BESIEGED AMERICAN MISSILE BASE...
WITNESS, COLONEL STEPHEN TREVOR, THE COMING OF OUR MASTER, THE WAR-GOD ARES-- AT HIS MOMENT OF GREATEST TRIUMPH!
LOOK UPON HIS WORKS, YE MIGHTY-- AND DESPAIR!
THIS JUST KEEPS GETTING MORE AND MORE INSANE!
POWERPLAY
PLOT & PENCILS: GEORGE PÉREZ • SCRIPT: LEN WEIN
INKS: BRUCE PATTERSON • LETTERS: JOHN COSTANZA
COLORS: TATJANA WOOD • EDITING: KAREN BERGER

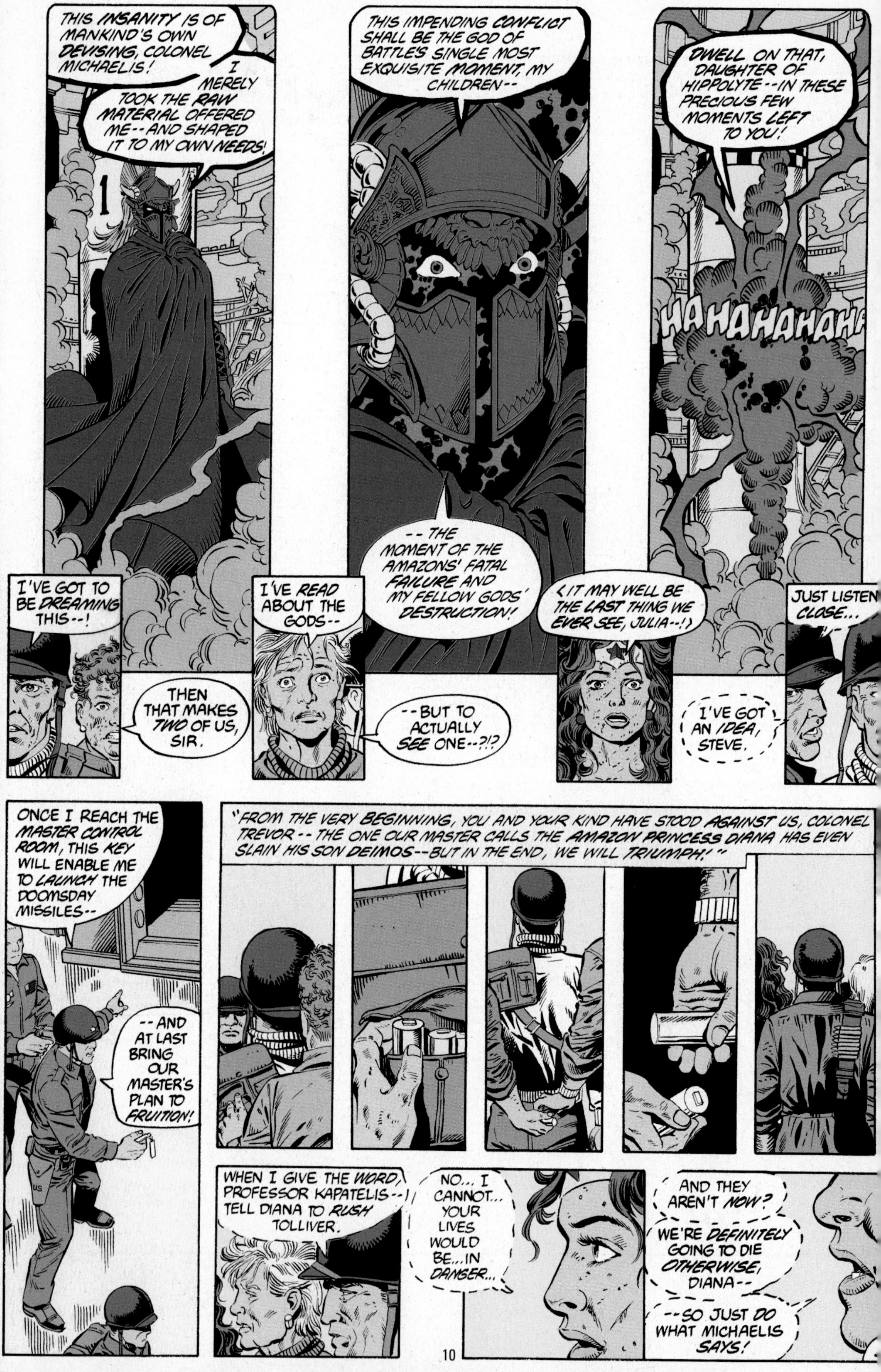
THIS INSANITY IS OF MANKIND'S OWN DEVISING, COLONEL MICHAELIS!
I MERELY TOOK THE RAW MATERIAL OFFERED ME--AND SHAPED IT TO MY OWN NEEDS!
1
THIS IMPENDING CONFLICT SHALL BE THE GOD OF BATTLE'S SINGLE MOST EXQUISITE MOMENT, MY CHILDREN--
--THE MOMENT OF THE AMAZONS' FATAL FAILURE AND MY FELLOW GODS' DESTRUCTION!
DWELL ON THAT, DAUGHTER OF HIPPOLYTE--IN THESE PRECIOUS FEW MOMENTS LEFT TO YOU!
HAHAHAHAHAH
I'VE GOT TO BE DREAMING THIS--!
THEN THAT MAKES TWO OF US, SIR.
I'VE READ ABOUT THE GODS--
--BUT TO ACTUALLY SEE ONE--?!?
<IT MAY WELL BE THE LAST THING WE EVER SEE, JULIA--!>
I'VE GOT AN IDEA, STEVE.
JUST LISTEN CLOSE...
ONCE I REACH THE MASTER CONTROL ROOM, THIS KEY WILL ENABLE ME TO LAUNCH THE DOOMSDAY MISSILES--
--AND AT LAST BRING OUR MASTER'S PLAN TO FRUITION!
"FROM THE VERY BEGINNING, YOU AND YOUR KIND HAVE STOOD AGAINST US, COLONEL TREVOR--THE ONE OUR MASTER CALLS THE AMAZON PRINCESS DIANA HAS EVEN SLAIN HIS SON DEIMOS--BUT IN THE END, WE WILL TRIUMPH!"
US
WHEN I GIVE THE WORD, PROFESSOR KAPATELIS--TELL DIANA TO RUSH TOLLIVER.
NO... I CANNOT... YOUR LIVES WOULD BE...IN DANGER...
AND THEY AREN'T NOW?
WE'RE DEFINITELY GOING TO DIE OTHERWISE, DIANA--
--SO JUST DO WHAT MICHAELIS SAYS!

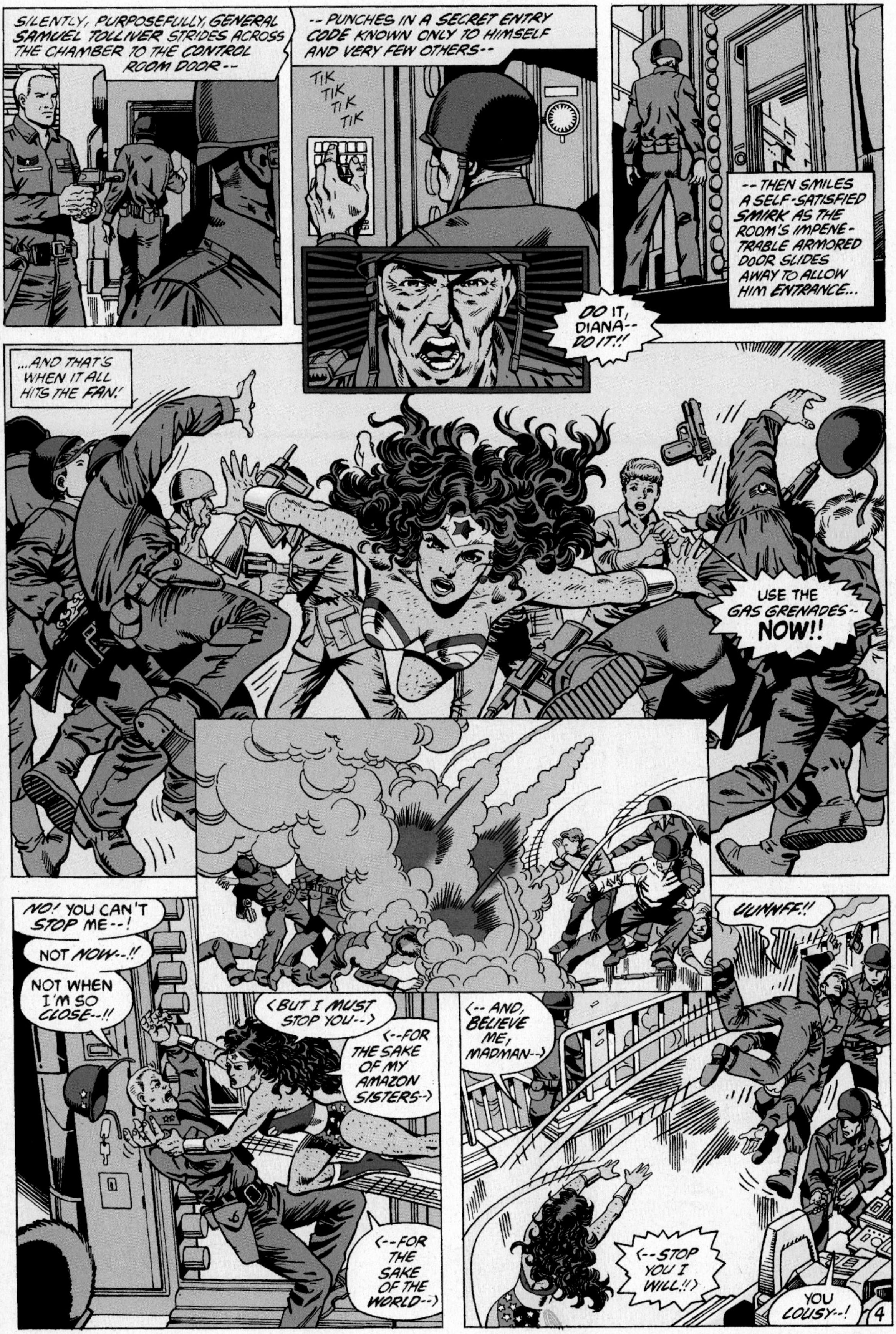

SILENTLY, PURPOSEFULLY, GENERAL SAMUEL TOLLIVER STRIDES ACROSS THE CHAMBER TO THE CONTROL ROOM DOOR--
--PUNCHES IN A SECRET ENTRY CODE KNOWN ONLY TO HIMSELF AND VERY FEW OTHERS--
TIK TIK TIK TIK
--THEN SMILES A SELF-SATISFIED SMIRK AS THE ROOM'S IMPENETRABLE ARMORED DOOR SLIDES AWAY TO ALLOW HIM ENTRANCE...
DO IT, DIANA-- DO IT!!
...AND THAT'S WHEN IT ALL HITS THE FAN!
USE THE GAS GRENADES-- NOW!!
NO! YOU CAN'T STOP ME--!
NOT NOW--!!
NOT WHEN I'M SO CLOSE--!!
<BUT I MUST STOP YOU-->
<--FOR THE SAKE OF MY AMAZON SISTERS-->
<--FOR THE SAKE OF THE WORLD-->
<--AND, BELIEVE ME, MADMAN-->
UUNNFF!!
<--STOP YOU I WILL!!>
YOU LOUSY--!
4

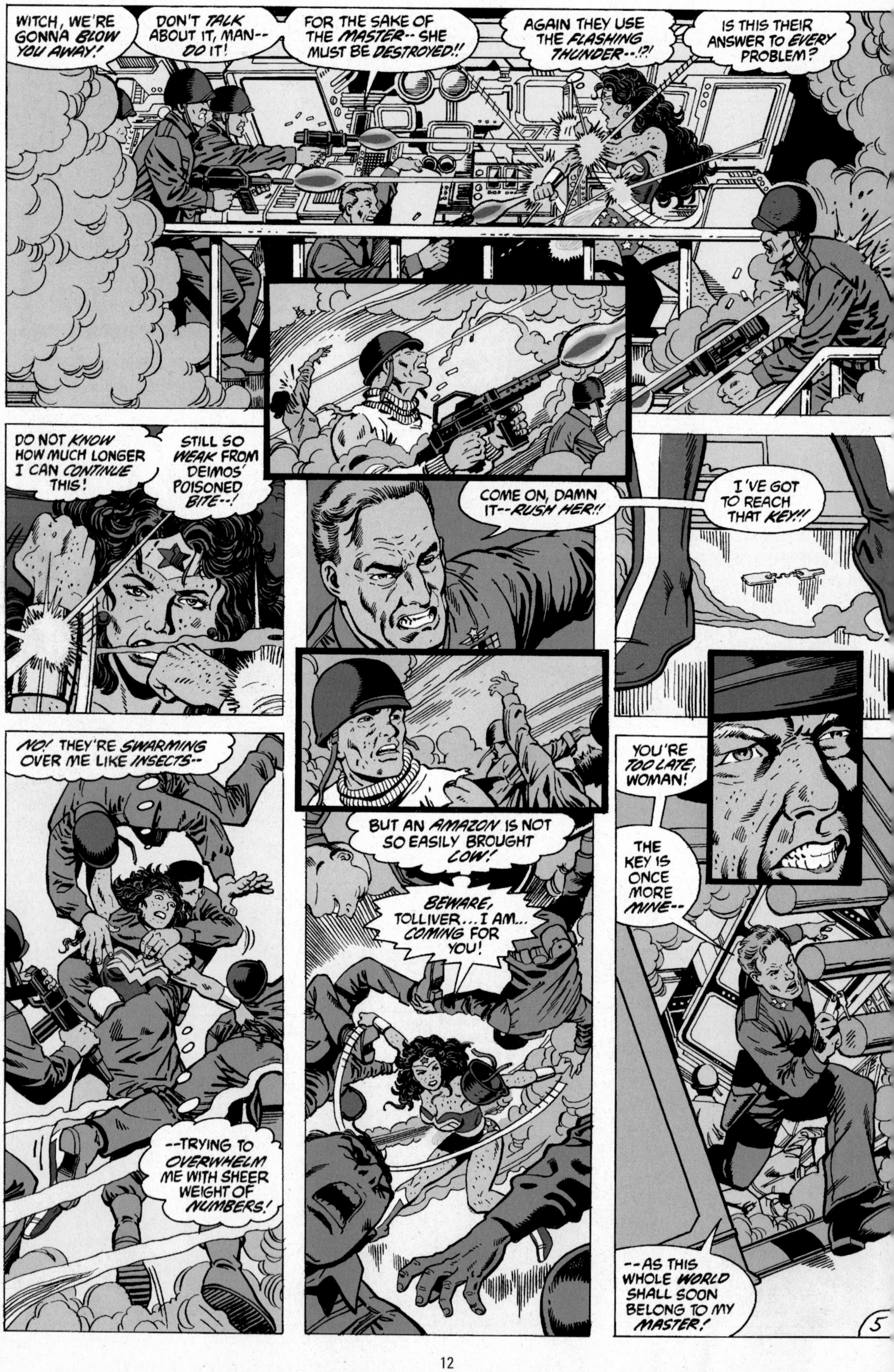
WITCH, WE'RE GONNA BLOW YOU AWAY!
DON'T TALK ABOUT IT, MAN-- DO IT!
FOR THE SAKE OF THE MASTER-- SHE MUST BE DESTROYED!!
AGAIN THEY USE THE FLASHING THUNDER--!?!
IS THIS THEIR ANSWER TO EVERY PROBLEM?
DO NOT KNOW HOW MUCH LONGER I CAN CONTINUE THIS!
STILL SO WEAK FROM DEIMOS' POISONED BITE--!
COME ON, DAMN IT--RUSH HER!!
I'VE GOT TO REACH THAT KEY!!
NO! THEY'RE SWARMING OVER ME LIKE INSECTS--
--TRYING TO OVERWHELM ME WITH SHEER WEIGHT OF NUMBERS!
BUT AN AMAZON IS NOT SO EASILY BROUGHT LOW!
BEWARE, TOLLIVER... I AM... COMING FOR YOU!
YOU'RE TOO LATE, WOMAN!
THE KEY IS ONCE MORE MINE--
--AS THIS WHOLE WORLD SHALL SOON BELONG TO MY MASTER!
5

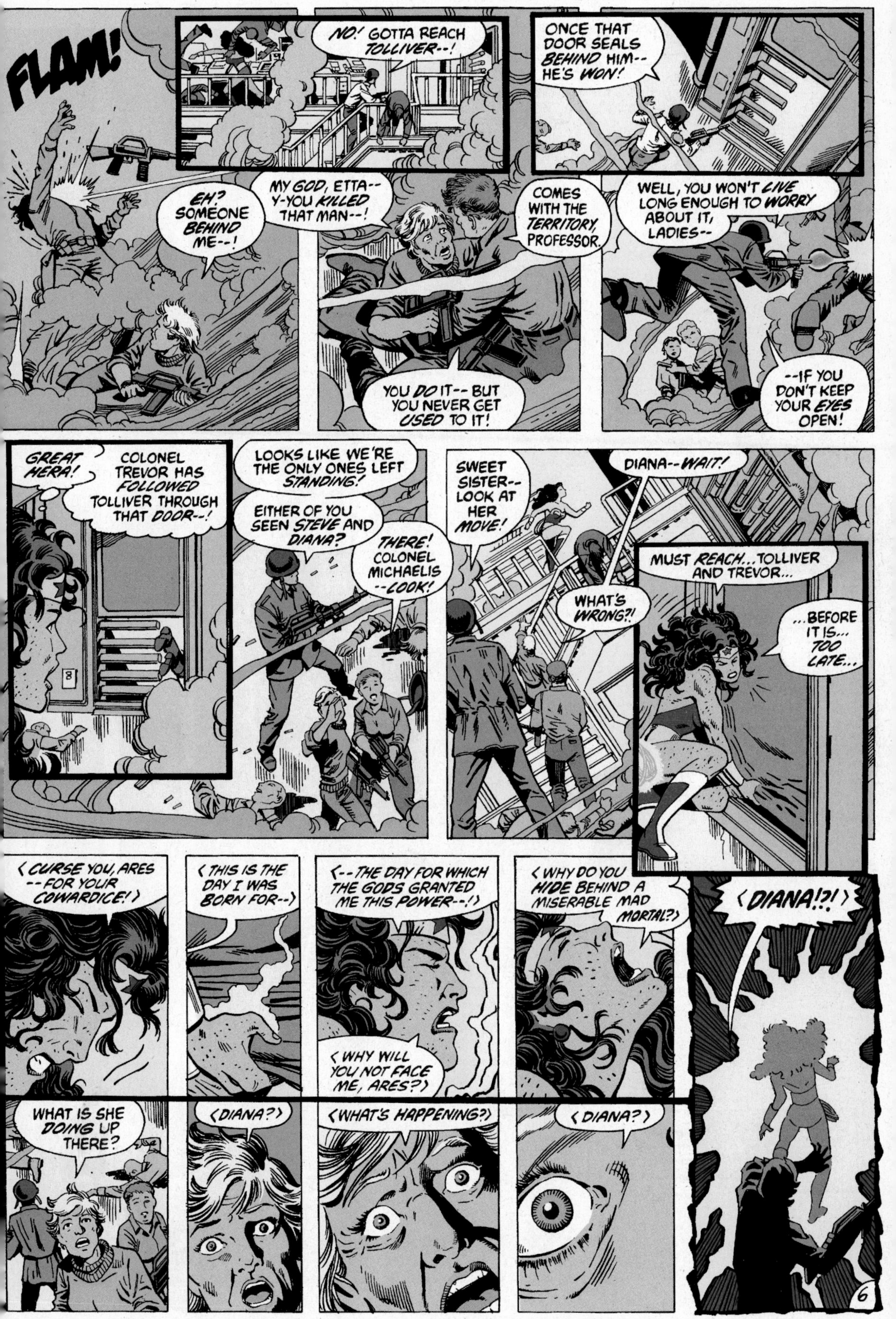
FLAM!
NO! GOTTA REACH TOLLIVER--!
ONCE THAT DOOR SEALS BEHIND HIM-- HE'S WON!
EH? SOMEONE BEHIND ME--!
MY GOD, ETTA-- Y-YOU KILLED THAT MAN--!
COMES WITH THE TERRITORY, PROFESSOR.
YOU DO IT-- BUT YOU NEVER GET USED TO IT!
WELL, YOU WON'T LIVE LONG ENOUGH TO WORRY ABOUT IT, LADIES--
--IF YOU DON'T KEEP YOUR EYES OPEN!
GREAT HERA!
COLONEL TREVOR HAS FOLLOWED TOLLIVER THROUGH THAT DOOR--!
LOOKS LIKE WE'RE THE ONLY ONES LEFT STANDING!
EITHER OF YOU SEEN STEVE AND DIANA?
THERE! COLONEL MICHAELIS --LOOK!
SWEET SISTER-- LOOK AT HER MOVE!
DIANA--WAIT!
WHAT'S WRONG?!
MUST REACH... TOLLIVER AND TREVOR...
...BEFORE IT IS... TOO LATE...
‹CURSE YOU, ARES --FOR YOUR COWARDICE!›
‹THIS IS THE DAY I WAS BORN FOR--›
‹--THE DAY FOR WHICH THE GODS GRANTED ME THIS POWER--!›
‹WHY WILL YOU NOT FACE ME, ARES?›
‹WHY DO YOU HIDE BEHIND A MISERABLE MAD MORTAL?›
‹DIANA!?!›
WHAT IS SHE DOING UP THERE?
‹DIANA?›
‹WHAT'S HAPPENING?›
‹DIANA?›
6

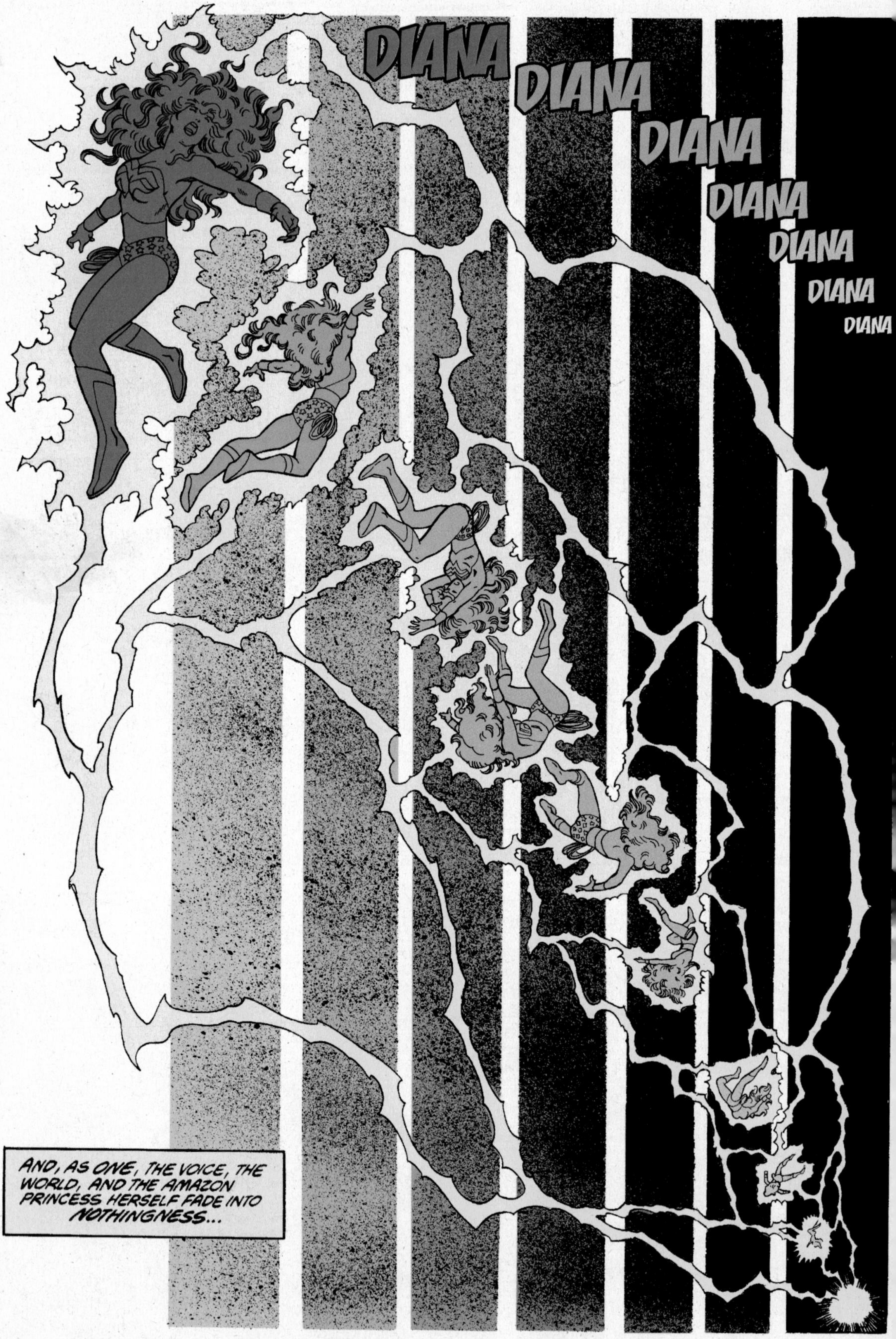
DIANA
DIANA
DIANA
DIANA
DIANA
DIANA
DIANA
AND, AS ONE, THE VOICE, THE WORLD, AND THE AMAZON PRINCESS HERSELF FADE INTO NOTHINGNESS...

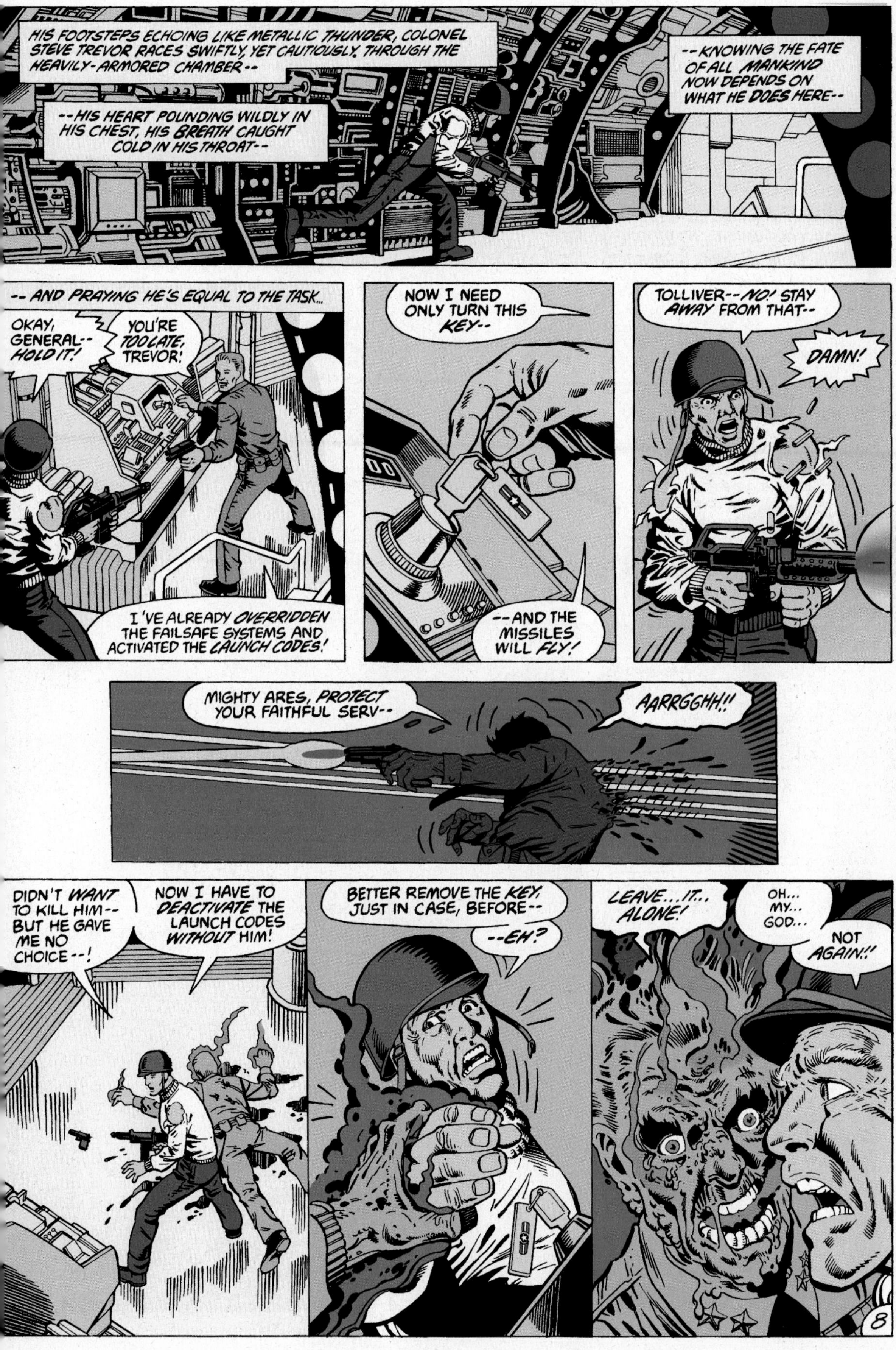

HIS FOOTSTEPS ECHOING LIKE METALLIC THUNDER, COLONEL STEVE TREVOR RACES SWIFTLY, YET CAUTIOUSLY, THROUGH THE HEAVILY-ARMORED CHAMBER--
--HIS HEART POUNDING WILDLY IN HIS CHEST, HIS BREATH CAUGHT COLD IN HIS THROAT--
--KNOWING THE FATE OF ALL MANKIND NOW DEPENDS ON WHAT HE DOES HERE--
--AND PRAYING HE'S EQUAL TO THE TASK...
OKAY, GENERAL--HOLD IT!
YOU'RE TOO LATE, TREVOR!
I'VE ALREADY OVERRIDDEN THE FAILSAFE SYSTEMS AND ACTIVATED THE LAUNCH CODES!
NOW I NEED ONLY TURN THIS KEY--
--AND THE MISSILES WILL FLY!
TOLLIVER--NO! STAY AWAY FROM THAT--
DAMN!
MIGHTY ARES, PROTECT YOUR FAITHFUL SERV--
AARRGGHH!!
DIDN'T WANT TO KILL HIM--BUT HE GAVE ME NO CHOICE--!
NOW I HAVE TO DEACTIVATE THE LAUNCH CODES WITHOUT HIM!
BETTER REMOVE THE KEY, JUST IN CASE, BEFORE--
--EH?
LEAVE... IT... ALONE!
OH... MY... GOD...
NOT AGAIN!!
8

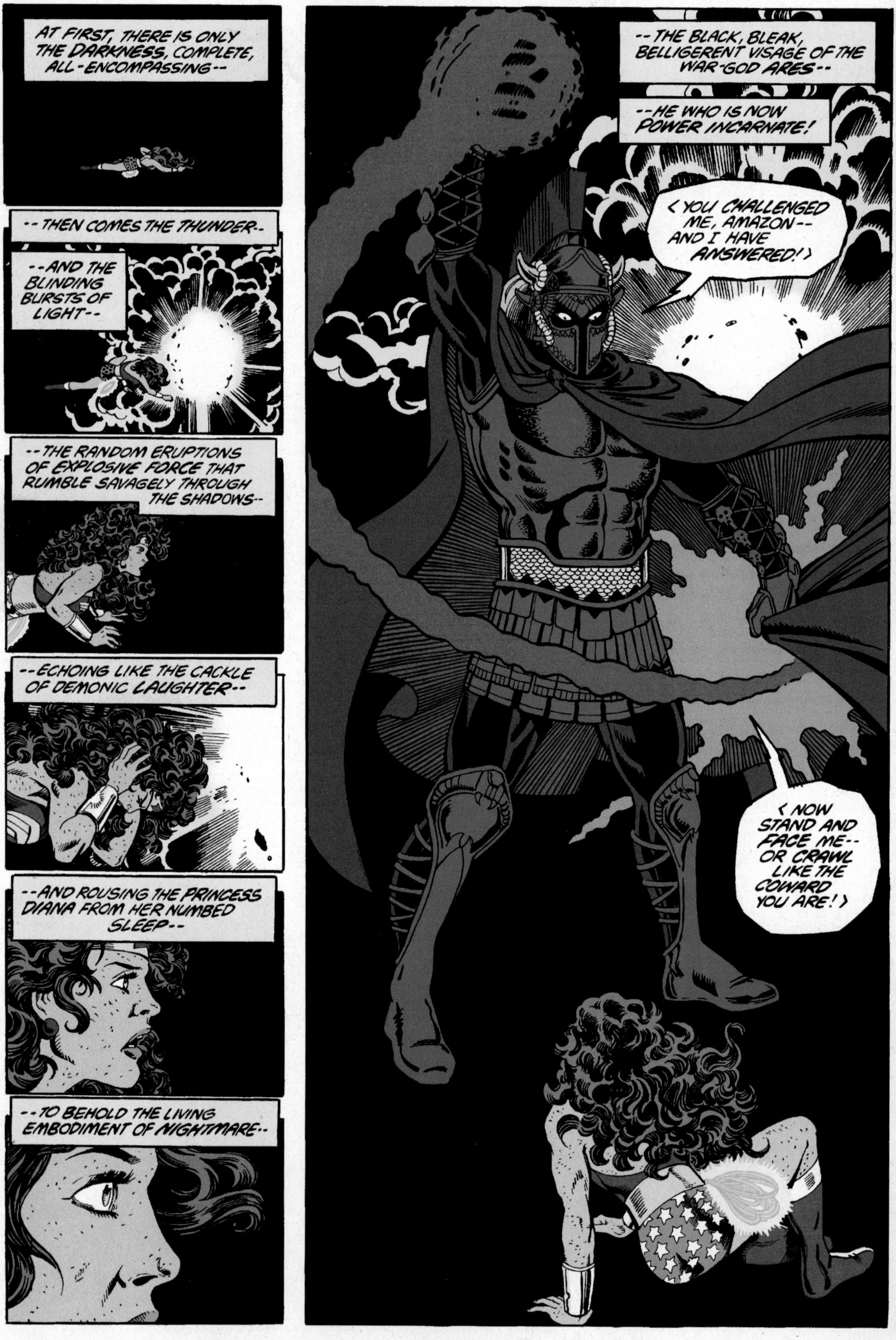
AT FIRST, THERE IS ONLY THE DARKNESS, COMPLETE, ALL-ENCOMPASSING--
--THEN COMES THE THUNDER--
--AND THE BLINDING BURSTS OF LIGHT--
--THE RANDOM ERUPTIONS OF EXPLOSIVE FORCE THAT RUMBLE SAVAGELY THROUGH THE SHADOWS--
--ECHOING LIKE THE CACKLE OF DEMONIC LAUGHTER--
--AND ROUSING THE PRINCESS DIANA FROM HER NUMBED SLEEP--
--TO BEHOLD THE LIVING EMBODIMENT OF NIGHTMARE--
--THE BLACK, BLEAK, BELLIGERENT VISAGE OF THE WAR-GOD ARES--
--HE WHO IS NOW POWER INCARNATE!
<YOU CHALLENGED ME, AMAZON-- AND I HAVE ANSWERED!>
<NOW STAND AND FACE ME-- OR CRAWL LIKE THE COWARD YOU ARE!>

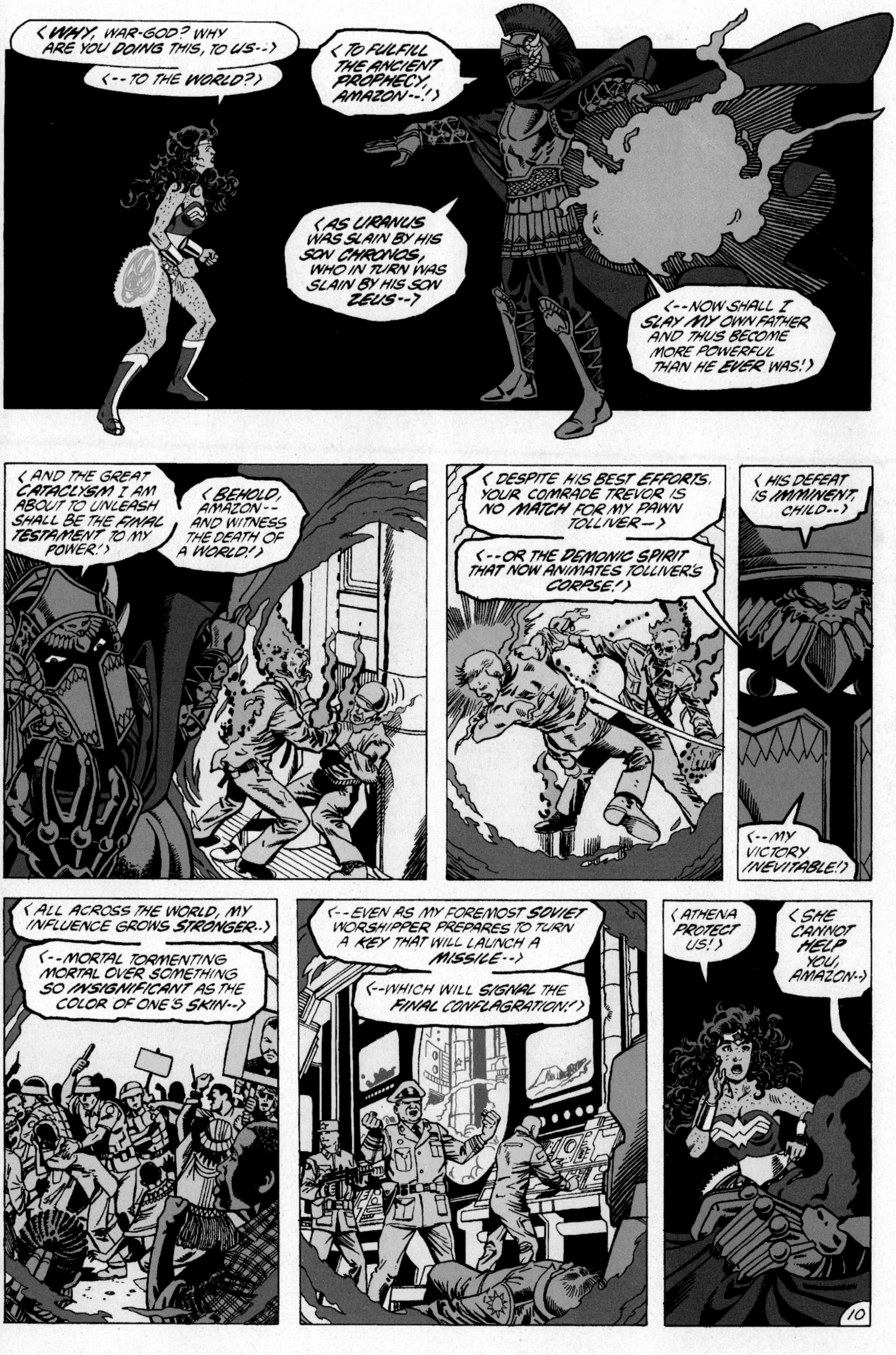

<WHY, WAR-GOD? WHY ARE YOU DOING THIS, TO US-->
<--TO THE WORLD?>
<TO FULFILL THE ANCIENT PROPHECY, AMAZON--!>
<AS URANUS WAS SLAIN BY HIS SON CHRONOS, WHO IN TURN WAS SLAIN BY HIS SON ZEUS-->
<--NOW SHALL I SLAY MY OWN FATHER AND THUS BECOME MORE POWERFUL THAN HE EVER WAS!>
<AND THE GREAT CATACLYSM I AM ABOUT TO UNLEASH SHALL BE THE FINAL TESTAMENT TO MY POWER!>
<BEHOLD, AMAZON-- AND WITNESS THE DEATH OF A WORLD!>
<DESPITE HIS BEST EFFORTS, YOUR COMRADE TREVOR IS NO MATCH FOR MY PAWN TOLLIVER-->
<--OR THE DEMONIC SPIRIT THAT NOW ANIMATES TOLLIVER'S CORPSE!>
<HIS DEFEAT IS IMMINENT, CHILD-->
<--MY VICTORY INEVITABLE!>
<ALL ACROSS THE WORLD, MY INFLUENCE GROWS STRONGER-->
<--MORTAL TORMENTING MORTAL OVER SOMETHING SO INSIGNIFICANT AS THE COLOR OF ONE'S SKIN-->
<--EVEN AS MY FOREMOST SOVIET WORSHIPPER PREPARES TO TURN A KEY THAT WILL LAUNCH A MISSILE-->
<--WHICH WILL SIGNAL THE FINAL CONFLAGRATION!>
<ATHENA PROTECT US!>
<SHE CANNOT HELP YOU, AMAZON-->
10

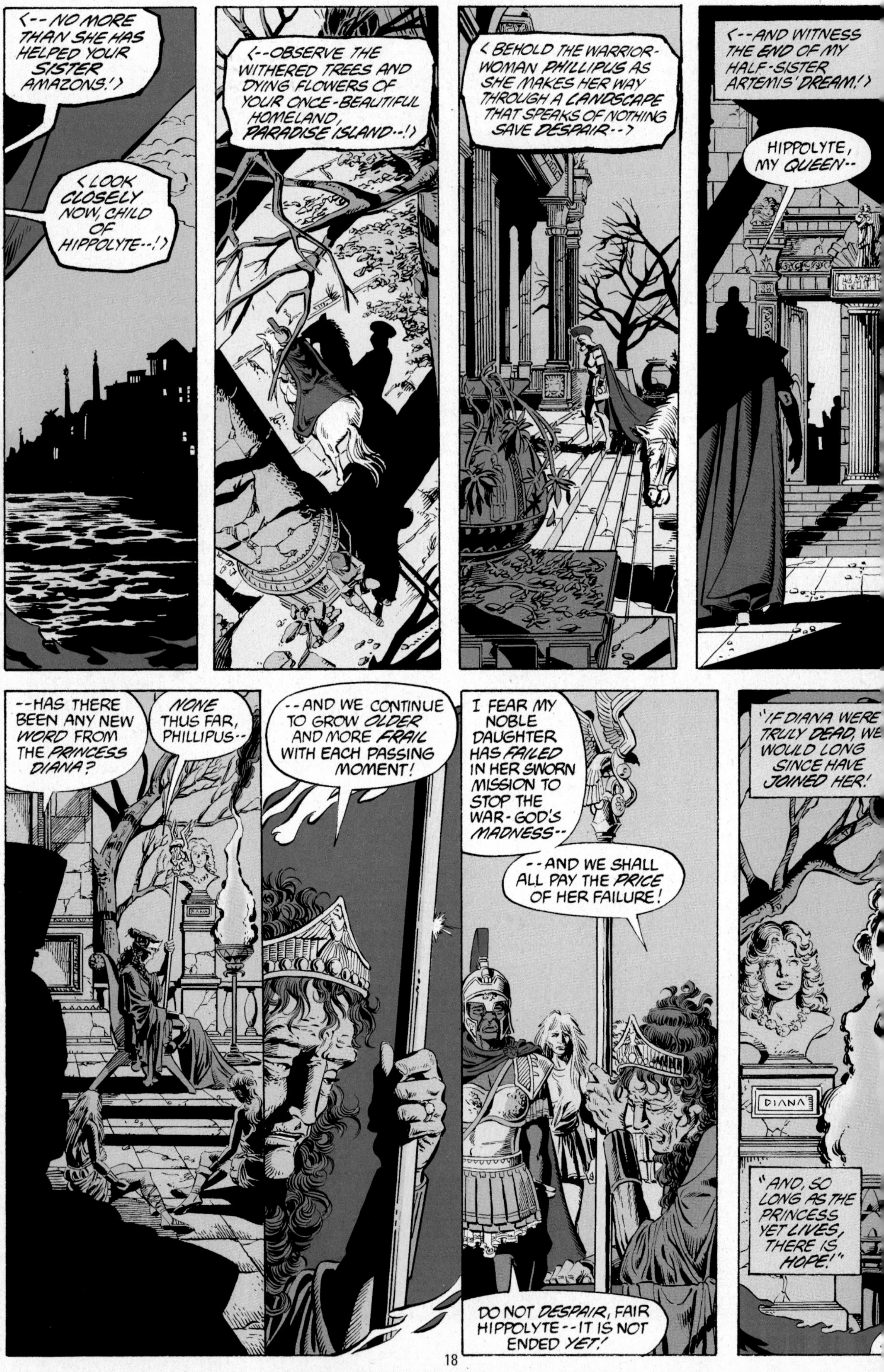
<--NO MORE THAN SHE HAS HELPED YOUR SISTER AMAZONS!>
<LOOK CLOSELY NOW, CHILD OF HIPPOLYTE--!>
<--OBSERVE THE WITHERED TREES AND DYING FLOWERS OF YOUR ONCE-BEAUTIFUL HOMELAND, PARADISE ISLAND--!>
<BEHOLD THE WARRIOR-WOMAN PHILLIPUS AS SHE MAKES HER WAY THROUGH A LANDSCAPE THAT SPEAKS OF NOTHING SAVE DESPAIR-->
<--AND WITNESS THE END OF MY HALF-SISTER ARTEMIS' DREAM!>
HIPPOLYTE, MY QUEEN--
--HAS THERE BEEN ANY NEW WORD FROM THE PRINCESS DIANA?
NONE THUS FAR, PHILLIPUS--
--AND WE CONTINUE TO GROW OLDER AND MORE FRAIL WITH EACH PASSING MOMENT!
I FEAR MY NOBLE DAUGHTER HAS FAILED IN HER SWORN MISSION TO STOP THE WAR-GOD'S MADNESS--
--AND WE SHALL ALL PAY THE PRICE OF HER FAILURE!
DO NOT DESPAIR, FAIR HIPPOLYTE--IT IS NOT ENDED YET!
"IF DIANA WERE TRULY DEAD, WE WOULD LONG SINCE HAVE JOINED HER!
DIANA
"AND, SO LONG AS THE PRINCESS YET LIVES, THERE IS HOPE!"

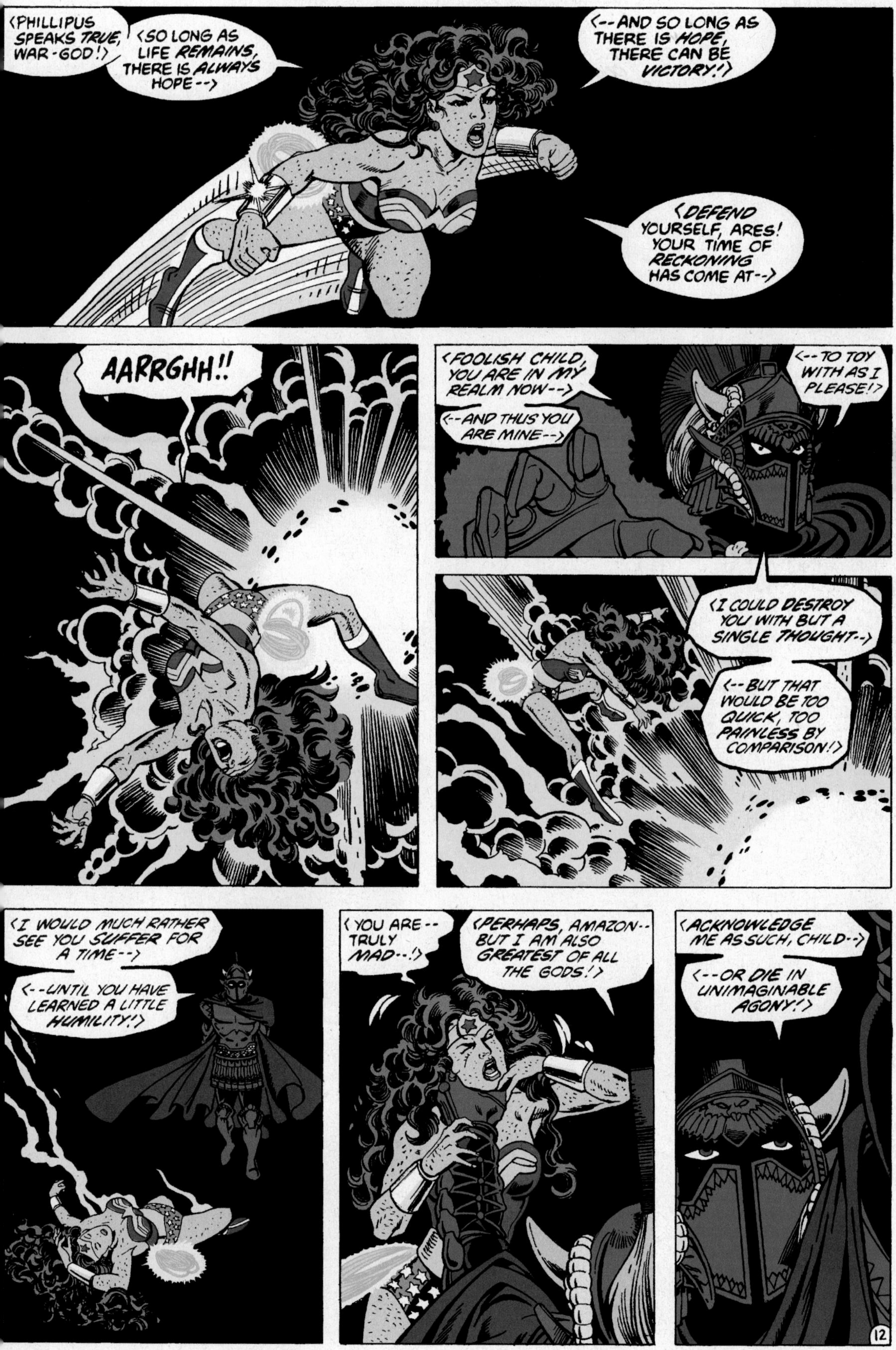

‹PHILLIPUS SPEAKS TRUE, WAR-GOD!›
‹SO LONG AS LIFE REMAINS, THERE IS ALWAYS HOPE--›
‹--AND SO LONG AS THERE IS HOPE, THERE CAN BE VICTORY!›
‹DEFEND YOURSELF, ARES! YOUR TIME OF RECKONING HAS COME AT--›
AARRGHH!!
‹FOOLISH CHILD, YOU ARE IN MY REALM NOW--›
‹--AND THUS YOU ARE MINE--›
‹--TO TOY WITH AS I PLEASE!›
‹I COULD DESTROY YOU WITH BUT A SINGLE THOUGHT--›
‹--BUT THAT WOULD BE TOO QUICK, TOO PAINLESS BY COMPARISON!›
‹I WOULD MUCH RATHER SEE YOU SUFFER FOR A TIME--›
‹--UNTIL YOU HAVE LEARNED A LITTLE HUMILITY!›
‹YOU ARE--TRULY MAD--!›
‹PERHAPS, AMAZON--BUT I AM ALSO GREATEST OF ALL THE GODS!›
‹ACKNOWLEDGE ME AS SUCH, CHILD--›
‹--OR DIE IN UNIMAGINABLE AGONY!›
12

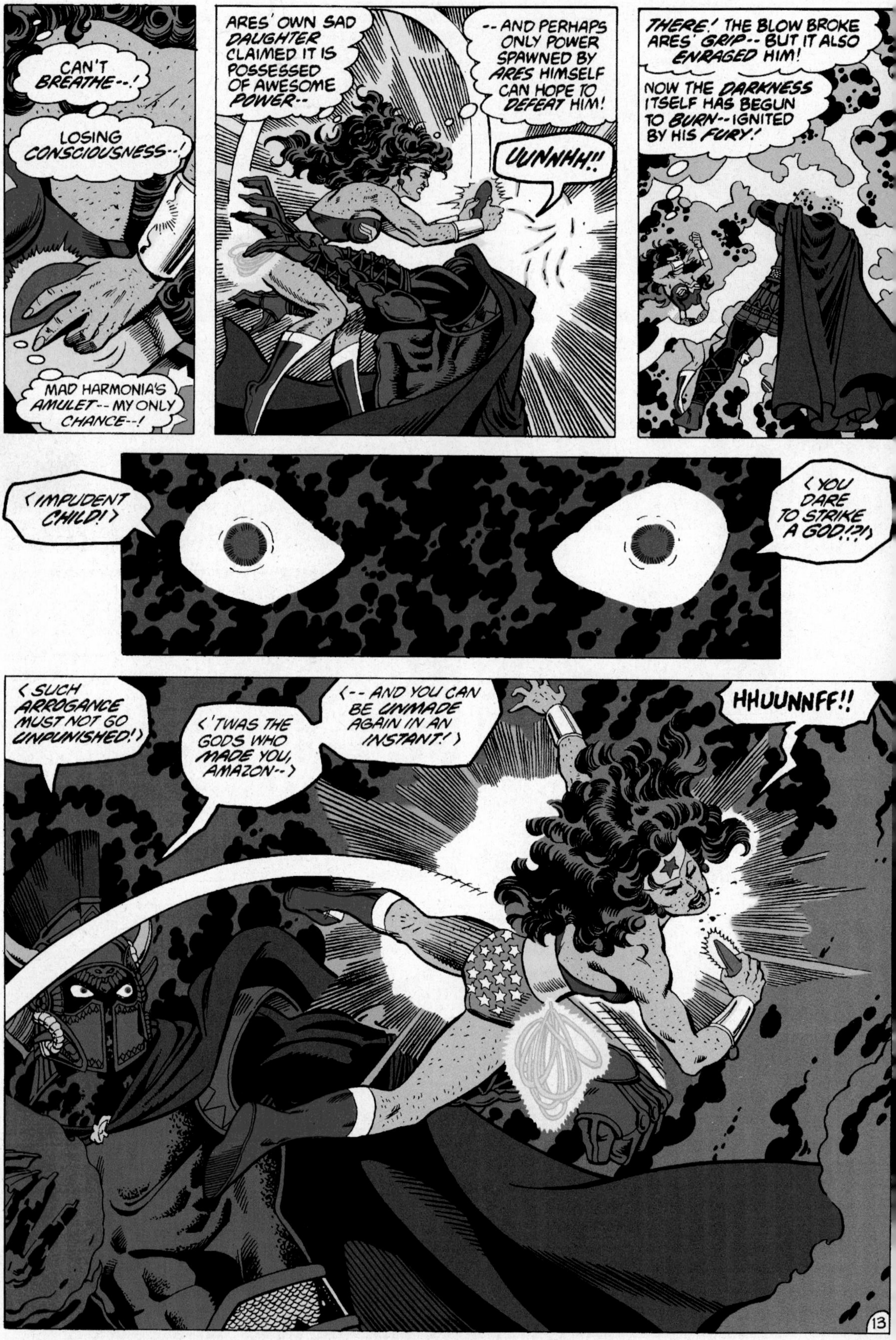

CAN'T BREATHE--!
LOSING CONSCIOUSNESS--!
MAD HARMONIA'S AMULET--MY ONLY CHANCE--!
ARES' OWN SAD DAUGHTER CLAIMED IT IS POSSESSED OF AWESOME POWER--
--AND PERHAPS ONLY POWER SPAWNED BY ARES HIMSELF CAN HOPE TO DEFEAT HIM!
UUNNHH!!
THERE! THE BLOW BROKE ARES' GRIP--BUT IT ALSO ENRAGED HIM!
NOW THE DARKNESS ITSELF HAS BEGUN TO BURN--IGNITED BY HIS FURY!
<IMPUDENT CHILD!>
<YOU DARE TO STRIKE A GOD!?!>
<SUCH ARROGANCE MUST NOT GO UNPUNISHED!>
<'TWAS THE GODS WHO MADE YOU, AMAZON-->
<--AND YOU CAN BE UNMADE AGAIN IN AN INSTANT!>
HHUUNNFF!!
13

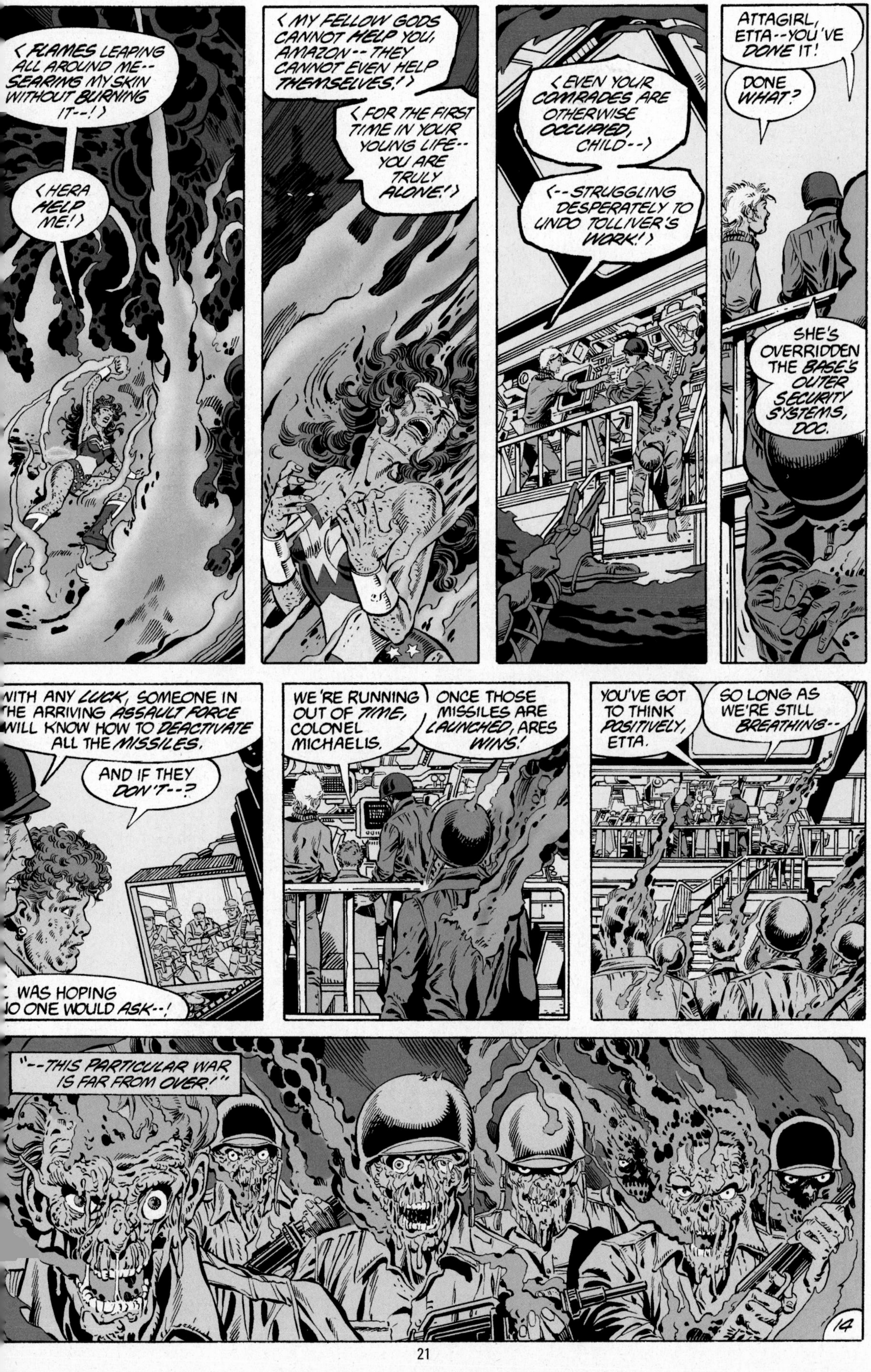
<FLAMES LEAPING ALL AROUND ME-- SEARING MY SKIN WITHOUT BURNING IT--!>
<HERA HELP ME!>
<MY FELLOW GODS CANNOT HELP YOU, AMAZON--THEY CANNOT EVEN HELP THEMSELVES!>
<FOR THE FIRST TIME IN YOUR YOUNG LIFE-- YOU ARE TRULY ALONE!>
<EVEN YOUR COMRADES ARE OTHERWISE OCCUPIED, CHILD-->
<--STRUGGLING DESPERATELY TO UNDO TOLLIVER'S WORK!>
ATTAGIRL, ETTA--YOU'VE DONE IT!
DONE WHAT?
SHE'S OVERRIDDEN THE BASE'S OUTER SECURITY SYSTEMS, DOC.
WITH ANY LUCK, SOMEONE IN THE ARRIVING ASSAULT FORCE WILL KNOW HOW TO DEACTIVATE ALL THE MISSILES.
AND IF THEY DON'T--?
WAS HOPING NO ONE WOULD ASK--!
WE'RE RUNNING OUT OF TIME, COLONEL MICHAELIS.
ONCE THOSE MISSILES ARE LAUNCHED, ARES WINS!
YOU'VE GOT TO THINK POSITIVELY, ETTA.
SO LONG AS WE'RE STILL BREATHING--
"--THIS PARTICULAR WAR IS FAR FROM OVER!"
14

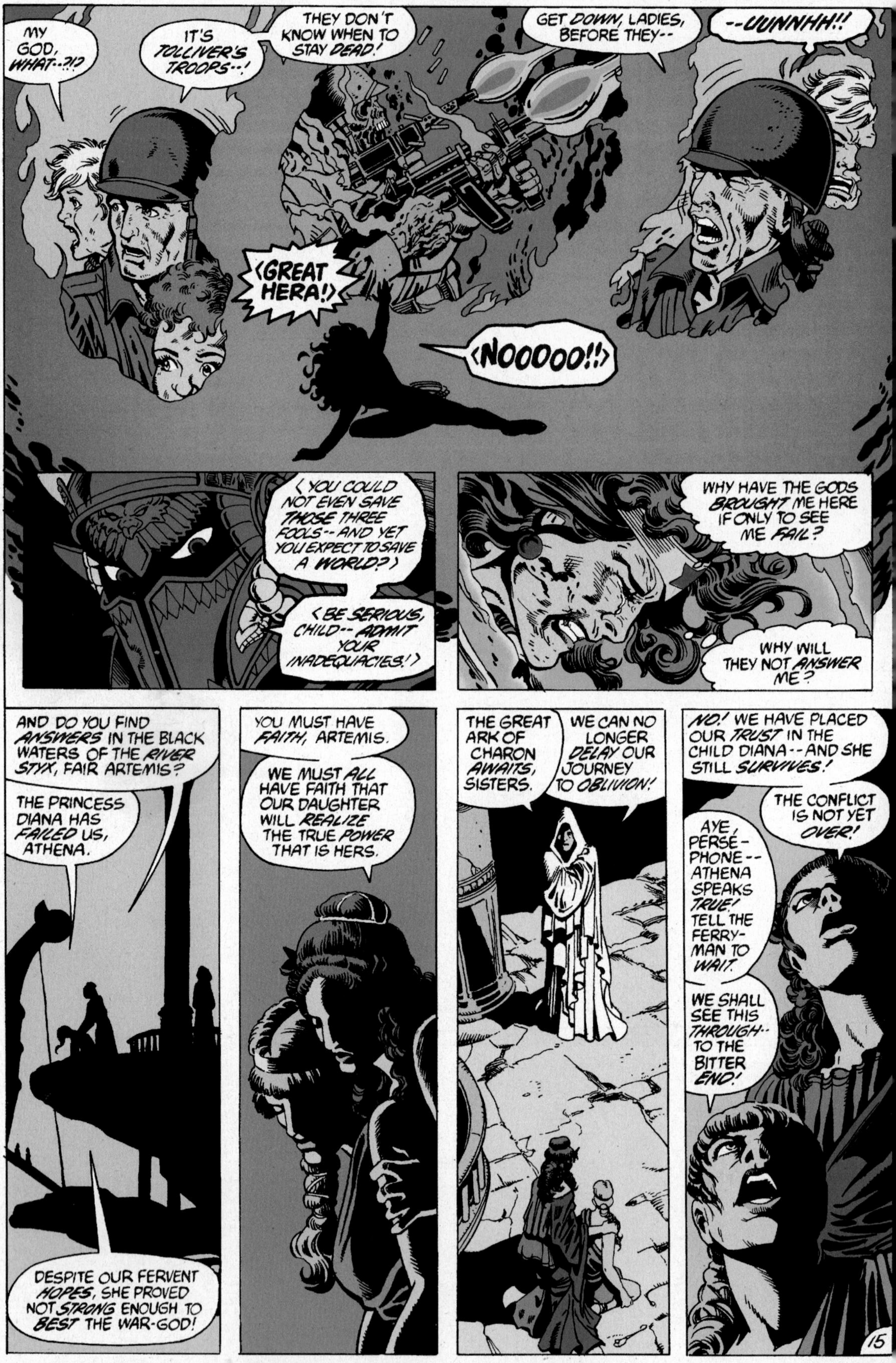
MY GOD, WHAT--?!?
IT'S TOLLIVER'S TROOPS--!
THEY DON'T KNOW WHEN TO STAY DEAD!
GET DOWN, LADIES, BEFORE THEY--
--UUNNHH!!
‹GREAT HERA!›
‹NOOOOO!!›
‹YOU COULD NOT EVEN SAVE THOSE THREE FOOLS--AND YET YOU EXPECT TO SAVE A WORLD?›
‹BE SERIOUS, CHILD--ADMIT YOUR INADEQUACIES!›
WHY HAVE THE GODS BROUGHT ME HERE IF ONLY TO SEE ME FAIL?
WHY WILL THEY NOT ANSWER ME?
AND DO YOU FIND ANSWERS IN THE BLACK WATERS OF THE RIVER STYX, FAIR ARTEMIS?
THE PRINCESS DIANA HAS FAILED US, ATHENA.
DESPITE OUR FERVENT HOPES, SHE PROVED NOT STRONG ENOUGH TO BEST THE WAR-GOD!
YOU MUST HAVE FAITH, ARTEMIS.
WE MUST ALL HAVE FAITH THAT OUR DAUGHTER WILL REALIZE THE TRUE POWER THAT IS HERS.
THE GREAT ARK OF CHARON AWAITS, SISTERS.
WE CAN NO LONGER DELAY OUR JOURNEY TO OBLIVION!
NO! WE HAVE PLACED OUR TRUST IN THE CHILD DIANA--AND SHE STILL SURVIVES!
THE CONFLICT IS NOT YET OVER!
AYE, PERSE-PHONE--ATHENA SPEAKS TRUE! TELL THE FERRY-MAN TO WAIT.
WE SHALL SEE THIS THROUGH--TO THE BITTER END!
15

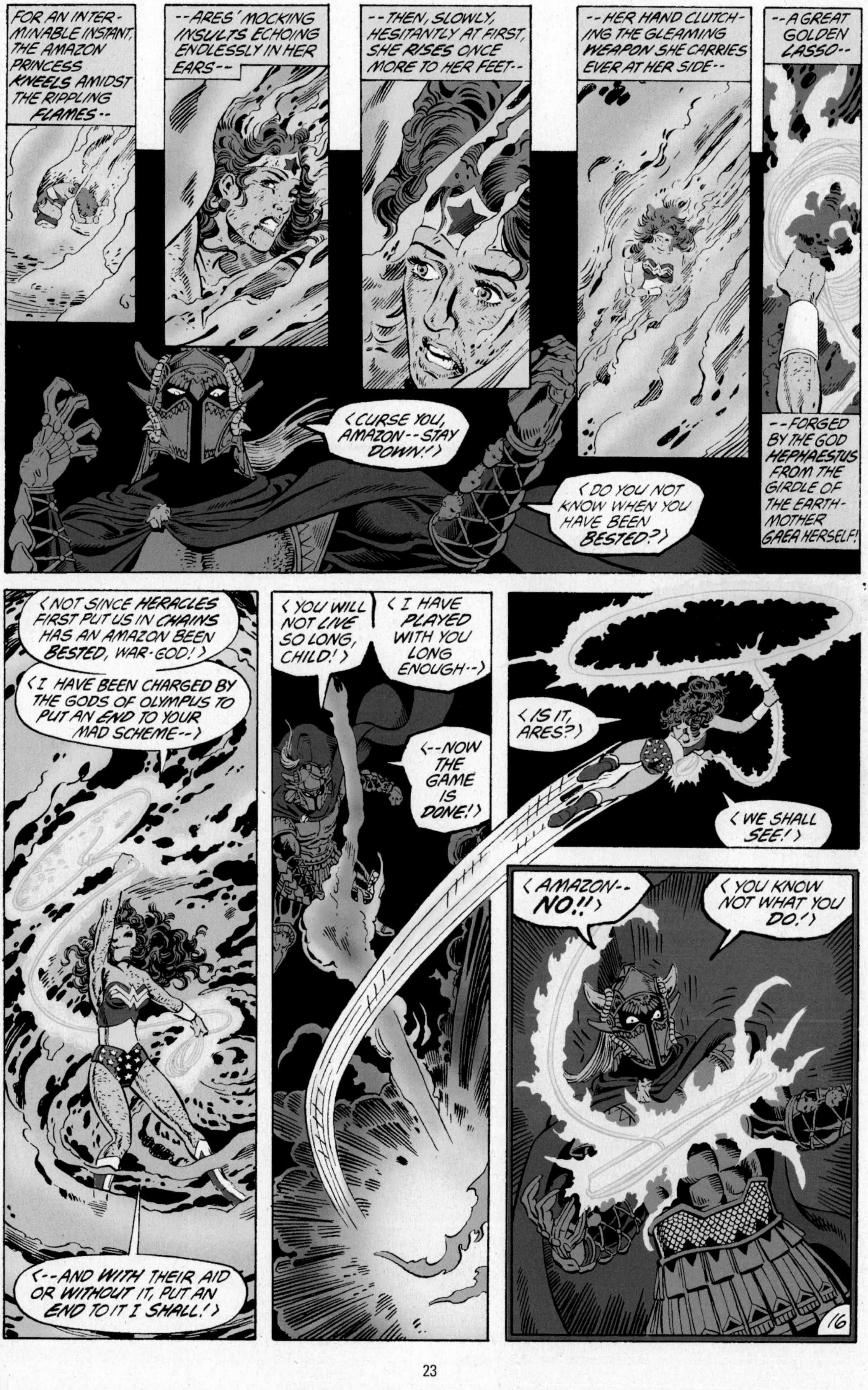
FOR AN INTERMINABLE INSTANT, THE AMAZON PRINCESS KNEELS AMIDST THE RIPPLING FLAMES--
--ARES' MOCKING INSULTS ECHOING ENDLESSLY IN HER EARS--
--THEN, SLOWLY, HESITANTLY AT FIRST, SHE RISES ONCE MORE TO HER FEET--
--HER HAND CLUTCHING THE GLEAMING WEAPON SHE CARRIES EVER AT HER SIDE--
--A GREAT GOLDEN LASSO--
<CURSE YOU, AMAZON--STAY DOWN!>
<DO YOU NOT KNOW WHEN YOU HAVE BEEN BESTED?>
--FORGED BY THE GOD HEPHAESTUS FROM THE GIRDLE OF THE EARTH-MOTHER GAEA HERSELF!
<NOT SINCE HERACLES FIRST PUT US IN CHAINS HAS AN AMAZON BEEN BESTED, WAR-GOD!>
<I HAVE BEEN CHARGED BY THE GODS OF OLYMPUS TO PUT AN END TO YOUR MAD SCHEME-->
<--AND WITH THEIR AID OR WITHOUT IT, PUT AN END TO IT I SHALL!>
<YOU WILL NOT LIVE SO LONG, CHILD!>
<I HAVE PLAYED WITH YOU LONG ENOUGH-->
<--NOW THE GAME IS DONE!>
<IS IT, ARES?>
<WE SHALL SEE!>
<AMAZON--NO!!>
<YOU KNOW NOT WHAT YOU DO!>
16

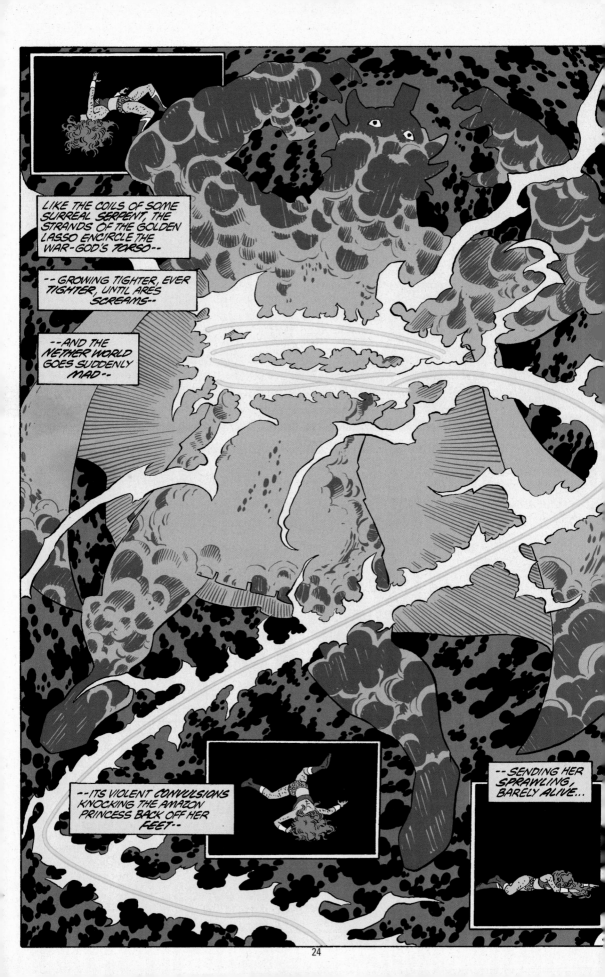

LIKE THE COILS OF SOME SURREAL SERPENT, THE STRANDS OF THE GOLDEN LASSO ENCIRCLE THE WAR-GOD'S *TORSO*--

-- GROWING TIGHTER, EVER TIGHTER, UNTIL ARES *SCREAMS*--

--AND THE *NETHER WORLD* GOES SUDDENLY *MAD*--

--ITS VIOLENT *CONVULSIONS* KNOCKING THE AMAZON PRINCESS BACK OFF HER *FEET*--

-- SENDING HER *SPRAWLING, BARELY ALIVE...*

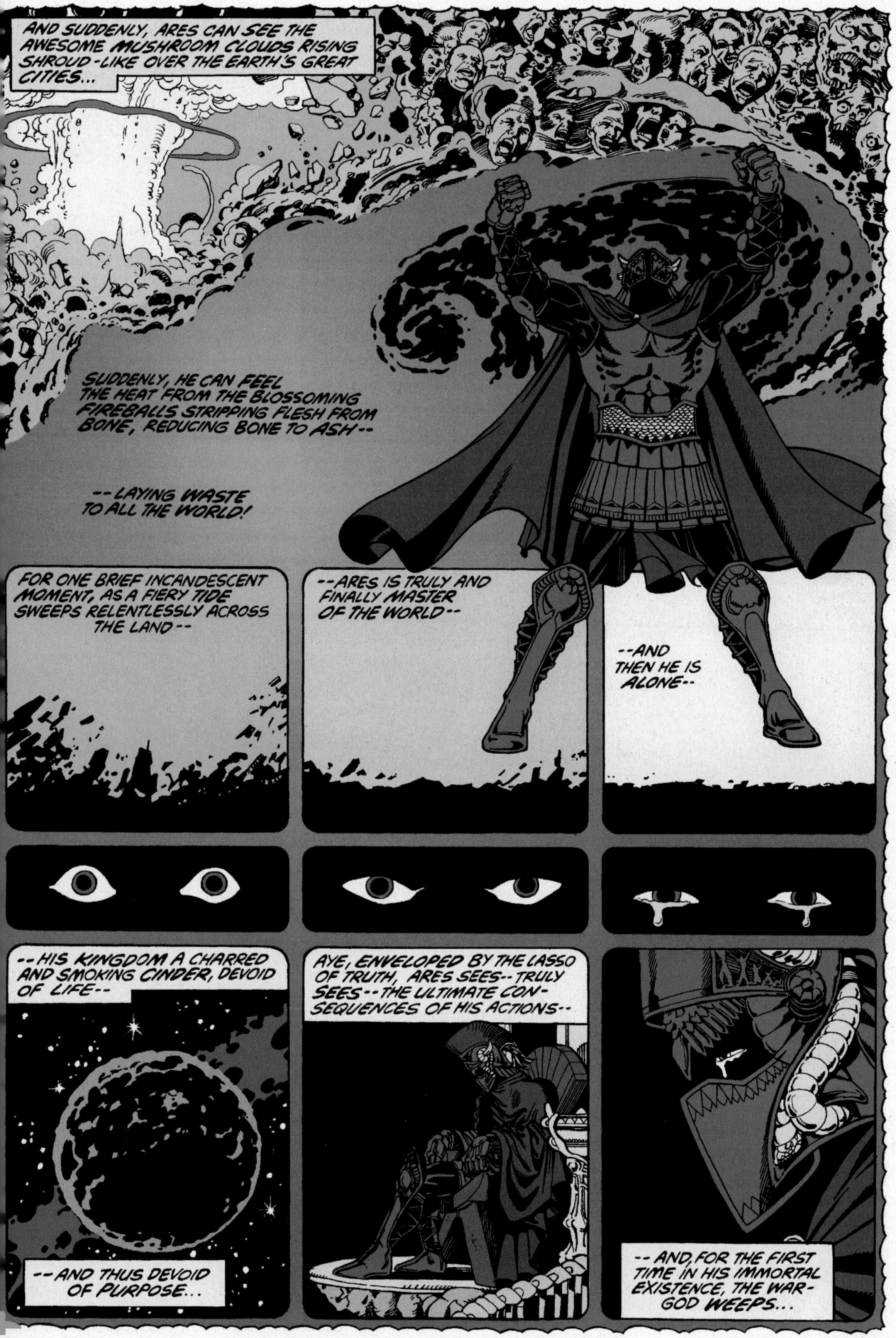
AND SUDDENLY, ARES CAN SEE THE AWESOME MUSHROOM CLOUDS RISING SHROUD-LIKE OVER THE EARTH'S GREAT CITIES...
SUDDENLY, HE CAN FEEL THE HEAT FROM THE BLOSSOMING FIREBALLS STRIPPING FLESH FROM BONE, REDUCING BONE TO ASH--
--LAYING WASTE TO ALL THE WORLD!
FOR ONE BRIEF INCANDESCENT MOMENT, AS A FIERY TIDE SWEEPS RELENTLESSLY ACROSS THE LAND--
--ARES IS TRULY AND FINALLY MASTER OF THE WORLD--
--AND THEN HE IS ALONE--
--HIS KINGDOM A CHARRED AND SMOKING CINDER, DEVOID OF LIFE--
--AND THUS DEVOID OF PURPOSE...
AYE, ENVELOPED BY THE LASSO OF TRUTH, ARES SEES--TRULY SEES--THE ULTIMATE CONSEQUENCES OF HIS ACTIONS--
--AND, FOR THE FIRST TIME IN HIS IMMORTAL EXISTENCE, THE WAR-GOD WEEPS...

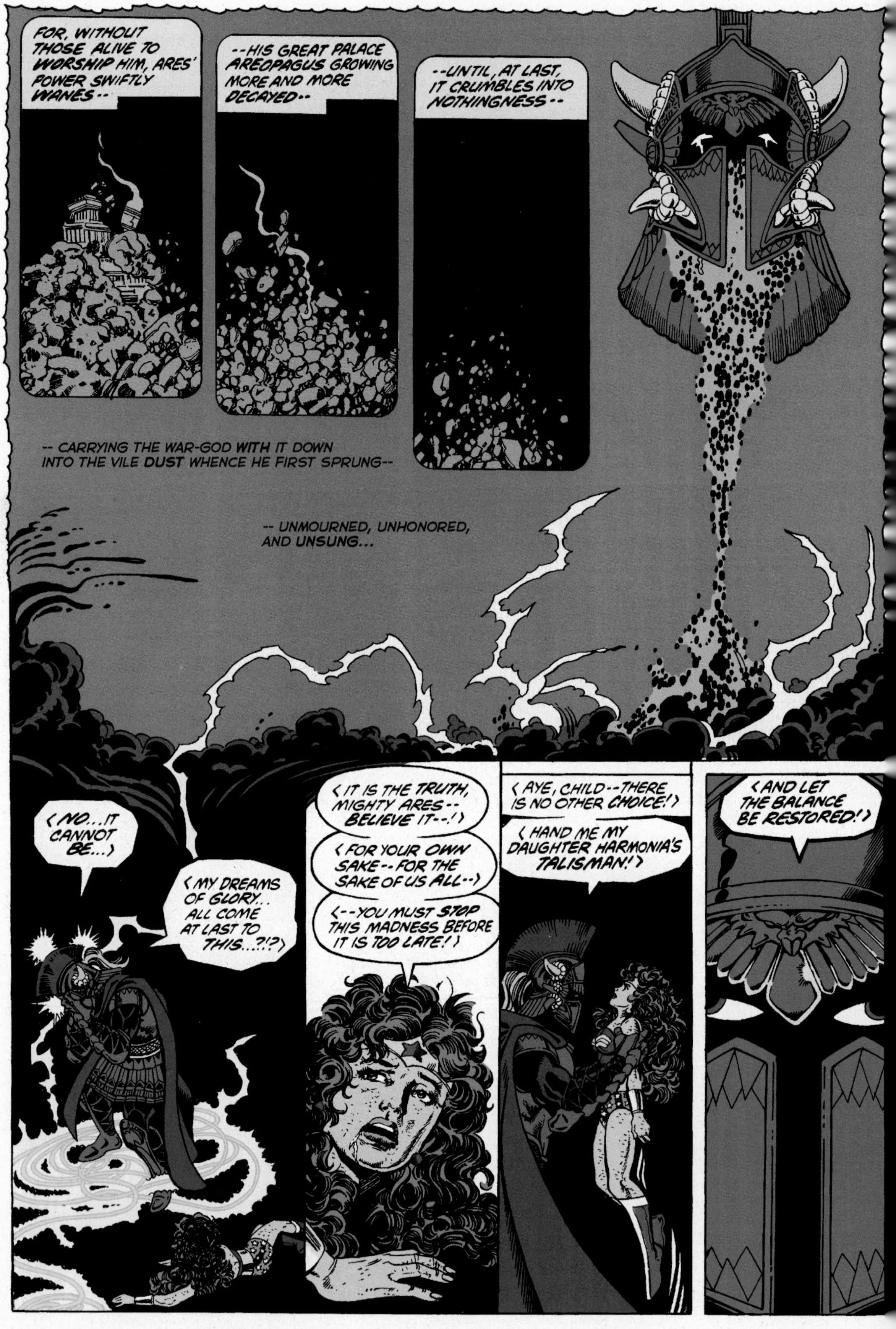

FOR, WITHOUT THOSE ALIVE TO WORSHIP HIM, ARES' POWER SWIFTLY WANES--
--HIS GREAT PALACE AREOPAGUS GROWING MORE AND MORE DECAYED--
--UNTIL, AT LAST, IT CRUMBLES INTO NOTHINGNESS--
-- CARRYING THE WAR-GOD WITH IT DOWN INTO THE VILE DUST WHENCE HE FIRST SPRUNG--
-- UNMOURNED, UNHONORED, AND UNSUNG...
‹NO...IT CANNOT BE...›
‹MY DREAMS OF GLORY.. ALL COME AT LAST TO THIS...?!?›
‹IT IS THE TRUTH, MIGHTY ARES-- BELIEVE IT--!›
‹FOR YOUR OWN SAKE--FOR THE SAKE OF US ALL--›
‹--YOU MUST STOP THIS MADNESS BEFORE IT IS TOO LATE!›
‹AYE, CHILD--THERE IS NO OTHER CHOICE!›
‹HAND ME MY DAUGHTER HARMONIA'S TALISMAN!›
‹AND LET THE BALANCE BE RESTORED!›

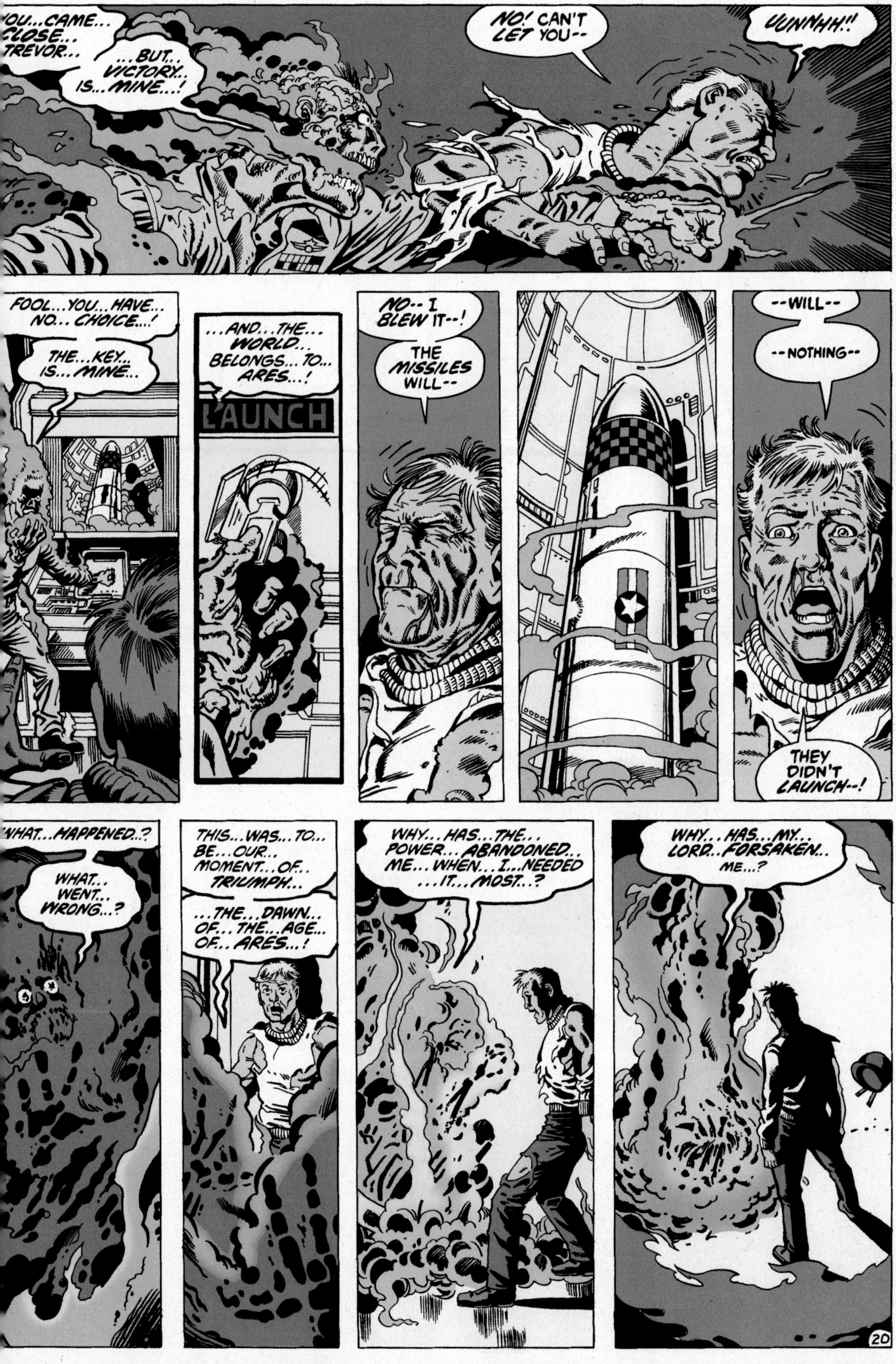
YOU...CAME... CLOSE... TREVOR...
...BUT... VICTORY... IS...MINE...!
NO! CAN'T LET YOU--
UUNNHH!!
FOOL...YOU...HAVE... NO...CHOICE...!
THE...KEY... IS...MINE...
...AND...THE... WORLD... BELONGS...TO... ARES...!
LAUNCH
NO-- I BLEW IT--!
THE MISSILES WILL--
--WILL--
--NOTHING--
THEY DIDN'T LAUNCH--!
WHAT...HAPPENED..?
WHAT... WENT... WRONG...?
THIS...WAS...TO... BE...OUR... MOMENT...OF... TRIUMPH...
...THE...DAWN... OF...THE...AGE... OF...ARES...!
WHY...HAS...THE... POWER...ABANDONED... ME...WHEN...I...NEEDED ...IT...MOST...?
WHY...HAS...MY... LORD...FORSAKEN... ME...?
20

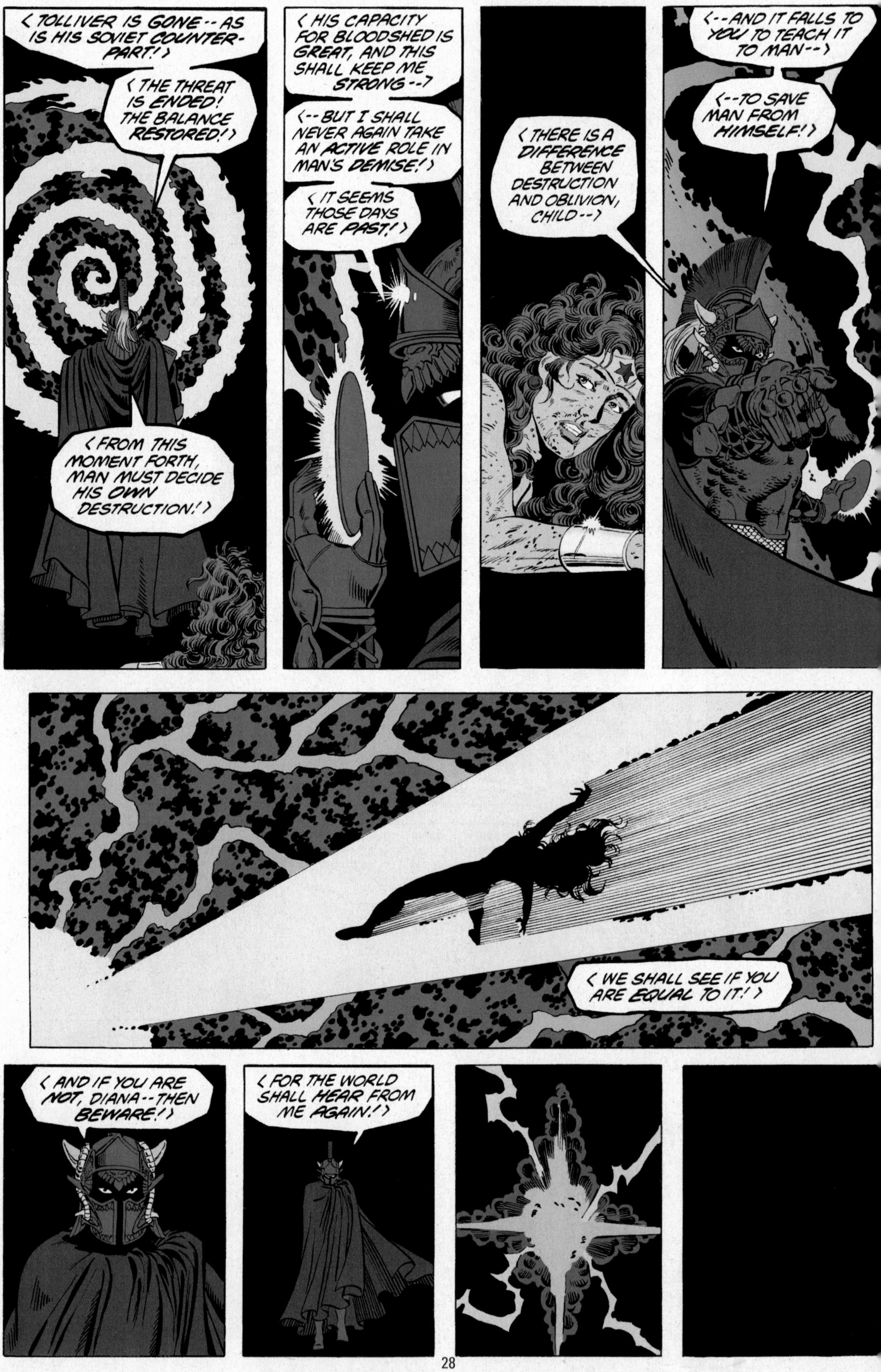

< TOLLIVER IS GONE -- AS IS HIS SOVIET COUNTERPART! >
< THE THREAT IS ENDED! THE BALANCE RESTORED! >
< FROM THIS MOMENT FORTH, MAN MUST DECIDE HIS OWN DESTRUCTION! >
< HIS CAPACITY FOR BLOODSHED IS GREAT, AND THIS SHALL KEEP ME STRONG -- >
< -- BUT I SHALL NEVER AGAIN TAKE AN ACTIVE ROLE IN MAN'S DEMISE! >
< IT SEEMS THOSE DAYS ARE PAST! >
< THERE IS A DIFFERENCE BETWEEN DESTRUCTION AND OBLIVION, CHILD -- >
< -- AND IT FALLS TO YOU TO TEACH IT TO MAN -- >
< -- TO SAVE MAN FROM HIMSELF! >
< WE SHALL SEE IF YOU ARE EQUAL TO IT! >
< AND IF YOU ARE NOT, DIANA -- THEN BEWARE! >
< FOR THE WORLD SHALL HEAR FROM ME AGAIN! >

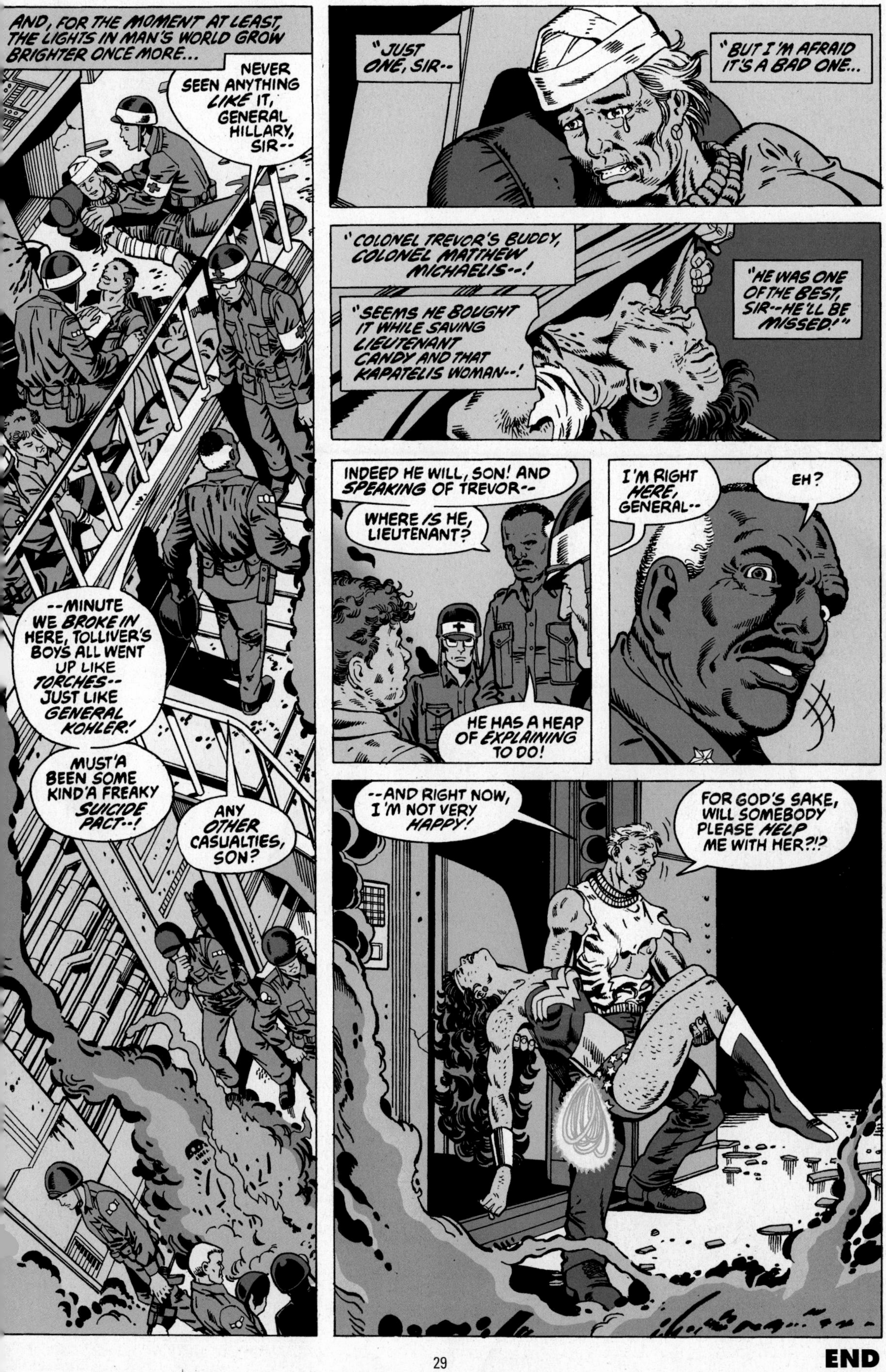
AND, FOR THE MOMENT AT LEAST, THE LIGHTS IN MAN'S WORLD GROW BRIGHTER ONCE MORE...
NEVER SEEN ANYTHING LIKE IT, GENERAL HILLARY, SIR--
--MINUTE WE BROKE IN HERE, TOLLIVER'S BOYS ALL WENT UP LIKE TORCHES--JUST LIKE GENERAL KOHLER!
MUST'A BEEN SOME KIND'A FREAKY SUICIDE PACT--!
ANY OTHER CASUALTIES, SON?
"JUST ONE, SIR--
"BUT I'M AFRAID IT'S A BAD ONE...
"COLONEL TREVOR'S BUDDY, COLONEL MATTHEW MICHAELIS--!
"SEEMS HE BOUGHT IT WHILE SAVING LIEUTENANT CANDY AND THAT KAPATELIS WOMAN--!
"HE WAS ONE OF THE BEST, SIR--HE'LL BE MISSED!"
INDEED HE WILL, SON! AND SPEAKING OF TREVOR--
WHERE IS HE, LIEUTENANT?
HE HAS A HEAP OF EXPLAINING TO DO!
I'M RIGHT HERE, GENERAL--
EH?
--AND RIGHT NOW, I'M NOT VERY HAPPY!
FOR GOD'S SAKE, WILL SOMEBODY PLEASE HELP ME WITH HER?!?

END

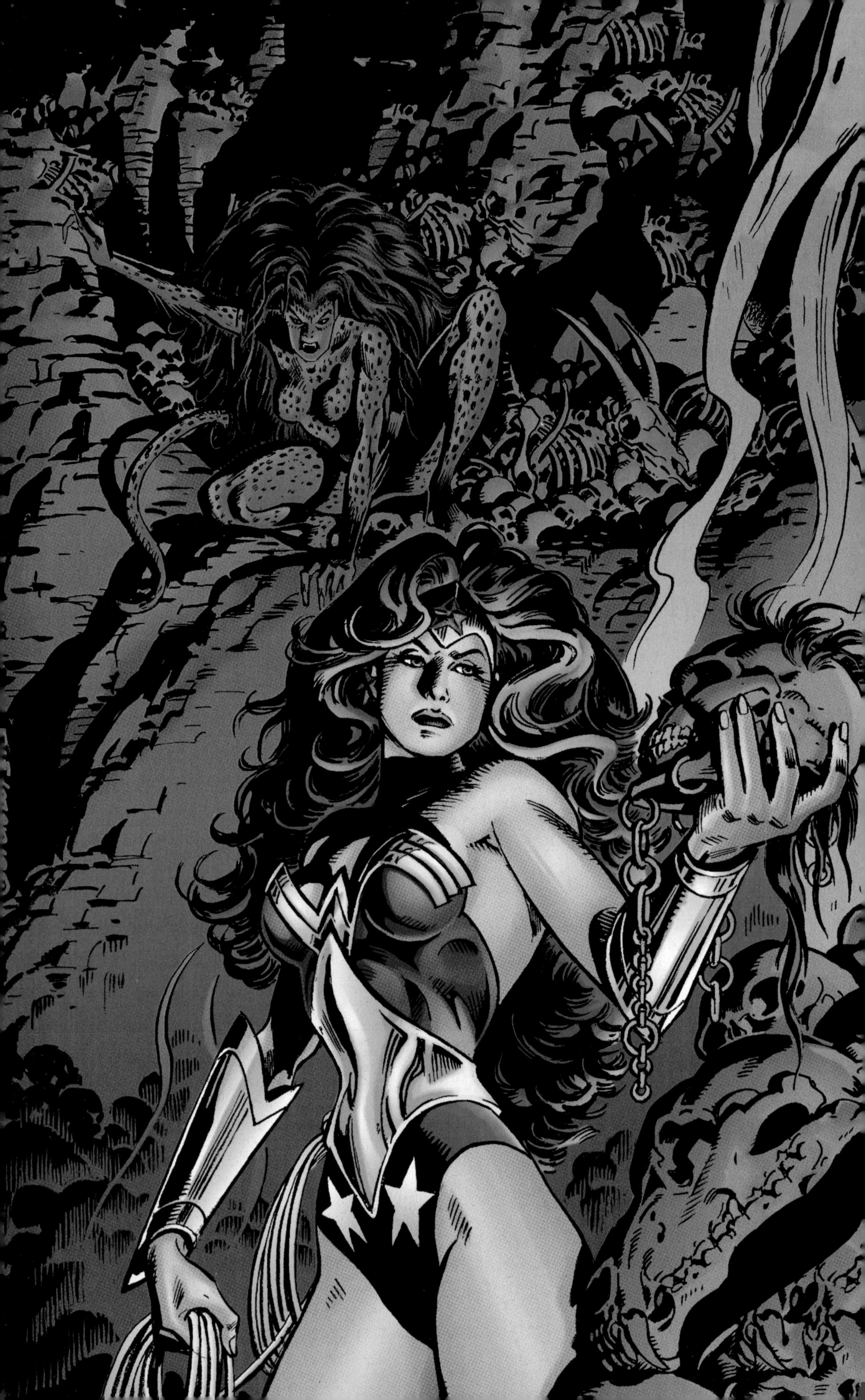

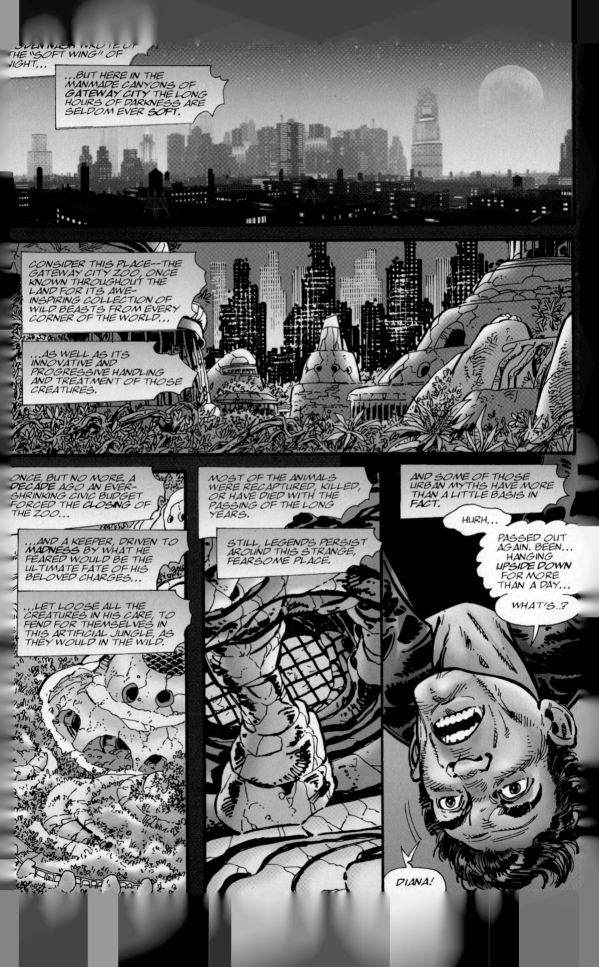

OGDEN NASH WROTE OF
THE "SOFT WING" OF
NIGHT...

...BUT HERE IN THE
MANMADE CANYONS OF
GATEWAY CITY THE LONG
HOURS OF DARKNESS ARE
SELDOM EVER SOFT.

CONSIDER THIS PLACE--THE
GATEWAY CITY ZOO, ONCE
KNOWN THROUGHOUT THE
LAND FOR ITS AWE-
INSPIRING COLLECTION OF
WILD BEASTS FROM EVERY
CORNER OF THE WORLD...

...AS WELL AS ITS
INNOVATIVE AND
PROGRESSIVE HANDLING
AND TREATMENT OF THOSE
CREATURES.

ONCE, BUT NO MORE. A
DECADE AGO AN EVER-
SHRINKING CIVIC BUDGET
FORCED THE CLOSING OF
THE ZOO...

...AND A KEEPER, DRIVEN TO
MADNESS BY WHAT HE
FEARED WOULD BE THE
ULTIMATE FATE OF HIS
BELOVED CHARGES...

...LET LOOSE ALL THE
CREATURES IN HIS CARE, TO
FEND FOR THEMSELVES IN
THIS ARTIFICIAL JUNGLE, AS
THEY WOULD IN THE WILD.

MOST OF THE ANIMALS
WERE RECAPTURED, KILLED,
OR HAVE DIED WITH THE
PASSING OF THE LONG
YEARS.

STILL, LEGENDS PERSIST
AROUND THIS STRANGE,
FEARSOME PLACE.

AND SOME OF THOSE
URBAN MYTHS HAVE MORE
THAN A LITTLE BASIS IN
FACT.

HURH...

PASSED OUT
AGAIN. BEEN...
HANGING
UPSIDE DOWN
FOR MORE
THAN A DAY...

WHAT'S..?

DIANA!

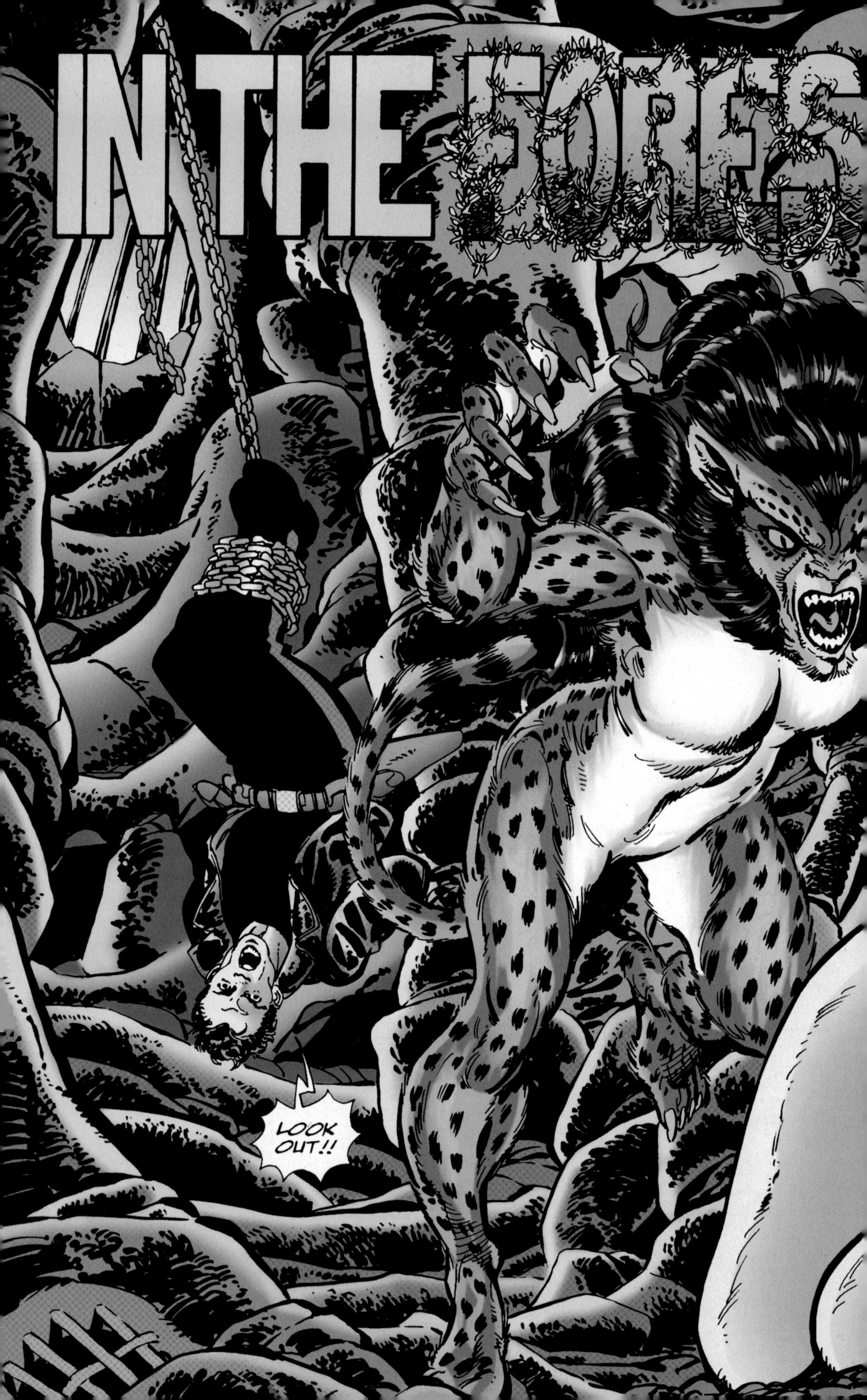
IN THE FORES
LOOK OUT!!

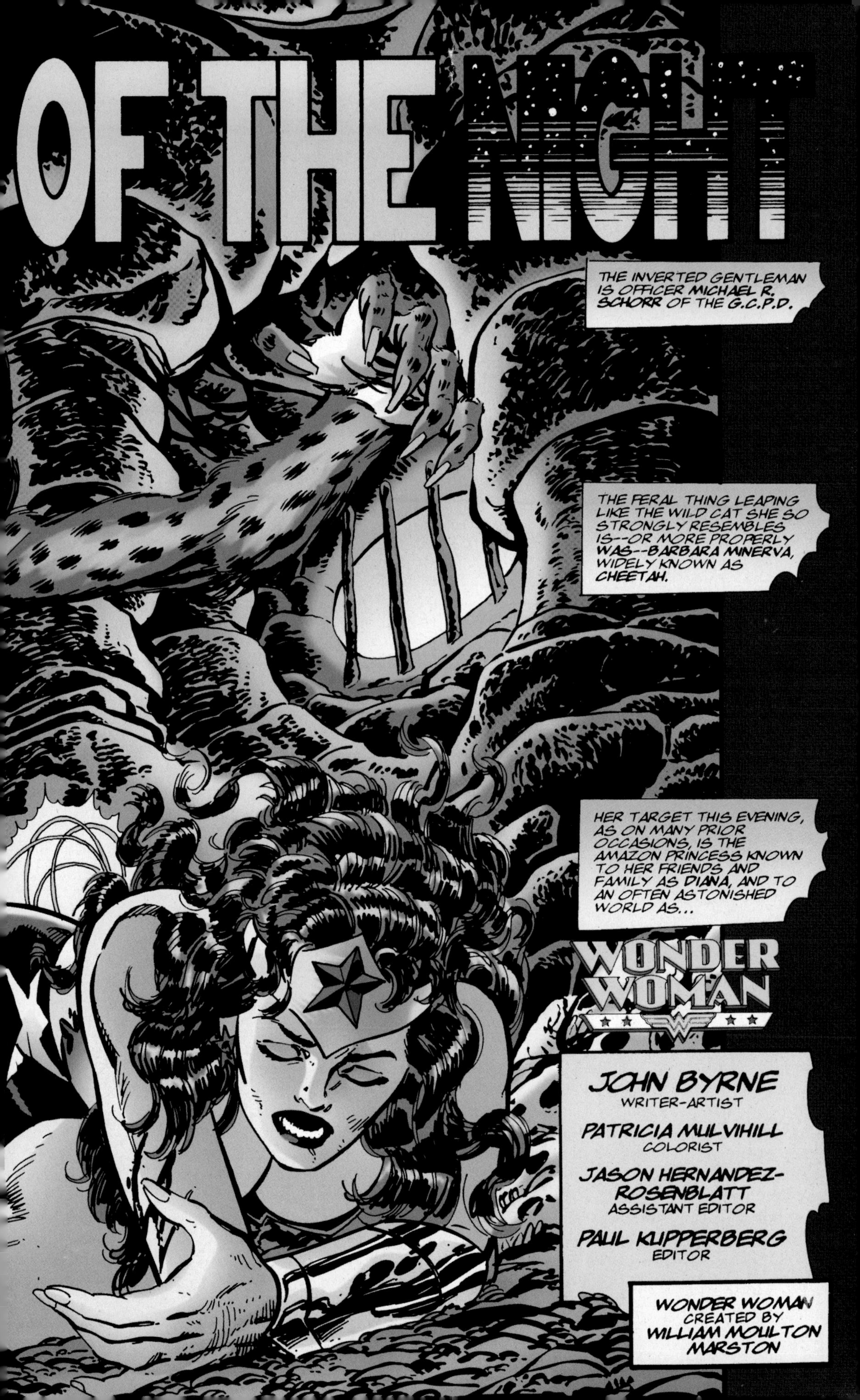
OF THE NIGHT
THE INVERTED GENTLEMAN IS OFFICER MICHAEL R. SCHORR OF THE G.C.P.D.
THE FERAL THING LEAPING LIKE THE WILD CAT SHE SO STRONGLY RESEMBLES IS--OR MORE PROPERLY WAS--BARBARA MINERVA, WIDELY KNOWN AS CHEETAH.
HER TARGET THIS EVENING, AS ON MANY PRIOR OCCASIONS, IS THE AMAZON PRINCESS KNOWN TO HER FRIENDS AND FAMILY AS DIANA, AND TO AN OFTEN ASTONISHED WORLD AS...
WONDER WOMAN
JOHN BYRNE
WRITER-ARTIST
PATRICIA MULVIHILL
COLORIST
JASON HERNANDEZ-ROSENBLATT
ASSISTANT EDITOR
PAUL KUPPERBERG
EDITOR
WONDER WOMAN CREATED BY WILLIAM MOULTON MARSTON

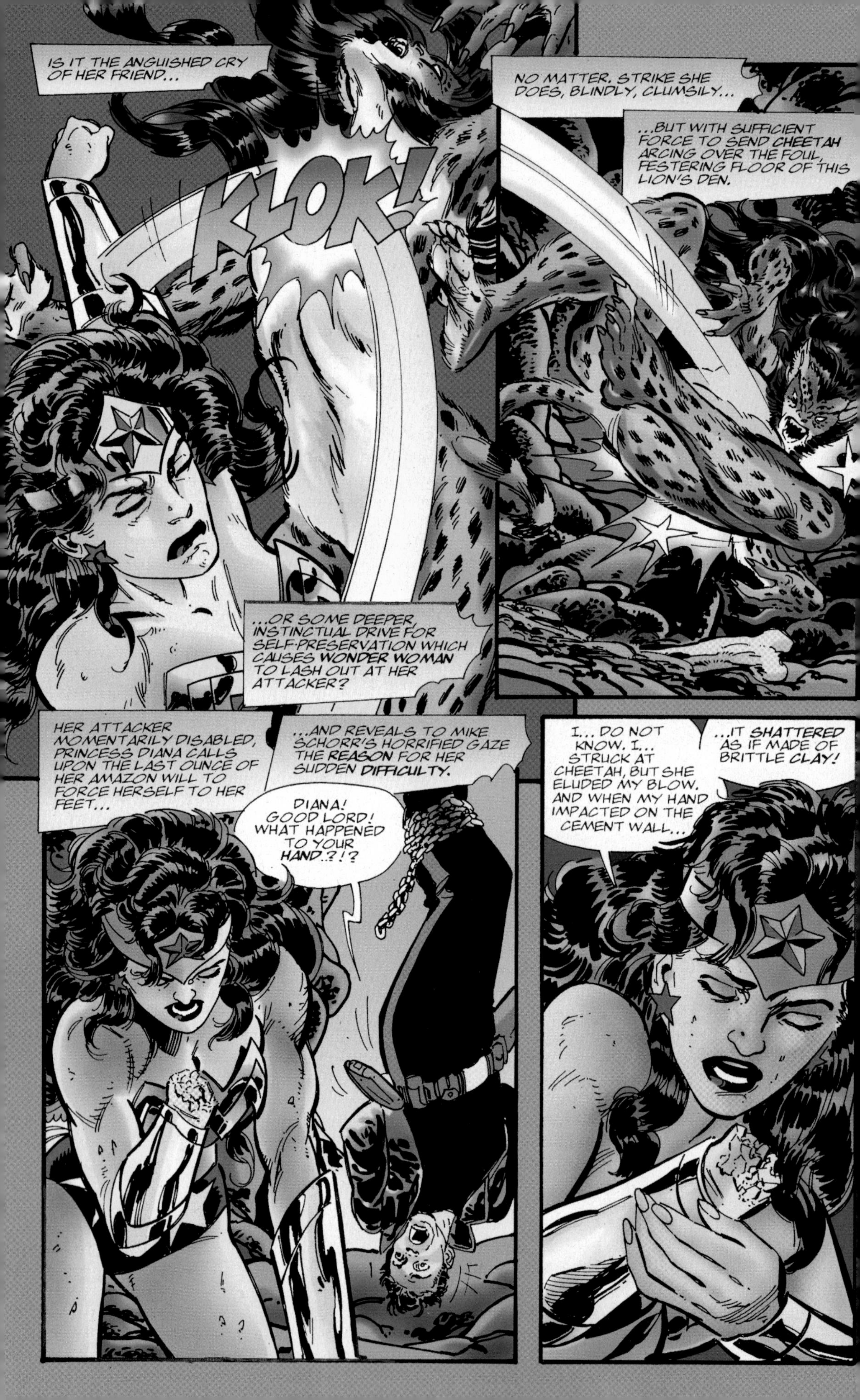
IS IT THE ANGUISHED CRY OF HER FRIEND...
KLOK!
...OR SOME DEEPER, INSTINCTUAL DRIVE FOR SELF-PRESERVATION WHICH CAUSES WONDER WOMAN TO LASH OUT AT HER ATTACKER?
NO MATTER. STRIKE SHE DOES, BLINDLY, CLUMSILY...
...BUT WITH SUFFICIENT FORCE TO SEND CHEETAH ARCING OVER THE FOUL, FESTERING FLOOR OF THIS LION'S DEN.
HER ATTACKER MOMENTARILY DISABLED, PRINCESS DIANA CALLS UPON THE LAST OUNCE OF HER AMAZON WILL TO FORCE HERSELF TO HER FEET...
...AND REVEALS TO MIKE SCHORR'S HORRIFIED GAZE THE REASON FOR HER SUDDEN DIFFICULTY.
DIANA! GOOD LORD! WHAT HAPPENED TO YOUR HAND..?!?
I... DO NOT KNOW. I... STRUCK AT CHEETAH, BUT SHE ELUDED MY BLOW. AND WHEN MY HAND IMPACTED ON THE CEMENT WALL...
...IT SHATTERED AS IF MADE OF BRITTLE CLAY!

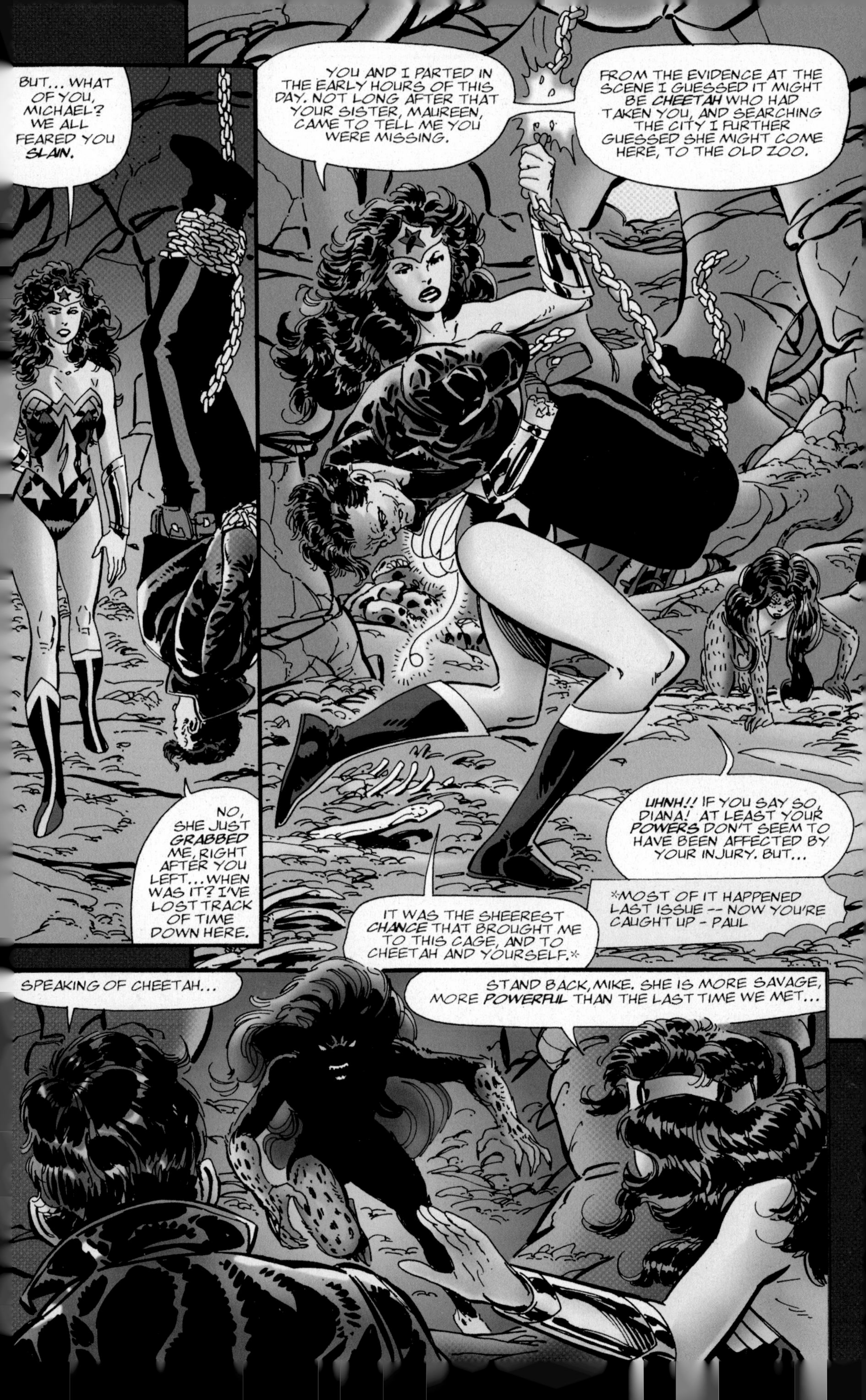
BUT... WHAT OF YOU, MICHAEL? WE ALL FEARED YOU SLAIN.
NO, SHE JUST GRABBED ME, RIGHT AFTER YOU LEFT... WHEN WAS IT? I'VE LOST TRACK OF TIME DOWN HERE.
YOU AND I PARTED IN THE EARLY HOURS OF THIS DAY. NOT LONG AFTER THAT YOUR SISTER, MAUREEN, CAME TO TELL ME YOU WERE MISSING.
FROM THE EVIDENCE AT THE SCENE I GUESSED IT MIGHT BE CHEETAH WHO HAD TAKEN YOU, AND SEARCHING THE CITY I FURTHER GUESSED SHE MIGHT COME HERE, TO THE OLD ZOO.
IT WAS THE SHEEREST CHANCE THAT BROUGHT ME TO THIS CAGE, AND TO CHEETAH AND YOURSELF.*
UHNH!! IF YOU SAY SO, DIANA! AT LEAST YOUR POWERS DON'T SEEM TO HAVE BEEN AFFECTED BY YOUR INJURY. BUT...
*MOST OF IT HAPPENED LAST ISSUE -- NOW YOU'RE CAUGHT UP - PAUL
SPEAKING OF CHEETAH...
STAND BACK, MIKE. SHE IS MORE SAVAGE, MORE POWERFUL THAN THE LAST TIME WE MET...

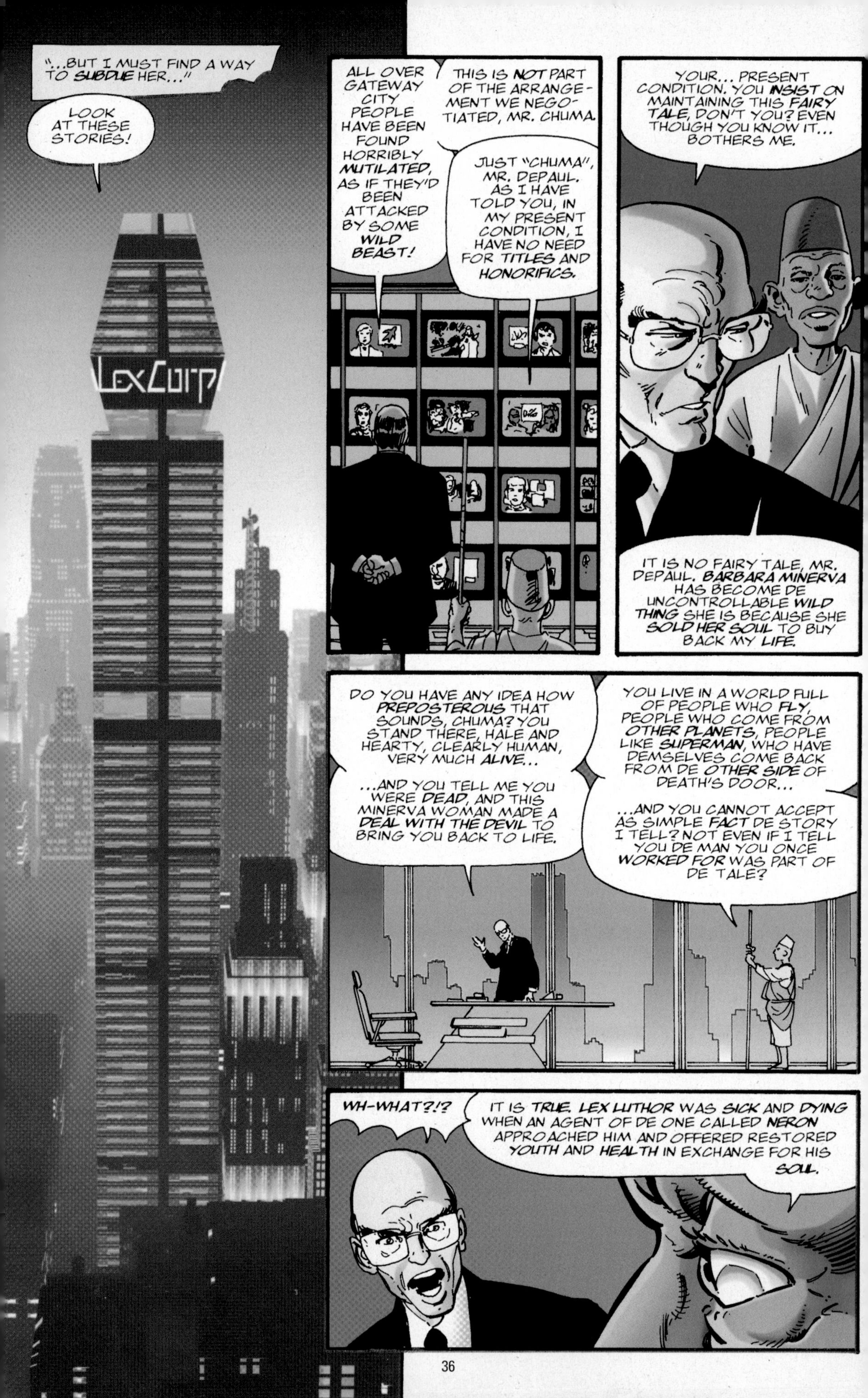
"...BUT I MUST FIND A WAY TO SUBDUE HER..."
LOOK AT THESE STORIES!
LEXCORP
ALL OVER GATEWAY CITY PEOPLE HAVE BEEN FOUND HORRIBLY MUTILATED, AS IF THEY'D BEEN ATTACKED BY SOME WILD BEAST!
THIS IS NOT PART OF THE ARRANGEMENT WE NEGOTIATED, MR. CHUMA.
JUST "CHUMA", MR. DEPAUL. AS I HAVE TOLD YOU, IN MY PRESENT CONDITION, I HAVE NO NEED FOR TITLES AND HONORIFICS.
YOUR... PRESENT CONDITION. YOU INSIST ON MAINTAINING THIS FAIRY TALE, DON'T YOU? EVEN THOUGH YOU KNOW IT... BOTHERS ME.
IT IS NO FAIRY TALE, MR. DEPAUL. BARBARA MINERVA HAS BECOME DE UNCONTROLLABLE WILD THING SHE IS BECAUSE SHE SOLD HER SOUL TO BUY BACK MY LIFE.
DO YOU HAVE ANY IDEA HOW PREPOSTEROUS THAT SOUNDS, CHUMA? YOU STAND THERE, HALE AND HEARTY, CLEARLY HUMAN, VERY MUCH ALIVE...
...AND YOU TELL ME YOU WERE DEAD, AND THIS MINERVA WOMAN MADE A DEAL WITH THE DEVIL TO BRING YOU BACK TO LIFE.
YOU LIVE IN A WORLD FULL OF PEOPLE WHO FLY, PEOPLE WHO COME FROM OTHER PLANETS, PEOPLE LIKE SUPERMAN, WHO HAVE DEMSELVES COME BACK FROM DE OTHER SIDE OF DEATH'S DOOR...
...AND YOU CANNOT ACCEPT AS SIMPLE FACT DE STORY I TELL? NOT EVEN IF I TELL YOU DE MAN YOU ONCE WORKED FOR WAS PART OF DE TALE?
WH-WHAT?!?
IT IS TRUE. LEX LUTHOR WAS SICK AND DYING WHEN AN AGENT OF DE ONE CALLED NERON APPROACHED HIM AND OFFERED RESTORED YOUTH AND HEALTH IN EXCHANGE FOR HIS SOUL.

"LUTHOR DID NOT BELIEVE HIMSELF TO HAVE A SOUL TO BARTER, AND SO HE ACCEPTED NERON'S OFFER.

"HE WAS ONE OF MANY.

"ANOTHER WAS MY MISTRESS. BARBARA MINERVA GAVE UP HER SOUL ON DE OFFER OF NERON TO RESTORE MY LIFE.

"SHE BELIEVED DAT I WAS DE ONLY ONE WHO COULD BRIDLE DE RAGING BEAST DAT WAS HER OTHER SELF.

"AT FIRST IT SEEMED ALL WOULD WORK OUT AS BARBARA HOPED IT WOULD.

"SHE STILL UNDERWENT DE TRANS-FORMATION TO CHEETAH, BUT WITH MY HELP SHE WAS ABLE TO CONTROL IT ONCE MORE.

"DEN AS NOW, SHE WAS ABLE TO SENSE DE DARKNESS DAT SQUATS AT DE CENTER OF SOME MEN'S SOULS...

"...AND DEN AS NOW IT WAS ONLY DIS HUMAN REFUSE ON WHICH SHE PREYED.

"BUT WITH EACH NIGHT'S HUNT DE TRUE COST OF NERON'S BARGAIN BECAME MORE AND MORE APPARENT.

"WITH NO HUMAN SOUL TO ACT AS A BARRIER AGAINST DEM, THE MOST BASE AND SAVAGE OF HER ANIMAL INSTINCTS BEGAN SLOWLY TO OVERWHELM BARBARA MINERVA.

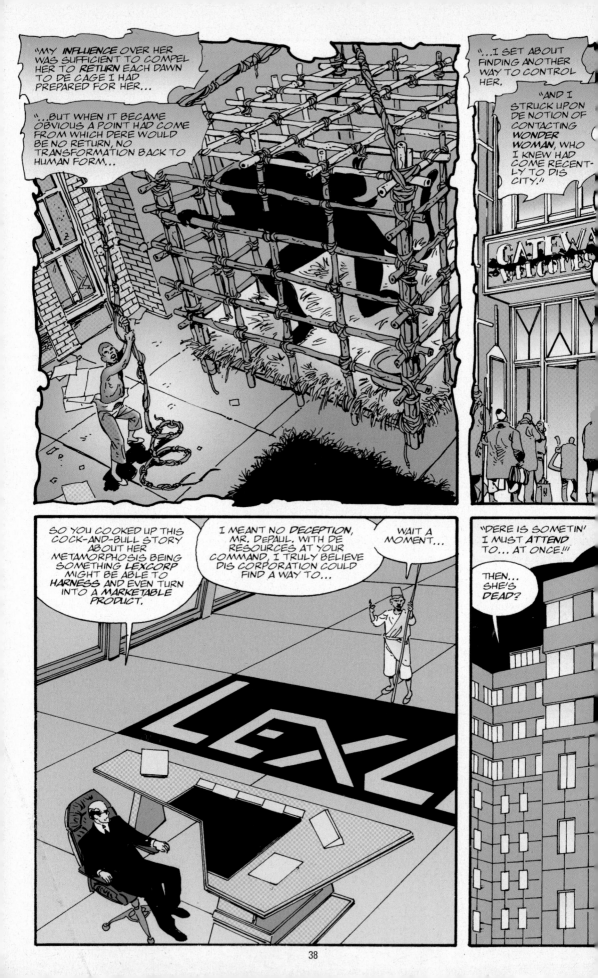

"MY *INFLUENCE* OVER HER WAS SUFFICIENT TO COMPEL HER TO *RETURN* EACH DAWN TO DE CAGE I HAD PREPARED FOR HER..."

"...BUT WHEN IT BECAME OBVIOUS A POINT HAD COME FROM WHICH DERE WOULD BE NO RETURN, NO TRANSFORMATION BACK TO HUMAN FORM..."

"...I SET ABOUT FINDING ANOTHER WAY TO CONTROL HER.

"AND I STRUCK UPON DE NOTION OF CONTACTING *WONDER WOMAN*, WHO I KNEW HAD COME RECENTLY TO DIS CITY."

GATEWA
WELCOMES

SO YOU COOKED UP THIS COCK-AND-BULL STORY ABOUT HER METAMORPHOSIS BEING SOMETHING *LEXCORP* MIGHT BE ABLE TO *HARNESS* AND EVEN TURN INTO A *MARKETABLE PRODUCT.*

I MEANT NO *DECEPTION,* MR. DEPAUL. WITH DE RESOURCES AT YOUR COMMAND, I TRULY BELIEVE DIS CORPORATION COULD FIND A WAY TO...

WAIT A MOMENT...

LEX

"DERE IS SOMETIN' I MUST *ATTEND* TO... AT ONCE.!!!

THEN... SHE'S *DEAD?*

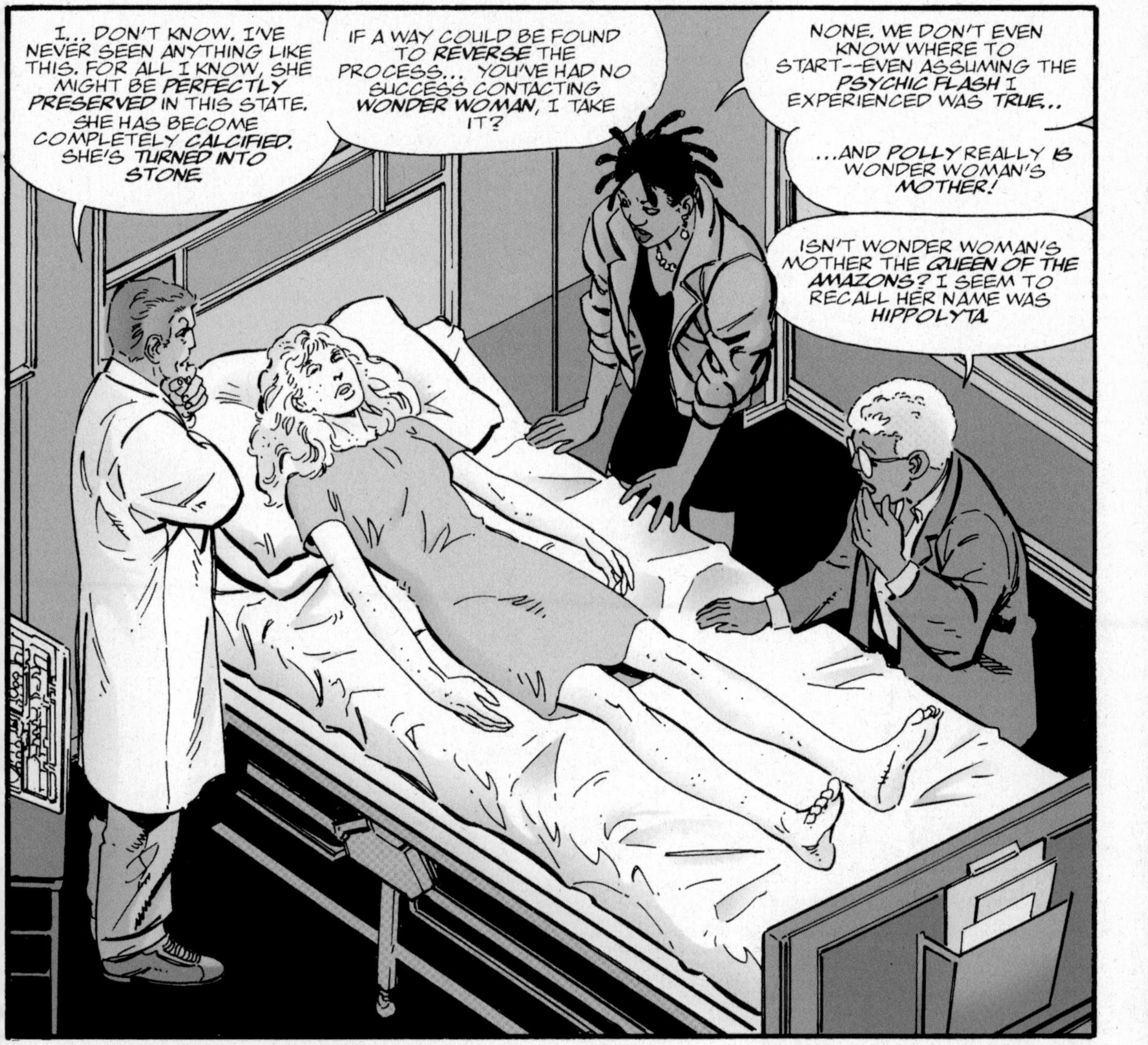
I... DON'T KNOW. I'VE NEVER SEEN ANYTHING LIKE THIS. FOR ALL I KNOW, SHE MIGHT BE PERFECTLY PRESERVED IN THIS STATE. SHE HAS BECOME COMPLETELY CALCIFIED. SHE'S TURNED INTO STONE.
IF A WAY COULD BE FOUND TO REVERSE THE PROCESS... YOU'VE HAD NO SUCCESS CONTACTING WONDER WOMAN, I TAKE IT?
NONE. WE DON'T EVEN KNOW WHERE TO START--EVEN ASSUMING THE PSYCHIC FLASH I EXPERIENCED WAS TRUE...
...AND POLLY REALLY IS WONDER WOMAN'S MOTHER!
ISN'T WONDER WOMAN'S MOTHER THE QUEEN OF THE AMAZONS? I SEEM TO RECALL HER NAME WAS HIPPOLYTA.

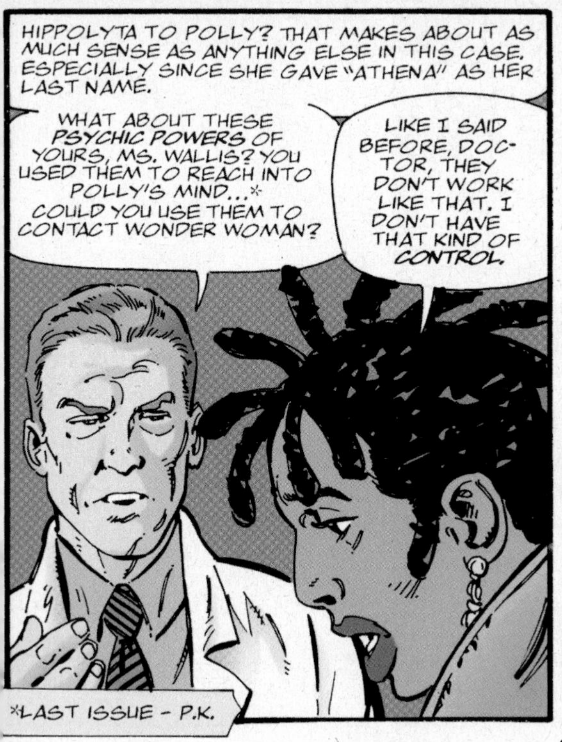
HIPPOLYTA TO POLLY? THAT MAKES ABOUT AS MUCH SENSE AS ANYTHING ELSE IN THIS CASE. ESPECIALLY SINCE SHE GAVE "ATHENA" AS HER LAST NAME.
WHAT ABOUT THESE PSYCHIC POWERS OF YOURS, MS. WALLIS? YOU USED THEM TO REACH INTO POLLY'S MIND...* COULD YOU USE THEM TO CONTACT WONDER WOMAN?
LIKE I SAID BEFORE, DOCTOR, THEY DON'T WORK LIKE THAT. I DON'T HAVE THAT KIND OF CONTROL.
*LAST ISSUE - P.K.

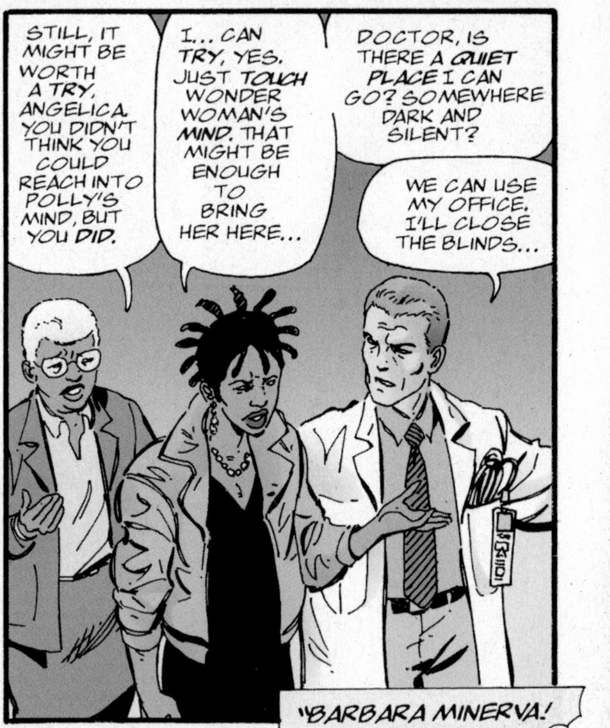
STILL, IT MIGHT BE WORTH A TRY, ANGELICA. YOU DIDN'T THINK YOU COULD REACH INTO POLLY'S MIND, BUT YOU DID.
I... CAN TRY, YES. JUST TOUCH WONDER WOMAN'S MIND. THAT MIGHT BE ENOUGH TO BRING HER HERE...
DOCTOR, IS THERE A QUIET PLACE I CAN GO? SOMEWHERE DARK AND SILENT?
WE CAN USE MY OFFICE. I'LL CLOSE THE BLINDS...
"BARBARA MINERVA!

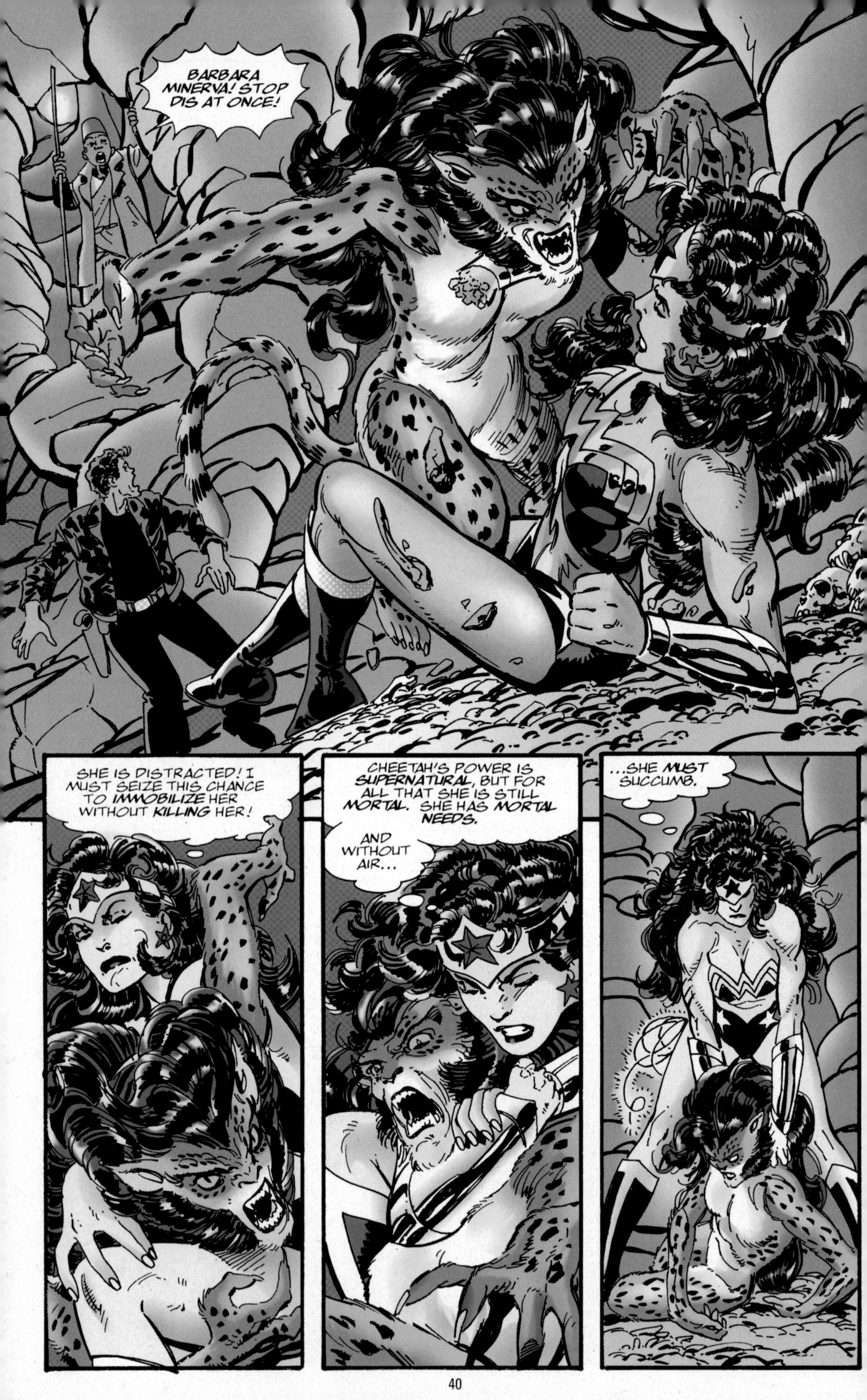
BARBARA MINERVA! STOP DIS AT ONCE!
SHE IS DISTRACTED! I MUST SEIZE THIS CHANCE TO IMMOBILIZE HER WITHOUT KILLING HER!
CHEETAH'S POWER IS SUPERNATURAL, BUT FOR ALL THAT SHE IS STILL MORTAL. SHE HAS MORTAL NEEDS.
AND WITHOUT AIR...
...SHE MUST SUCCUMB.

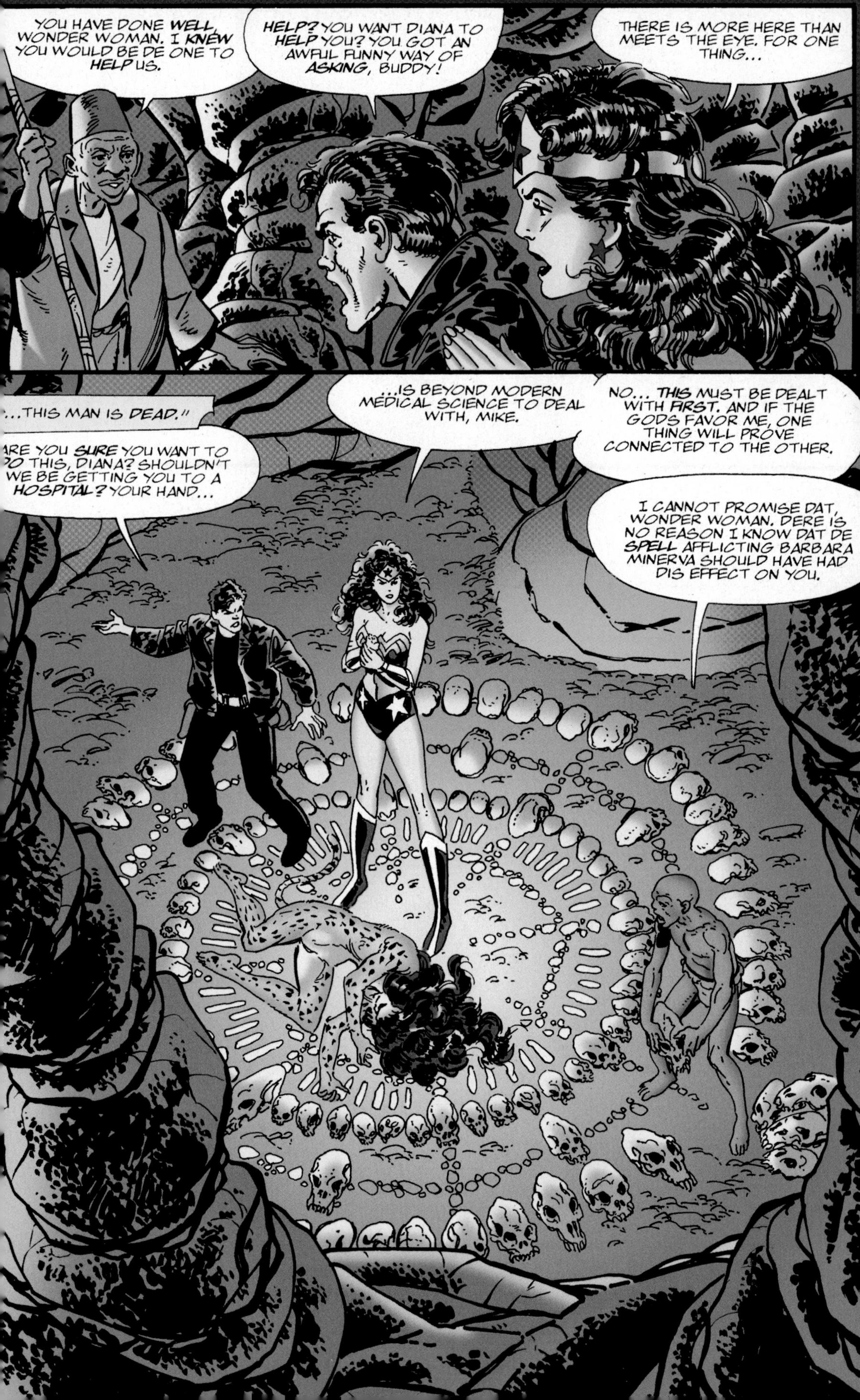
YOU HAVE DONE WELL, WONDER WOMAN. I KNEW YOU WOULD BE DE ONE TO HELP US.
HELP? YOU WANT DIANA TO HELP YOU? YOU GOT AN AWFUL FUNNY WAY OF ASKING, BUDDY!
THERE IS MORE HERE THAN MEETS THE EYE. FOR ONE THING...
...THIS MAN IS DEAD."
ARE YOU SURE YOU WANT TO DO THIS, DIANA? SHOULDN'T WE BE GETTING YOU TO A HOSPITAL? YOUR HAND...
...IS BEYOND MODERN MEDICAL SCIENCE TO DEAL WITH, MIKE.
NO... THIS MUST BE DEALT WITH FIRST. AND IF THE GODS FAVOR ME, ONE THING WILL PROVE CONNECTED TO THE OTHER.
I CANNOT PROMISE DAT, WONDER WOMAN. DERE IS NO REASON I KNOW DAT DE SPELL AFFLICTING BARBARA MINERVA SHOULD HAVE HAD DIS EFFECT ON YOU.

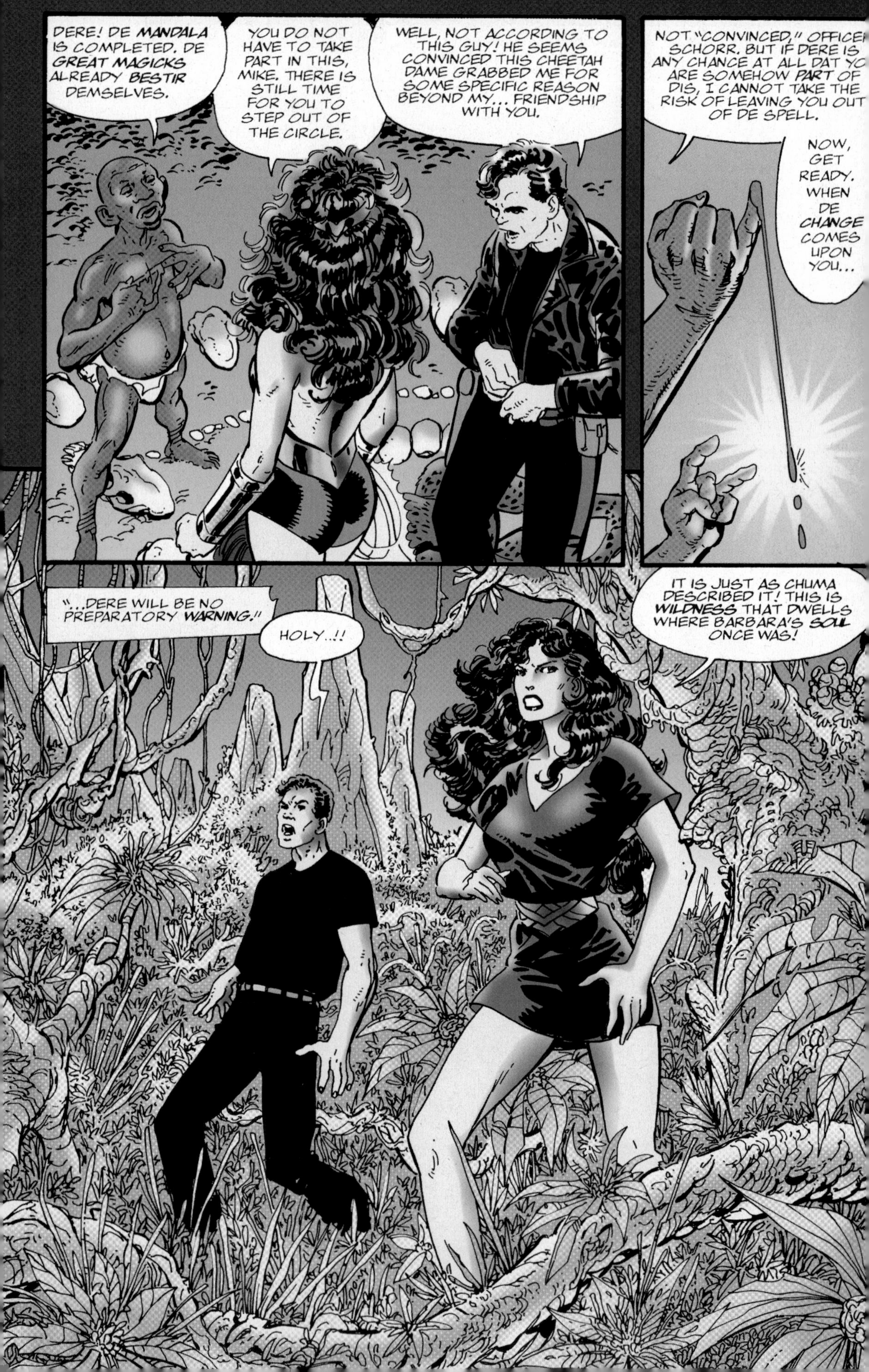
DERE! DE MANDALA IS COMPLETED. DE GREAT MAGICKS ALREADY BESTIR DEMSELVES.
YOU DO NOT HAVE TO TAKE PART IN THIS, MIKE. THERE IS STILL TIME FOR YOU TO STEP OUT OF THE CIRCLE.
WELL, NOT ACCORDING TO THIS GUY! HE SEEMS CONVINCED THIS CHEETAH DAME GRABBED ME FOR SOME SPECIFIC REASON BEYOND MY... FRIENDSHIP WITH YOU.
NOT "CONVINCED," OFFICER SCHORR. BUT IF DERE IS ANY CHANCE AT ALL DAT YOU ARE SOMEHOW PART OF DIS, I CANNOT TAKE THE RISK OF LEAVING YOU OUT OF DE SPELL...
NOW, GET READY. WHEN DE CHANGE COMES UPON YOU...
"...DERE WILL BE NO PREPARATORY WARNING!"
HOLY..!!
IT IS JUST AS CHUMA DESCRIBED IT! THIS IS WILDNESS THAT DWELLS WHERE BARBARA'S SOUL ONCE WAS!

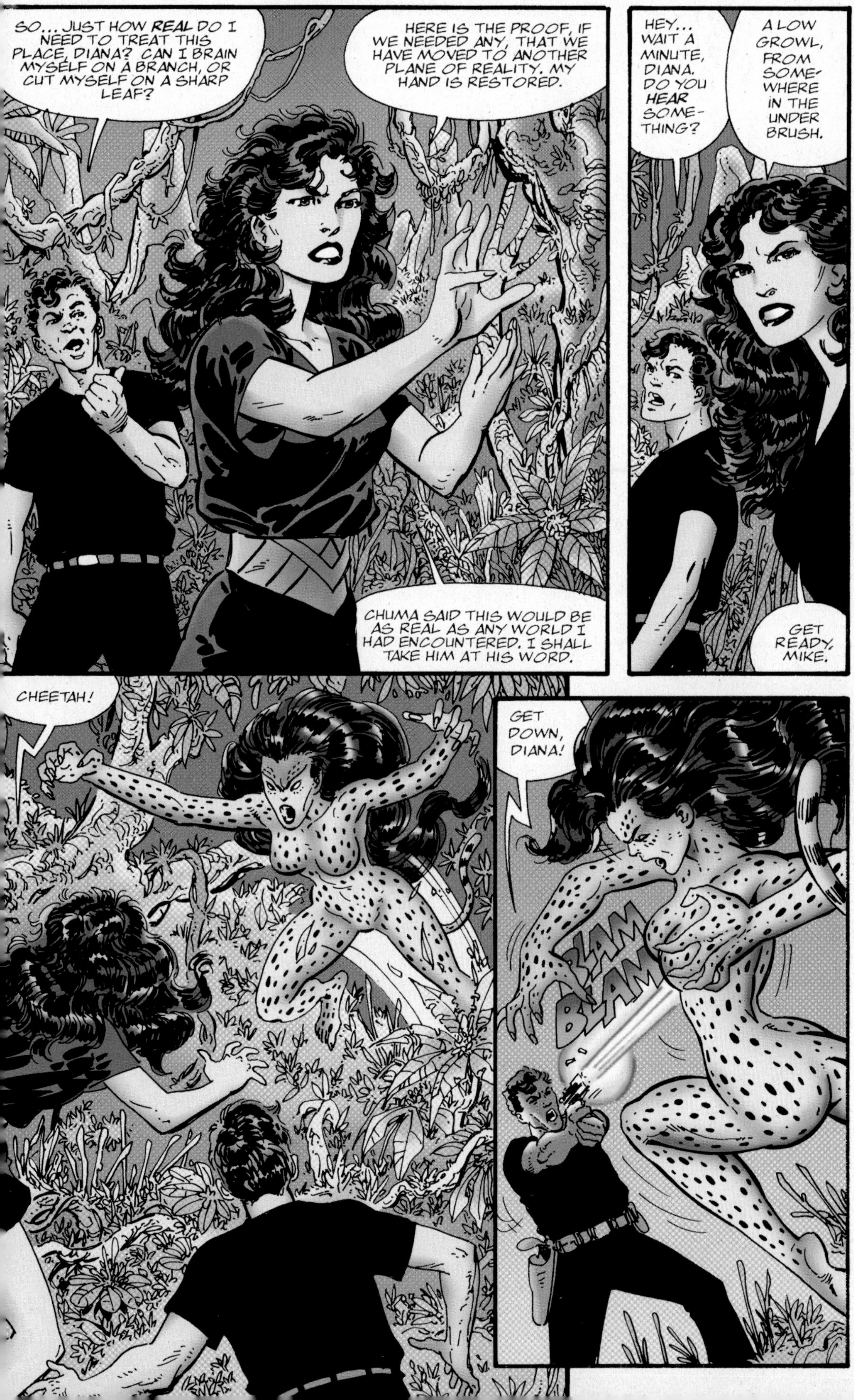
SO... JUST HOW REAL DO I NEED TO TREAT THIS PLACE, DIANA? CAN I BRAIN MYSELF ON A BRANCH, OR CUT MYSELF ON A SHARP LEAF?
HERE IS THE PROOF, IF WE NEEDED ANY, THAT WE HAVE MOVED TO ANOTHER PLANE OF REALITY. MY HAND IS RESTORED.
CHUMA SAID THIS WOULD BE AS REAL AS ANY WORLD I HAD ENCOUNTERED. I SHALL TAKE HIM AT HIS WORD.
HEY... WAIT A MINUTE, DIANA. DO YOU HEAR SOME-THING?
A LOW GROWL, FROM SOME-WHERE IN THE UNDER BRUSH.
GET READY, MIKE.
CHEETAH!
GET DOWN, DIANA!
BLAM BLAM

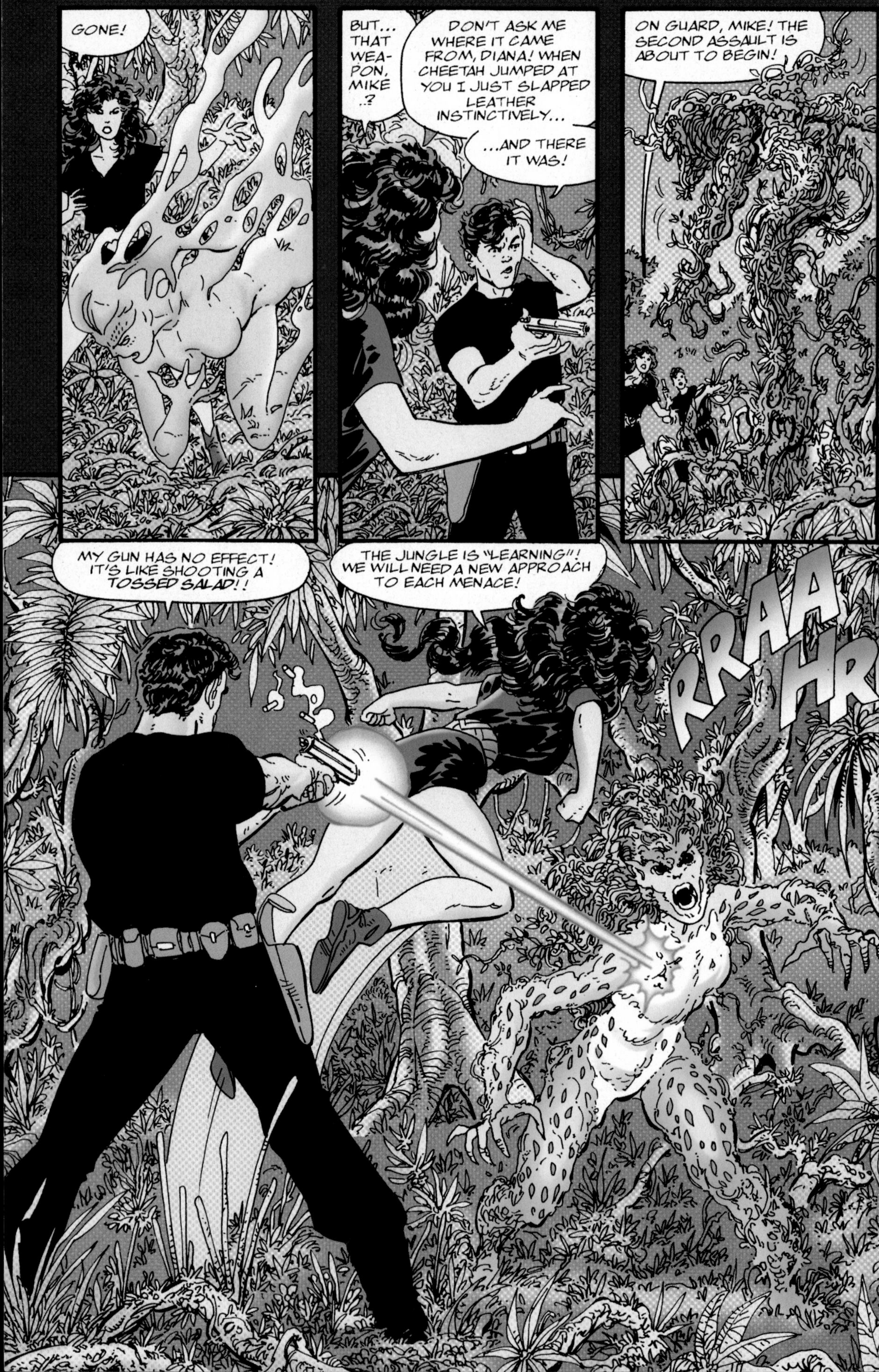
GONE!
BUT... THAT WEAPON, MIKE ..?
DON'T ASK ME WHERE IT CAME FROM, DIANA! WHEN CHEETAH JUMPED AT YOU I JUST SLAPPED LEATHER INSTINCTIVELY...
...AND THERE IT WAS!
ON GUARD, MIKE! THE SECOND ASSAULT IS ABOUT TO BEGIN!
MY GUN HAS NO EFFECT! IT'S LIKE SHOOTING A TOSSED SALAD!!
THE JUNGLE IS "LEARNING"! WE WILL NEED A NEW APPROACH TO EACH MENACE!
RRAA HR

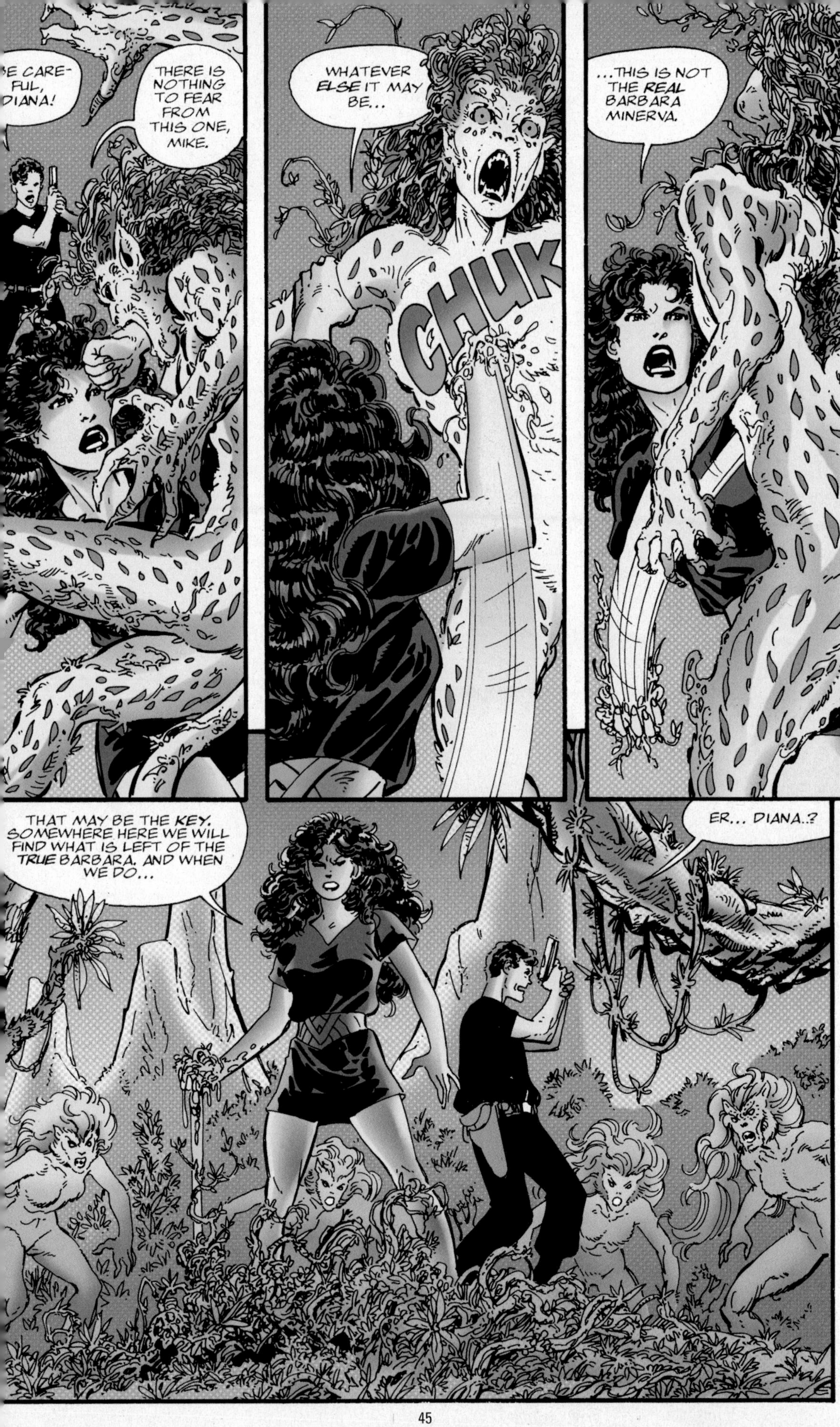

BE CARE-FUL, DIANA!
THERE IS NOTHING TO FEAR FROM THIS ONE, MIKE.
WHATEVER ELSE IT MAY BE...
CHUK
...THIS IS NOT THE REAL BARBARA MINERVA.
THAT MAY BE THE KEY. SOMEWHERE HERE WE WILL FIND WHAT IS LEFT OF THE TRUE BARBARA. AND WHEN WE DO...
ER... DIANA..?

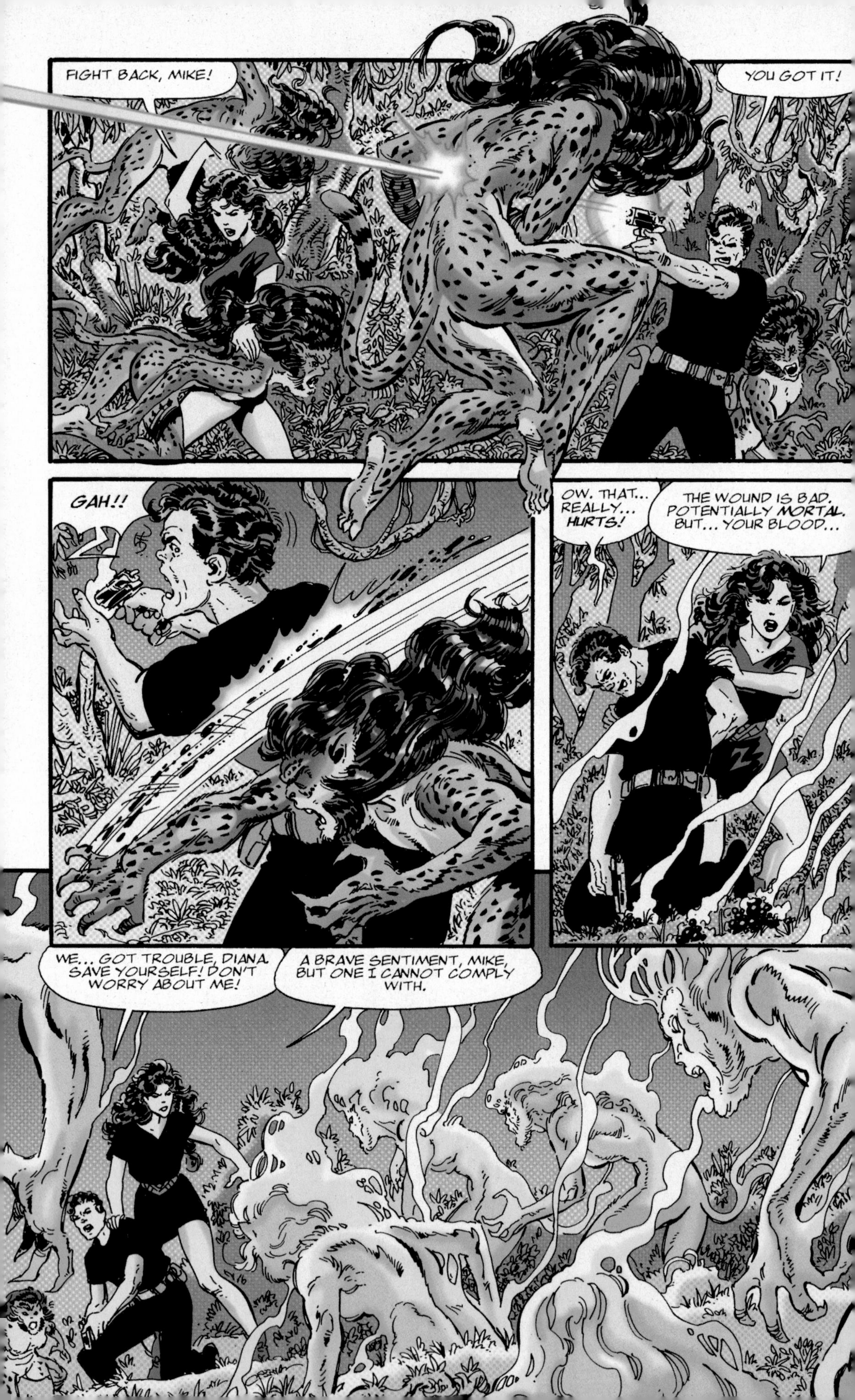
FIGHT BACK, MIKE!
YOU GOT IT!
GAH!!
OW. THAT... REALLY... HURTS!
THE WOUND IS BAD. POTENTIALLY MORTAL. BUT... YOUR BLOOD...
WE... GOT TROUBLE, DIANA. SAVE YOURSELF! DON'T WORRY ABOUT ME!
A BRAVE SENTIMENT, MIKE, BUT ONE I CANNOT COMPLY WITH.

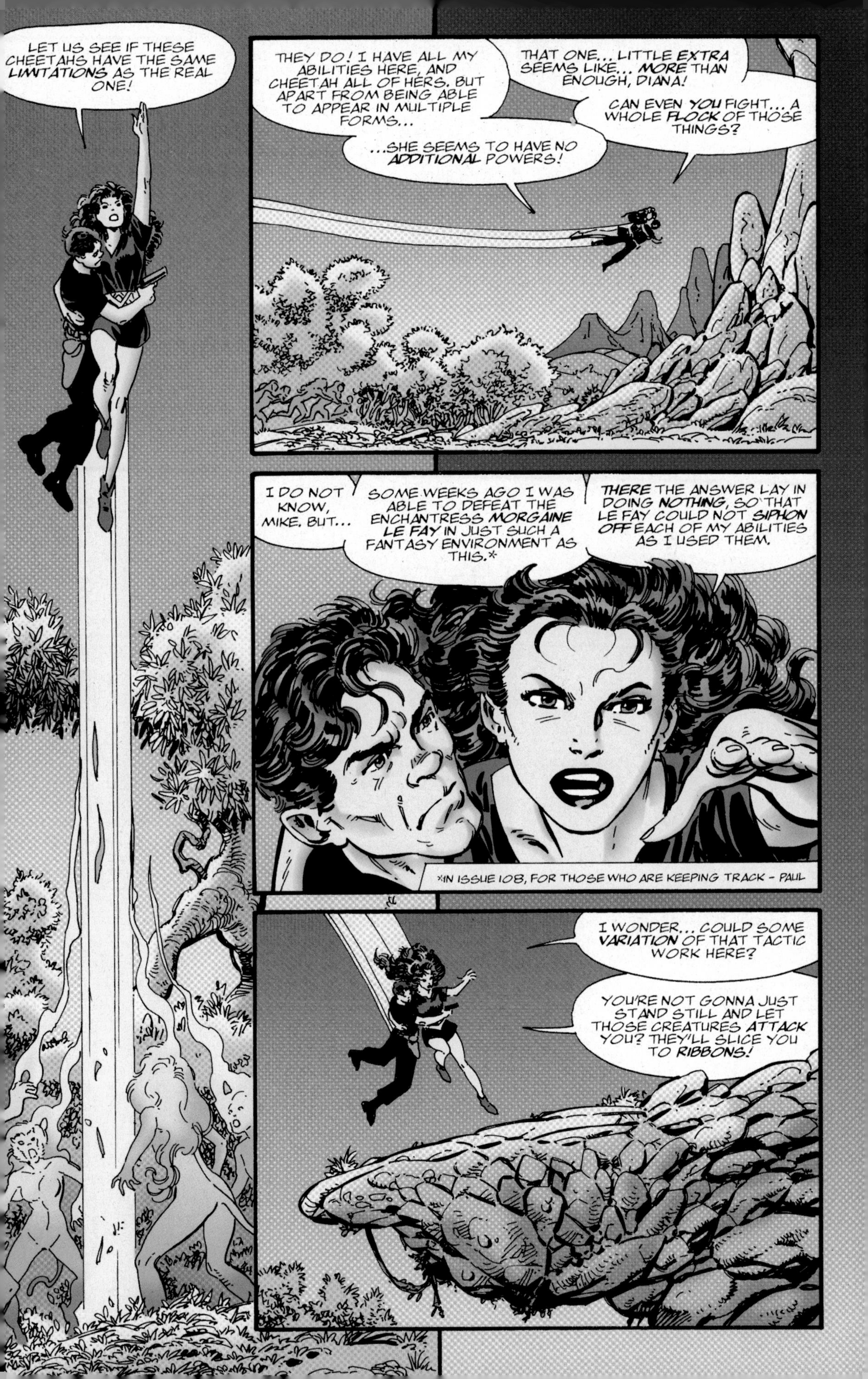
LET US SEE IF THESE CHEETAHS HAVE THE SAME LIMITATIONS AS THE REAL ONE!
THEY DO! I HAVE ALL MY ABILITIES HERE, AND CHEETAH ALL OF HERS. BUT APART FROM BEING ABLE TO APPEAR IN MULTIPLE FORMS...
...SHE SEEMS TO HAVE NO ADDITIONAL POWERS!
THAT ONE... LITTLE EXTRA SEEMS LIKE... MORE THAN ENOUGH, DIANA!
CAN EVEN YOU FIGHT... A WHOLE FLOCK OF THOSE THINGS?
I DO NOT KNOW, MIKE. BUT...
SOME WEEKS AGO I WAS ABLE TO DEFEAT THE ENCHANTRESS MORGAINE LE FAY IN JUST SUCH A FANTASY ENVIRONMENT AS THIS.*
THERE THE ANSWER LAY IN DOING NOTHING, SO THAT LE FAY COULD NOT SIPHON OFF EACH OF MY ABILITIES AS I USED THEM.
*IN ISSUE 108, FOR THOSE WHO ARE KEEPING TRACK - PAUL
I WONDER... COULD SOME VARIATION OF THAT TACTIC WORK HERE?
YOU'RE NOT GONNA JUST STAND STILL AND LET THOSE CREATURES ATTACK YOU? THEY'LL SLICE YOU TO RIBBONS!

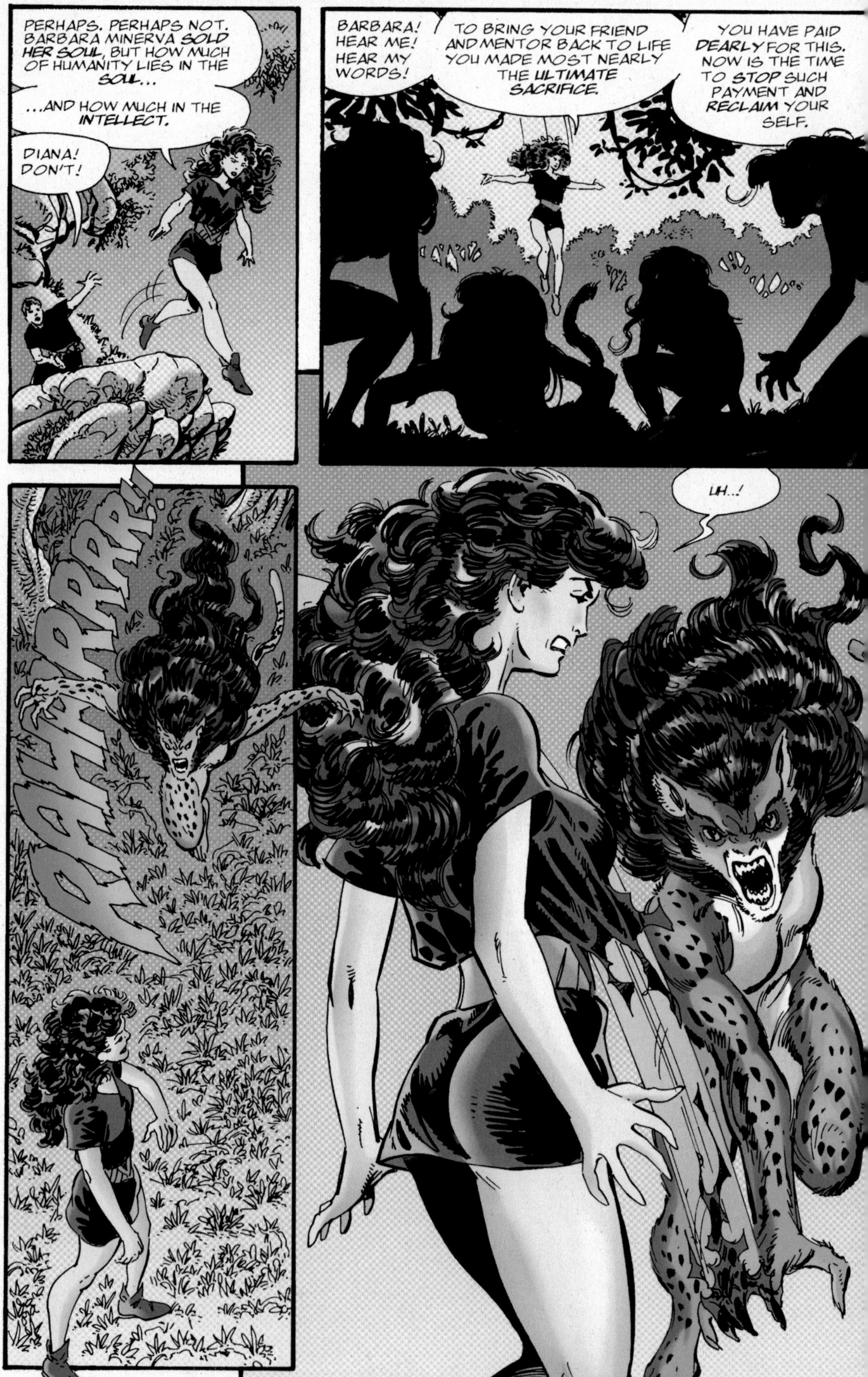
PERHAPS. PERHAPS NOT. BARBARA MINERVA SOLD HER SOUL, BUT HOW MUCH OF HUMANITY LIES IN THE SOUL...
...AND HOW MUCH IN THE INTELLECT.
DIANA! DON'T!
BARBARA! HEAR ME! HEAR MY WORDS!
TO BRING YOUR FRIEND AND MENTOR BACK TO LIFE YOU MADE MOST NEARLY THE ULTIMATE SACRIFICE.
YOU HAVE PAID DEARLY FOR THIS. NOW IS THE TIME TO STOP SUCH PAYMENT AND RECLAIM YOUR SELF.
RRAAHHRRR!
UH...!

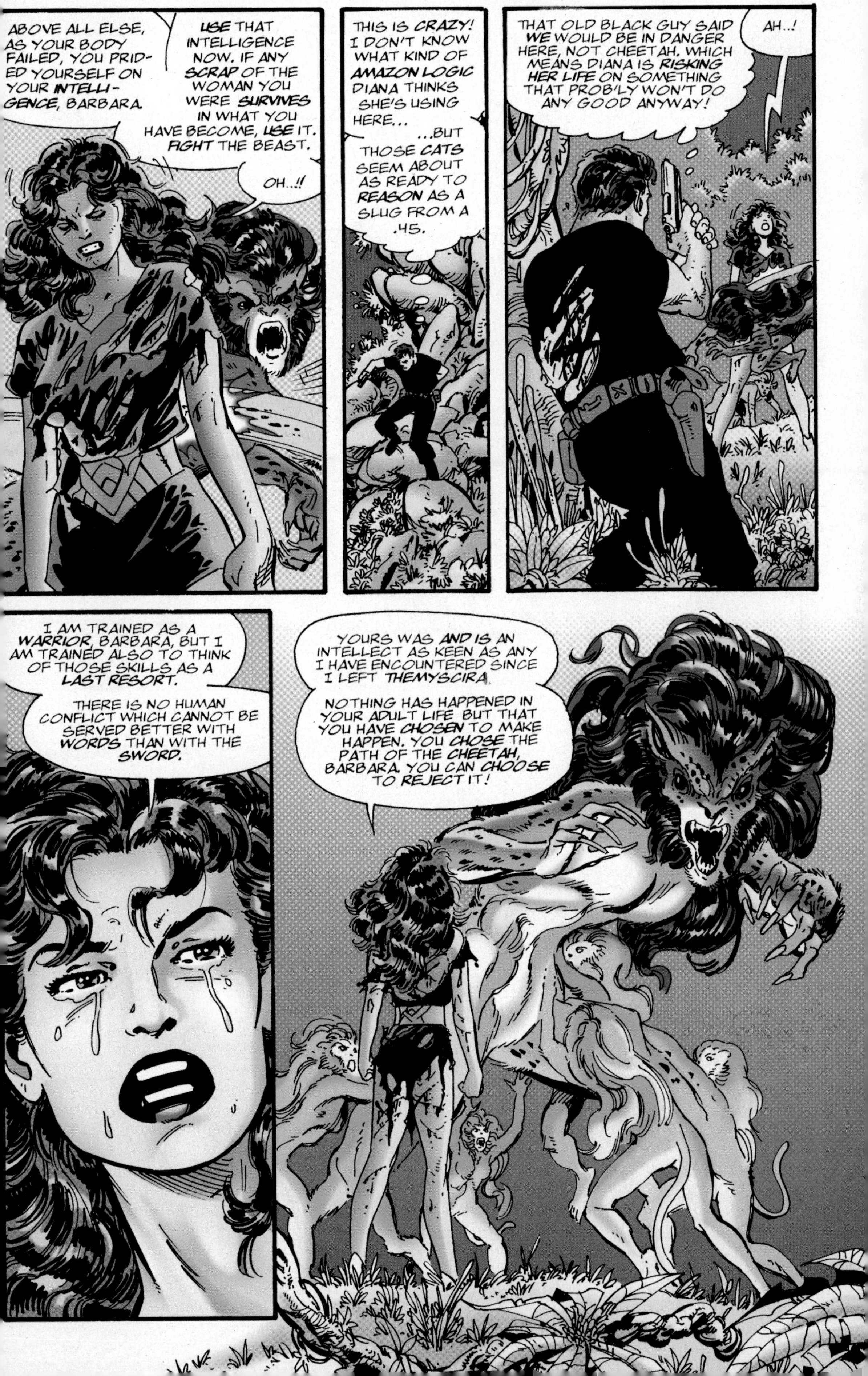
ABOVE ALL ELSE, AS YOUR BODY FAILED, YOU PRIDED YOURSELF ON YOUR INTELLIGENCE, BARBARA.
USE THAT INTELLIGENCE NOW. IF ANY SCRAP OF THE WOMAN YOU WERE SURVIVES IN WHAT YOU HAVE BECOME, USE IT. FIGHT THE BEAST.
OH...!!
THIS IS CRAZY! I DON'T KNOW WHAT KIND OF AMAZON LOGIC DIANA THINKS SHE'S USING HERE...
...BUT THOSE CATS SEEM ABOUT AS READY TO REASON AS A SLUG FROM A .45.
THAT OLD BLACK GUY SAID WE WOULD BE IN DANGER HERE, NOT CHEETAH. WHICH MEANS DIANA IS RISKING HER LIFE ON SOMETHING THAT PROB'LY WON'T DO ANY GOOD ANYWAY!
AH...!
I AM TRAINED AS A WARRIOR, BARBARA, BUT I AM TRAINED ALSO TO THINK OF THOSE SKILLS AS A LAST RESORT.
THERE IS NO HUMAN CONFLICT WHICH CANNOT BE SERVED BETTER WITH WORDS THAN WITH THE SWORD.
YOURS WAS AND IS AN INTELLECT AS KEEN AS ANY I HAVE ENCOUNTERED SINCE I LEFT THEMYSCIRA.
NOTHING HAS HAPPENED IN YOUR ADULT LIFE BUT THAT YOU HAVE CHOSEN TO MAKE HAPPEN. YOU CHOSE THE PATH OF THE CHEETAH, BARBARA. YOU CAN CHOOSE TO REJECT IT!

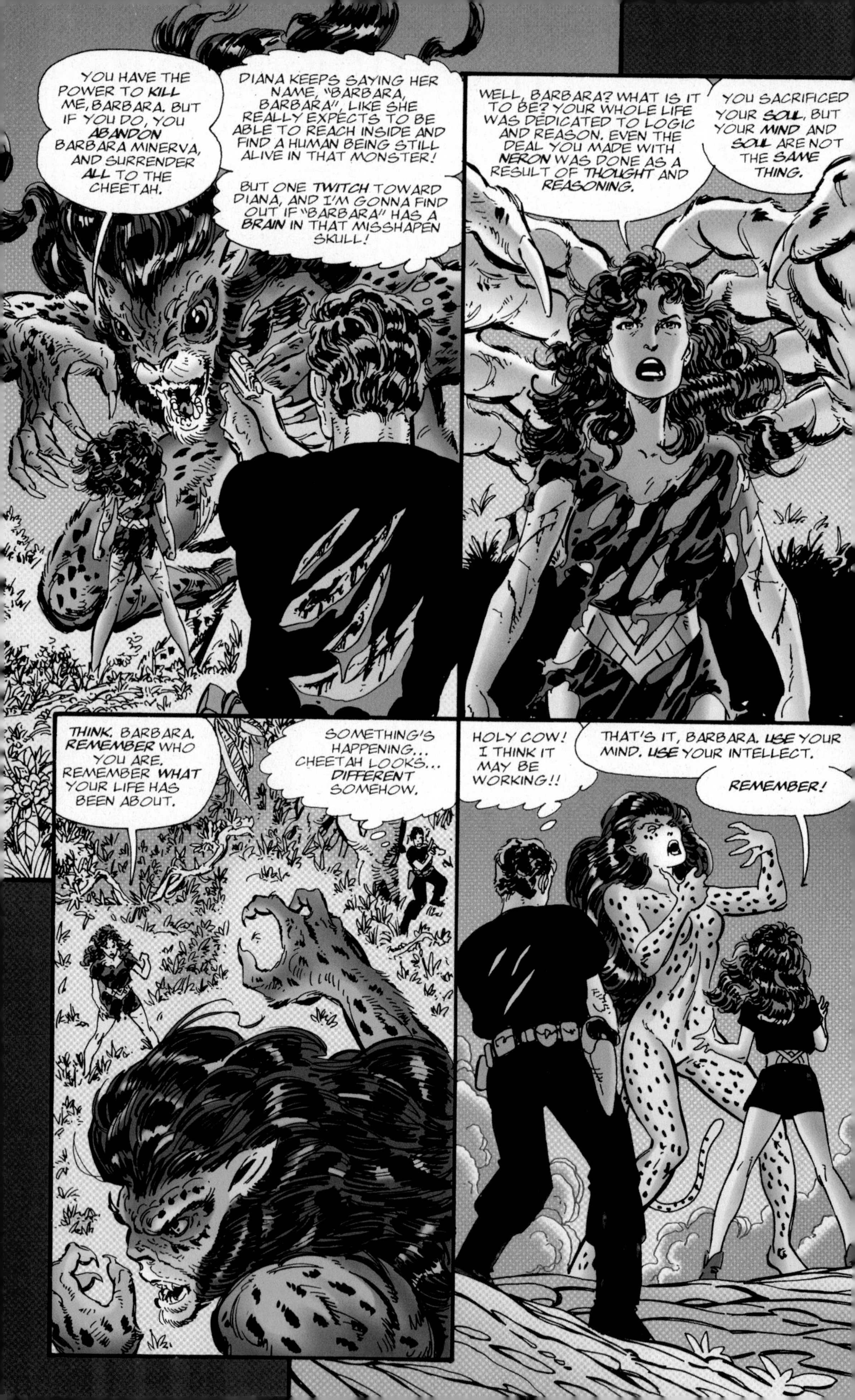
YOU HAVE THE POWER TO KILL ME, BARBARA. BUT IF YOU DO, YOU ABANDON BARBARA MINERVA, AND SURRENDER ALL TO THE CHEETAH.
DIANA KEEPS SAYING HER NAME, "BARBARA, BARBARA", LIKE SHE REALLY EXPECTS TO BE ABLE TO REACH INSIDE AND FIND A HUMAN BEING STILL ALIVE IN THAT MONSTER!
BUT ONE TWITCH TOWARD DIANA, AND I'M GONNA FIND OUT IF "BARBARA" HAS A BRAIN IN THAT MISSHAPEN SKULL!
WELL, BARBARA? WHAT IS IT TO BE? YOUR WHOLE LIFE WAS DEDICATED TO LOGIC AND REASON. EVEN THE DEAL YOU MADE WITH NERON WAS DONE AS A RESULT OF THOUGHT AND REASONING.
YOU SACRIFICED YOUR SOUL, BUT YOUR MIND AND SOUL ARE NOT THE SAME THING.
THINK, BARBARA. REMEMBER WHO YOU ARE. REMEMBER WHAT YOUR LIFE HAS BEEN ABOUT.
SOMETHING'S HAPPENING... CHEETAH LOOKS... DIFFERENT SOMEHOW.
HOLY COW! I THINK IT MAY BE WORKING!!
THAT'S IT, BARBARA. USE YOUR MIND. USE YOUR INTELLECT.
REMEMBER!

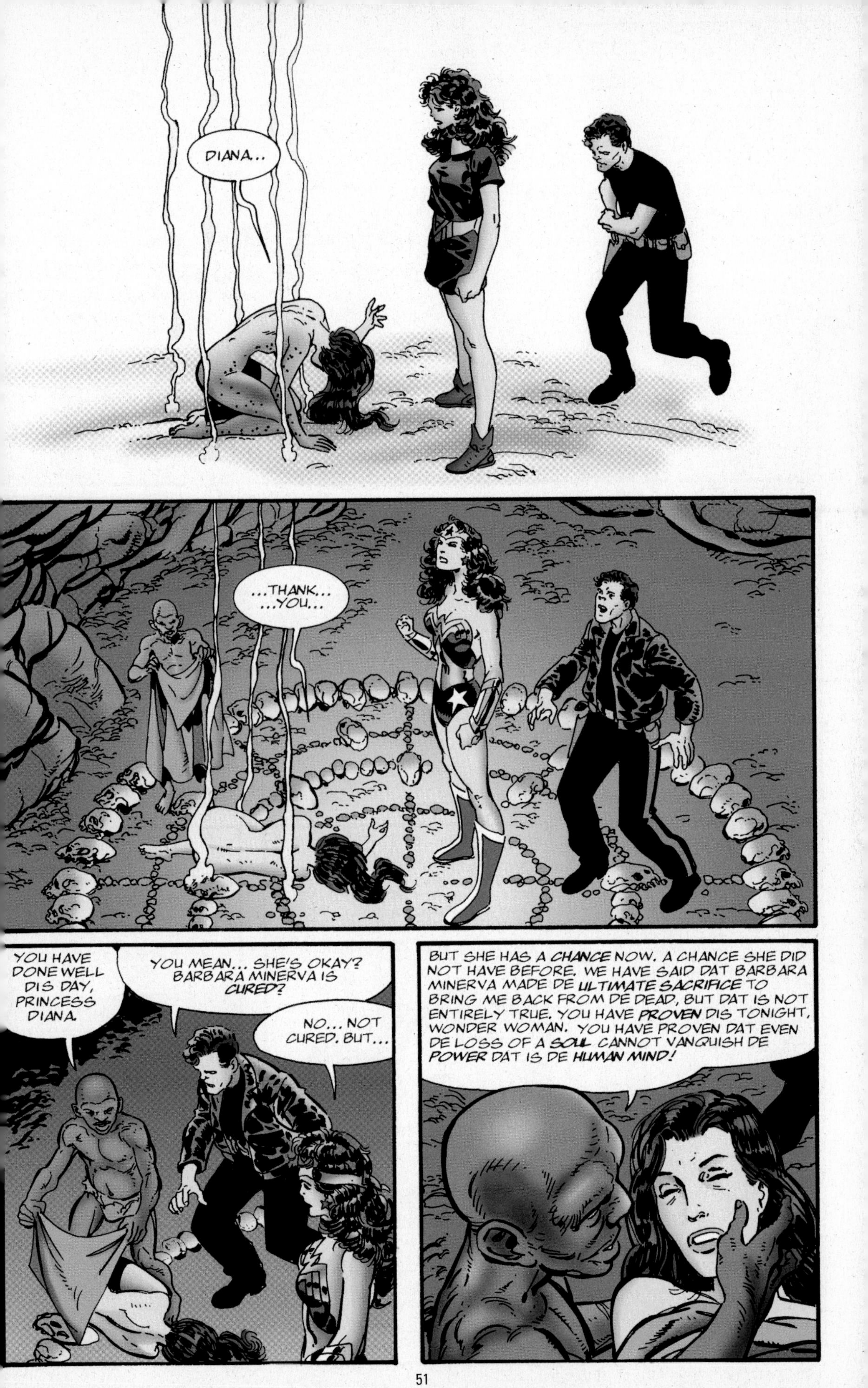
DIANA...
...THANK...
...YOU...
YOU HAVE DONE WELL DIS DAY, PRINCESS DIANA.
YOU MEAN... SHE'S OKAY? BARBARA MINERVA IS CURED?
NO... NOT CURED. BUT...
BUT SHE HAS A CHANCE NOW. A CHANCE SHE DID NOT HAVE BEFORE. WE HAVE SAID DAT BARBARA MINERVA MADE DE ULTIMATE SACRIFICE TO BRING ME BACK FROM DE DEAD, BUT DAT IS NOT ENTIRELY TRUE. YOU HAVE PROVEN DIS TONIGHT, WONDER WOMAN. YOU HAVE PROVEN DAT EVEN DE LOSS OF A SOUL CANNOT VANQUISH DE POWER DAT IS DE HUMAN MIND!

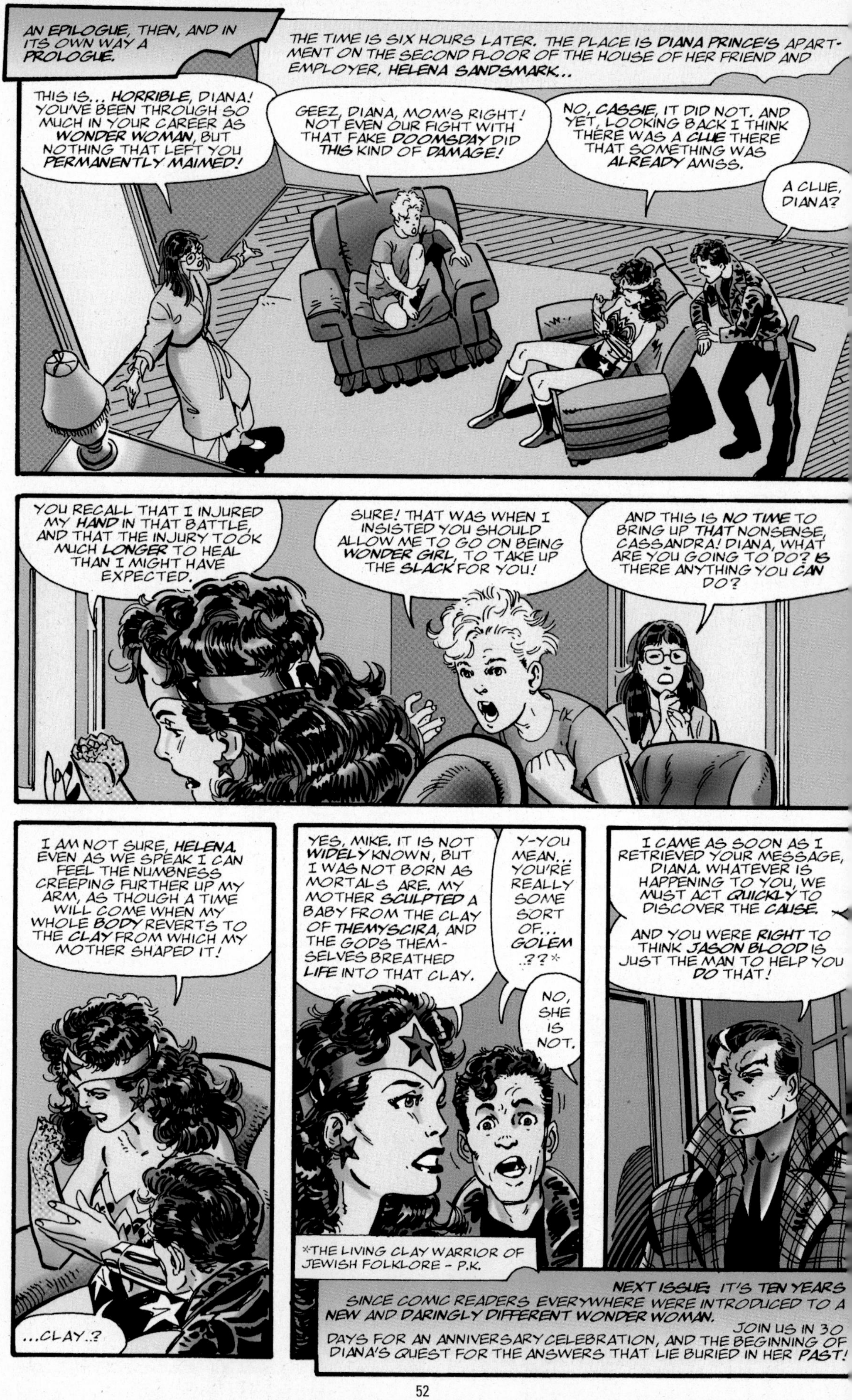
AN EPILOGUE, THEN, AND IN ITS OWN WAY A PROLOGUE.
THE TIME IS SIX HOURS LATER. THE PLACE IS DIANA PRINCE'S APARTMENT ON THE SECOND FLOOR OF THE HOUSE OF HER FRIEND AND EMPLOYER, HELENA SANDSMARK...
THIS IS... HORRIBLE, DIANA! YOU'VE BEEN THROUGH SO MUCH IN YOUR CAREER AS WONDER WOMAN, BUT NOTHING THAT LEFT YOU PERMANENTLY MAIMED!
GEEZ, DIANA, MOM'S RIGHT! NOT EVEN OUR FIGHT WITH THAT FAKE DOOMSDAY DID THIS KIND OF DAMAGE!
NO, CASSIE, IT DID NOT. AND YET, LOOKING BACK I THINK THERE WAS A CLUE THERE THAT SOMETHING WAS ALREADY AMISS.
A CLUE, DIANA?
YOU RECALL THAT I INJURED MY HAND IN THAT BATTLE, AND THAT THE INJURY TOOK MUCH LONGER TO HEAL THAN I MIGHT HAVE EXPECTED.
SURE! THAT WAS WHEN I INSISTED YOU SHOULD ALLOW ME TO GO ON BEING WONDER GIRL, TO TAKE UP THE SLACK FOR YOU!
AND THIS IS NO TIME TO BRING UP THAT NONSENSE, CASSANDRA! DIANA, WHAT ARE YOU GOING TO DO? IS THERE ANYTHING YOU CAN DO?
I AM NOT SURE, HELENA. EVEN AS WE SPEAK I CAN FEEL THE NUMBNESS CREEPING FURTHER UP MY ARM, AS THOUGH A TIME WILL COME WHEN MY WHOLE BODY REVERTS TO THE CLAY FROM WHICH MY MOTHER SHAPED IT!
...CLAY..?
YES, MIKE. IT IS NOT WIDELY KNOWN, BUT I WAS NOT BORN AS MORTALS ARE. MY MOTHER SCULPTED A BABY FROM THE CLAY OF THEMYSCIRA, AND THE GODS THEMSELVES BREATHED LIFE INTO THAT CLAY.
Y-YOU MEAN... YOU'RE REALLY SOME SORT OF... GOLEM ..??*
NO, SHE IS NOT.
*THE LIVING CLAY WARRIOR OF JEWISH FOLKLORE - P.K.
I CAME AS SOON AS I RETRIEVED YOUR MESSAGE, DIANA. WHATEVER IS HAPPENING TO YOU, WE MUST ACT QUICKLY TO DISCOVER THE CAUSE.
AND YOU WERE RIGHT TO THINK JASON BLOOD IS JUST THE MAN TO HELP YOU DO THAT!
NEXT ISSUE: IT'S TEN YEARS SINCE COMIC READERS EVERYWHERE WERE INTRODUCED TO A NEW AND DARINGLY DIFFERENT WONDER WOMAN.
JOIN US IN 30 DAYS FOR AN ANNIVERSARY CELEBRATION, AND THE BEGINNING OF DIANA'S QUEST FOR THE ANSWERS THAT LIE BURIED IN HER PAST!

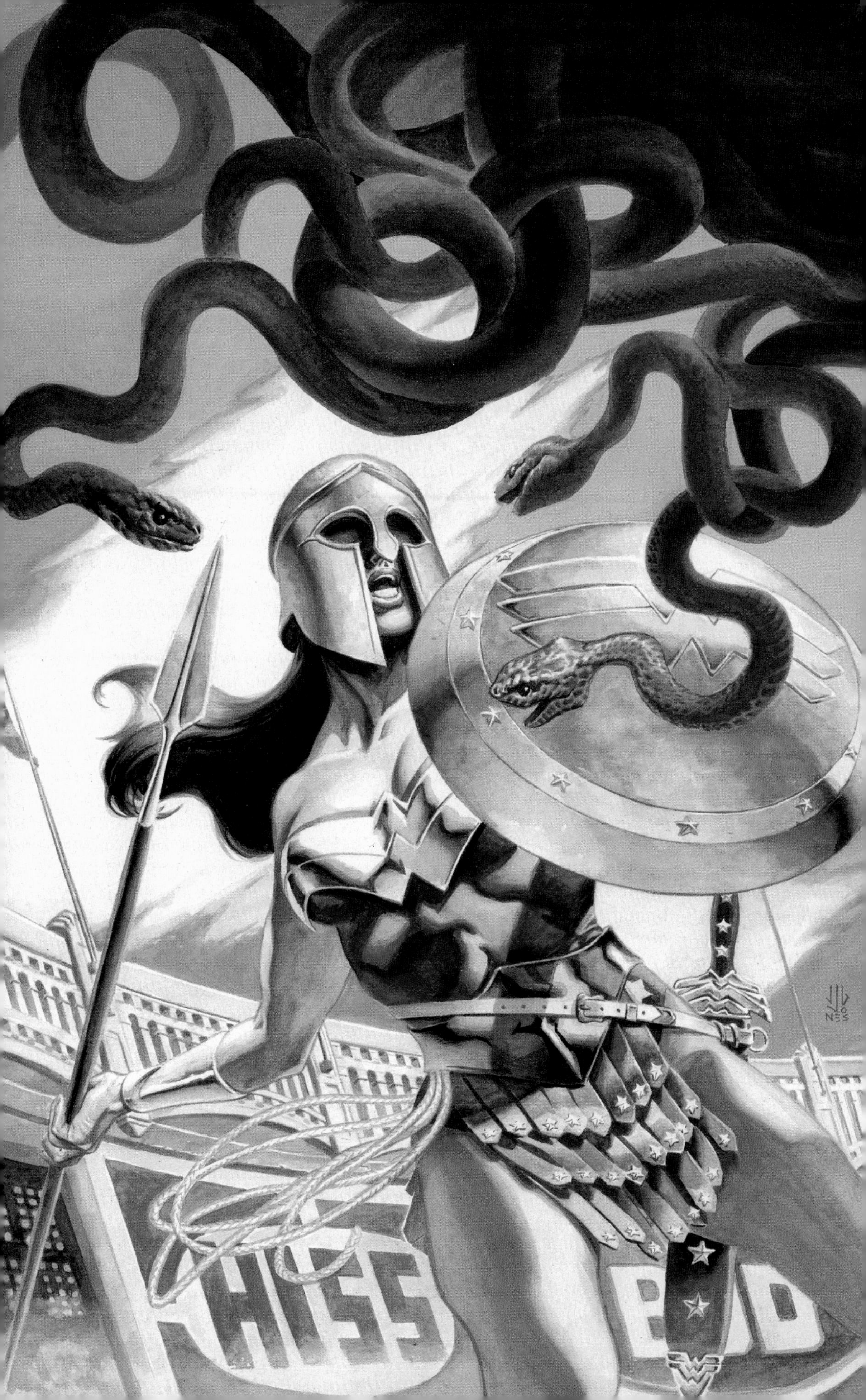
HISS

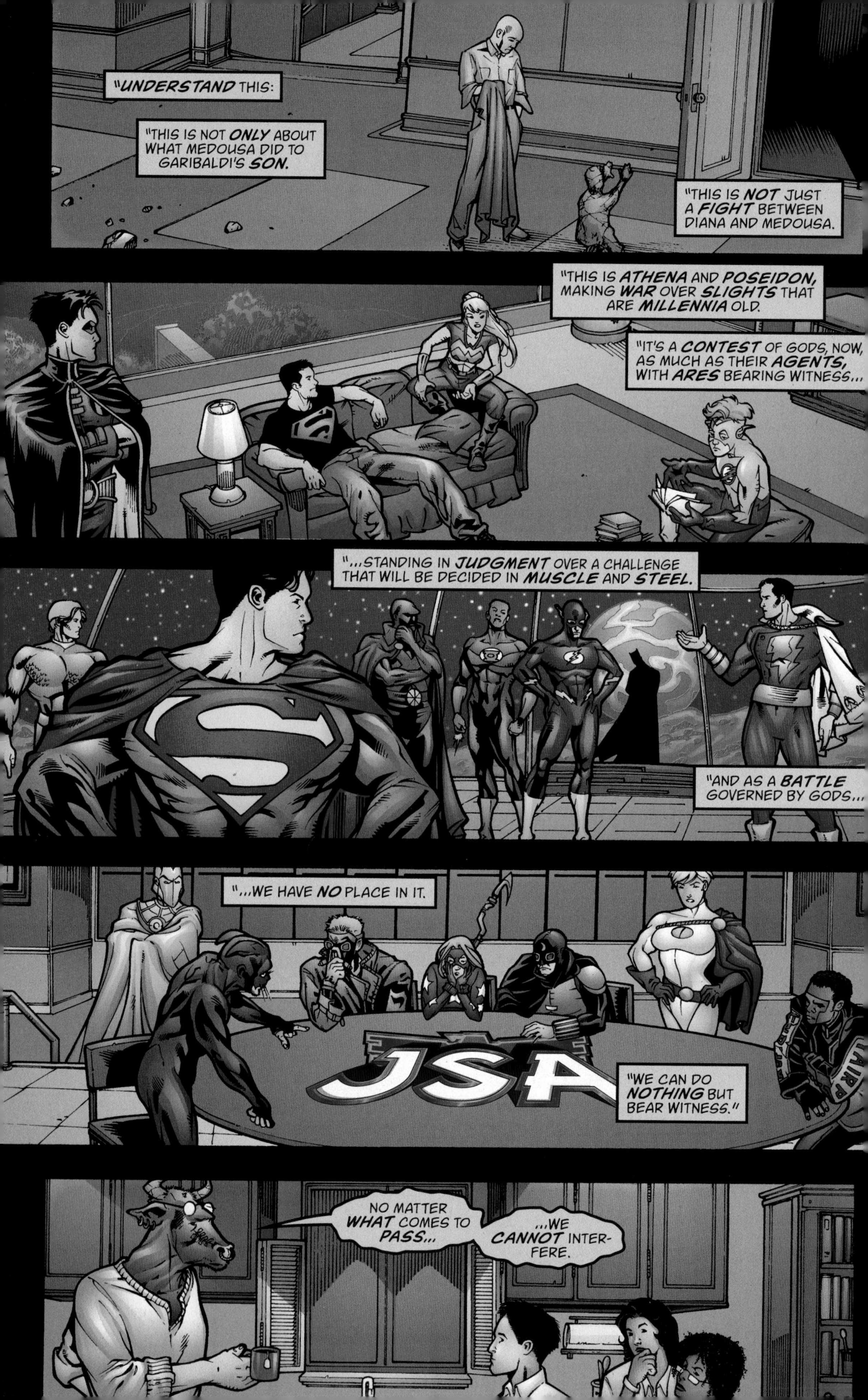
"UNDERSTAND THIS:
"THIS IS NOT ONLY ABOUT WHAT MEDOUSA DID TO GARIBALDI'S SON.
"THIS IS NOT JUST A FIGHT BETWEEN DIANA AND MEDOUSA.
"THIS IS ATHENA AND POSEIDON, MAKING WAR OVER SLIGHTS THAT ARE MILLENNIA OLD.
"IT'S A CONTEST OF GODS, NOW, AS MUCH AS THEIR AGENTS, WITH ARES BEARING WITNESS...
"...STANDING IN JUDGMENT OVER A CHALLENGE THAT WILL BE DECIDED IN MUSCLE AND STEEL.
"AND AS A BATTLE GOVERNED BY GODS...
"...WE HAVE NO PLACE IN IT.
JSA
"WE CAN DO NOTHING BUT BEAR WITNESS."
NO MATTER WHAT COMES TO PASS...
...WE CANNOT INTERFERE.

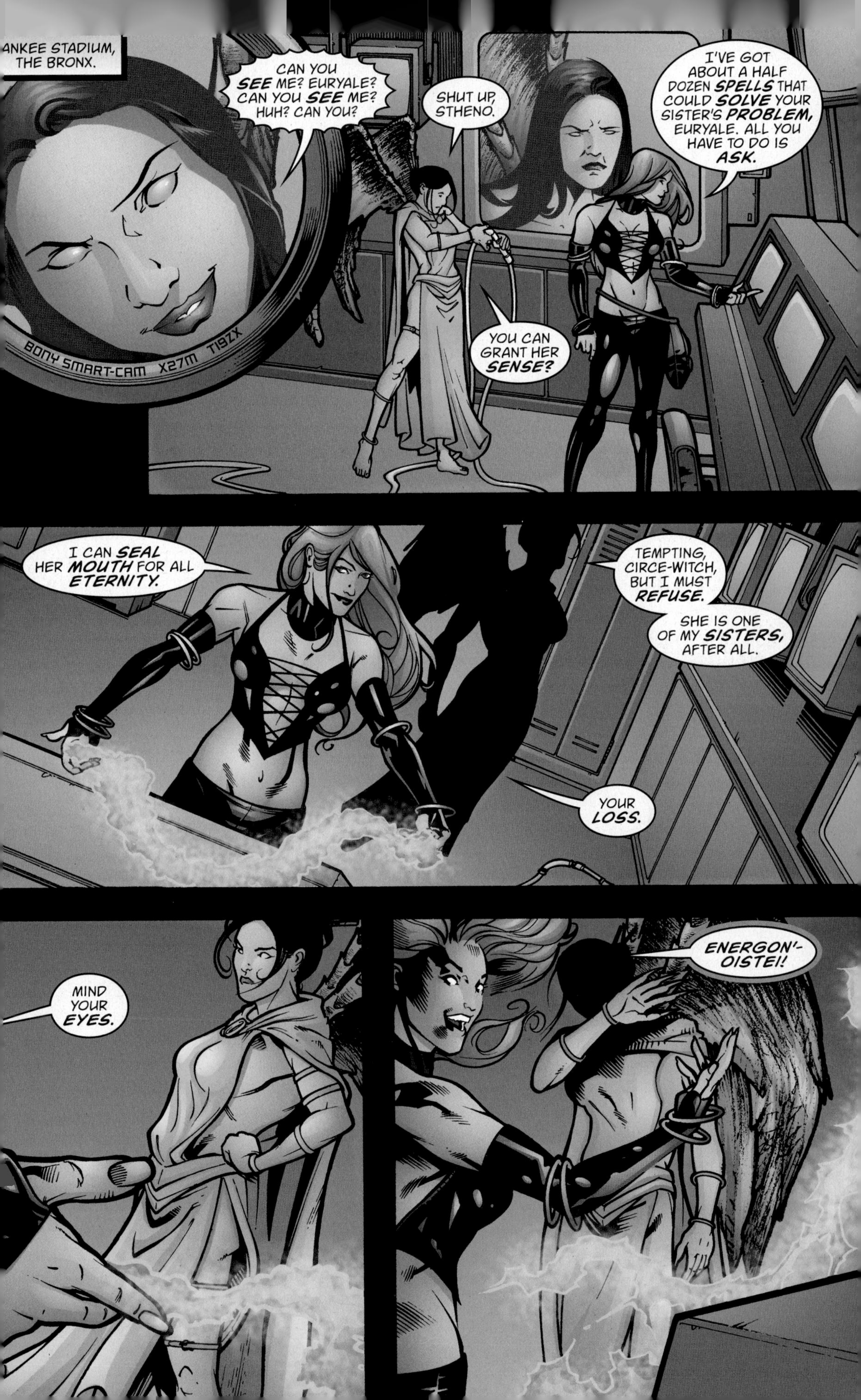
ANKEE STADIUM, THE BRONX.
CAN YOU SEE ME? EURYALE? CAN YOU SEE ME? HUH? CAN YOU?
SHUT UP, STHENO.
I'VE GOT ABOUT A HALF DOZEN SPELLS THAT COULD SOLVE YOUR SISTER'S PROBLEM, EURYALE. ALL YOU HAVE TO DO IS ASK.
BONY SMART-CAM X27M T19ZX
YOU CAN GRANT HER SENSE?
I CAN SEAL HER MOUTH FOR ALL ETERNITY.
TEMPTING, CIRCE-WITCH, BUT I MUST REFUSE.
SHE IS ONE OF MY SISTERS, AFTER ALL.
YOUR LOSS.
MIND YOUR EYES.
ENERGON'-OISTEI!

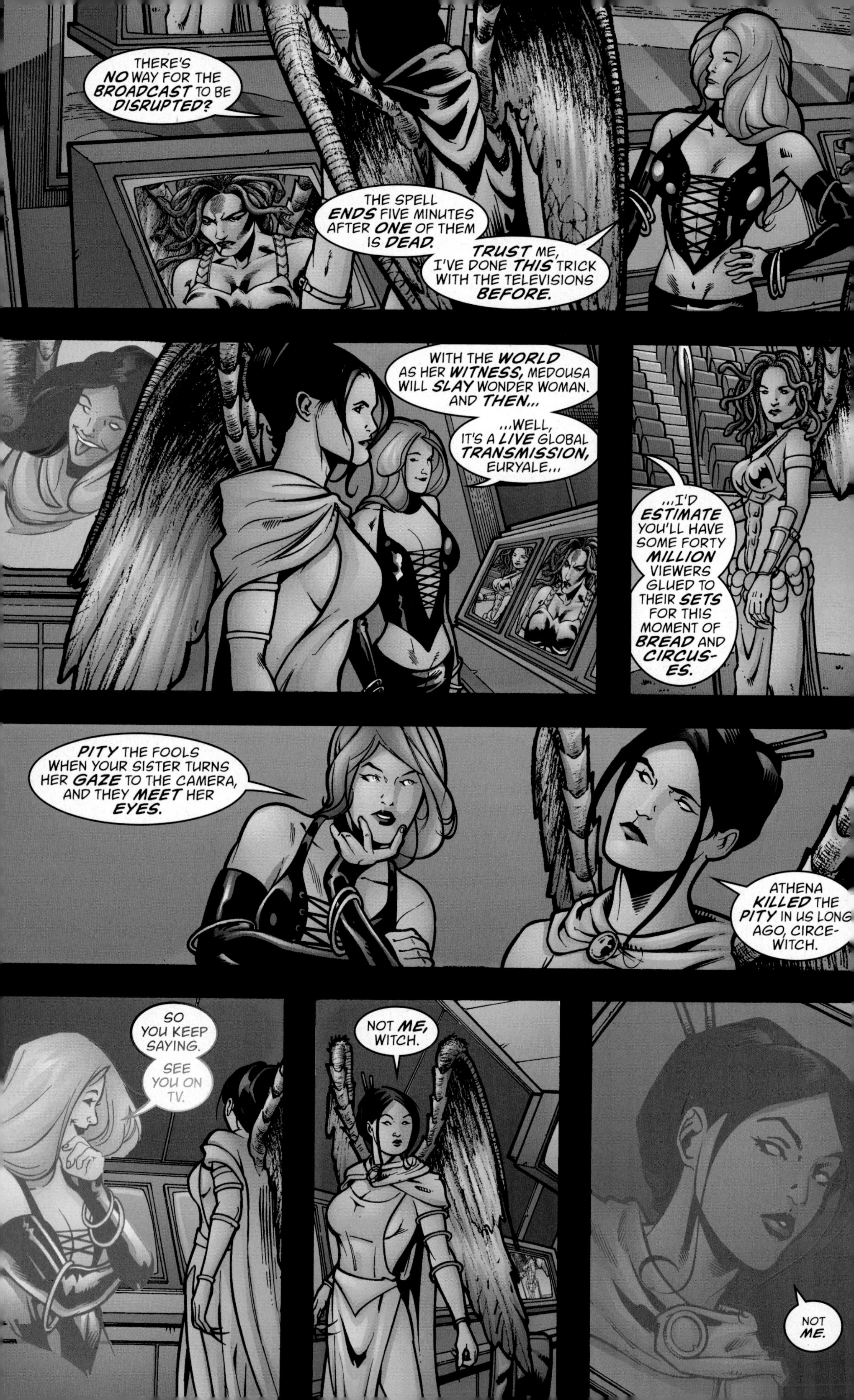

THERE'S NO WAY FOR THE BROADCAST TO BE DISRUPTED?
THE SPELL ENDS FIVE MINUTES AFTER ONE OF THEM IS DEAD.
TRUST ME, I'VE DONE THIS TRICK WITH THE TELEVISIONS BEFORE.
WITH THE WORLD AS HER WITNESS, MEDOUSA WILL SLAY WONDER WOMAN. AND THEN...
...WELL, IT'S A LIVE GLOBAL TRANSMISSION, EURYALE...
...I'D ESTIMATE YOU'LL HAVE SOME FORTY MILLION VIEWERS GLUED TO THEIR SETS FOR THIS MOMENT OF BREAD AND CIRCUS-ES.
PITY THE FOOLS WHEN YOUR SISTER TURNS HER GAZE TO THE CAMERA, AND THEY MEET HER EYES.
ATHENA KILLED THE PITY IN US LONG AGO, CIRCE-WITCH.
SO YOU KEEP SAYING.
SEE YOU ON TV.
NOT ME, WITCH.
NOT ME.

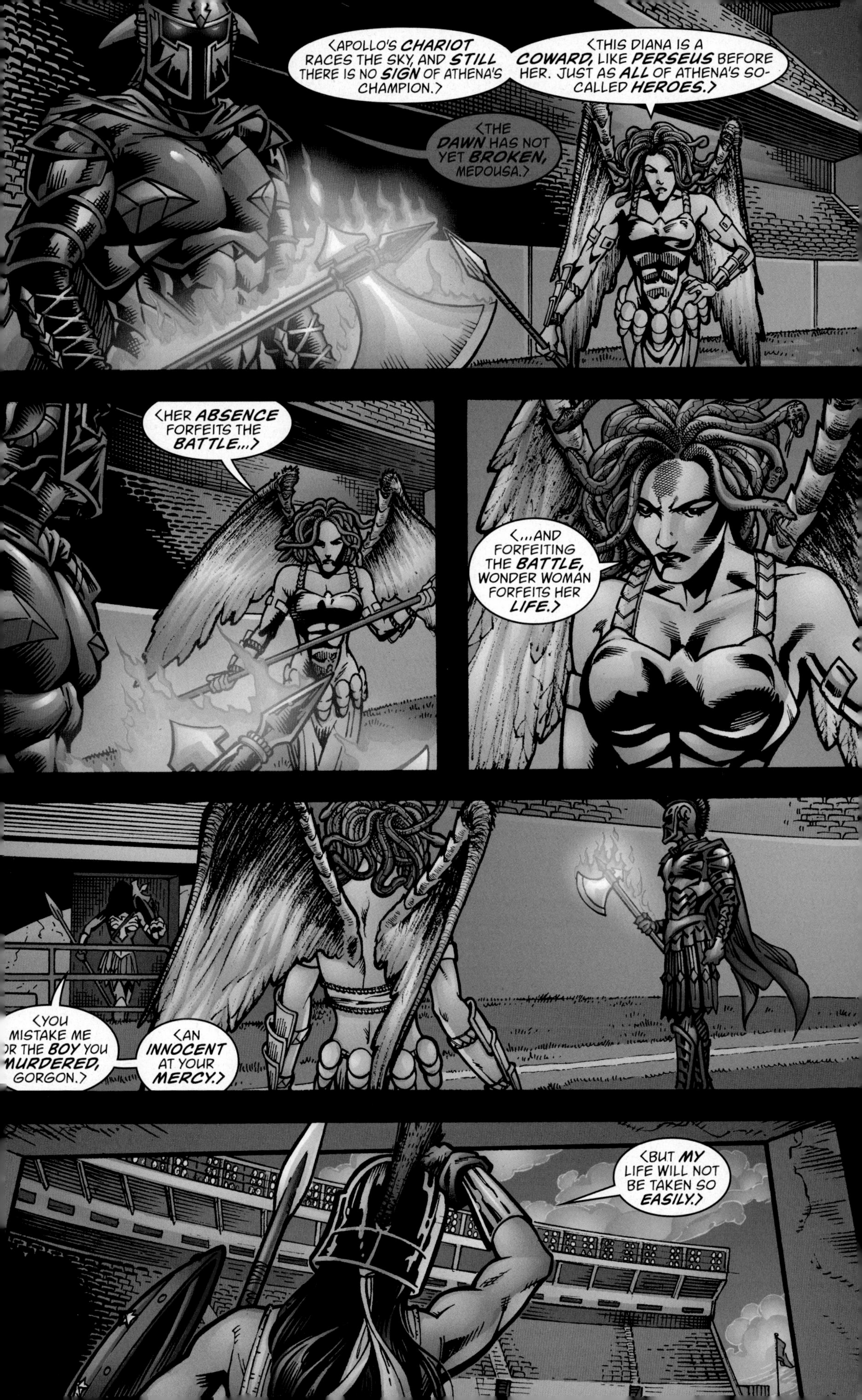

<APOLLO'S CHARIOT RACES THE SKY, AND STILL THERE IS NO SIGN OF ATHENA'S CHAMPION.>
<THIS DIANA IS A COWARD, LIKE PERSEUS BEFORE HER. JUST AS ALL OF ATHENA'S SO-CALLED HEROES.>
<THE DAWN HAS NOT YET BROKEN, MEDOUSA.>
<HER ABSENCE FORFEITS THE BATTLE...>
<...AND FORFEITING THE BATTLE, WONDER WOMAN FORFEITS HER LIFE.>
<YOU MISTAKE ME OR THE BOY YOU MURDERED, GORGON.>
<AN INNOCENT AT YOUR MERCY.>
<BUT MY LIFE WILL NOT BE TAKEN SO EASILY.>

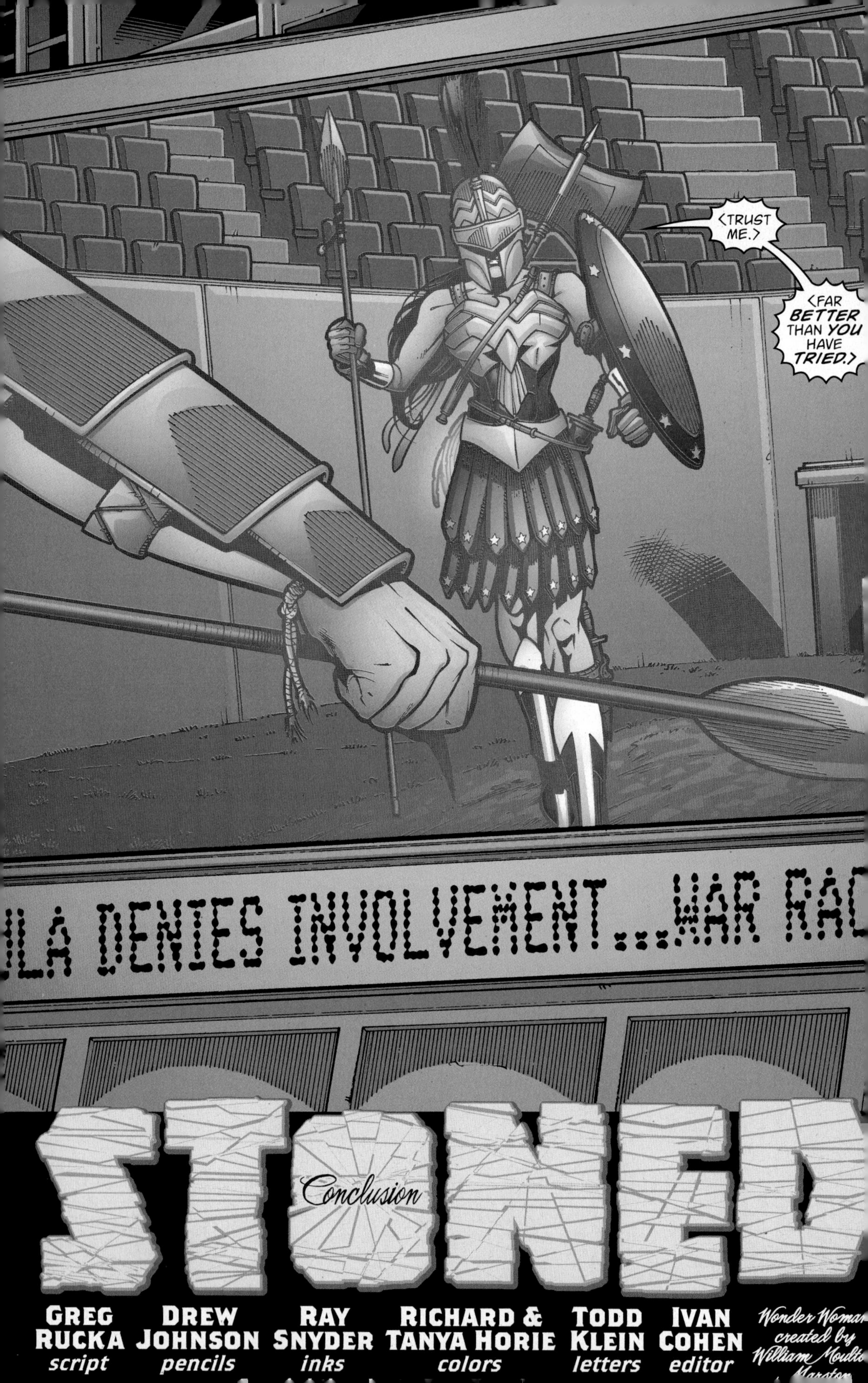
<TRUST ME.>
<FAR BETTER THAN YOU HAVE TRIED.>
DENIES INVOLVEMENT...
STONED
Conclusion
GREG RUCKA script
DREW JOHNSON pencils
RAY SNYDER inks
RICHARD & TANYA HORIE colors
TODD KLEIN letters
IVAN COHEN editor
created by

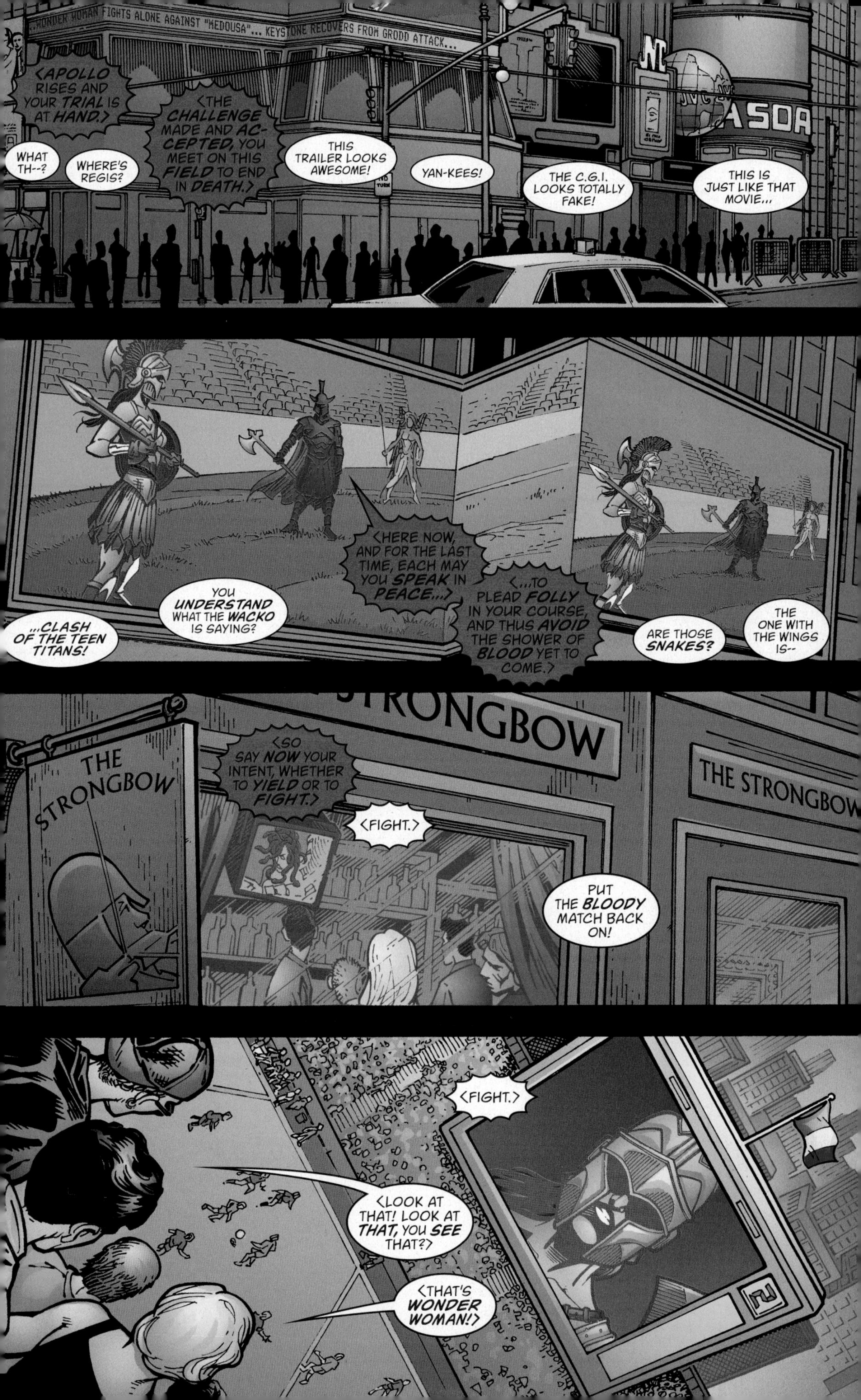
...WONDER WOMAN FIGHTS ALONE AGAINST "MEDOUSA"... KEYSTONE RECOVERS FROM GRODD ATTACK...
<APOLLO RISES AND YOUR TRIAL IS AT HAND.>
WHAT TH--?
WHERE'S REGIS?
<THE CHALLENGE MADE AND ACCEPTED, YOU MEET ON THIS FIELD TO END IN DEATH.>
THIS TRAILER LOOKS AWESOME!
YAN-KEES!
THE C.G.I. LOOKS TOTALLY FAKE!
THIS IS JUST LIKE THAT MOVIE...
ASOA
<HERE NOW, AND FOR THE LAST TIME, EACH MAY YOU SPEAK IN PEACE...>
...CLASH OF THE TEEN TITANS!
YOU UNDERSTAND WHAT THE WACKO IS SAYING?
<...TO PLEAD FOLLY IN YOUR COURSE, AND THUS AVOID THE SHOWER OF BLOOD YET TO COME.>
ARE THOSE SNAKES?
THE ONE WITH THE WINGS IS--
STRONGBOW
THE STRONGBOW
<SO SAY NOW YOUR INTENT, WHETHER TO YIELD OR TO FIGHT.>
THE STRONGBOW
<FIGHT.>
PUT THE BLOODY MATCH BACK ON!
<FIGHT.>
<LOOK AT THAT! LOOK AT THAT, YOU SEE THAT?>
<THAT'S WONDER WOMAN!>

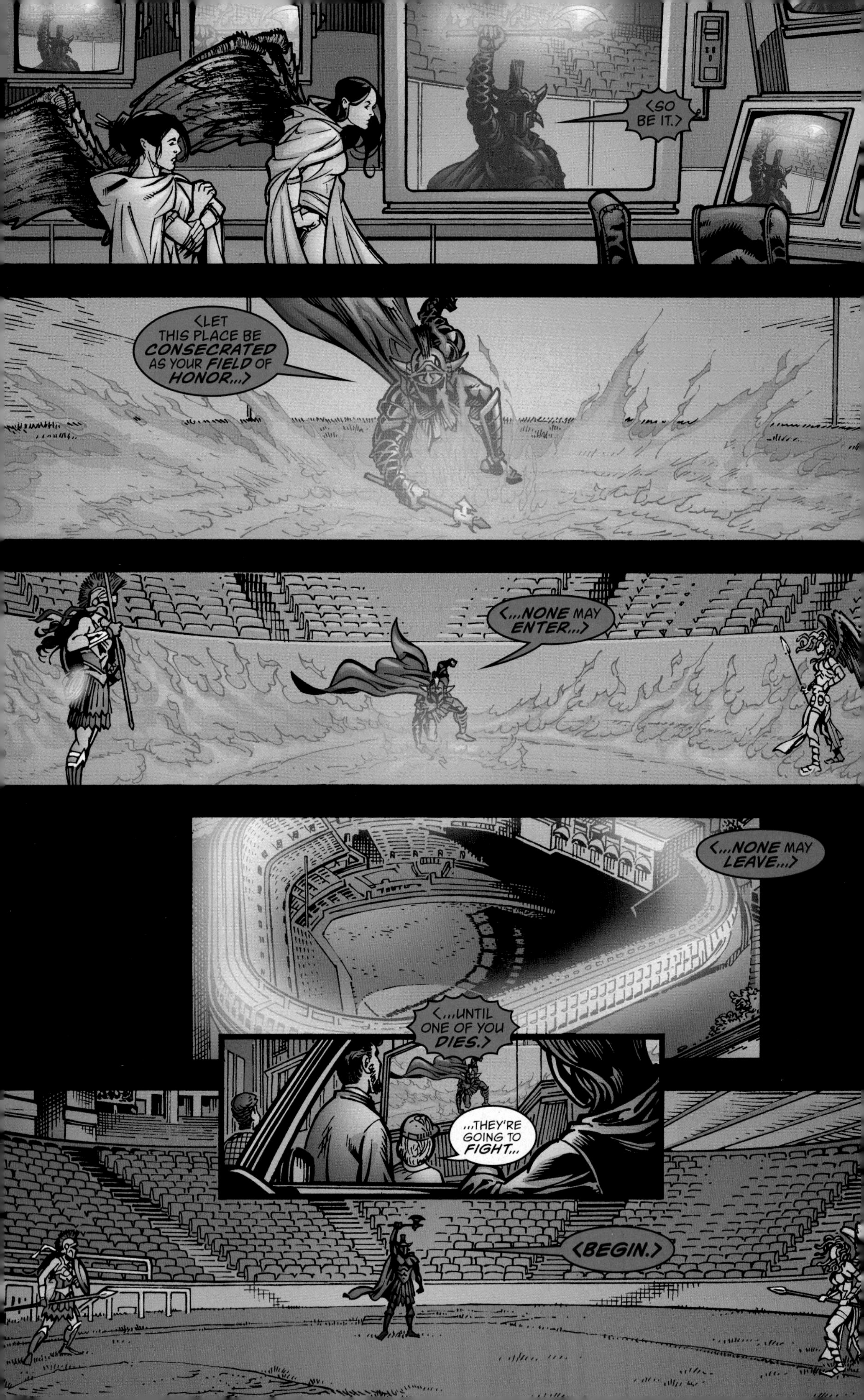
<SO BE IT.>
<LET THIS PLACE BE CONSECRATED AS YOUR FIELD OF HONOR...>
<...NONE MAY ENTER...>
<...NONE MAY LEAVE...>
<...UNTIL ONE OF YOU DIES.>
...THEY'RE GOING TO FIGHT...
<BEGIN.>

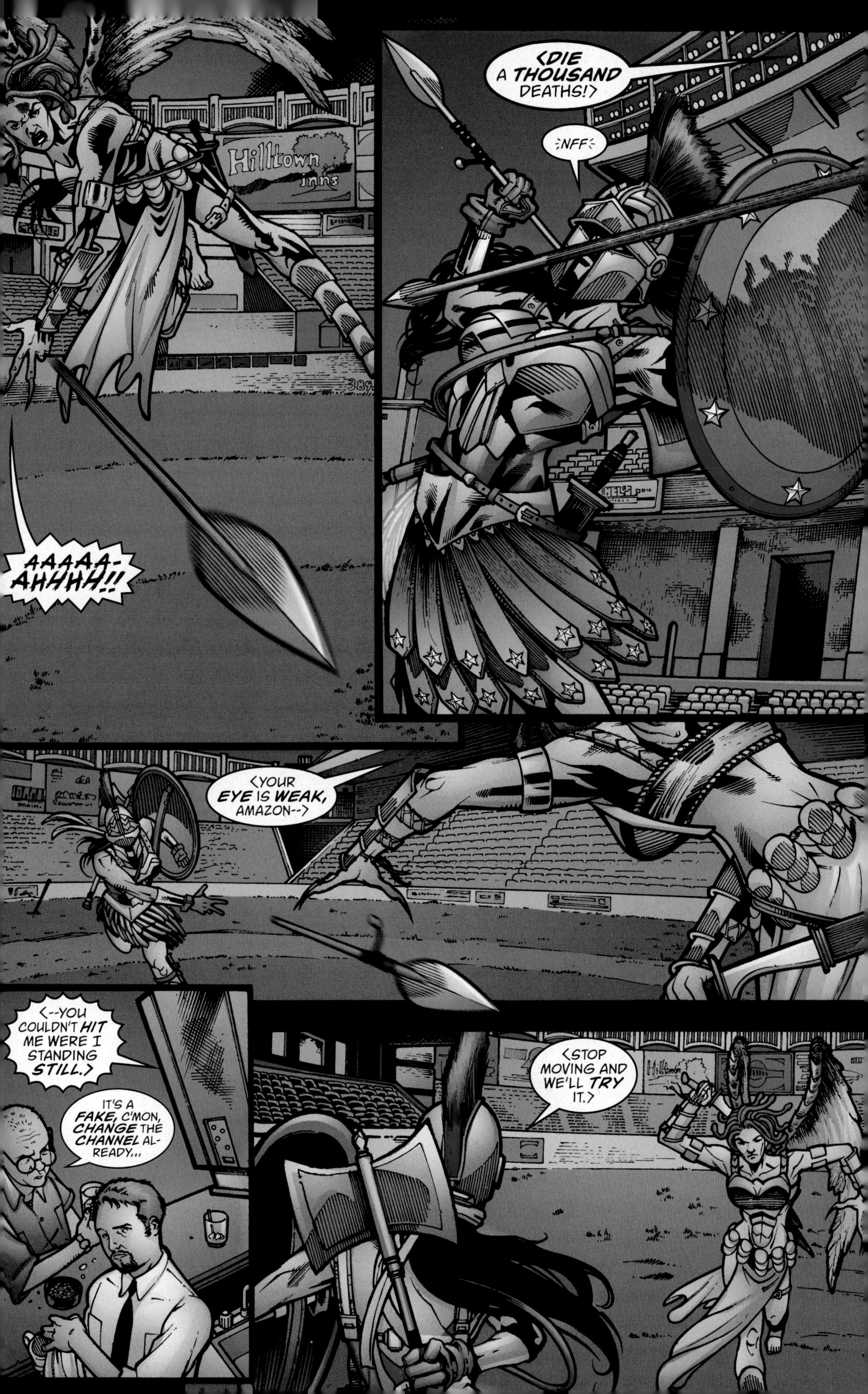
Hilltown inns
AAAAA-AHHHH!!
<DIE A THOUSAND DEATHS!>
NFF
<YOUR EYE IS WEAK, AMAZON-->
<--YOU COULDN'T HIT ME WERE I STANDING STILL.>
IT'S A FAKE, C'MON, CHANGE THE CHANNEL ALREADY...
<STOP MOVING AND WE'LL TRY IT.>

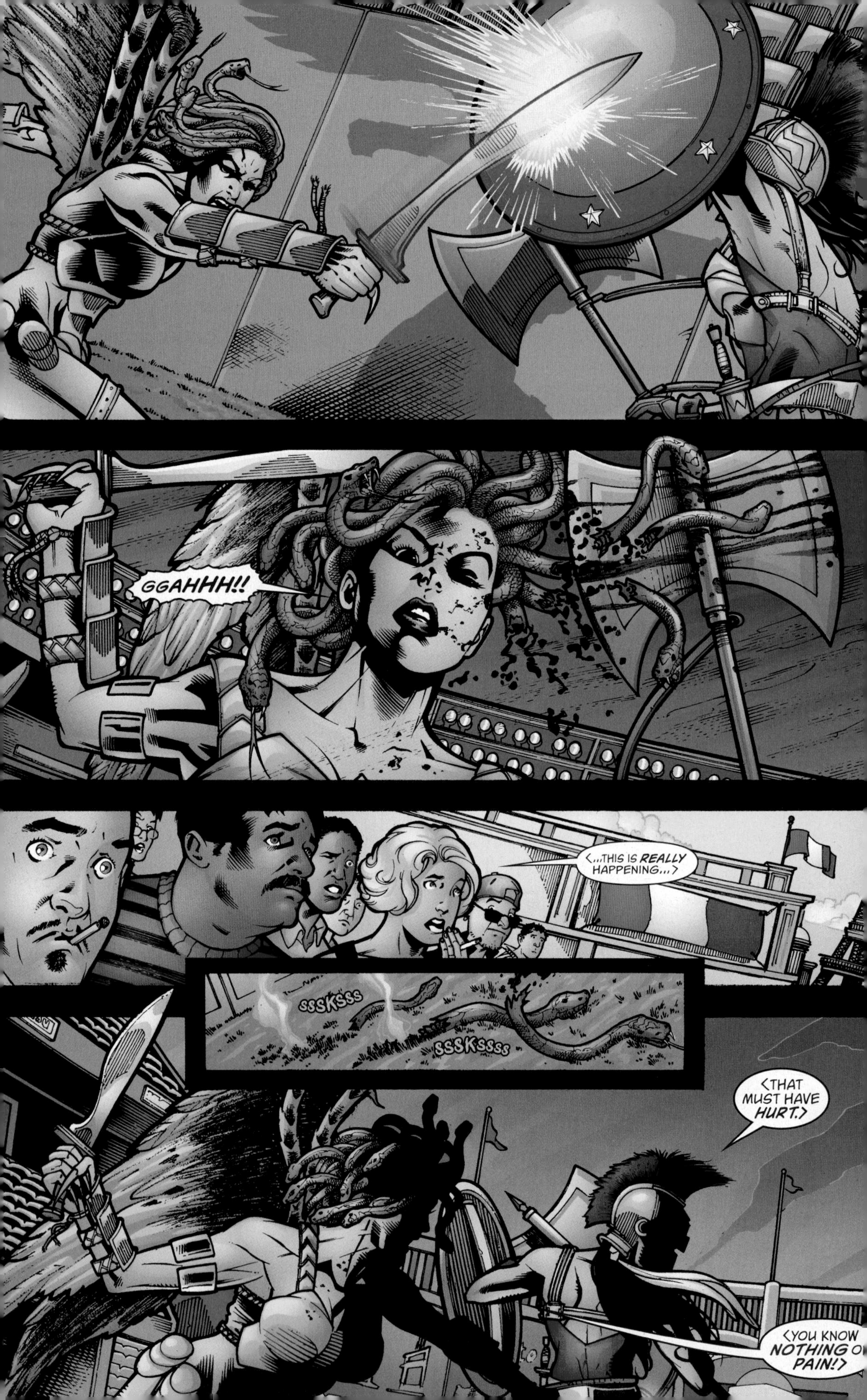
GGAHHH!!
<...THIS IS REALLY HAPPENING...>
SSSKSSS
SSSKSSSS
<THAT MUST HAVE HURT.>
<YOU KNOW NOTHING O
PAIN!>

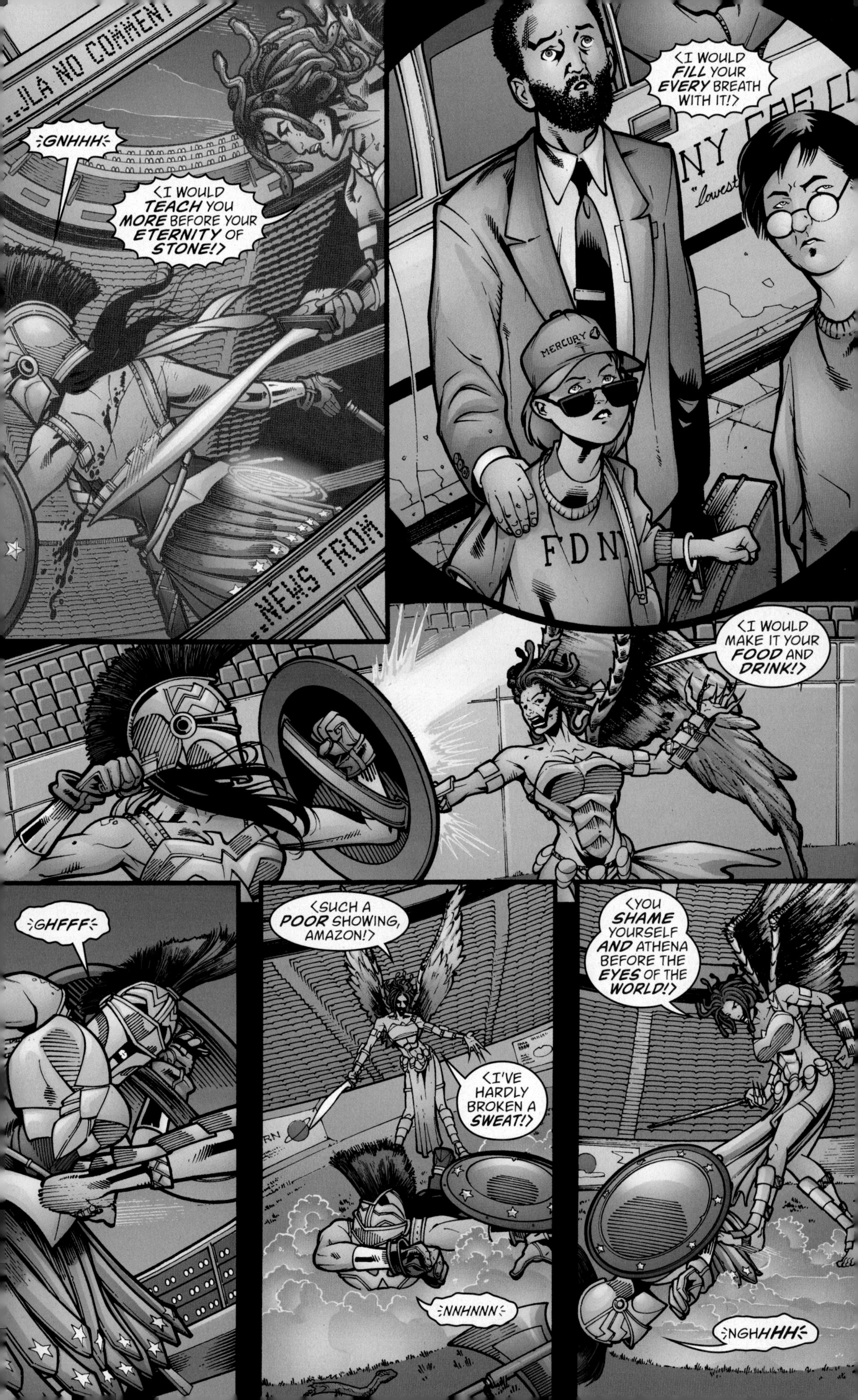
...JLA NO COMMENT
GNHHH
<I WOULD TEACH YOU MORE BEFORE YOUR ETERNITY OF STONE!>
NEWS FROM
<I WOULD FILL YOUR EVERY BREATH WITH IT!>
NY CAB
MERCURY
FDN
<I WOULD MAKE IT YOUR FOOD AND DRINK!>
GHFFF
<SUCH A POOR SHOWING, AMAZON!>
<I'VE HARDLY BROKEN A SWEAT!>
NNHNNN
<YOU SHAME YOURSELF AND ATHENA BEFORE THE EYES OF THE WORLD!>
NGHHHH

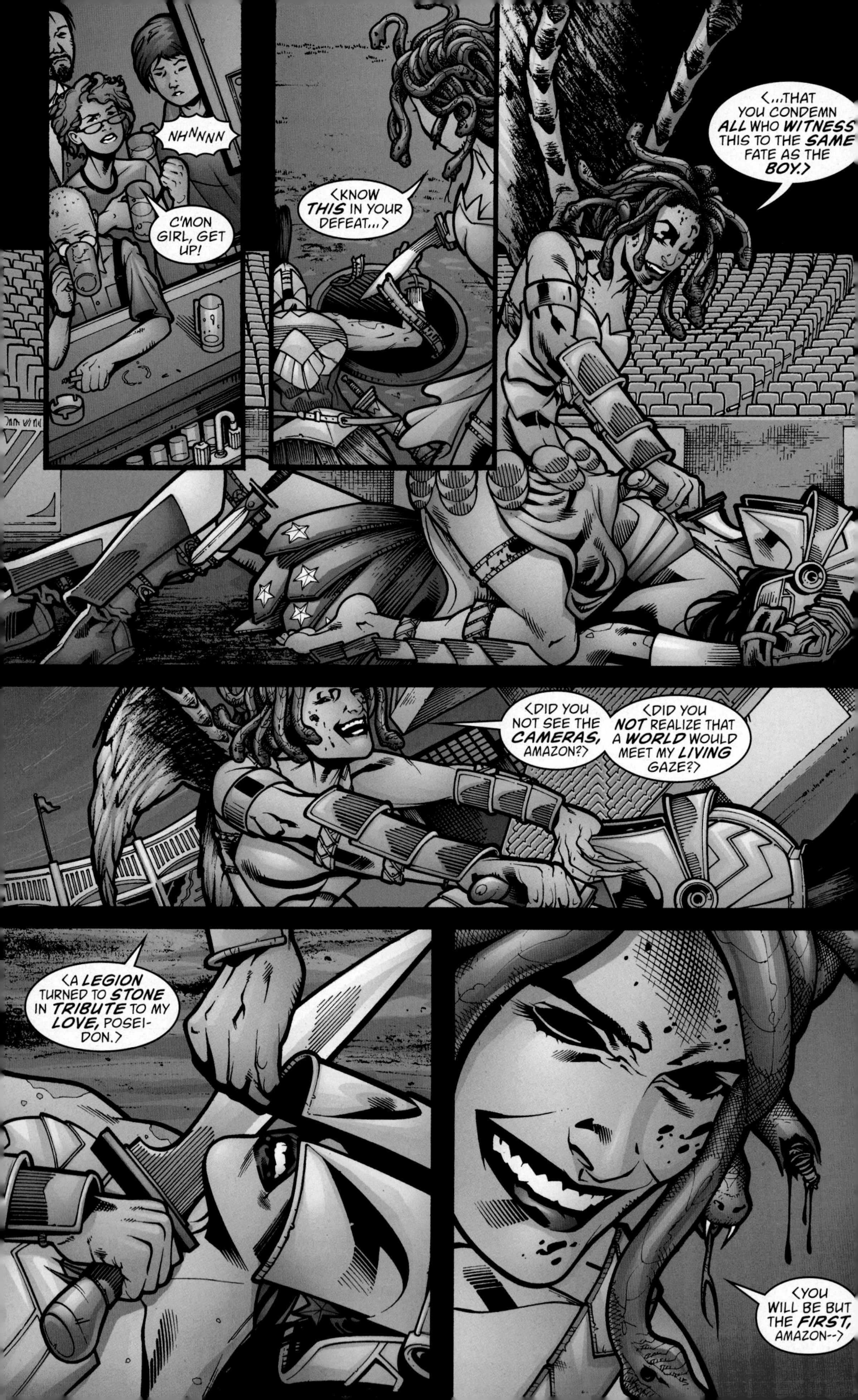

NHNNNN
C'MON GIRL, GET UP!
<KNOW THIS IN YOUR DEFEAT...>
<...THAT YOU CONDEMN ALL WHO WITNESS THIS TO THE SAME FATE AS THE BOY.>
<DID YOU NOT SEE THE CAMERAS, AMAZON?>
<DID YOU NOT REALIZE THAT A WORLD WOULD MEET MY LIVING GAZE?>
<A LEGION TURNED TO STONE IN TRIBUTE TO MY LOVE, POSEI-DON.>
<YOU WILL BE BUT THE FIRST, AMAZON-->

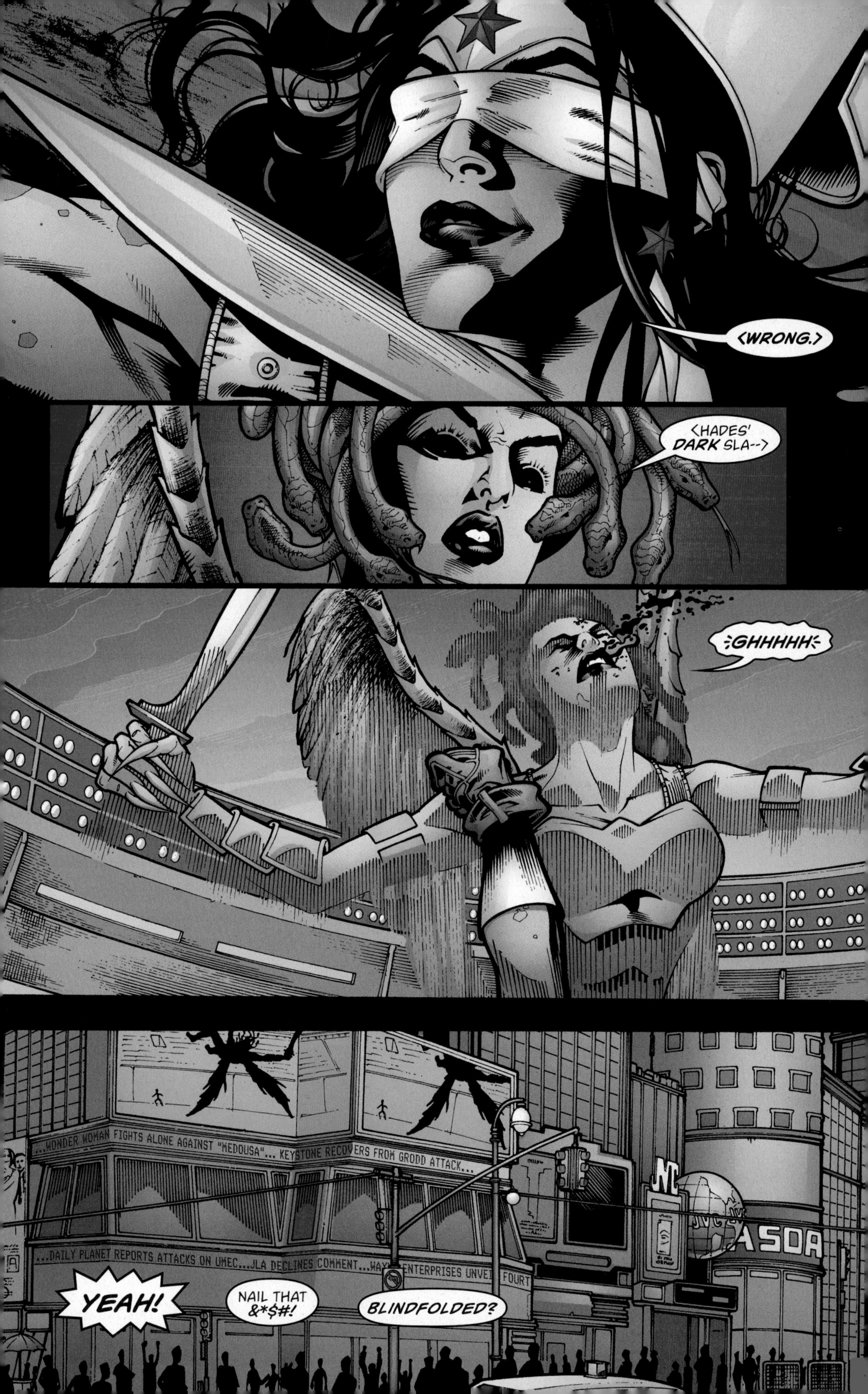

<WRONG.>
<HADES' DARK SLA-->
GHHHHH
...WONDER WOMAN FIGHTS ALONE AGAINST "MEDOUSA"... KEYSTONE RECOVERS FROM GRODD ATTACK...
...DAILY PLANET REPORTS ATTACKS ON UMEC...JLA DECLINES COMMENT...
YEAH!
NAIL THAT &*$#!
BLINDFOLDED?

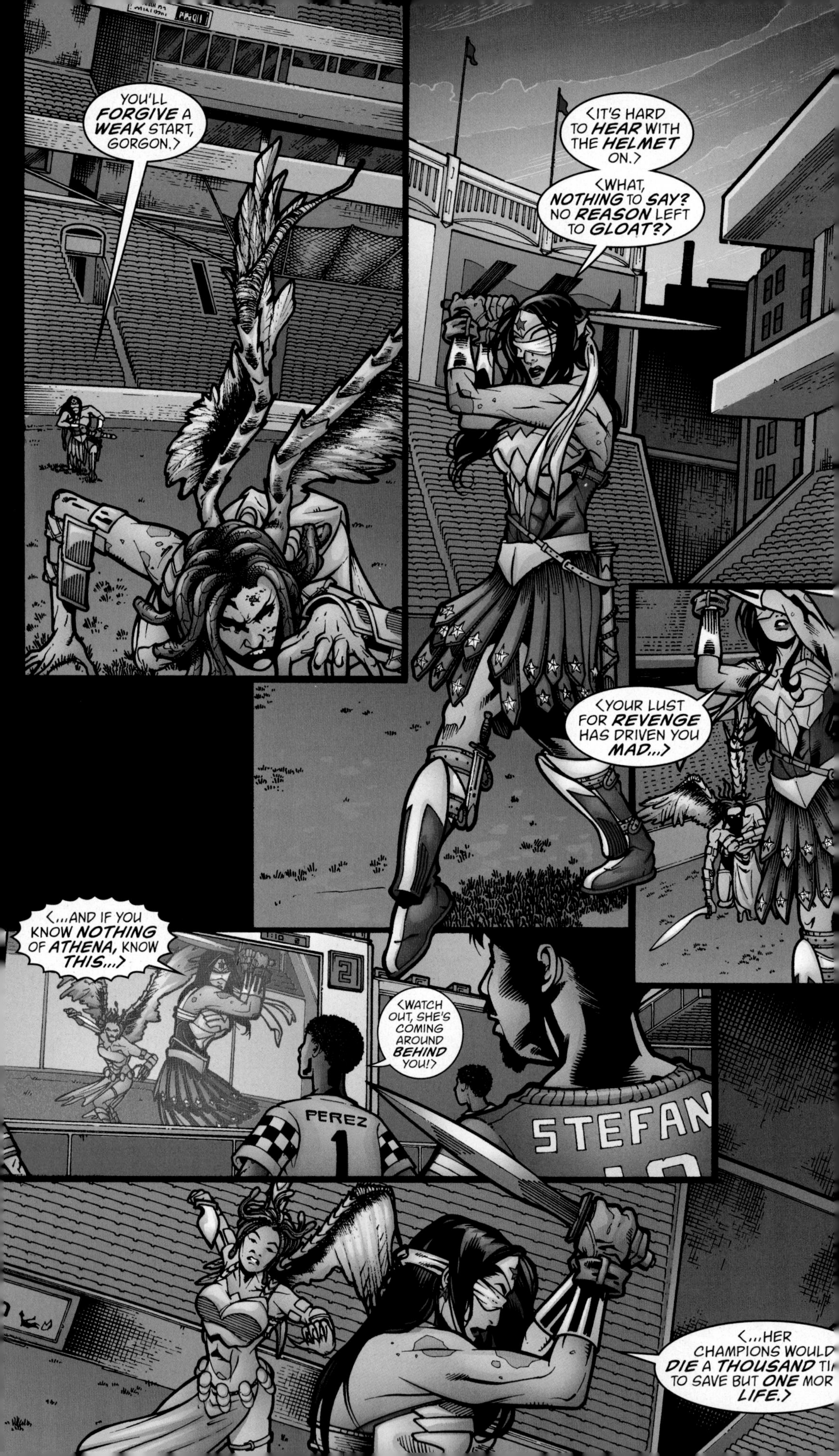

<YOU'LL FORGIVE A WEAK START, GORGON.>
<IT'S HARD TO HEAR WITH THE HELMET ON.>
<WHAT, NOTHING TO SAY? NO REASON LEFT TO GLOAT?>
<YOUR LUST FOR REVENGE HAS DRIVEN YOU MAD...>
<...AND IF YOU KNOW NOTHING OF ATHENA, KNOW THIS...>
<WATCH OUT, SHE'S COMING AROUND BEHIND YOU!>
PEREZ
1
STEFAN
<...HER CHAMPIONS WOULD DIE A THOUSAND TI
TO SAVE BUT ONE MOR
LIFE.>

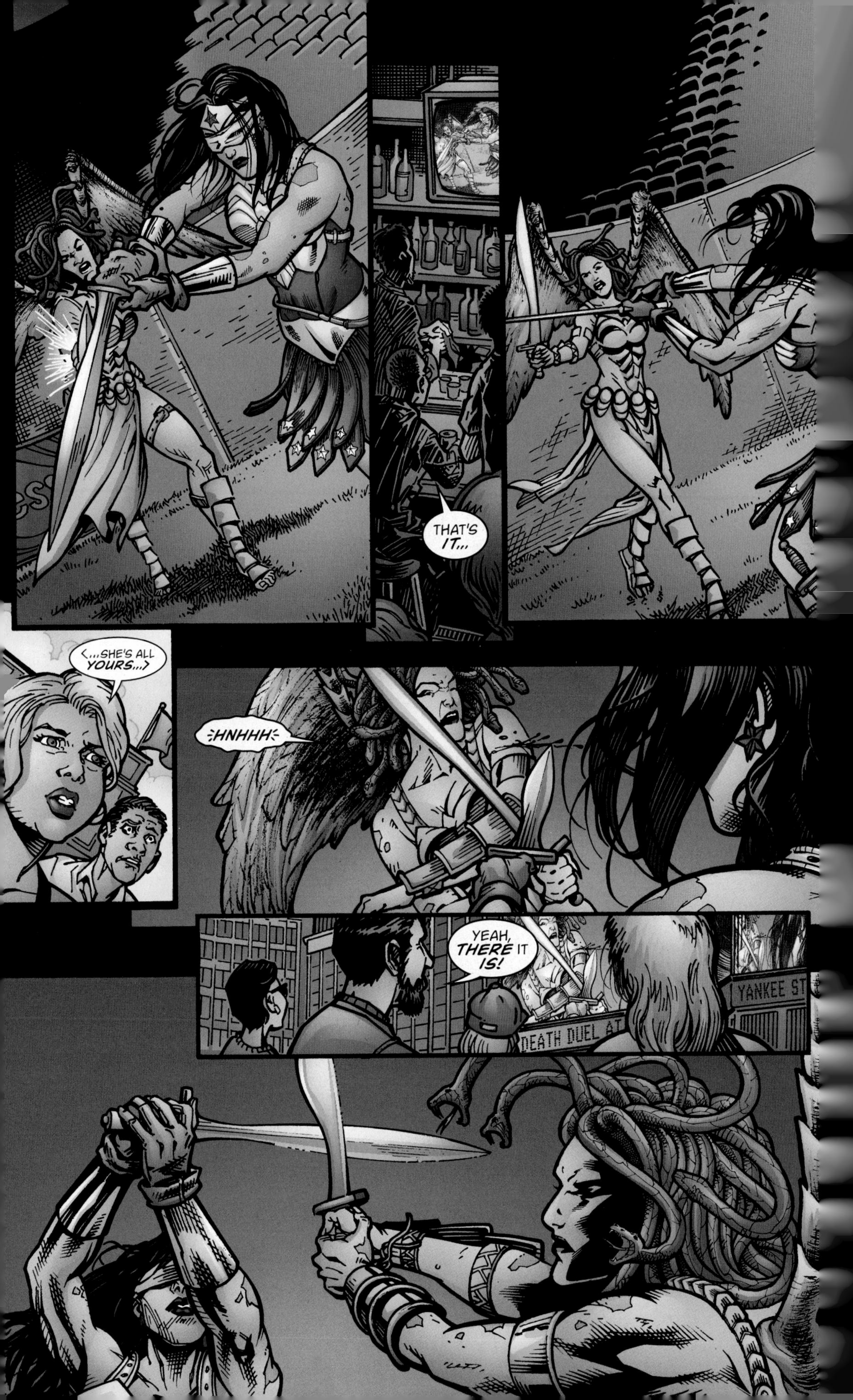
THAT'S IT...
<...SHE'S ALL YOURS...>
HNHHH
YEAH, THERE IT IS!
YANKEE ST
DEATH DUEL AT

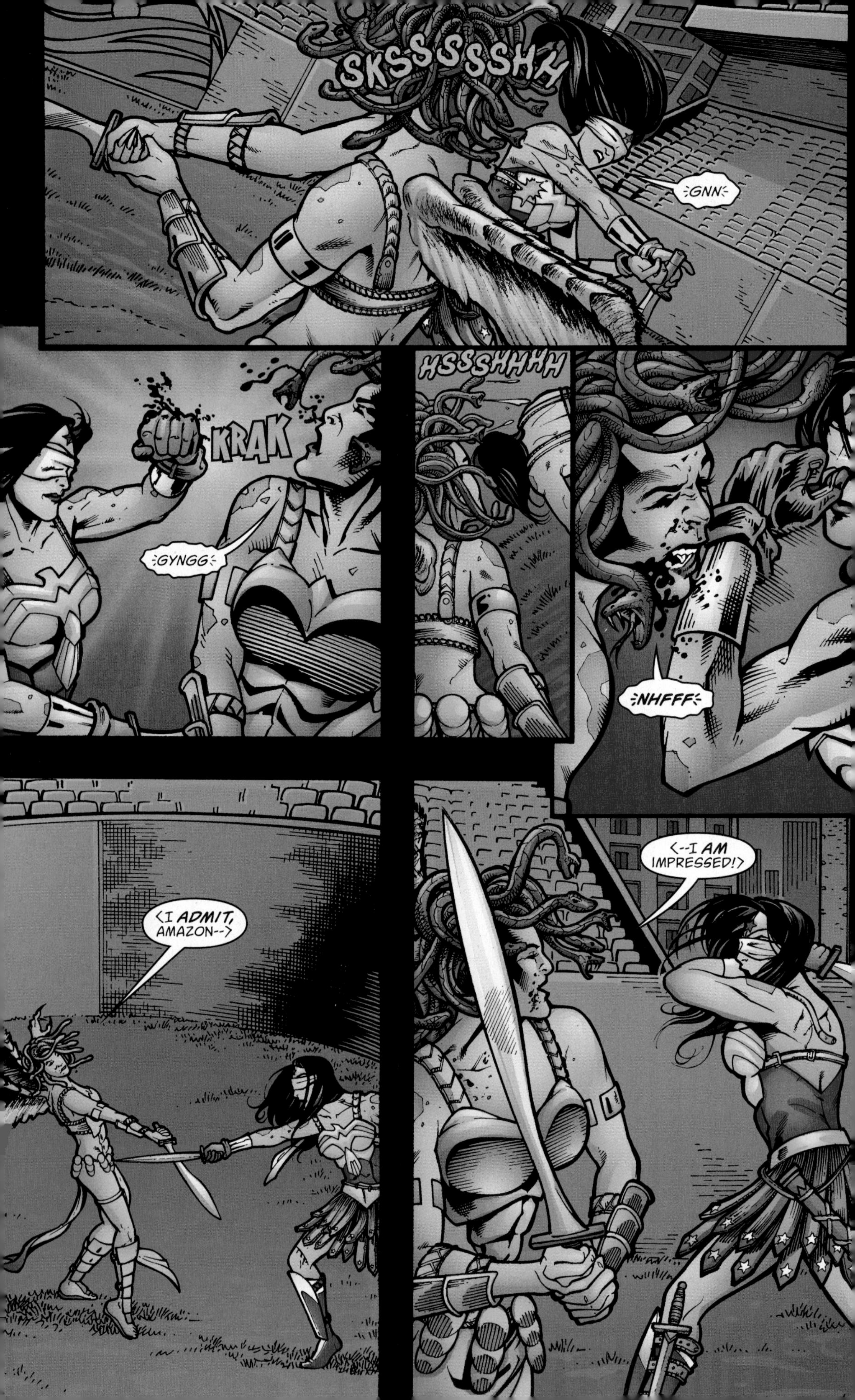
SKSSSSSHH
GNN
KRAK
GYNGG
HSSSHHHH
NHFFF
<I ADMIT, AMAZON-->
<--I AM IMPRESSED!>

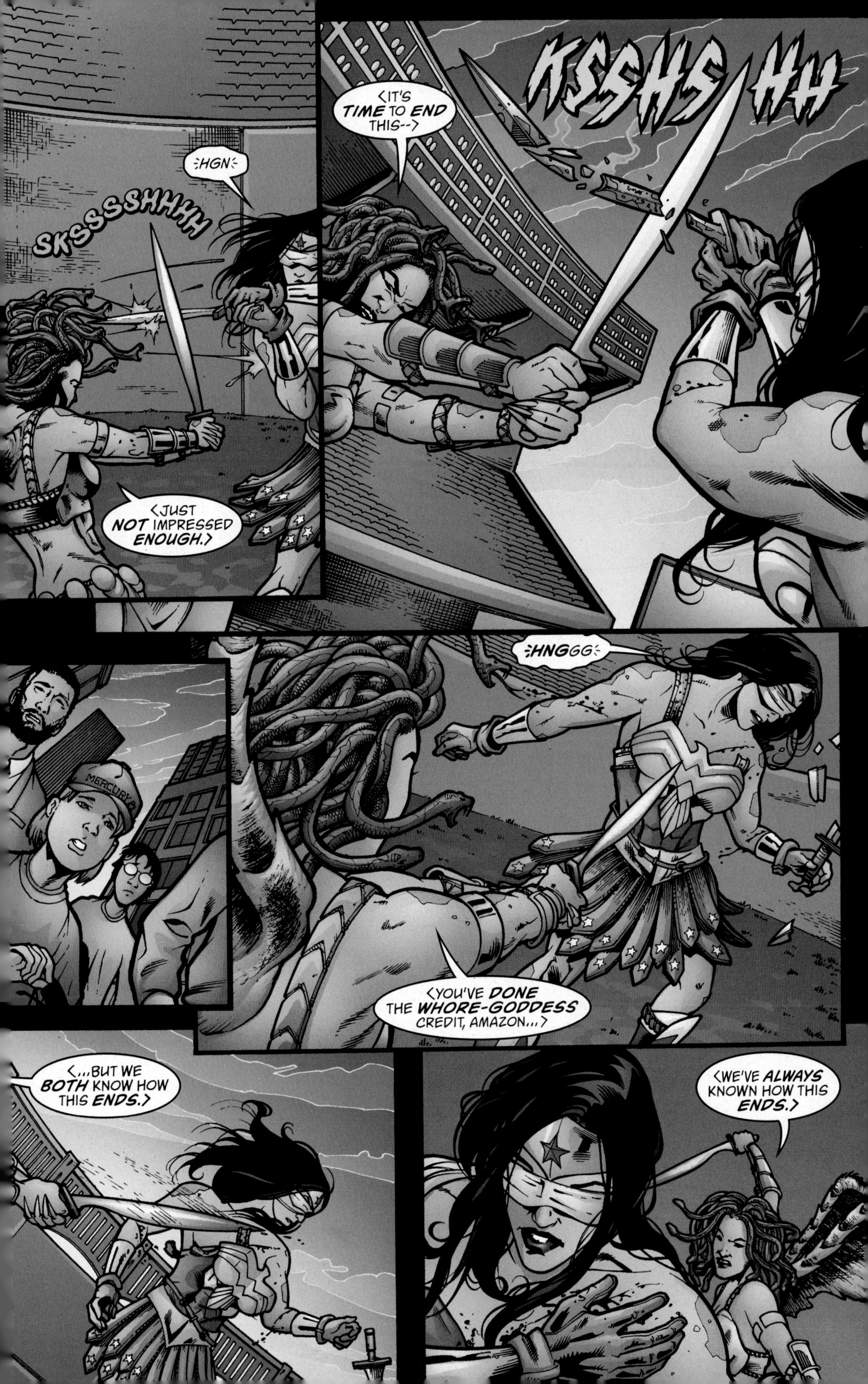
HGN
SKSSSSHHHH
<JUST NOT IMPRESSED ENOUGH.>
<IT'S TIME TO END THIS-->
KSSHS HH
HNGGG
<YOU'VE DONE THE WHORE-GODDESS CREDIT, AMAZON...>
MERCURY
<...BUT WE BOTH KNOW HOW THIS ENDS.>
<WE'VE ALWAYS KNOWN HOW THIS ENDS.>

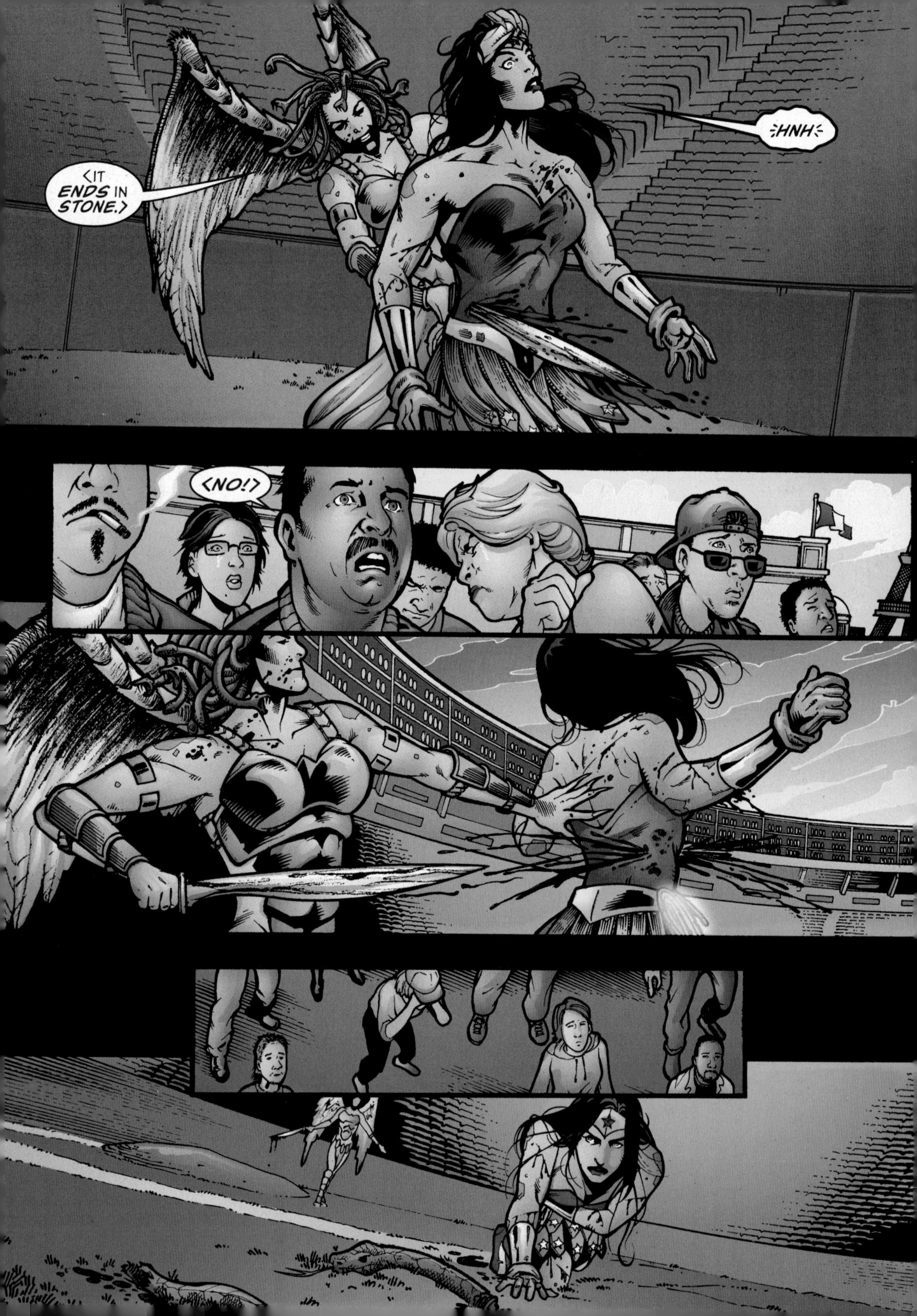
HNH
<IT ENDS IN STONE.>
<NO!>

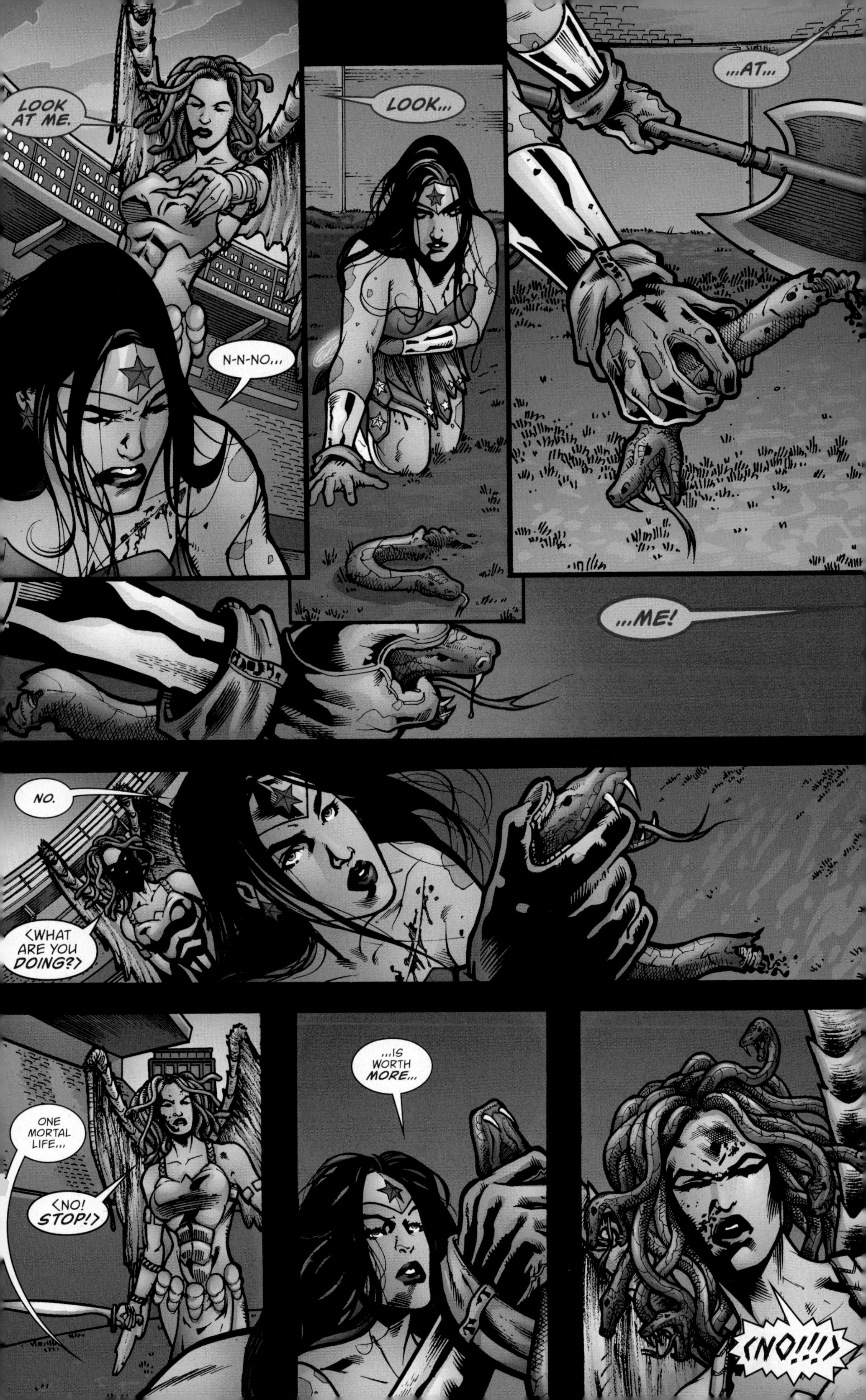
LOOK AT ME.
N-N-NO...
LOOK...
...AT...
...ME!
NO.
<WHAT ARE YOU DOING?>
ONE MORTAL LIFE...
<NO! STOP!>
...IS WORTH MORE...
<NO!!!>

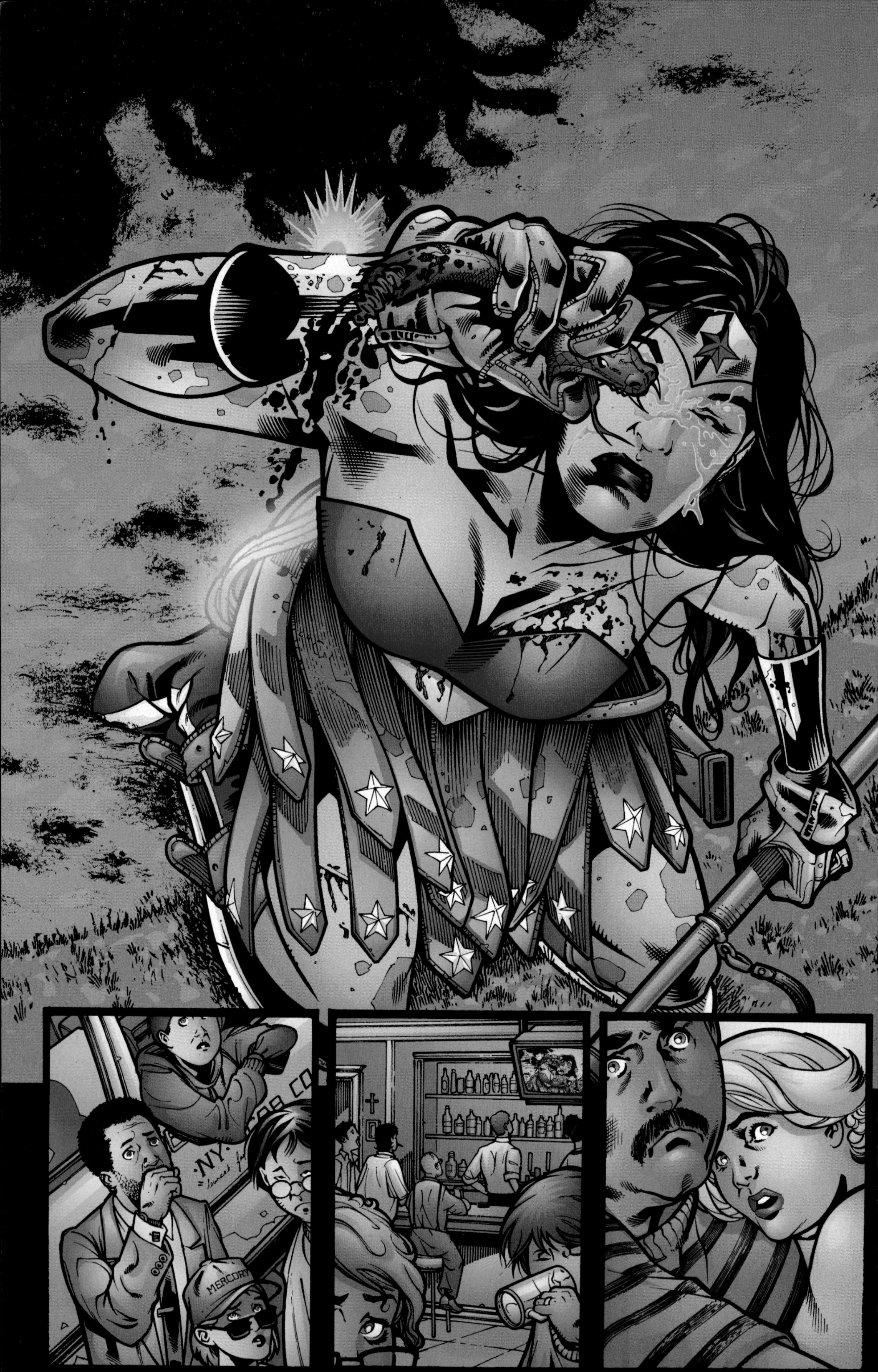
NY

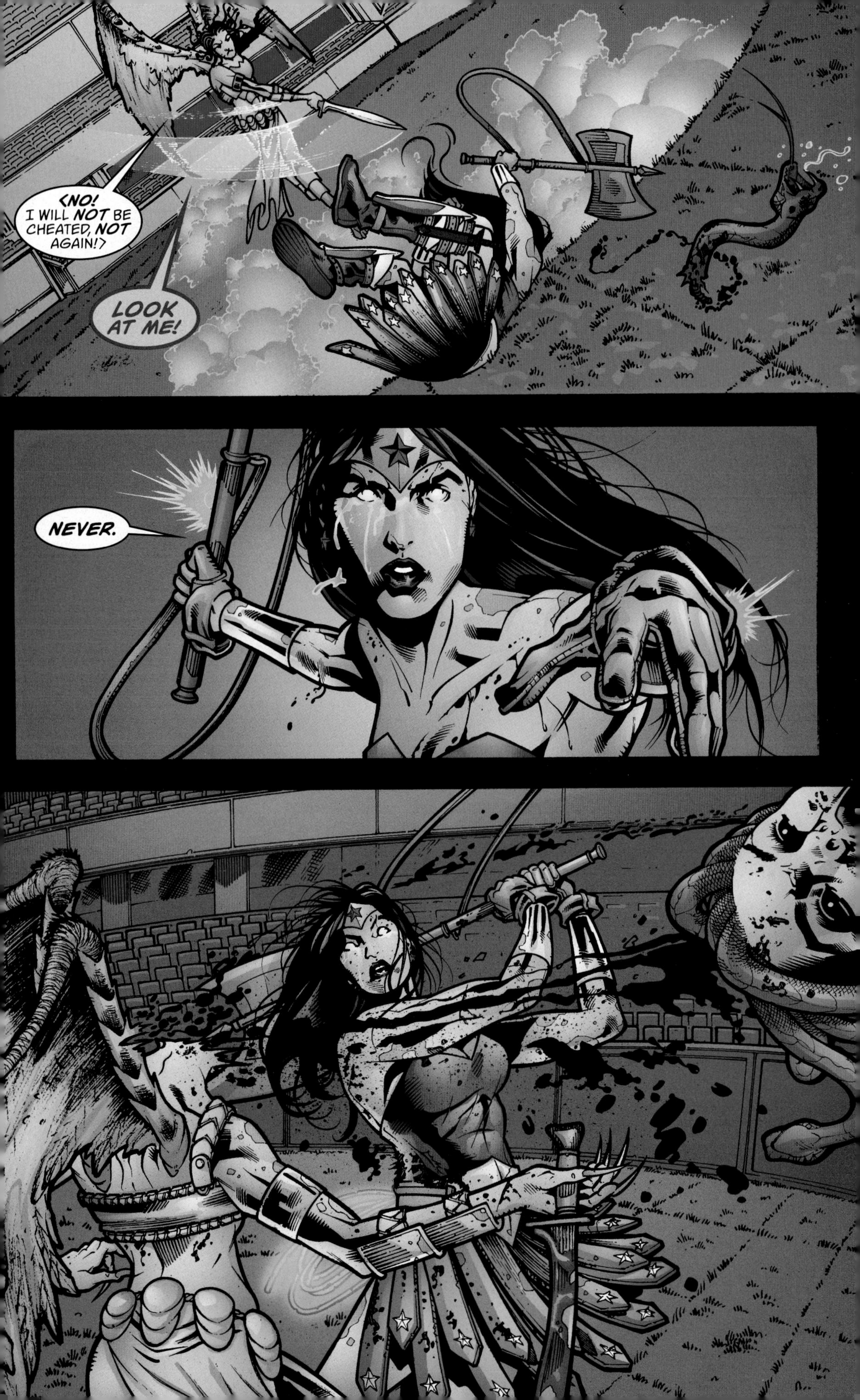

<NO! I WILL NOT BE CHEATED, NOT AGAIN!>
LOOK AT ME!
NEVER.

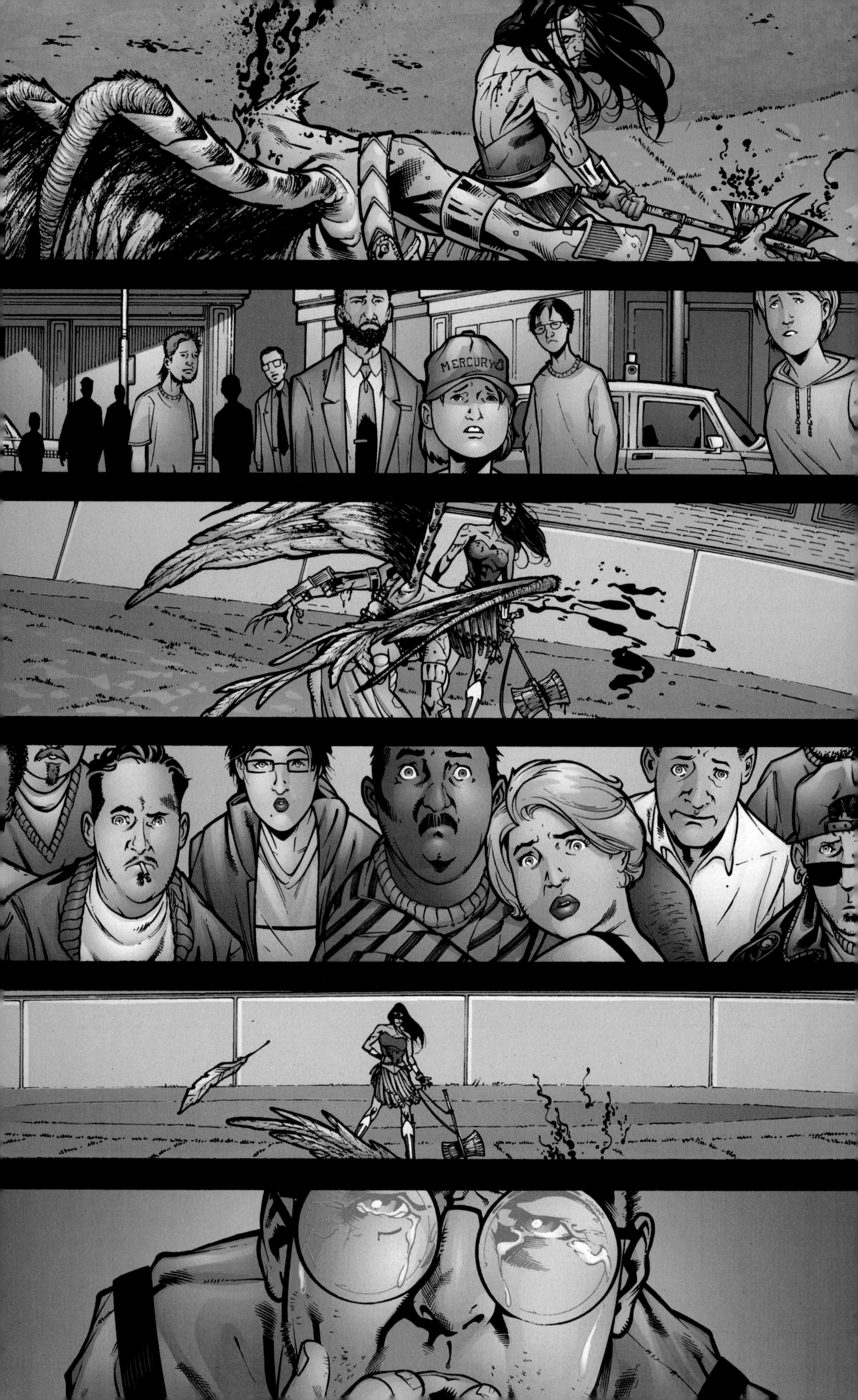
MERCURY

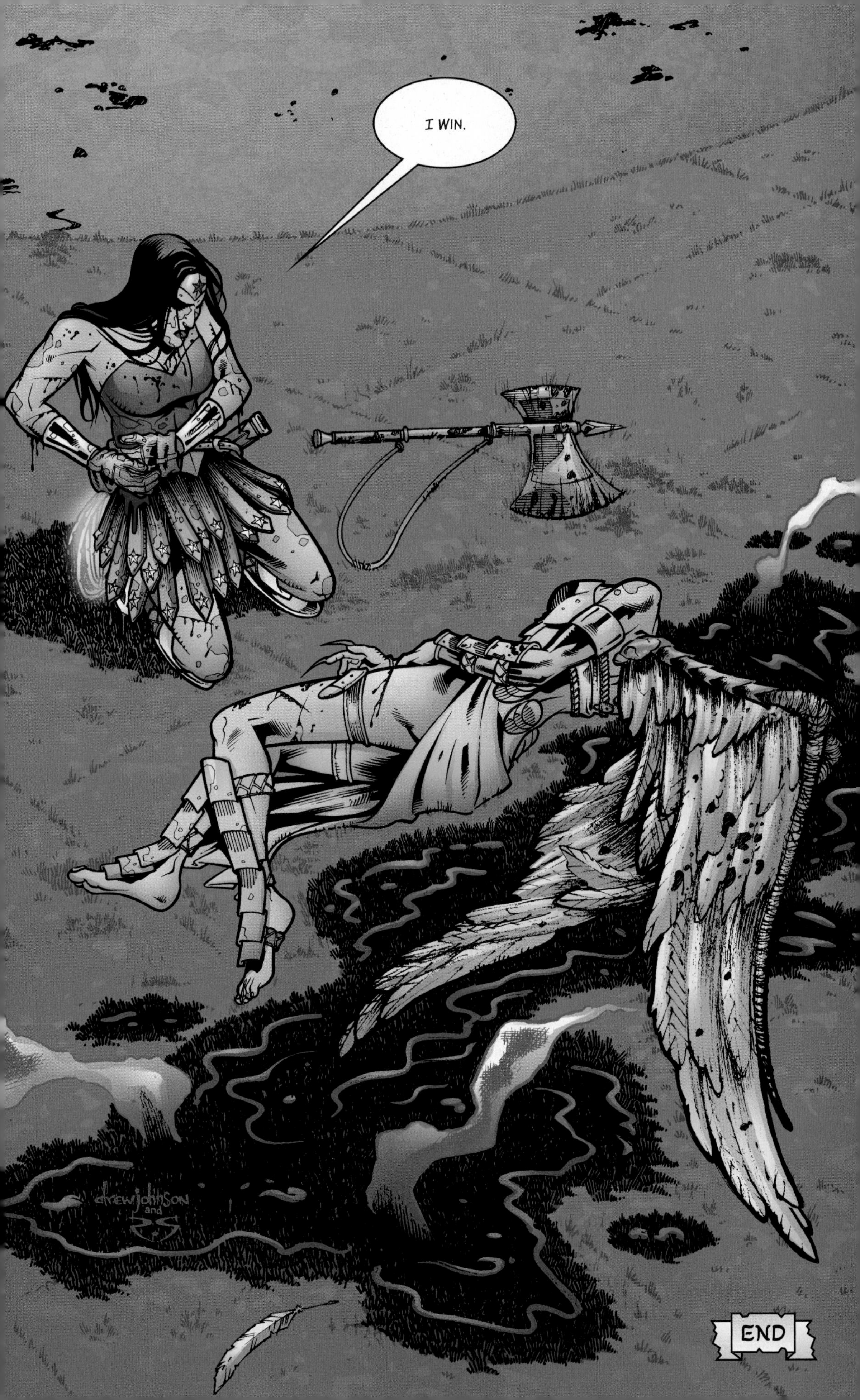
I WIN.
drewjohnson and
END

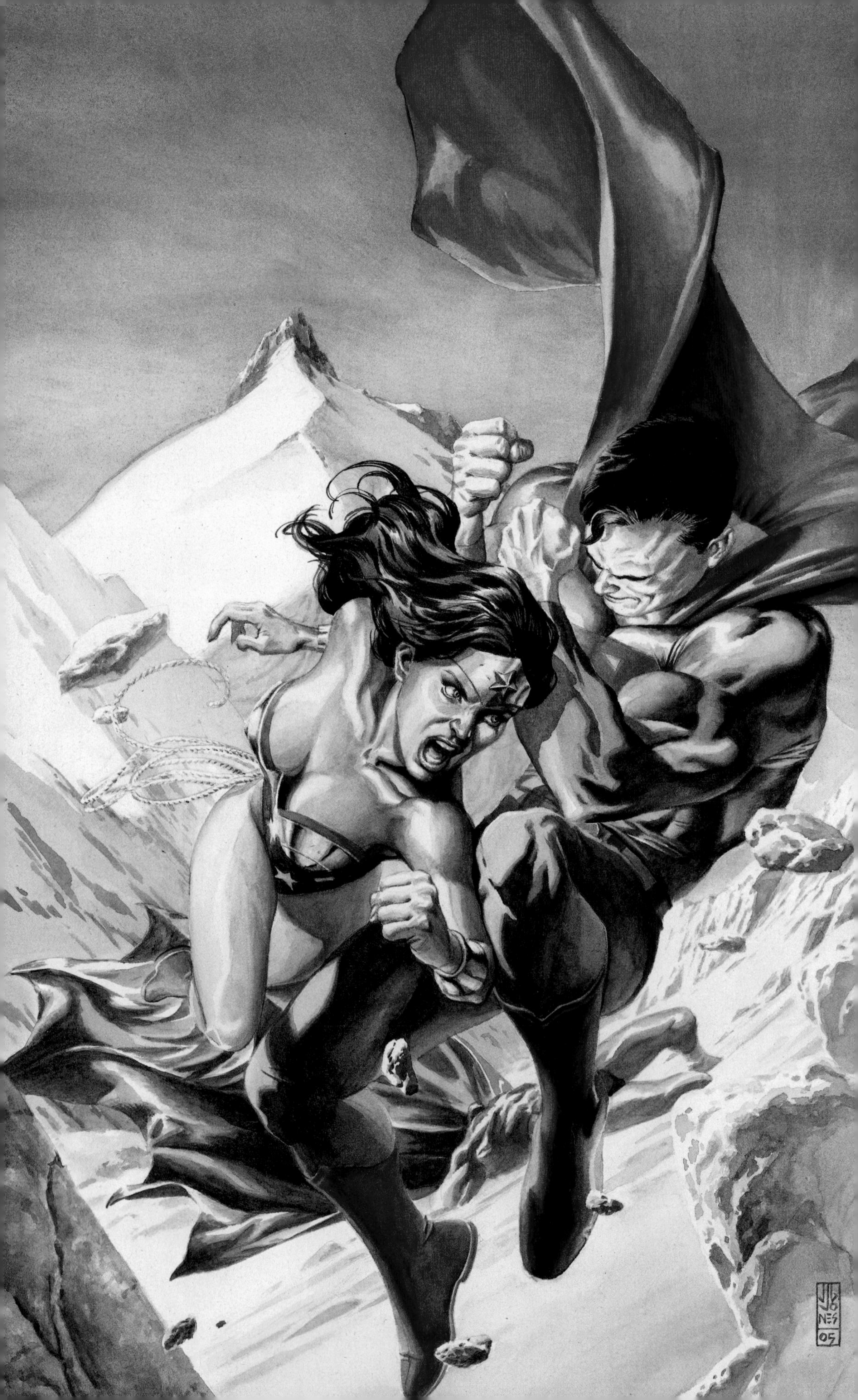

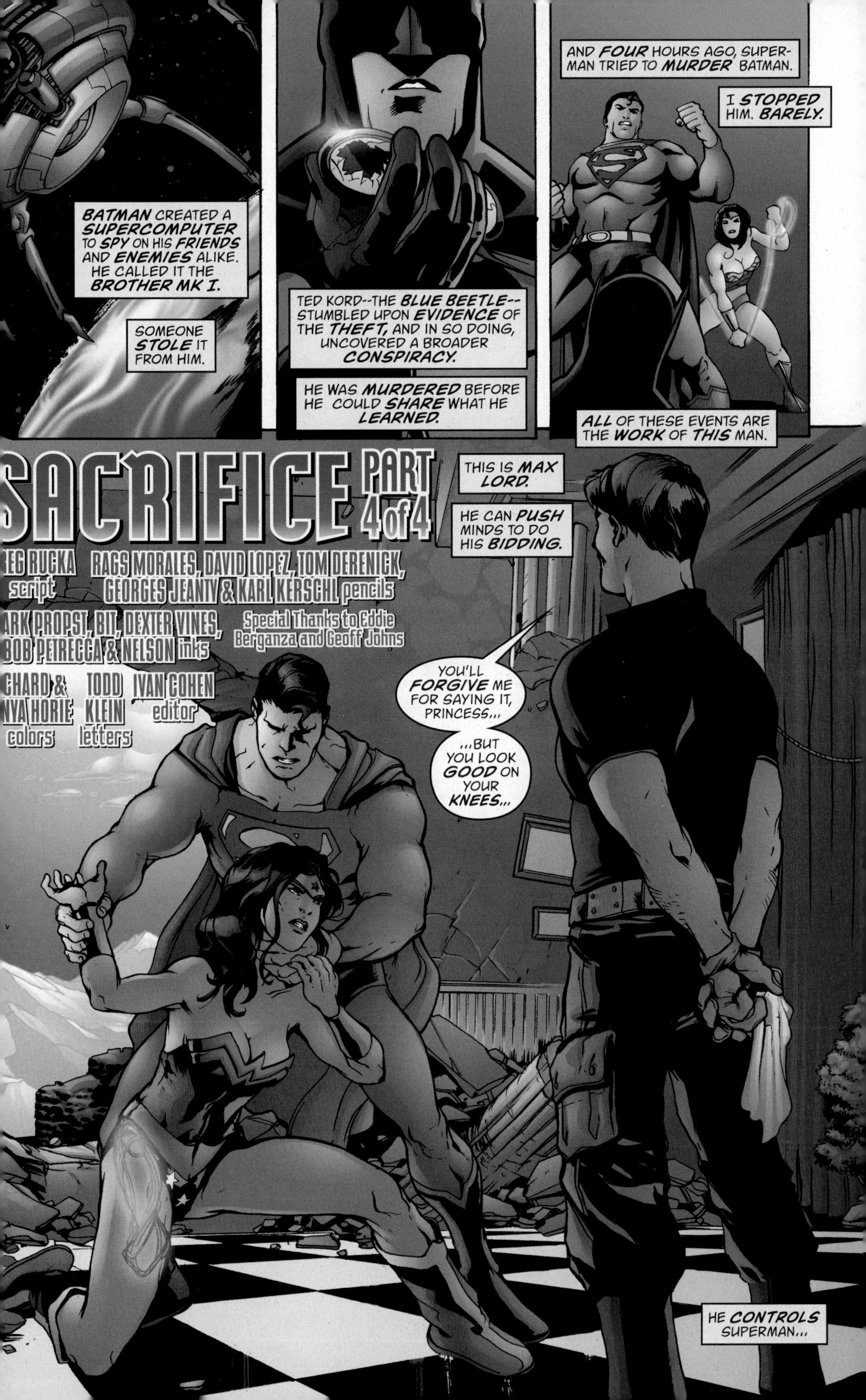

BATMAN CREATED A SUPERCOMPUTER TO SPY ON HIS FRIENDS AND ENEMIES ALIKE. HE CALLED IT THE BROTHER MK I.
SOMEONE STOLE IT FROM HIM.
TED KORD--THE BLUE BEETLE--STUMBLED UPON EVIDENCE OF THE THEFT, AND IN SO DOING, UNCOVERED A BROADER CONSPIRACY.
HE WAS MURDERED BEFORE HE COULD SHARE WHAT HE LEARNED.
AND FOUR HOURS AGO, SUPER-MAN TRIED TO MURDER BATMAN.
I STOPPED HIM. BARELY.
ALL OF THESE EVENTS ARE THE WORK OF THIS MAN.
SACRIFICE PART 4 of 4
EG RUCKA script
RAGS MORALES, DAVID LOPEZ, TOM DERENICK, GEORGES JEANTY & KARL KERSCHL pencils
ARK PROPST, BIT, DEXTER VINES, BOB PETRECCA & NELSON inks
Special Thanks to Eddie Berganza and Geoff Johns
CHARD & NYA HORIE colors
TODD KLEIN letters
IVAN COHEN editor
THIS IS MAX LORD.
HE CAN PUSH MINDS TO DO HIS BIDDING.
YOU'LL FORGIVE ME FOR SAYING IT, PRINCESS...
...BUT YOU LOOK GOOD ON YOUR KNEES...
HE CONTROLS SUPERMAN...

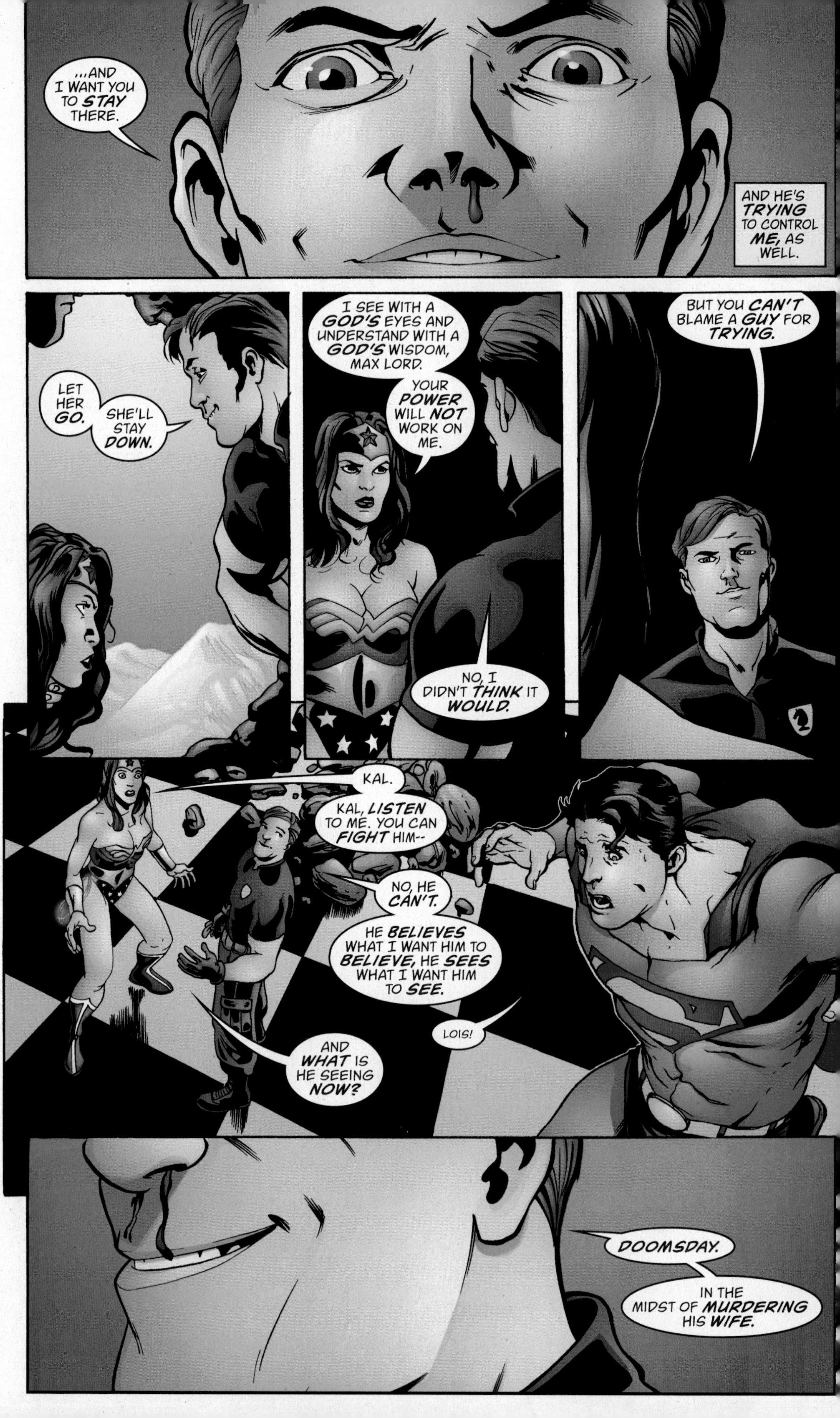
...AND I WANT YOU TO STAY THERE.
AND HE'S TRYING TO CONTROL ME, AS WELL.
LET HER GO.
SHE'LL STAY DOWN.
I SEE WITH A GOD'S EYES AND UNDERSTAND WITH A GOD'S WISDOM, MAX LORD.
YOUR POWER WILL NOT WORK ON ME.
NO, I DIDN'T THINK IT WOULD.
BUT YOU CAN'T BLAME A GUY FOR TRYING.
KAL.
KAL, LISTEN TO ME. YOU CAN FIGHT HIM--
NO, HE CAN'T.
HE BELIEVES WHAT I WANT HIM TO BELIEVE, HE SEES WHAT I WANT HIM TO SEE.
LOIS!
AND WHAT IS HE SEEING NOW?
DOOMSDAY.
IN THE MIDST OF MURDERING HIS WIFE.

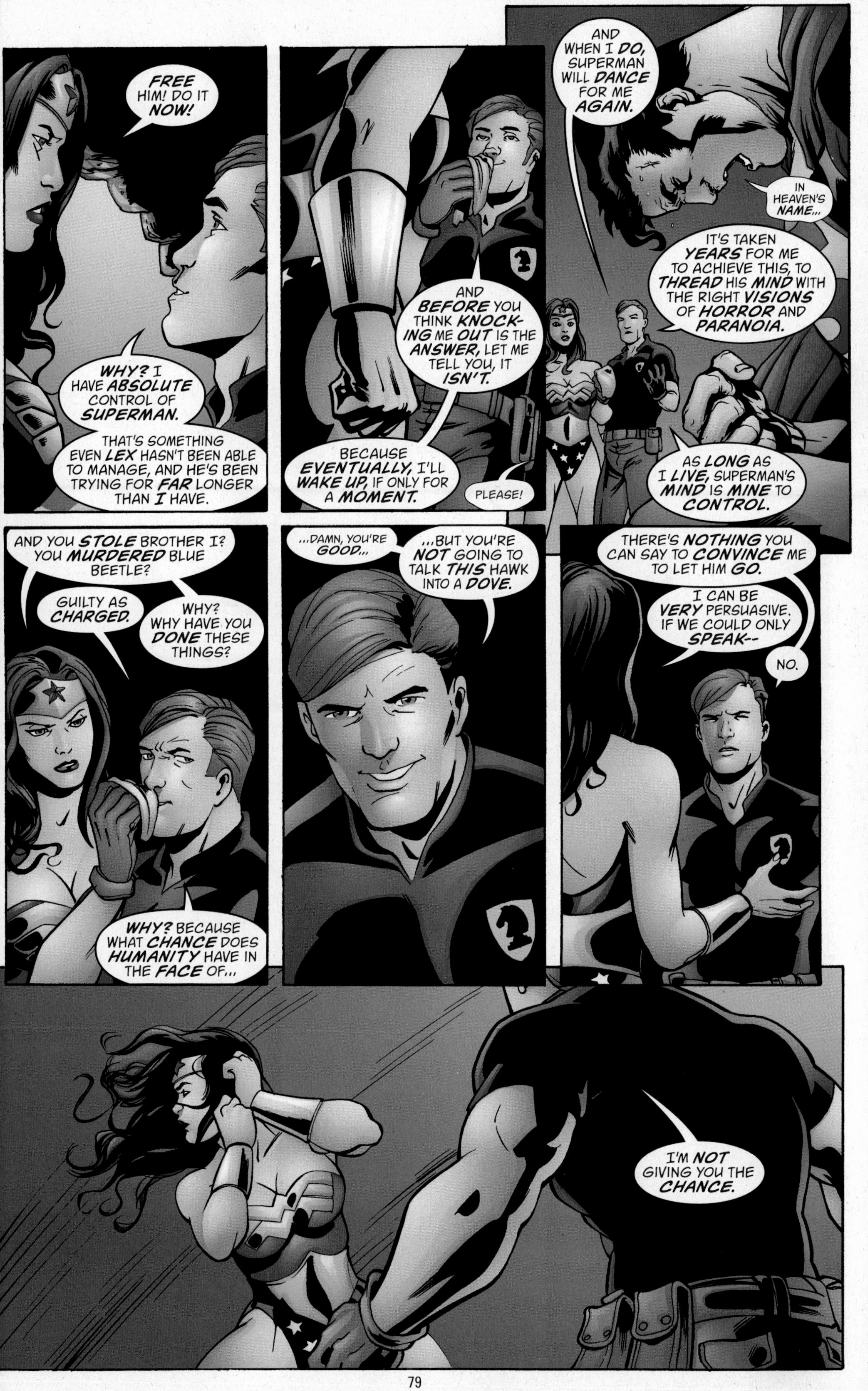
FREE HIM! DO IT NOW!
WHY? I HAVE ABSOLUTE CONTROL OF SUPERMAN.
THAT'S SOMETHING EVEN LEX HASN'T BEEN ABLE TO MANAGE, AND HE'S BEEN TRYING FOR FAR LONGER THAN I HAVE.
AND BEFORE YOU THINK KNOCKING ME OUT IS THE ANSWER, LET ME TELL YOU, IT ISN'T.
BECAUSE EVENTUALLY, I'LL WAKE UP, IF ONLY FOR A MOMENT.
PLEASE!
AND WHEN I DO, SUPERMAN WILL DANCE FOR ME AGAIN.
IN HEAVEN'S NAME...
IT'S TAKEN YEARS FOR ME TO ACHIEVE THIS, TO THREAD HIS MIND WITH THE RIGHT VISIONS OF HORROR AND PARANOIA.
AS LONG AS I LIVE, SUPERMAN'S MIND IS MINE TO CONTROL.
AND YOU STOLE BROTHER I? YOU MURDERED BLUE BEETLE?
GUILTY AS CHARGED.
WHY? WHY HAVE YOU DONE THESE THINGS?
WHY? BECAUSE WHAT CHANCE DOES HUMANITY HAVE IN THE FACE OF...
...DAMN, YOU'RE GOOD...
...BUT YOU'RE NOT GOING TO TALK THIS HAWK INTO A DOVE.
THERE'S NOTHING YOU CAN SAY TO CONVINCE ME TO LET HIM GO.
I CAN BE VERY PERSUASIVE. IF WE COULD ONLY SPEAK--
NO.
I'M NOT GIVING YOU THE CHANCE.

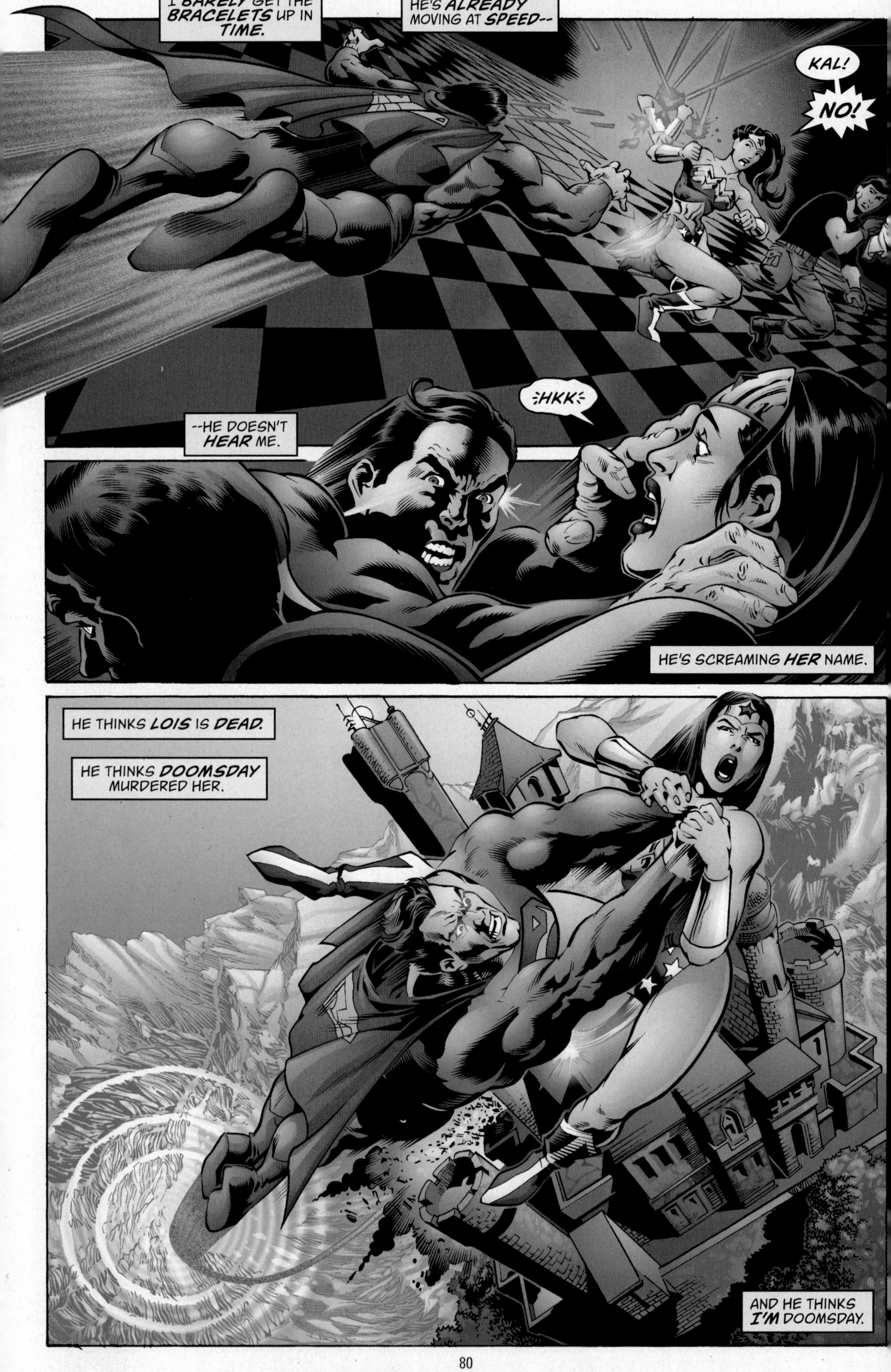
I BARELY GET THE BRACELETS UP IN TIME.
HE'S ALREADY MOVING AT SPEED--
KAL!
NO!
--HE DOESN'T HEAR ME.
HKK
HE'S SCREAMING HER NAME.
HE THINKS LOIS IS DEAD.
HE THINKS DOOMSDAY MURDERED HER.
AND HE THINKS I'M DOOMSDAY.

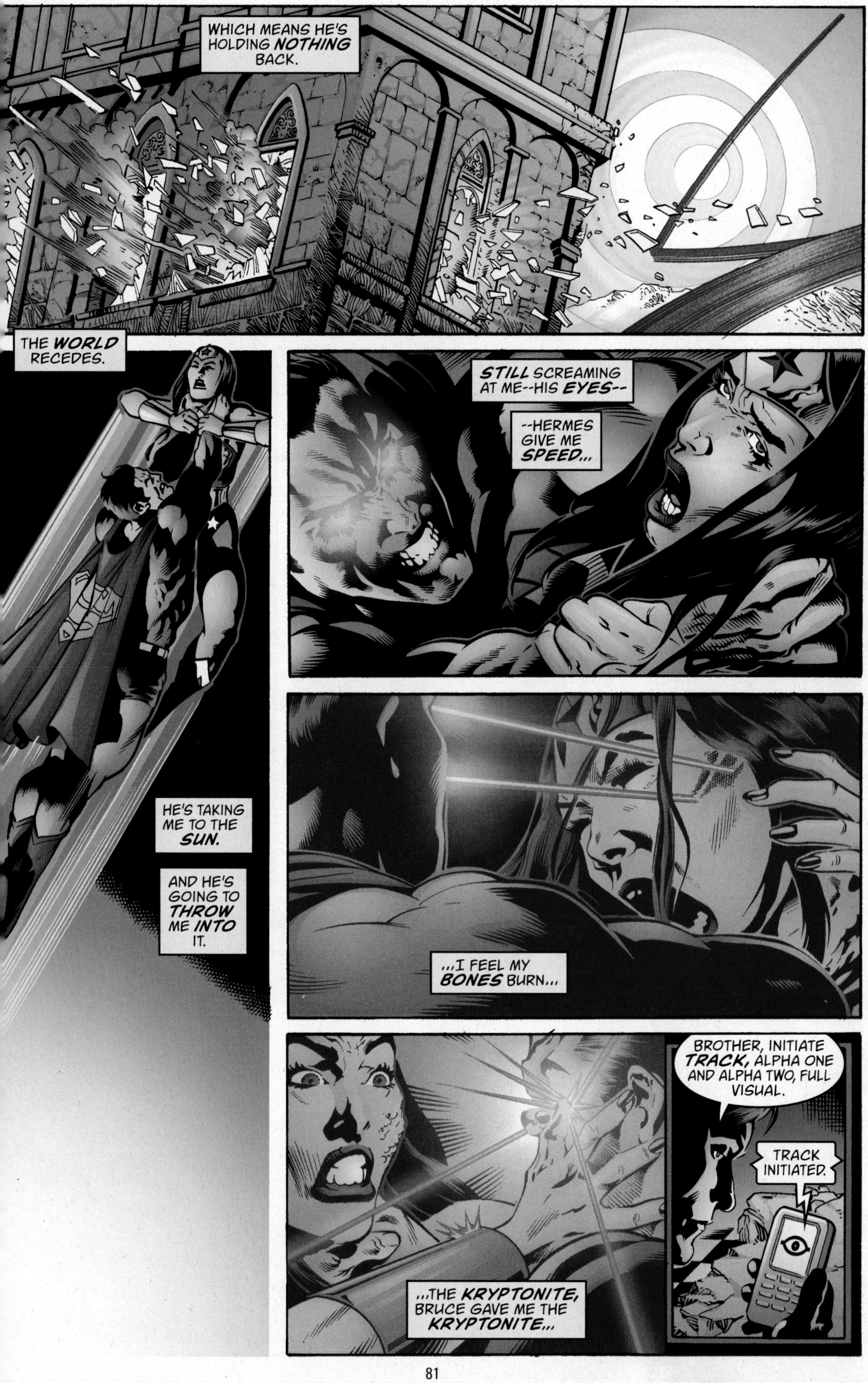

WHICH MEANS HE'S HOLDING NOTHING BACK.
THE WORLD RECEDES.
STILL SCREAMING AT ME--HIS EYES--
--HERMES GIVE ME SPEED...
HE'S TAKING ME TO THE SUN.
AND HE'S GOING TO THROW ME INTO IT.
...I FEEL MY BONES BURN...
...THE KRYPTONITE, BRUCE GAVE ME THE KRYPTONITE...
BROTHER, INITIATE TRACK, ALPHA ONE AND ALPHA TWO, FULL VISUAL.
TRACK INITIATED.

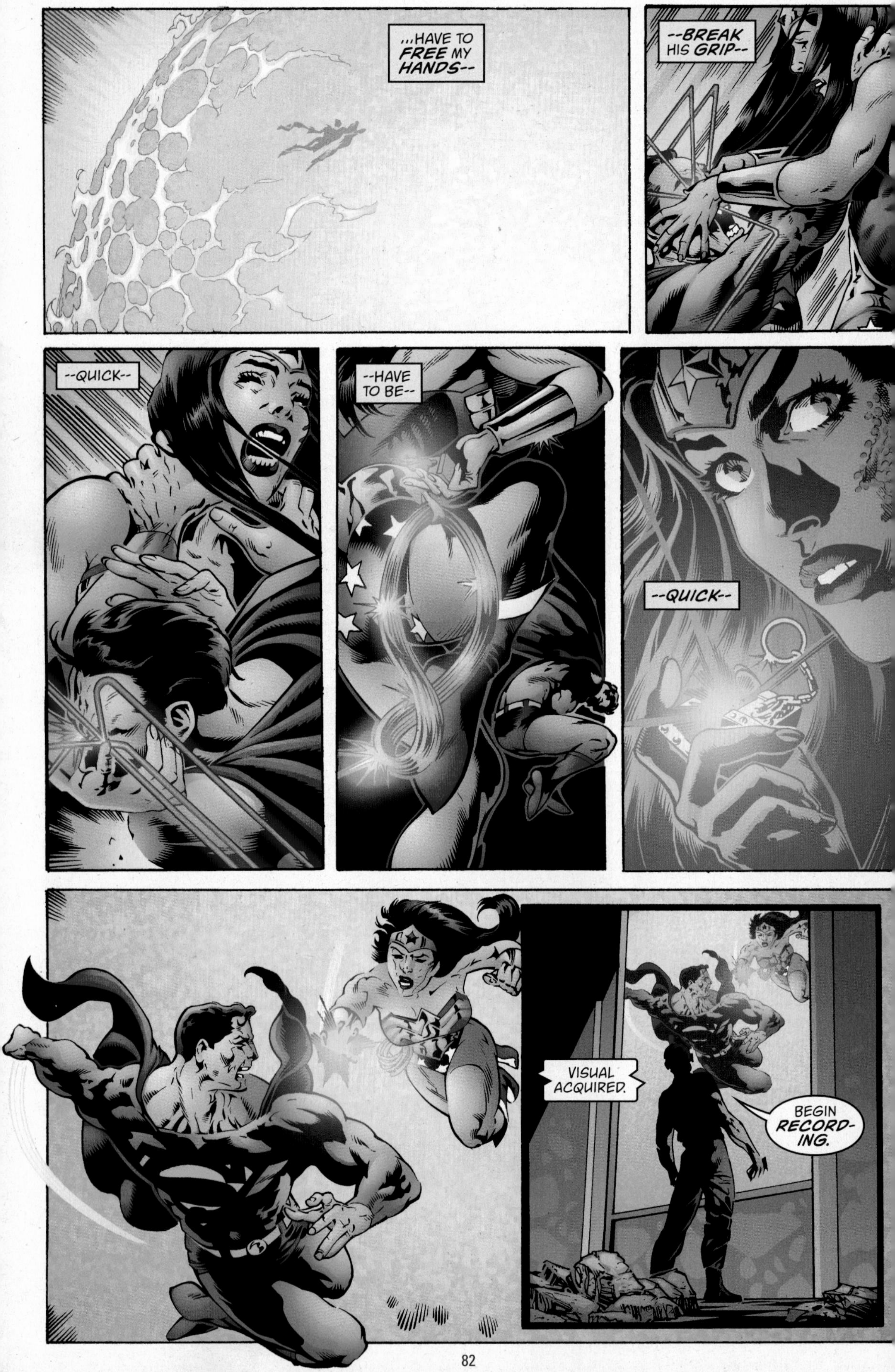
...HAVE TO FREE MY HANDS--
--BREAK HIS GRIP--
--QUICK--
--HAVE TO BE--
--QUICK--
VISUAL ACQUIRED.
BEGIN RECORDING.

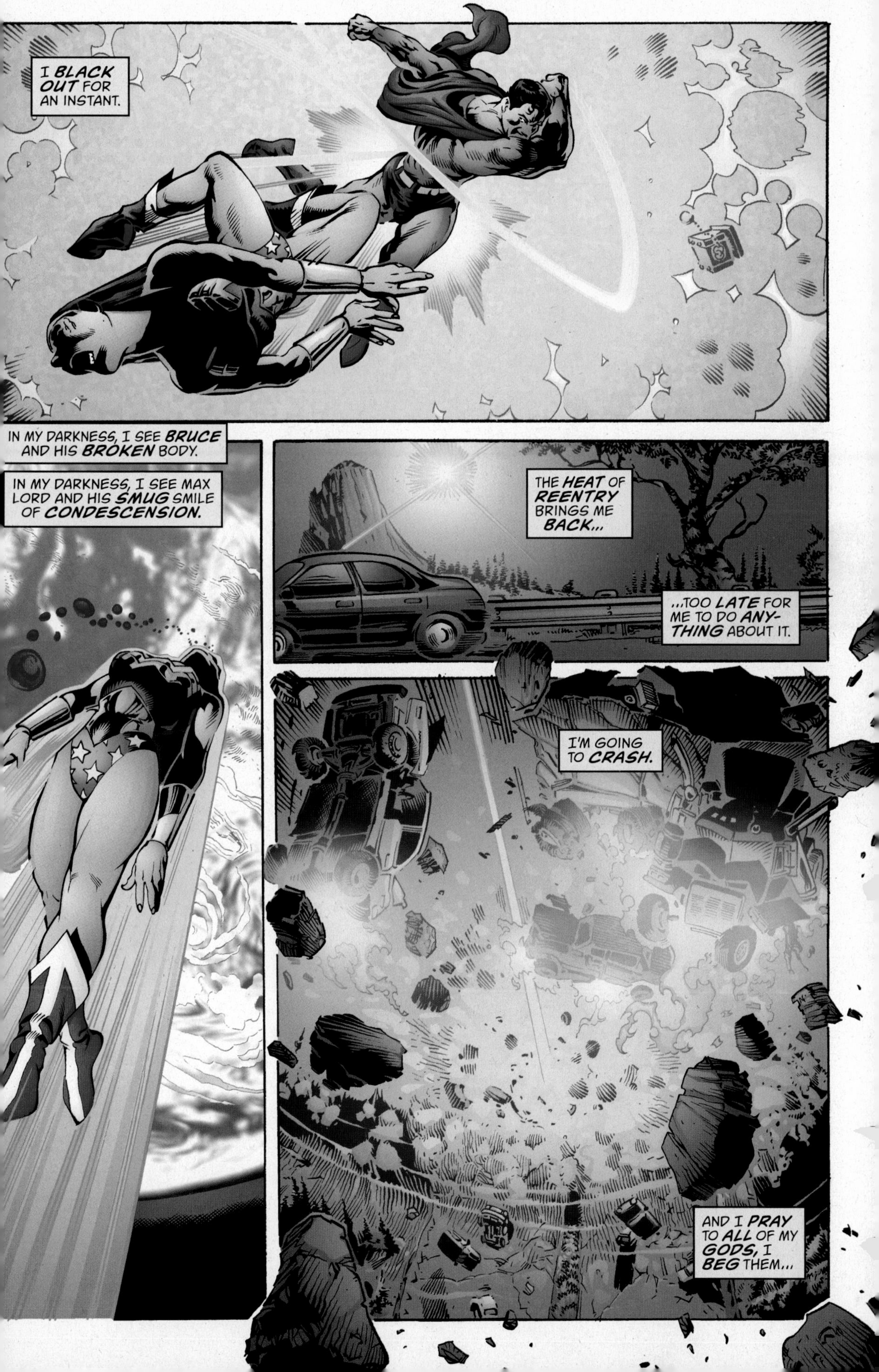
I BLACK OUT FOR AN INSTANT.
IN MY DARKNESS, I SEE BRUCE AND HIS BROKEN BODY.
IN MY DARKNESS, I SEE MAX LORD AND HIS SMUG SMILE OF CONDESCENSION.
THE HEAT OF REENTRY BRINGS ME BACK...
...TOO LATE FOR ME TO DO ANY-THING ABOUT IT.
I'M GOING TO CRASH.
AND I PRAY TO ALL OF MY GODS, I BEG THEM...

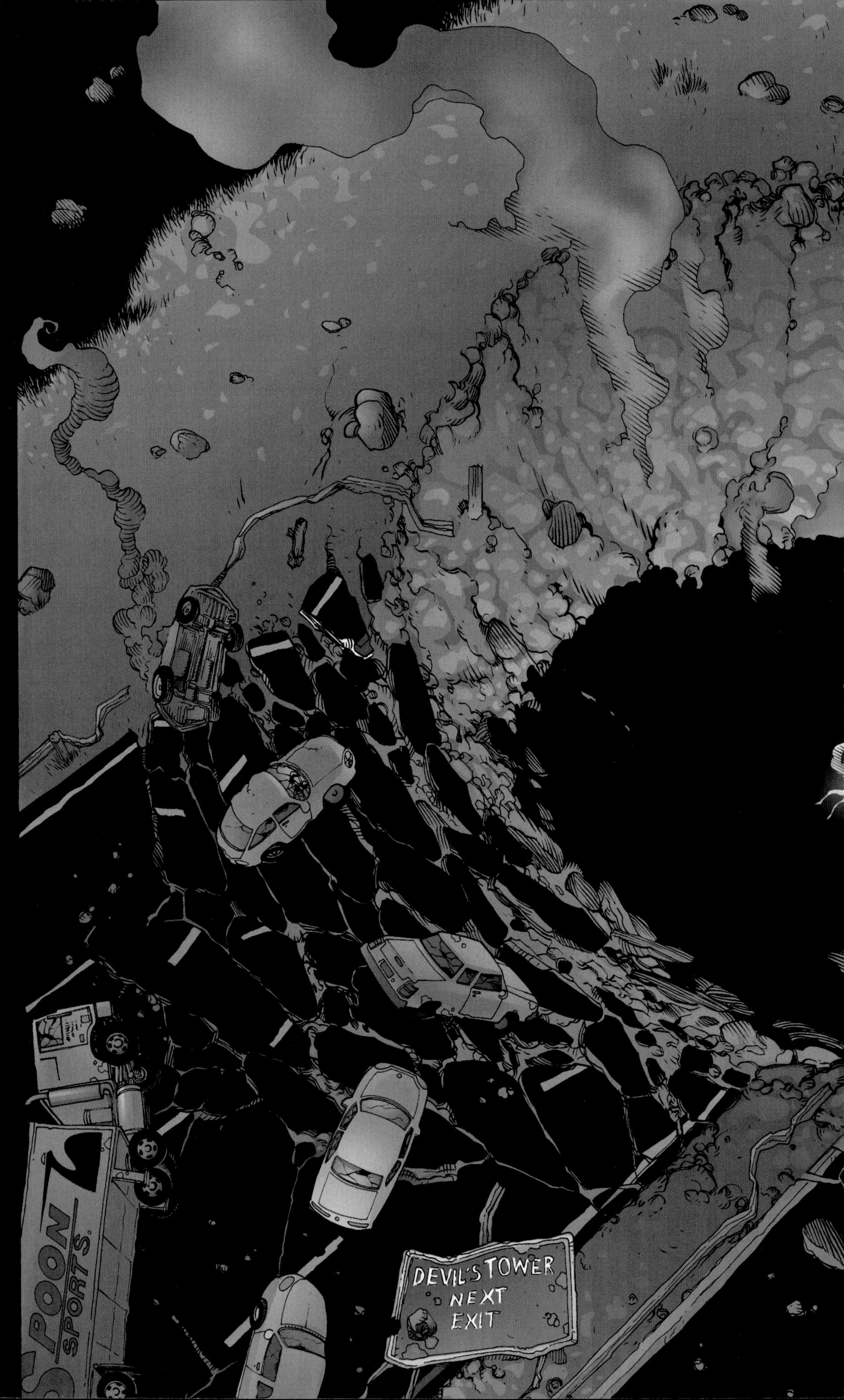
DEVIL'S TOWER
NEXT
EXIT
POON
SPORTS

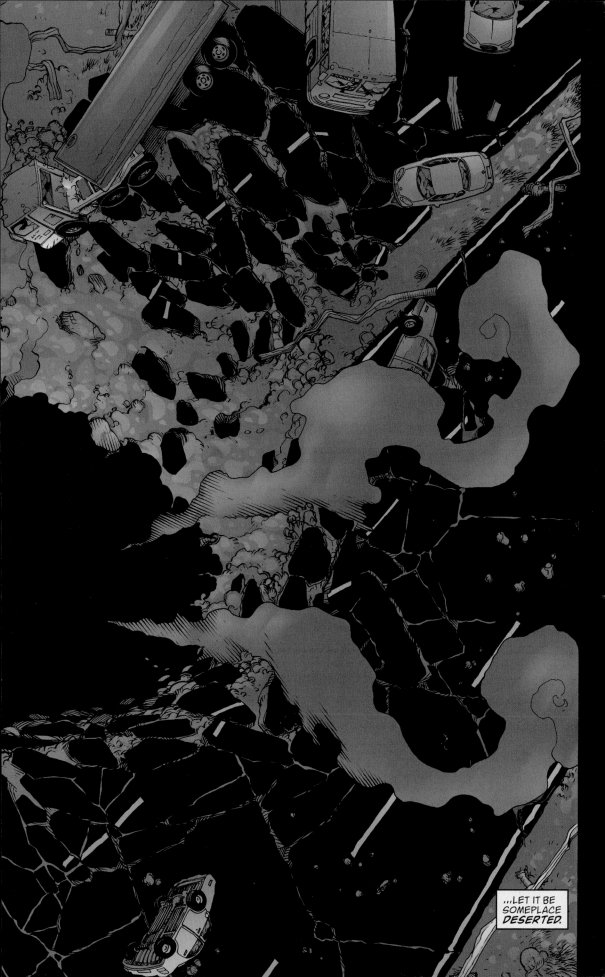

...LET IT BE SOMEPLACE *DESERTED.*

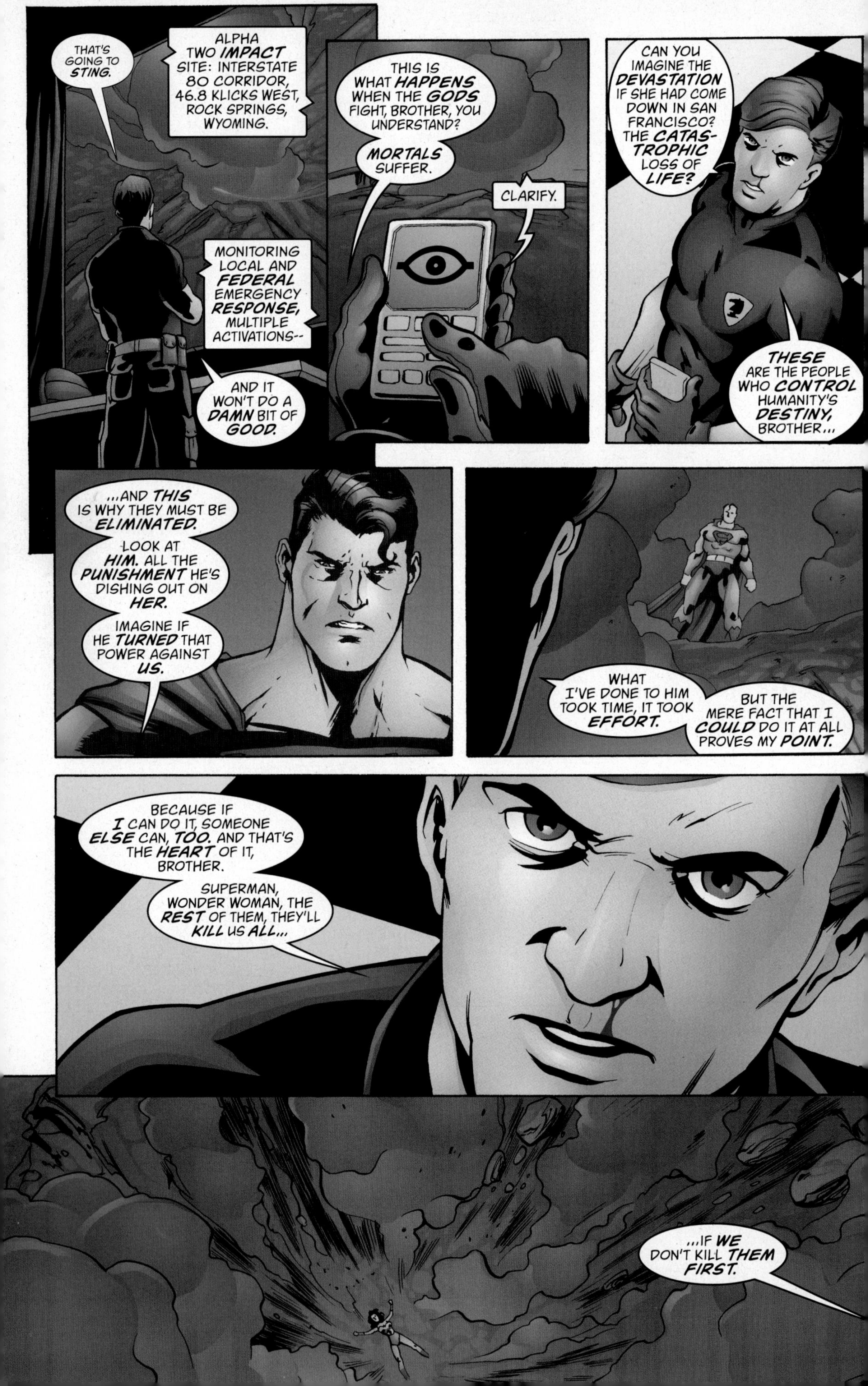

THAT'S GOING TO STING.
ALPHA TWO IMPACT SITE: INTERSTATE 80 CORRIDOR, 46.8 KLICKS WEST, ROCK SPRINGS, WYOMING.
MONITORING LOCAL AND FEDERAL EMERGENCY RESPONSE, MULTIPLE ACTIVATIONS--
AND IT WON'T DO A DAMN BIT OF GOOD.
THIS IS WHAT HAPPENS WHEN THE GODS FIGHT, BROTHER, YOU UNDERSTAND?
MORTALS SUFFER.
CLARIFY.
CAN YOU IMAGINE THE DEVASTATION IF SHE HAD COME DOWN IN SAN FRANCISCO? THE CATASTROPHIC LOSS OF LIFE?
THESE ARE THE PEOPLE WHO CONTROL HUMANITY'S DESTINY, BROTHER...
...AND THIS IS WHY THEY MUST BE ELIMINATED.
LOOK AT HIM. ALL THE PUNISHMENT HE'S DISHING OUT ON HER.
IMAGINE IF HE TURNED THAT POWER AGAINST US.
WHAT I'VE DONE TO HIM TOOK TIME, IT TOOK EFFORT.
BUT THE MERE FACT THAT I COULD DO IT AT ALL PROVES MY POINT.
BECAUSE IF I CAN DO IT, SOMEONE ELSE CAN, TOO. AND THAT'S THE HEART OF IT, BROTHER.
SUPERMAN, WONDER WOMAN, THE REST OF THEM, THEY'LL KILL US ALL...
...IF WE DON'T KILL THEM FIRST.

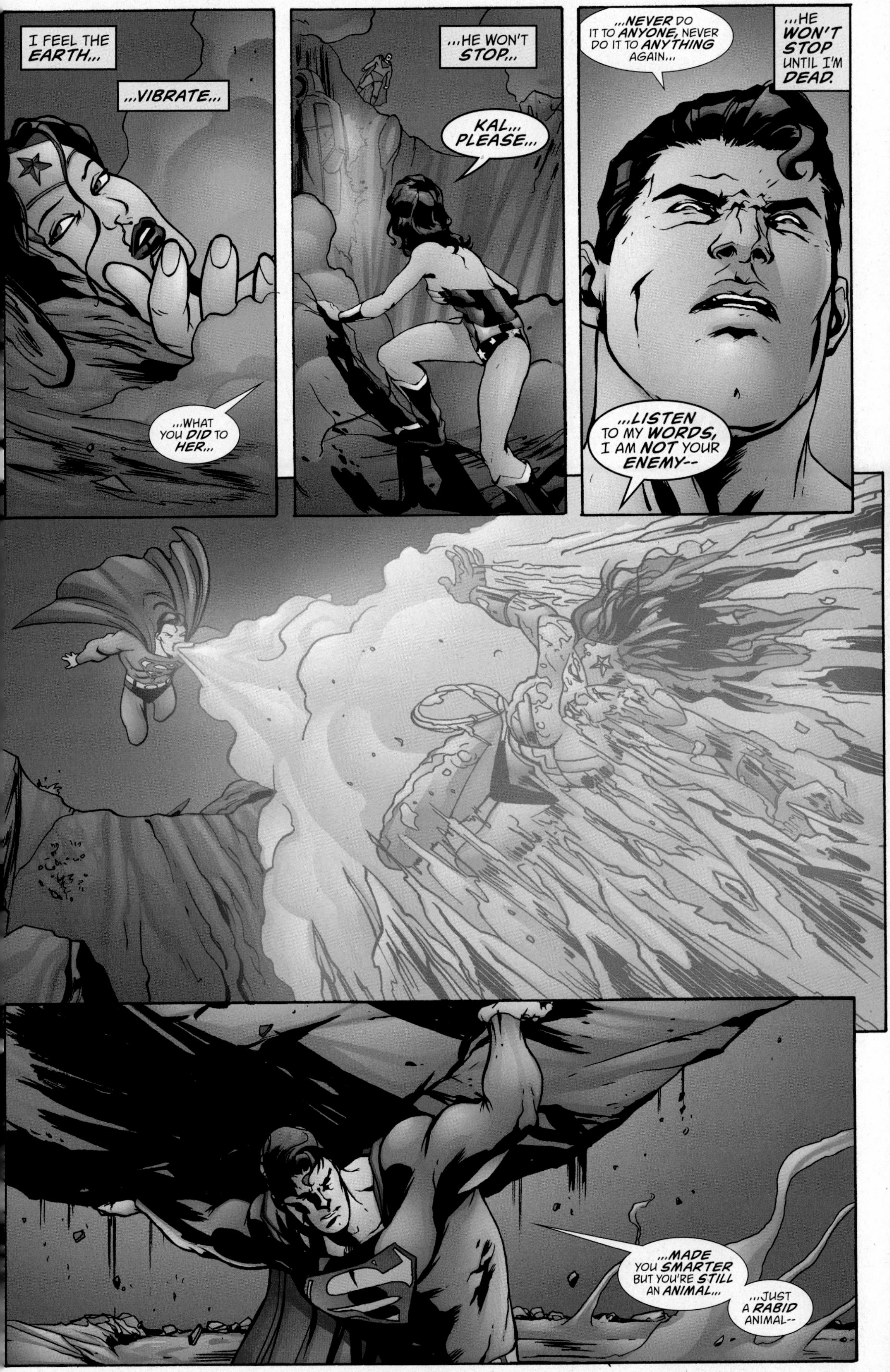

I FEEL THE EARTH...
...VIBRATE...
...WHAT YOU DID TO HER...
...HE WON'T STOP...
KAL... PLEASE...
...NEVER DO IT TO ANYONE, NEVER DO IT TO ANYTHING AGAIN...
...HE WON'T STOP UNTIL I'M DEAD.
...LISTEN TO MY WORDS, I AM NOT YOUR ENEMY--
...MADE YOU SMARTER BUT YOU'RE STILL AN ANIMAL...
...JUST A RABID ANIMAL--

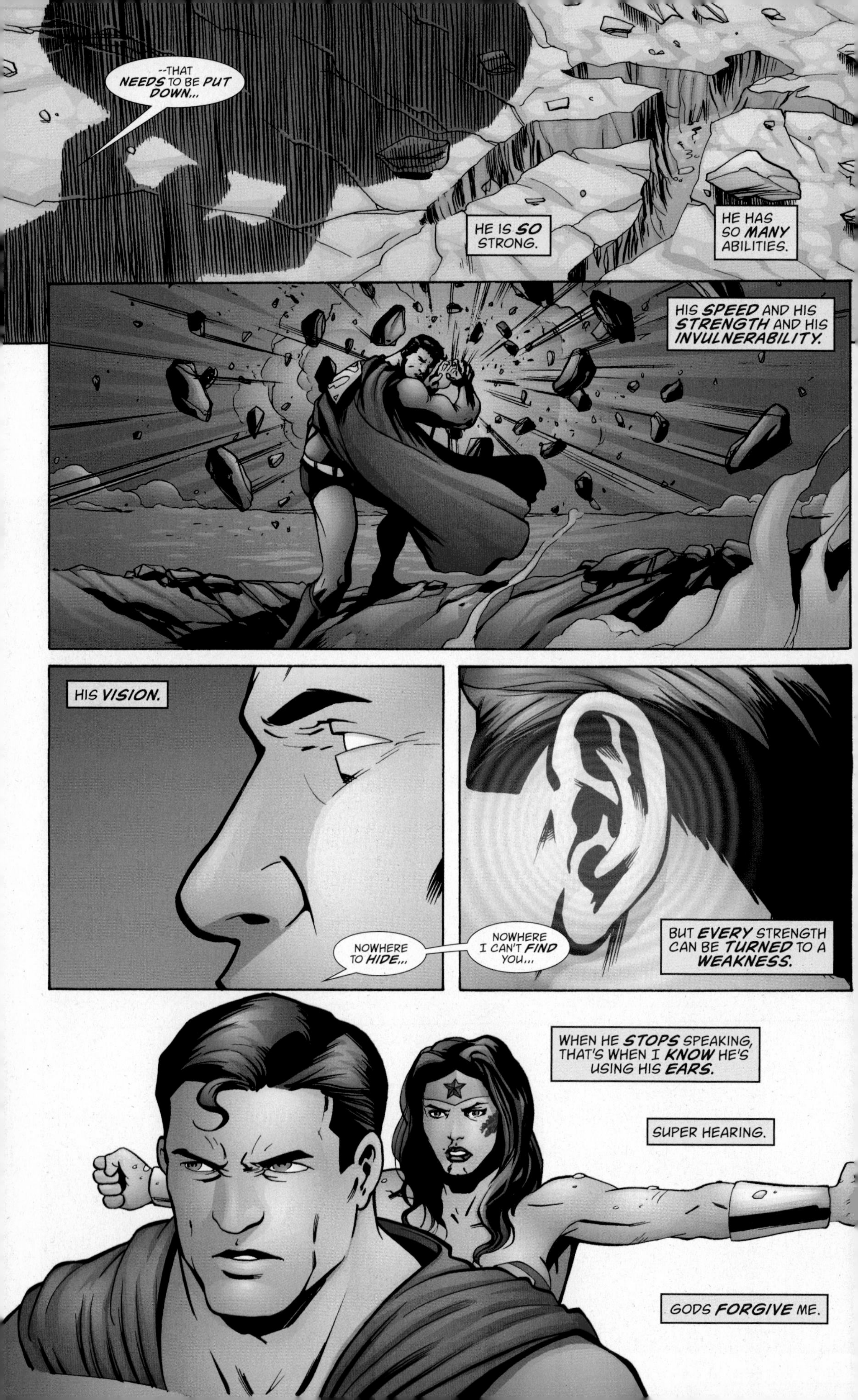
--THAT NEEDS TO BE PUT DOWN...
HE IS SO STRONG.
HE HAS SO MANY ABILITIES.
HIS SPEED AND HIS STRENGTH AND HIS INVULNERABILITY.
HIS VISION.
NOWHERE TO HIDE...
NOWHERE I CAN'T FIND YOU...
BUT EVERY STRENGTH CAN BE TURNED TO A WEAKNESS.
WHEN HE STOPS SPEAKING, THAT'S WHEN I KNOW HE'S USING HIS EARS.
SUPER HEARING.
GODS FORGIVE ME.

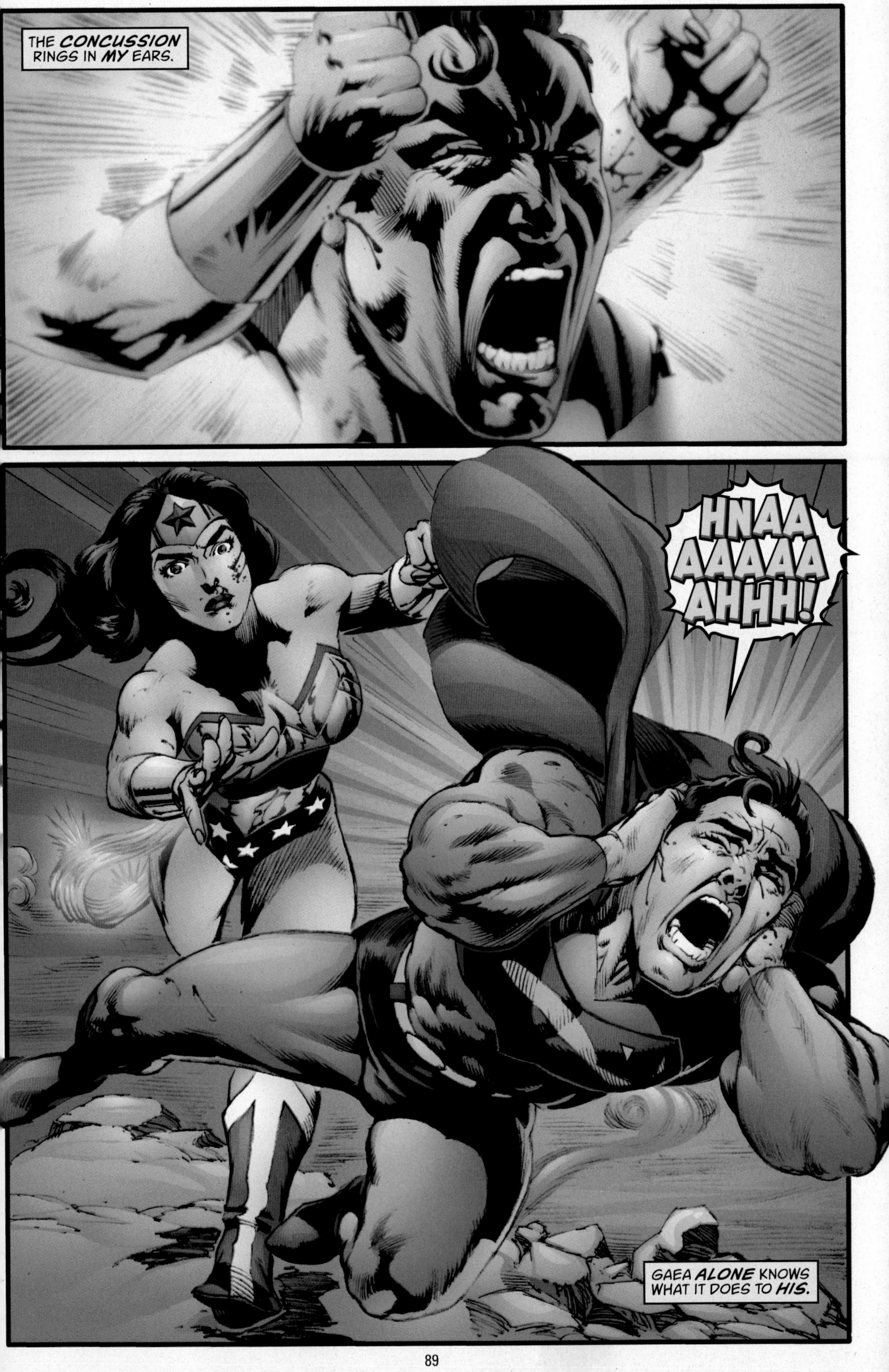
THE CONCUSSION RINGS IN MY EARS.
HNAA AAAAA AHHH!
GAEA ALONE KNOWS WHAT IT DOES TO HIS.

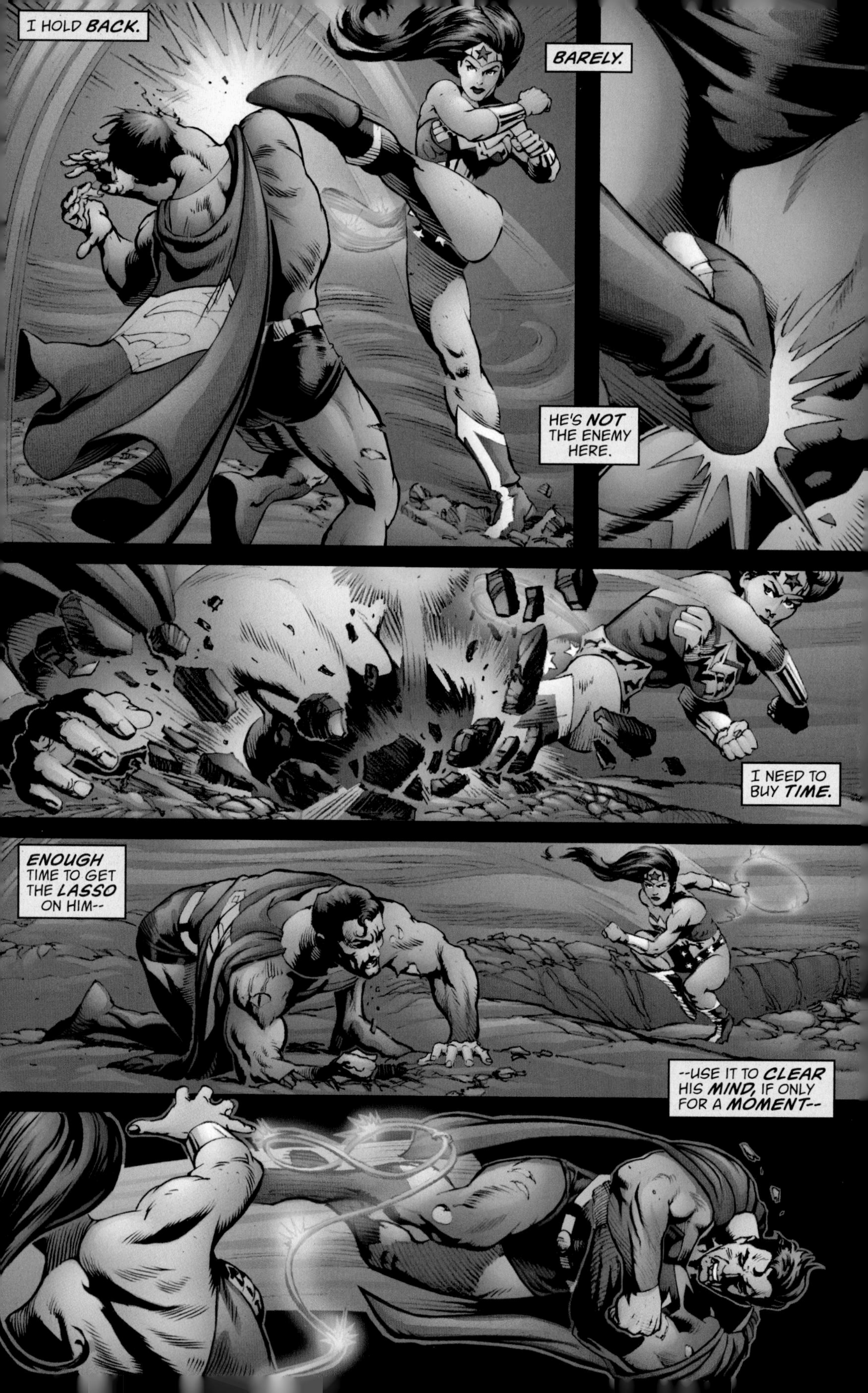
I HOLD BACK.
BARELY.
HE'S NOT THE ENEMY HERE.
I NEED TO BUY TIME.
ENOUGH TIME TO GET THE LASSO ON HIM--
--USE IT TO CLEAR HIS MIND, IF ONLY FOR A MOMENT--

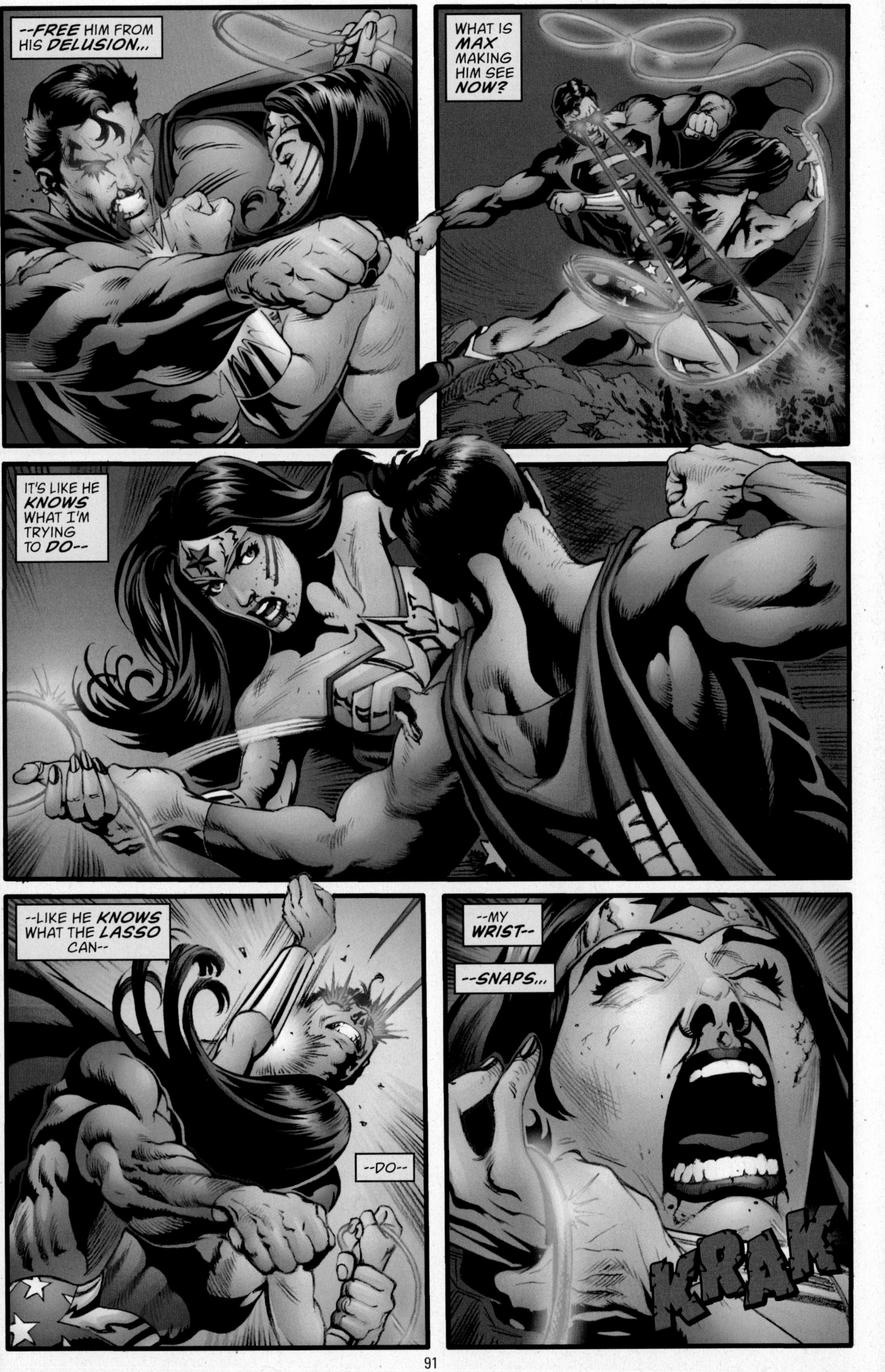
--FREE HIM FROM HIS DELUSION...
WHAT IS MAX MAKING HIM SEE NOW?
IT'S LIKE HE KNOWS WHAT I'M TRYING TO DO--
--LIKE HE KNOWS WHAT THE LASSO CAN--
--DO--
--MY WRIST--
--SNAPS...
KRAK

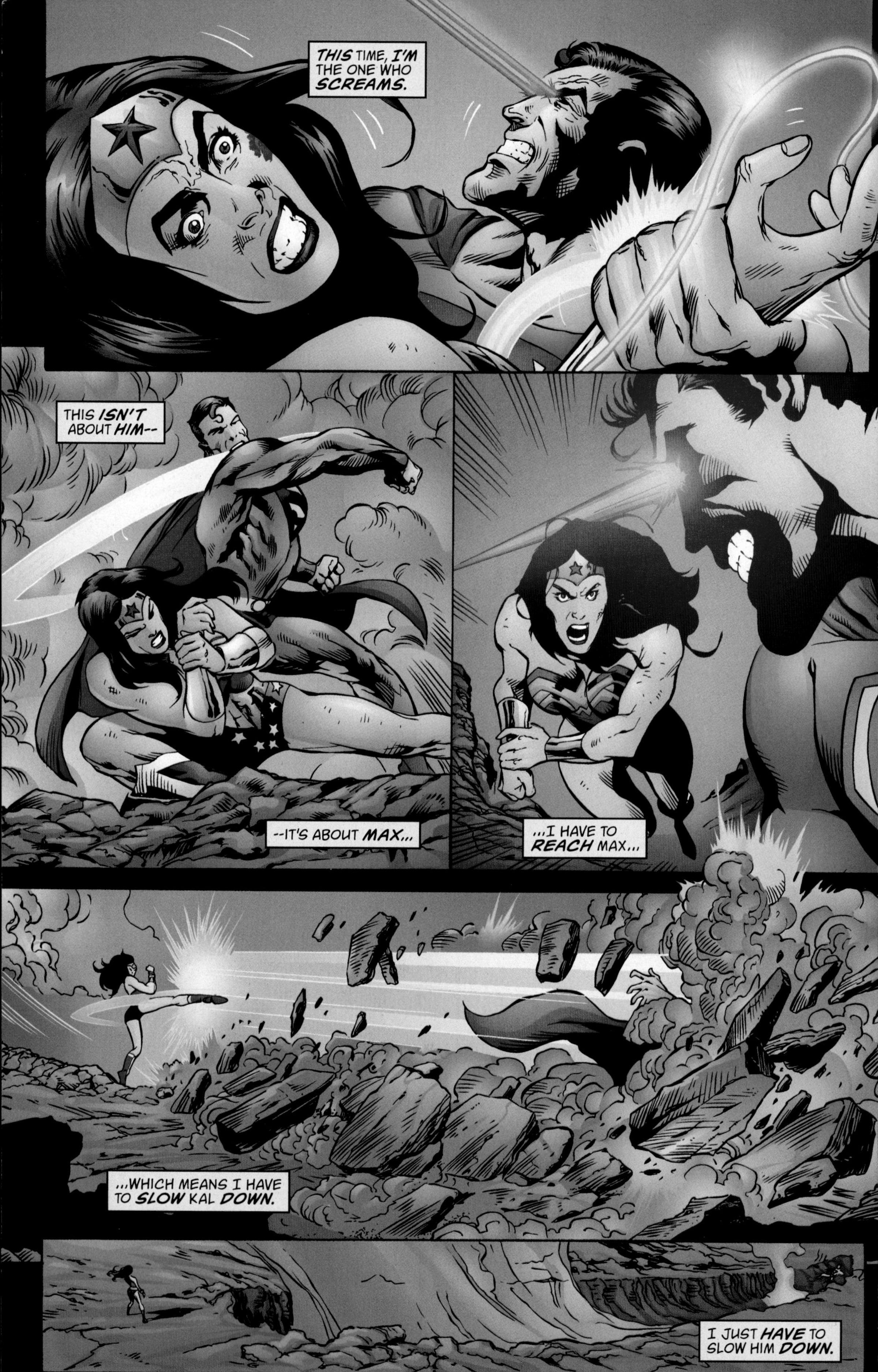
THIS TIME, I'M THE ONE WHO SCREAMS.
THIS ISN'T ABOUT HIM--
--IT'S ABOUT MAX...
...I HAVE TO REACH MAX...
...WHICH MEANS I HAVE TO SLOW KAL DOWN.
I JUST HAVE TO SLOW HIM DOWN.

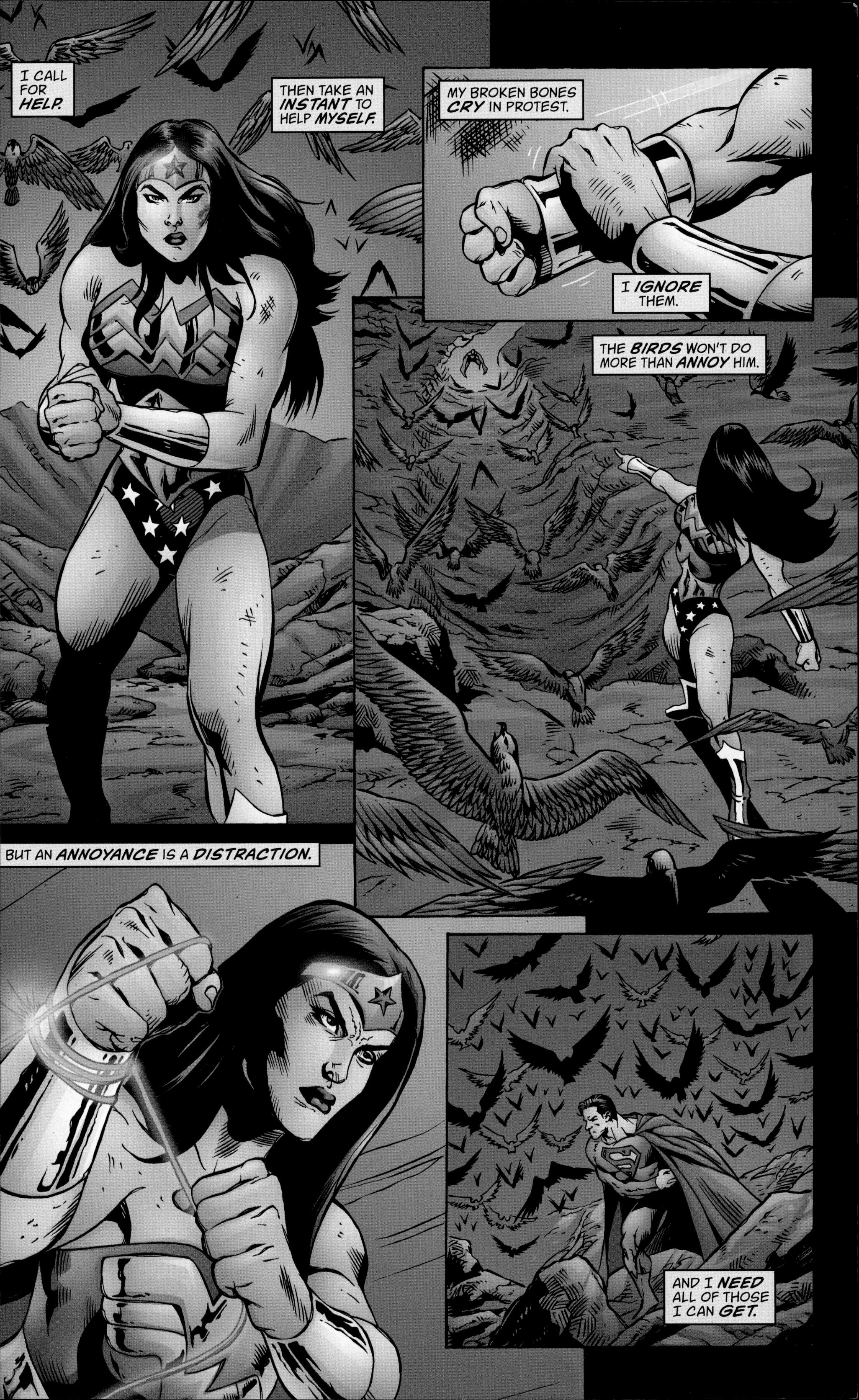
I CALL FOR HELP.
THEN TAKE AN INSTANT TO HELP MYSELF.
MY BROKEN BONES CRY IN PROTEST.
I IGNORE THEM.
THE BIRDS WON'T DO MORE THAN ANNOY HIM.
BUT AN ANNOYANCE IS A DISTRACTION.
AND I NEED ALL OF THOSE I CAN GET.

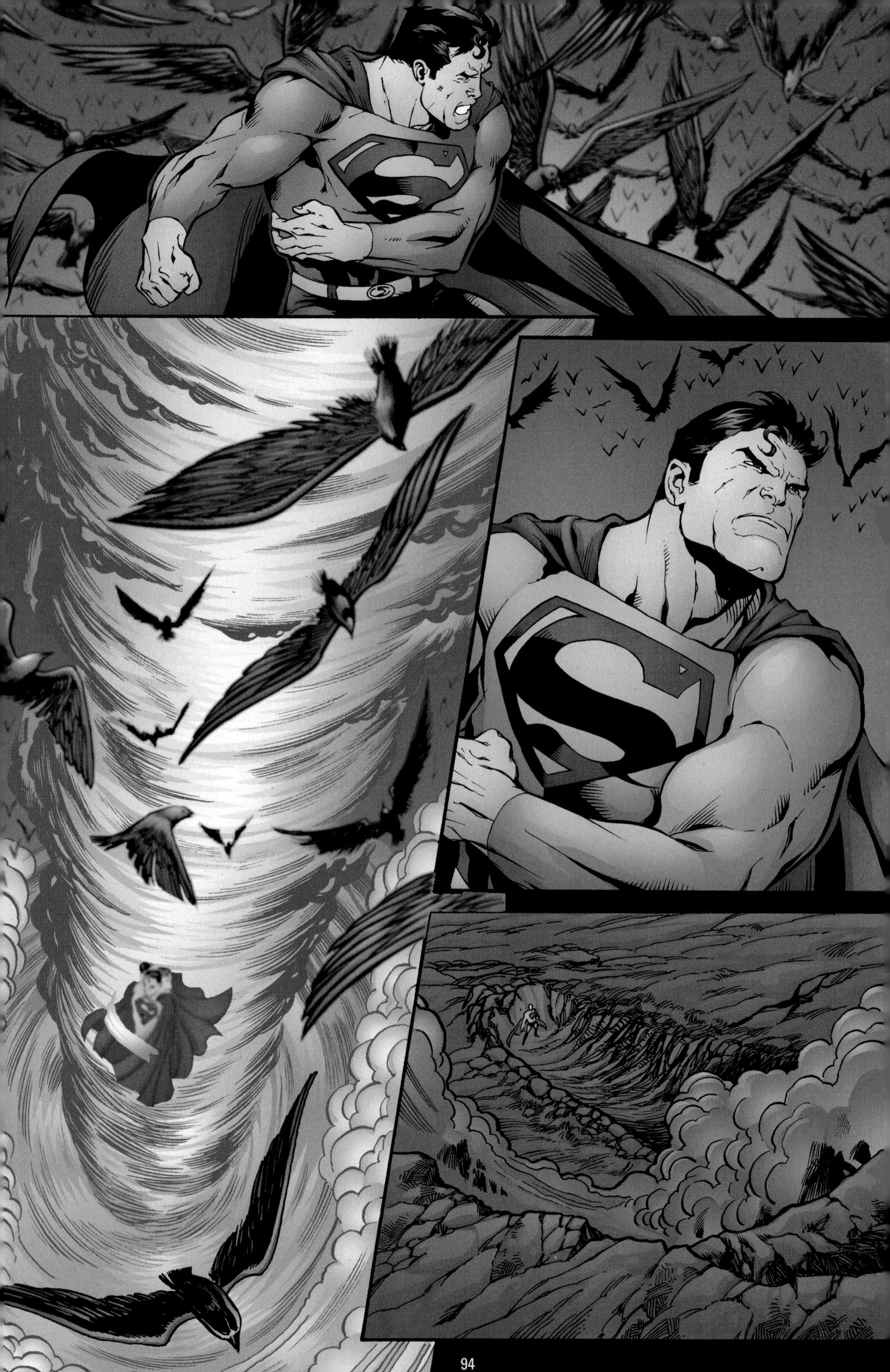

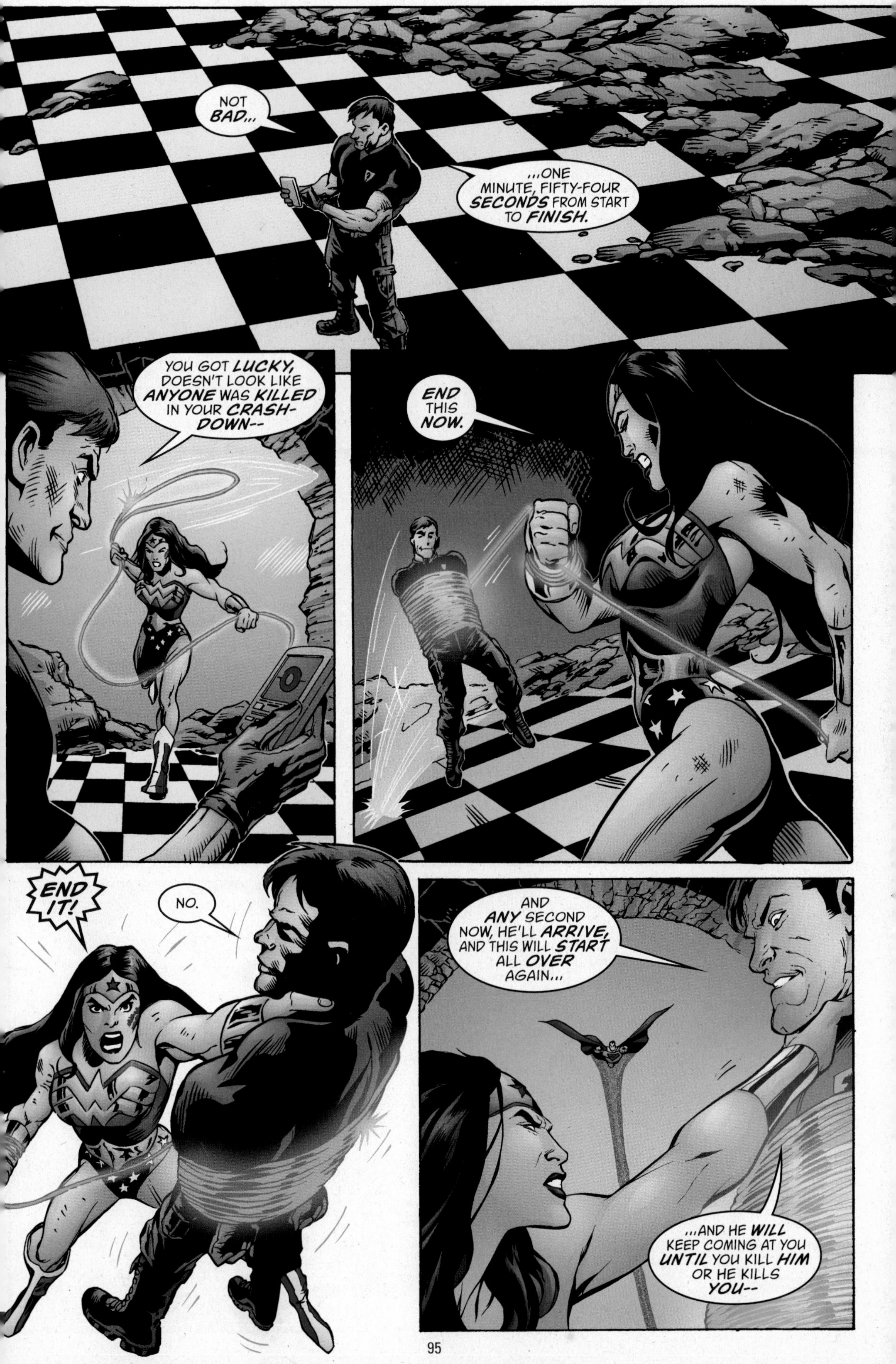
NOT BAD...
...ONE MINUTE, FIFTY-FOUR SECONDS FROM START TO FINISH.
YOU GOT LUCKY, DOESN'T LOOK LIKE ANYONE WAS KILLED IN YOUR CRASH-DOWN--
END THIS NOW.
END IT!
NO.
AND ANY SECOND NOW, HE'LL ARRIVE, AND THIS WILL START ALL OVER AGAIN...
...AND HE WILL KEEP COMING AT YOU UNTIL YOU KILL HIM OR HE KILLS YOU--

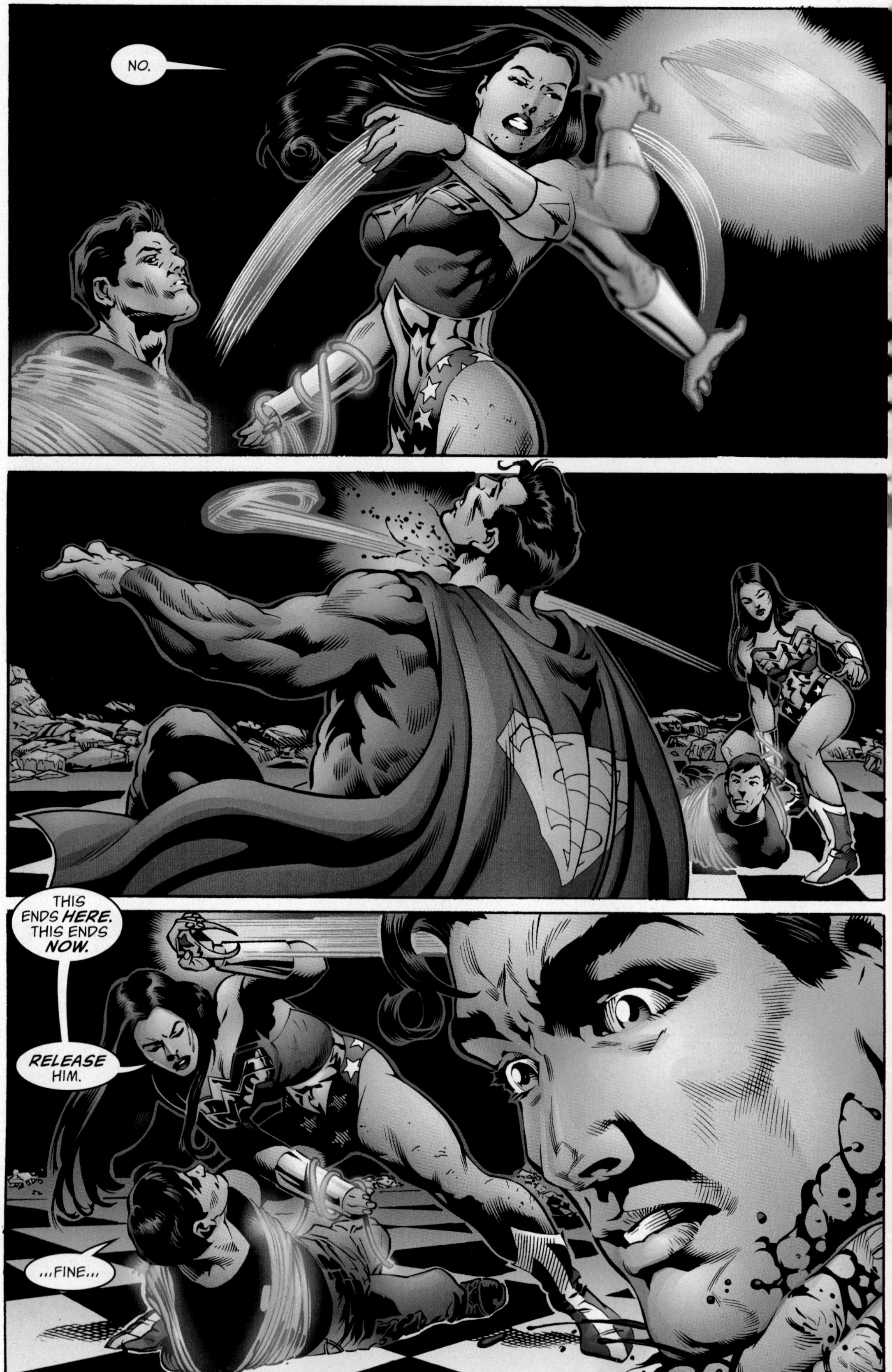
NO.
THIS ENDS HERE. THIS ENDS NOW.
RELEASE HIM.
...FINE...

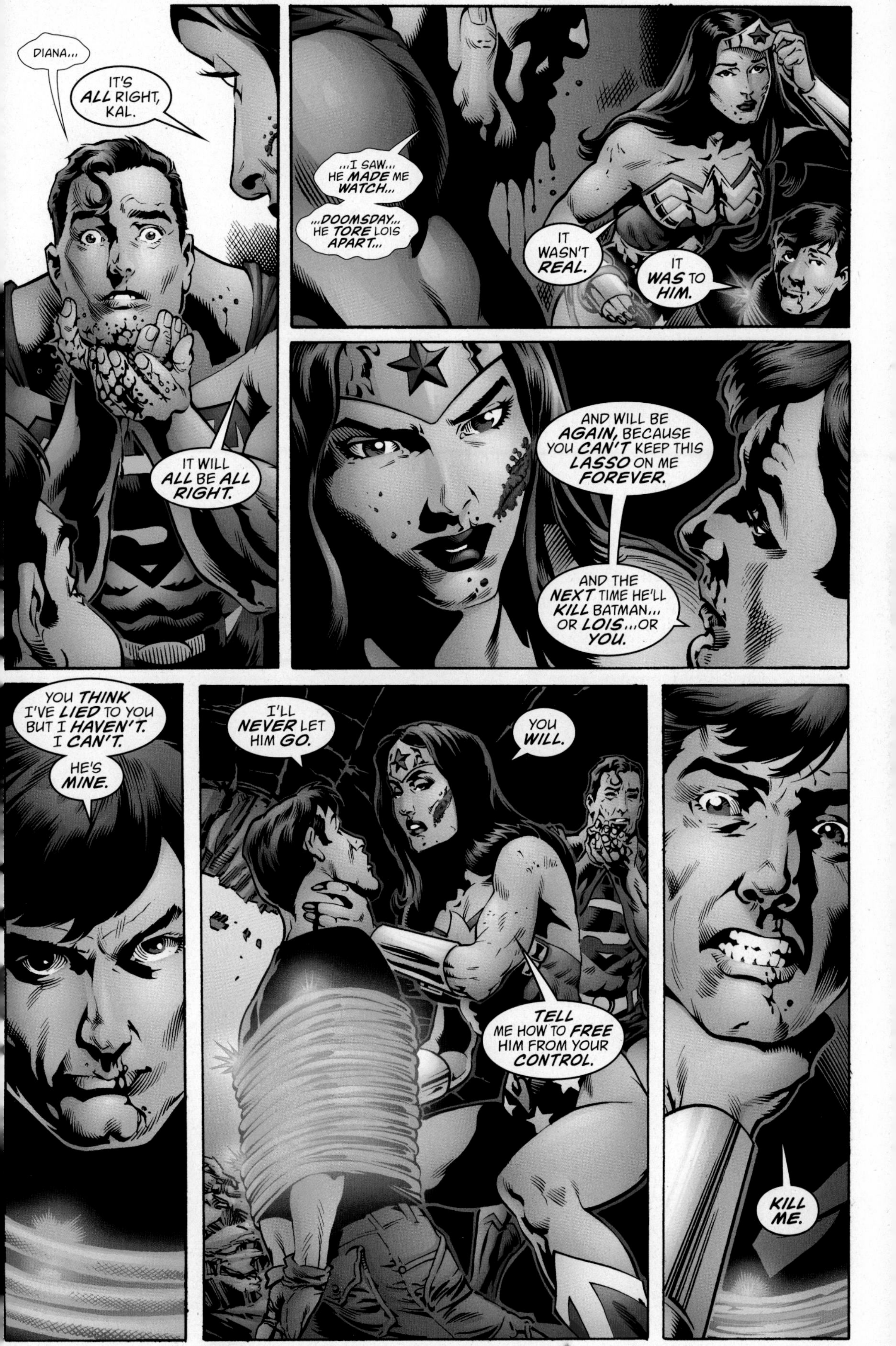
DIANA...
IT'S ALL RIGHT, KAL.
IT WILL ALL BE ALL RIGHT.
...I SAW... HE MADE ME WATCH...
...DOOMSDAY... HE TORE LOIS APART...
IT WASN'T REAL.
IT WAS TO HIM.
AND WILL BE AGAIN, BECAUSE YOU CAN'T KEEP THIS LASSO ON ME FOREVER.
AND THE NEXT TIME HE'LL KILL BATMAN... OR LOIS...OR YOU.
YOU THINK I'VE LIED TO YOU BUT I HAVEN'T. I CAN'T.
HE'S MINE.
I'LL NEVER LET HIM GO.
YOU WILL.
TELL ME HOW TO FREE HIM FROM YOUR CONTROL.
KILL ME.

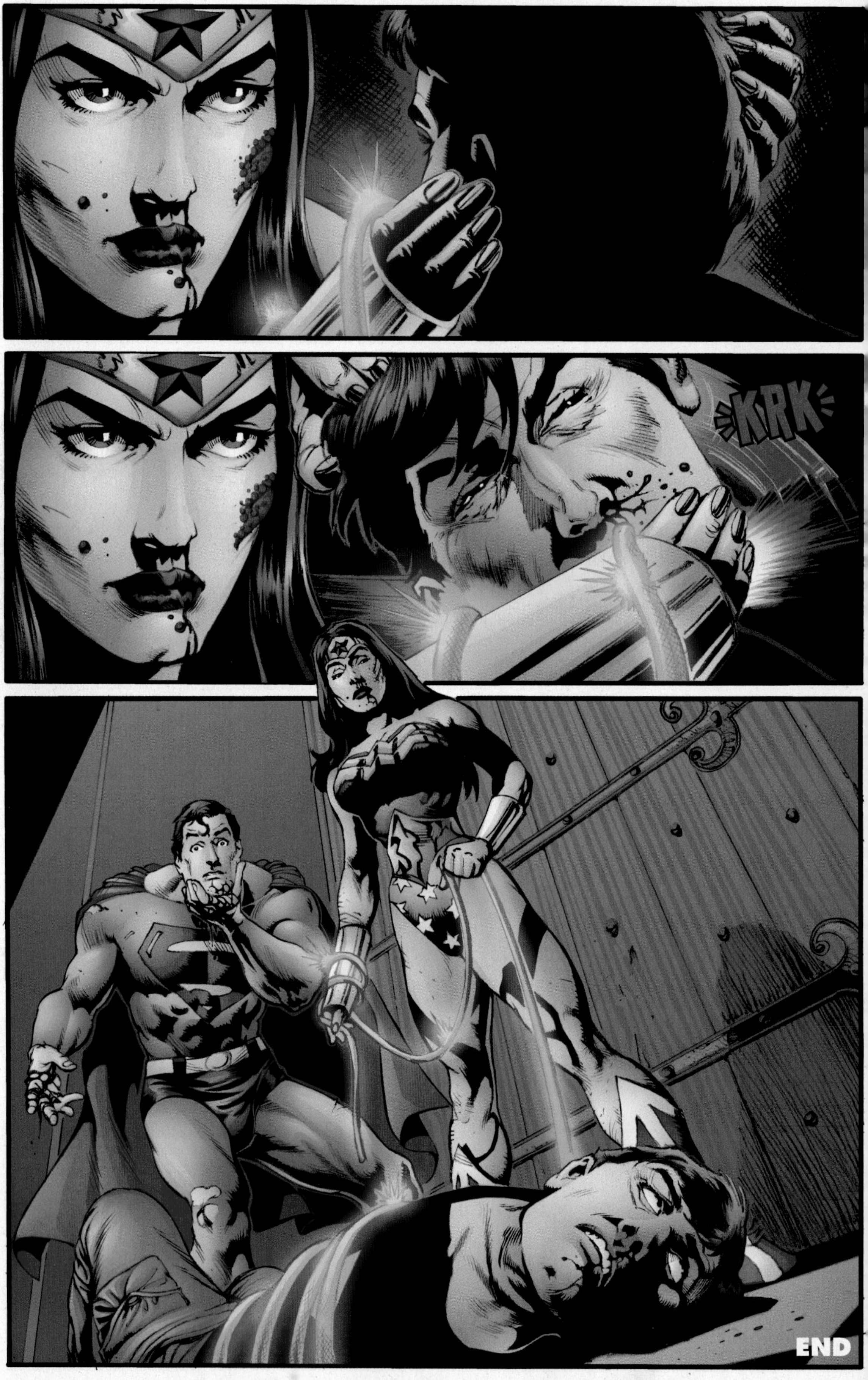
KRK
END

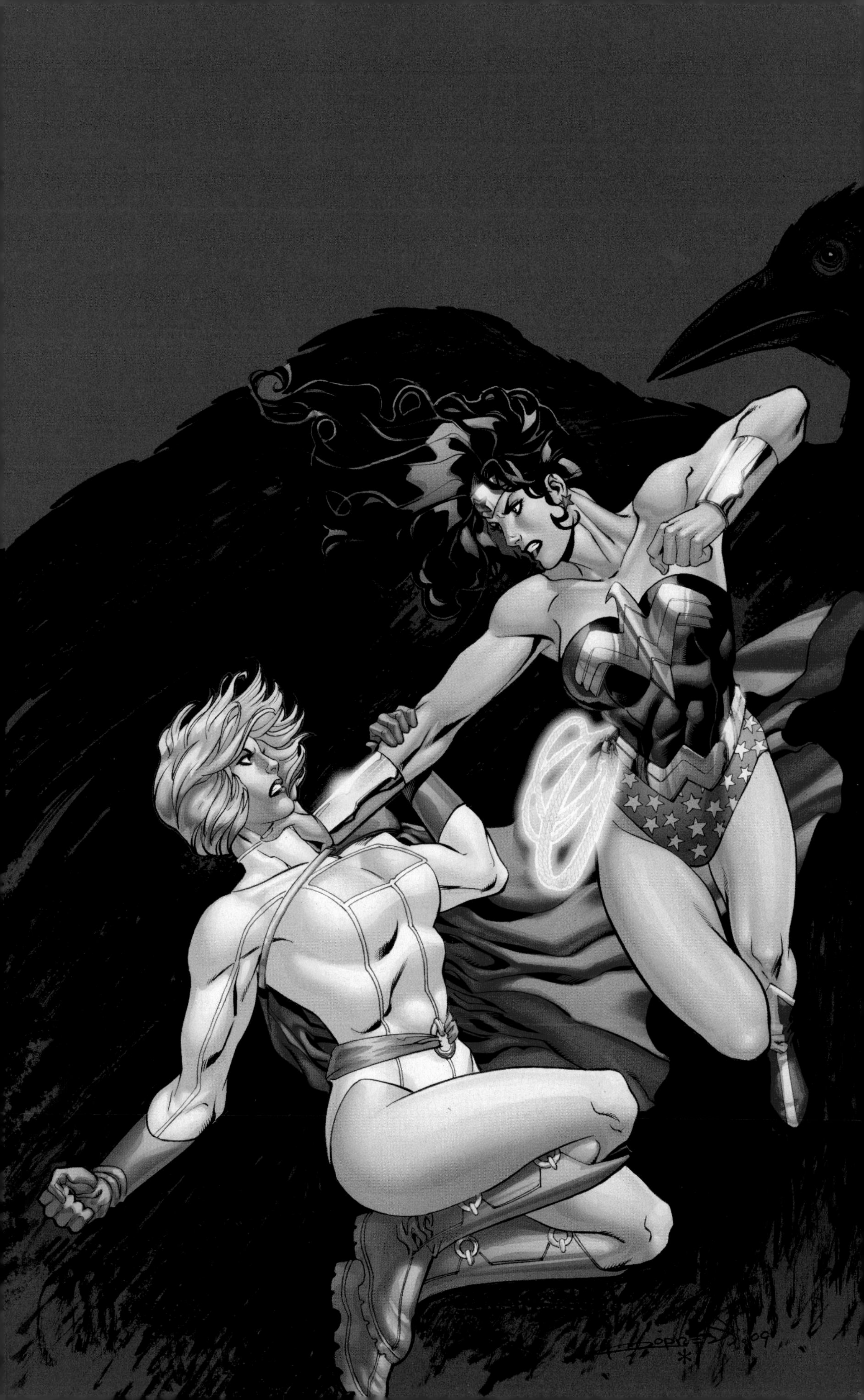

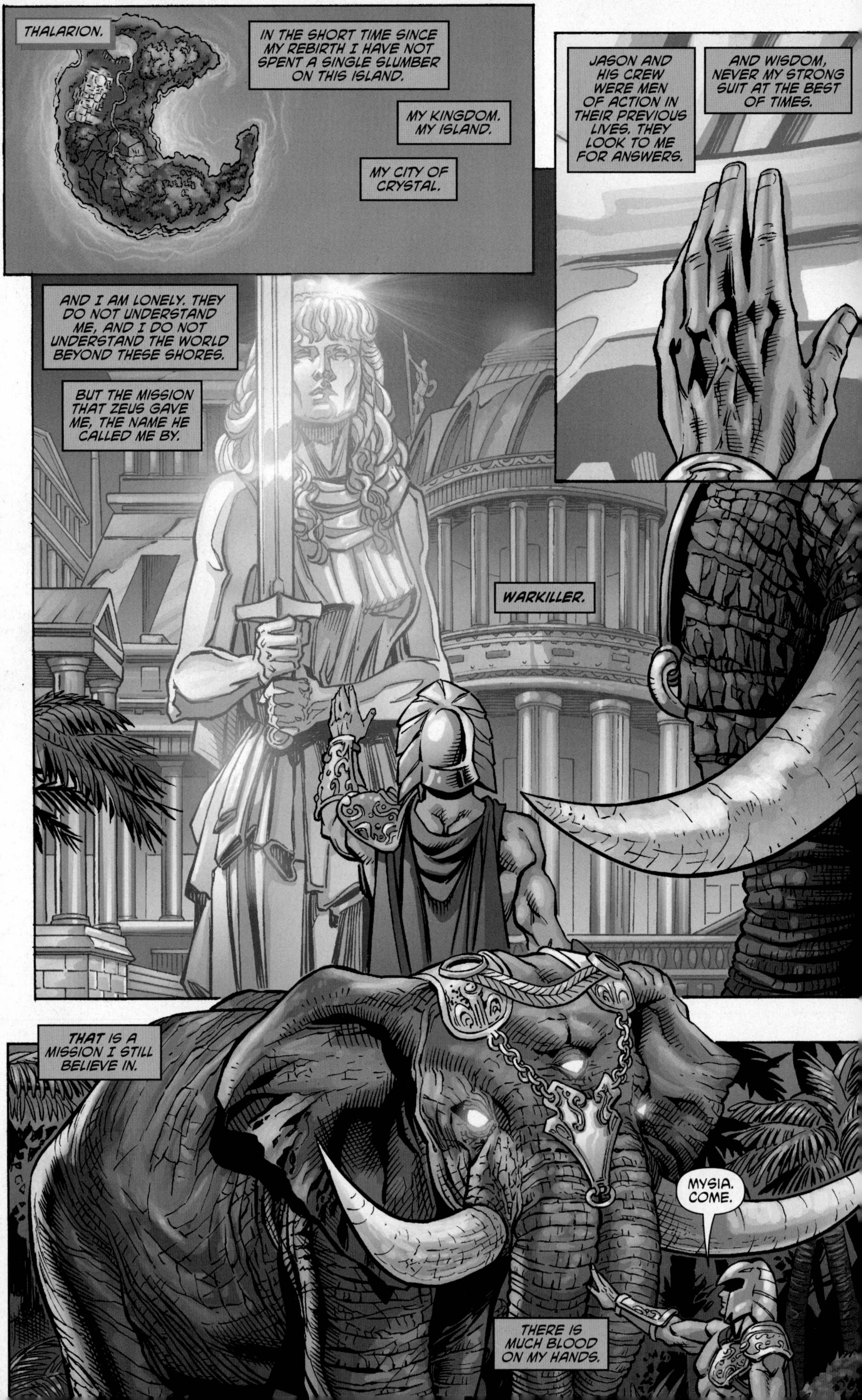
THALARION.
IN THE SHORT TIME SINCE MY REBIRTH I HAVE NOT SPENT A SINGLE SLUMBER ON THIS ISLAND.
MY KINGDOM. MY ISLAND.
MY CITY OF CRYSTAL.
JASON AND HIS CREW WERE MEN OF ACTION IN THEIR PREVIOUS LIVES. THEY LOOK TO ME FOR ANSWERS.
AND WISDOM, NEVER MY STRONG SUIT AT THE BEST OF TIMES.
AND I AM LONELY. THEY DO NOT UNDERSTAND ME, AND I DO NOT UNDERSTAND THE WORLD BEYOND THESE SHORES.
BUT THE MISSION THAT ZEUS GAVE ME, THE NAME HE CALLED ME BY.
WARKILLER.
THAT IS A MISSION I STILL BELIEVE IN.
MYSIA. COME.
THERE IS MUCH BLOOD ON MY HANDS.

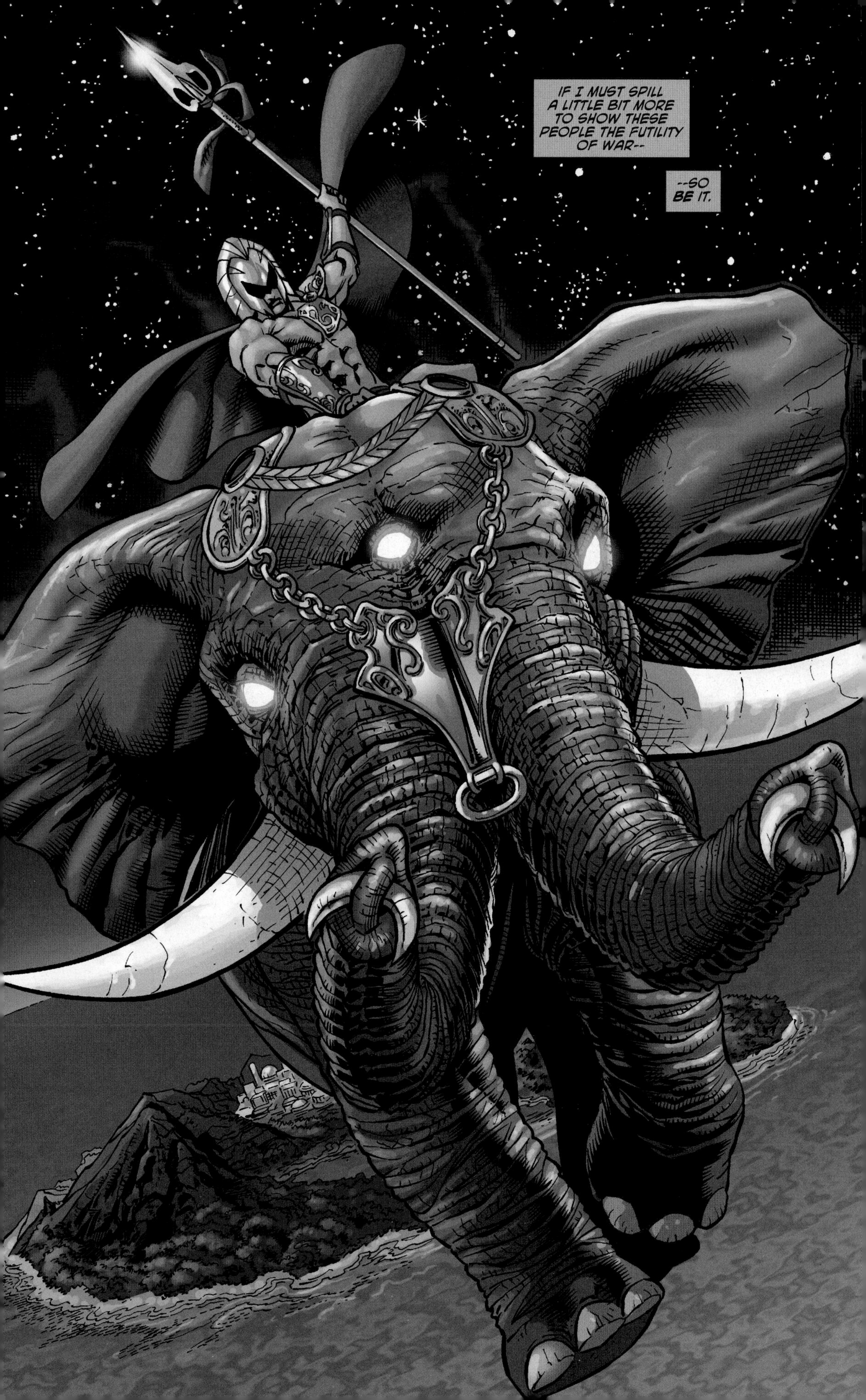
IF I MUST SPILL A LITTLE BIT MORE TO SHOW THESE PEOPLE THE FUTILITY OF WAR--
--SO BE IT.

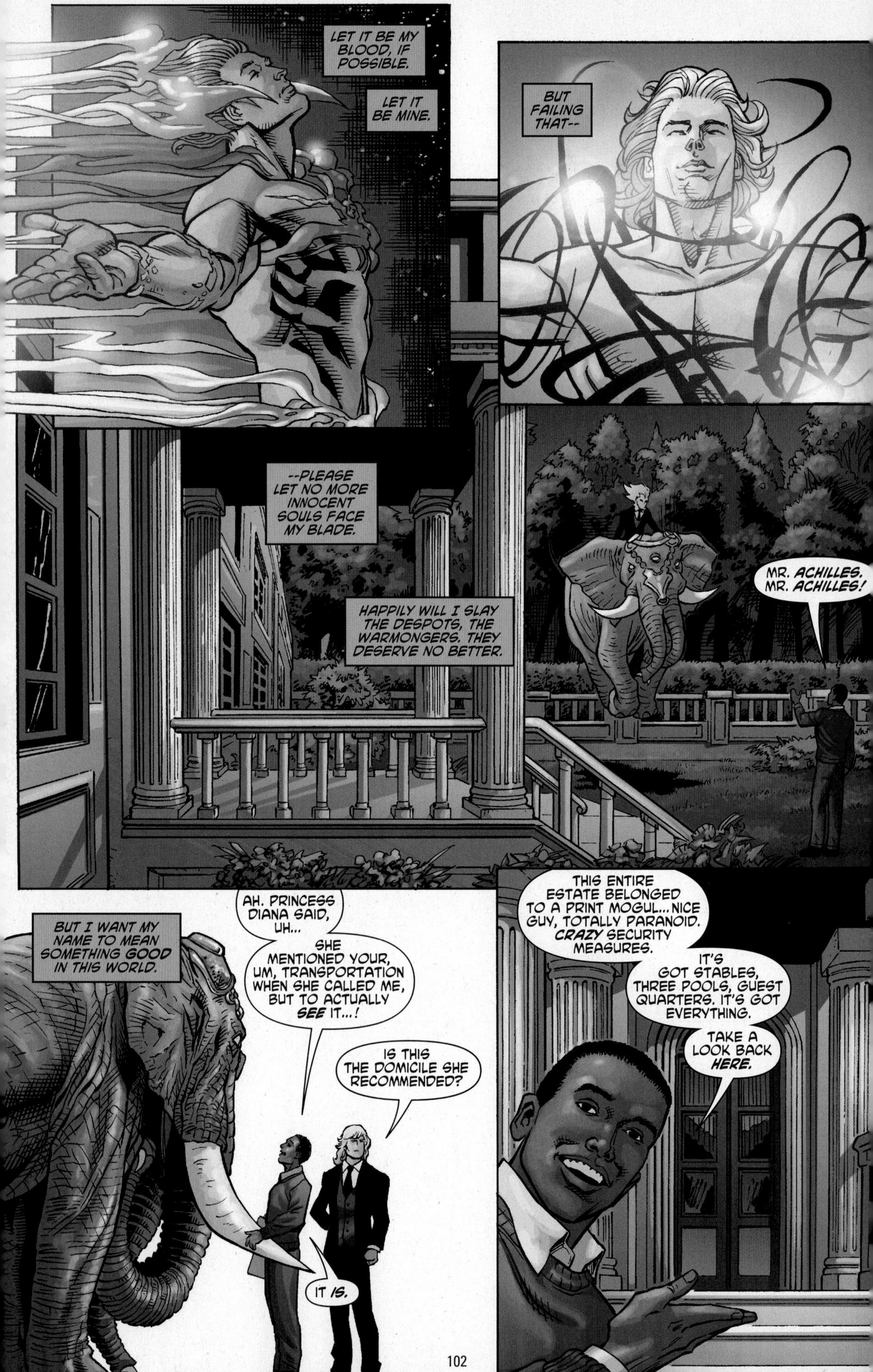

LET IT BE MY BLOOD, IF POSSIBLE.
LET IT BE MINE.
BUT FAILING THAT--
--PLEASE LET NO MORE INNOCENT SOULS FACE MY BLADE.
HAPPILY WILL I SLAY THE DESPOTS, THE WARMONGERS. THEY DESERVE NO BETTER.
MR. ACHILLES. MR. ACHILLES!
BUT I WANT MY NAME TO MEAN SOMETHING GOOD IN THIS WORLD.
AH. PRINCESS DIANA SAID, UH...
SHE MENTIONED YOUR, UM, TRANSPORTATION WHEN SHE CALLED ME, BUT TO ACTUALLY SEE IT...!
IS THIS THE DOMICILE SHE RECOMMENDED?
IT IS.
THIS ENTIRE ESTATE BELONGED TO A PRINT MOGUL... NICE GUY, TOTALLY PARANOID. CRAZY SECURITY MEASURES.
IT'S GOT STABLES, THREE POOLS, GUEST QUARTERS. IT'S GOT EVERYTHING.
TAKE A LOOK BACK HERE.

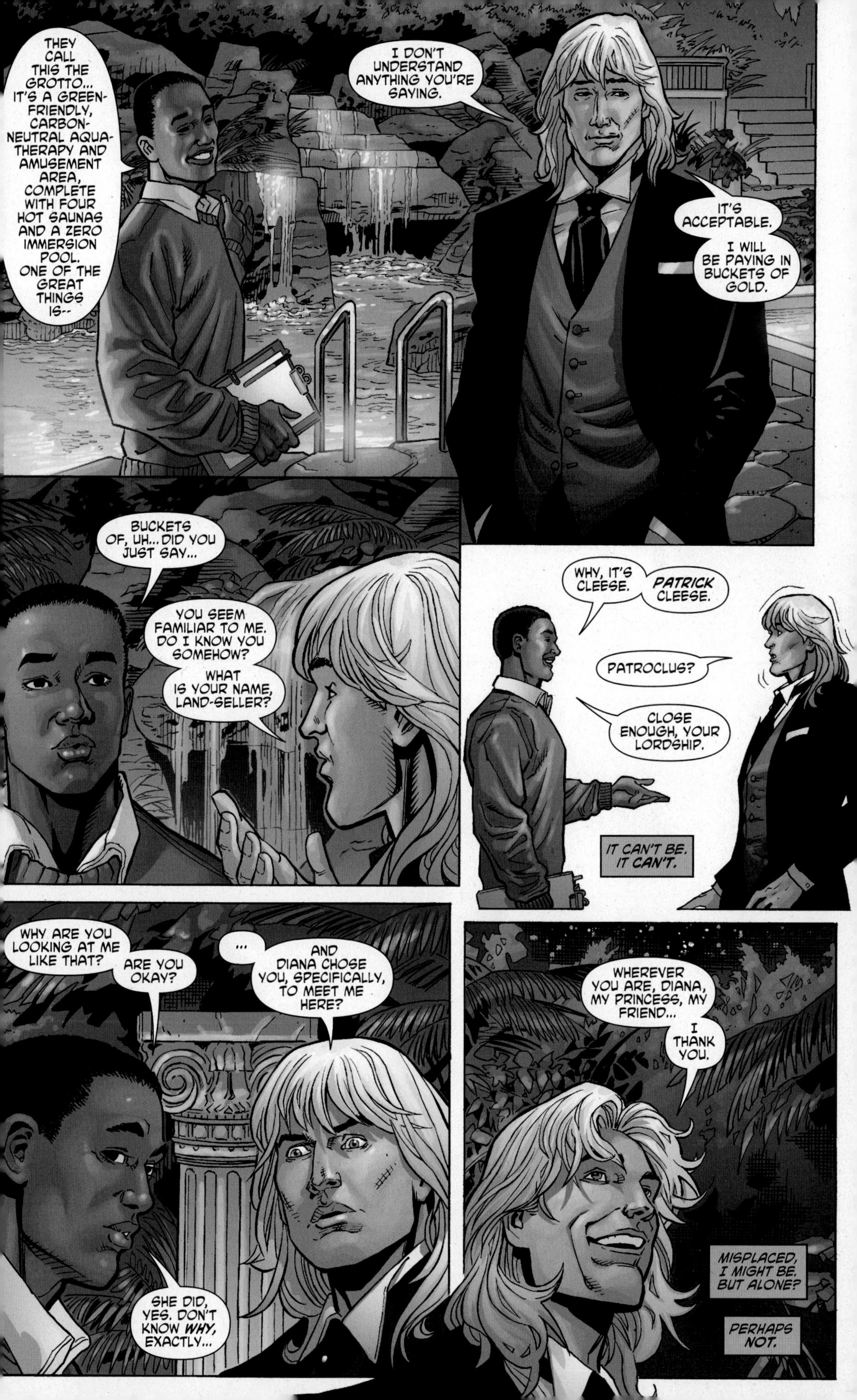
THEY CALL THIS THE GROTTO... IT'S A GREEN-FRIENDLY, CARBON-NEUTRAL AQUA-THERAPY AND AMUSEMENT AREA, COMPLETE WITH FOUR HOT SAUNAS AND A ZERO IMMERSION POOL. ONE OF THE GREAT THINGS IS--
I DON'T UNDERSTAND ANYTHING YOU'RE SAYING.
IT'S ACCEPTABLE.
I WILL BE PAYING IN BUCKETS OF GOLD.
BUCKETS OF, UH... DID YOU JUST SAY...
YOU SEEM FAMILIAR TO ME. DO I KNOW YOU SOMEHOW?
WHAT IS YOUR NAME, LAND-SELLER?
WHY, IT'S CLEESE.
PATRICK CLEESE.
PATROCLUS?
CLOSE ENOUGH, YOUR LORDSHIP.
IT CAN'T BE. IT CAN'T.
WHY ARE YOU LOOKING AT ME LIKE THAT?
ARE YOU OKAY?
...
AND DIANA CHOSE YOU, SPECIFICALLY, TO MEET ME HERE?
SHE DID, YES. DON'T KNOW WHY, EXACTLY...
WHEREVER YOU ARE, DIANA, MY PRINCESS, MY FRIEND...
I THANK YOU.
MISPLACED, I MIGHT BE. BUT ALONE?
PERHAPS NOT.

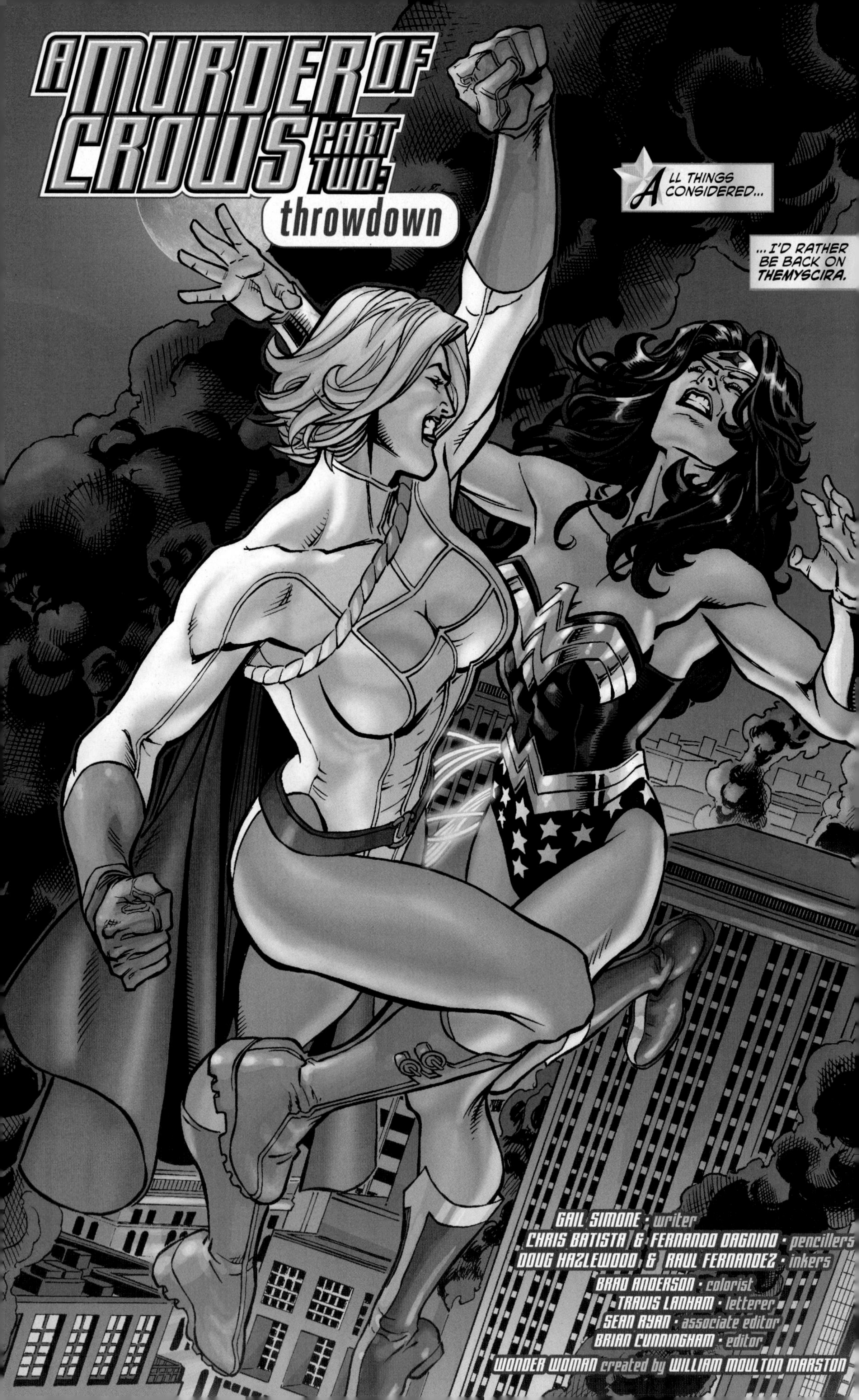
A MURDER OF CROWS PART TWO:
throwdown
ALL THINGS CONSIDERED...
...I'D RATHER BE BACK ON THEMYSCIRA.
GAIL SIMONE : writer
CHRIS BATISTA & FERNANDO DAGNINO : pencillers
DOUG HAZLEWOOD & RAUL FERNANDEZ : inkers
BRAD ANDERSON : colorist
TRAVIS LANHAM : letterer
SEAN RYAN : associate editor
BRIAN CUNNINGHAM : editor
WONDER WOMAN created by WILLIAM MOULTON MARSTON

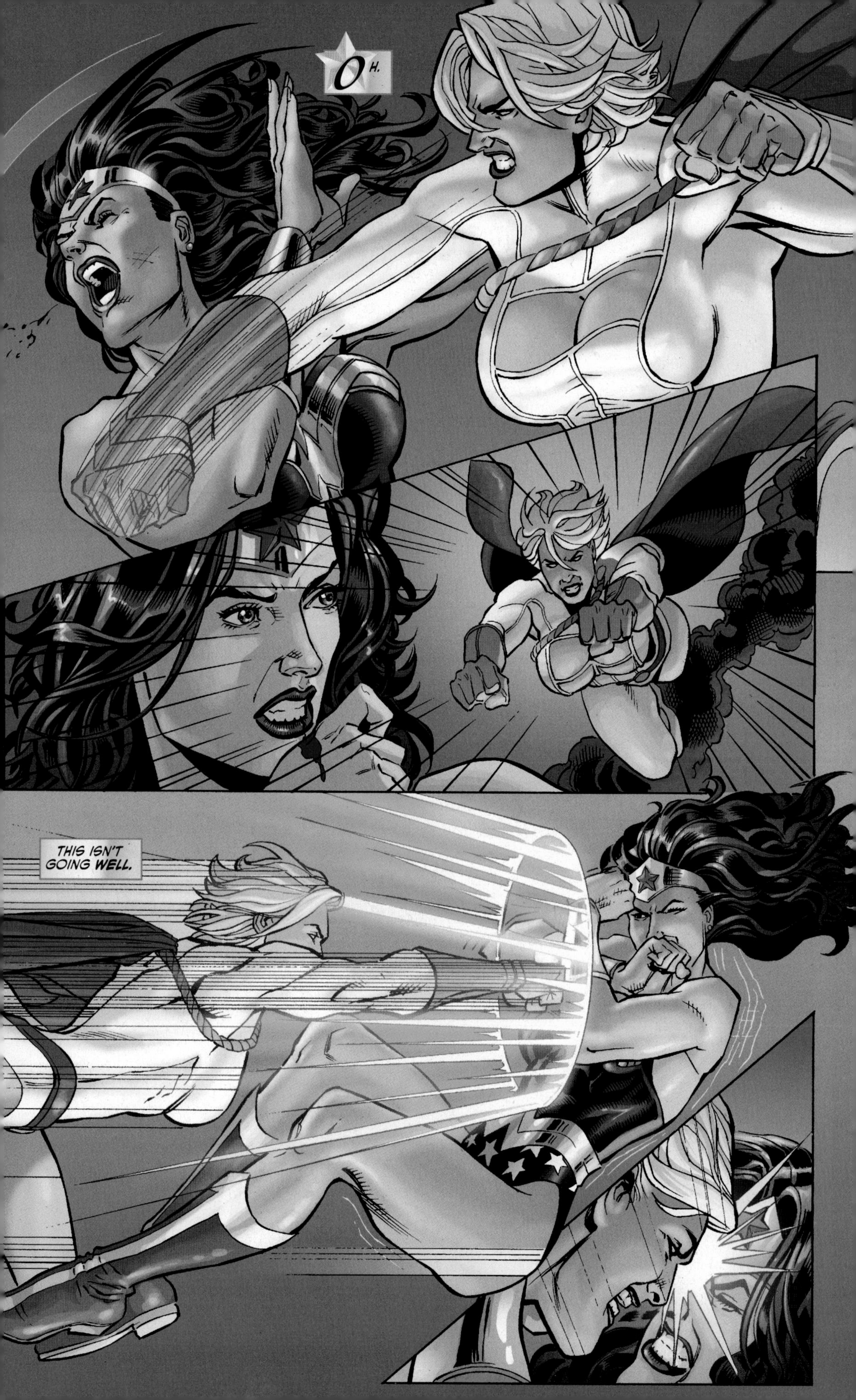
OH.
THIS ISN'T GOING WELL.

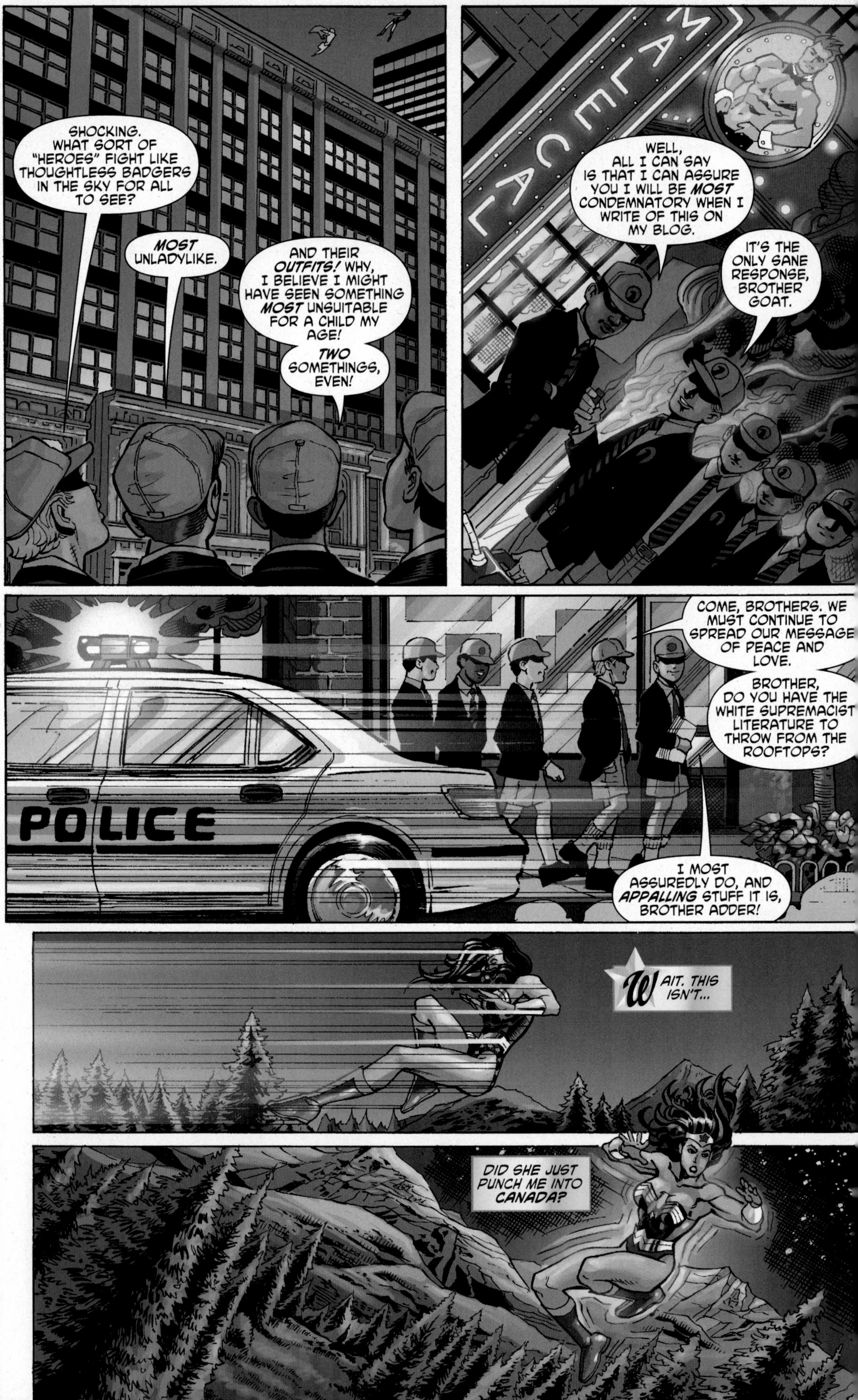
SHOCKING. WHAT SORT OF "HEROES" FIGHT LIKE THOUGHTLESS BADGERS IN THE SKY FOR ALL TO SEE?
MOST UNLADYLIKE.
AND THEIR OUTFITS! WHY, I BELIEVE I MIGHT HAVE SEEN SOMETHING MOST UNSUITABLE FOR A CHILD MY AGE!
TWO SOMETHINGS, EVEN!
WELL, ALL I CAN SAY IS THAT I CAN ASSURE YOU I WILL BE MOST CONDEMNATORY WHEN I WRITE OF THIS ON MY BLOG.
IT'S THE ONLY SANE RESPONSE, BROTHER GOAT.
COME, BROTHERS. WE MUST CONTINUE TO SPREAD OUR MESSAGE OF PEACE AND LOVE.
BROTHER, DO YOU HAVE THE WHITE SUPREMACIST LITERATURE TO THROW FROM THE ROOFTOPS?
POLICE
I MOST ASSUREDLY DO, AND APPALLING STUFF IT IS, BROTHER ADDER!
WAIT. THIS ISN'T...
DID SHE JUST PUNCH ME INTO CANADA?

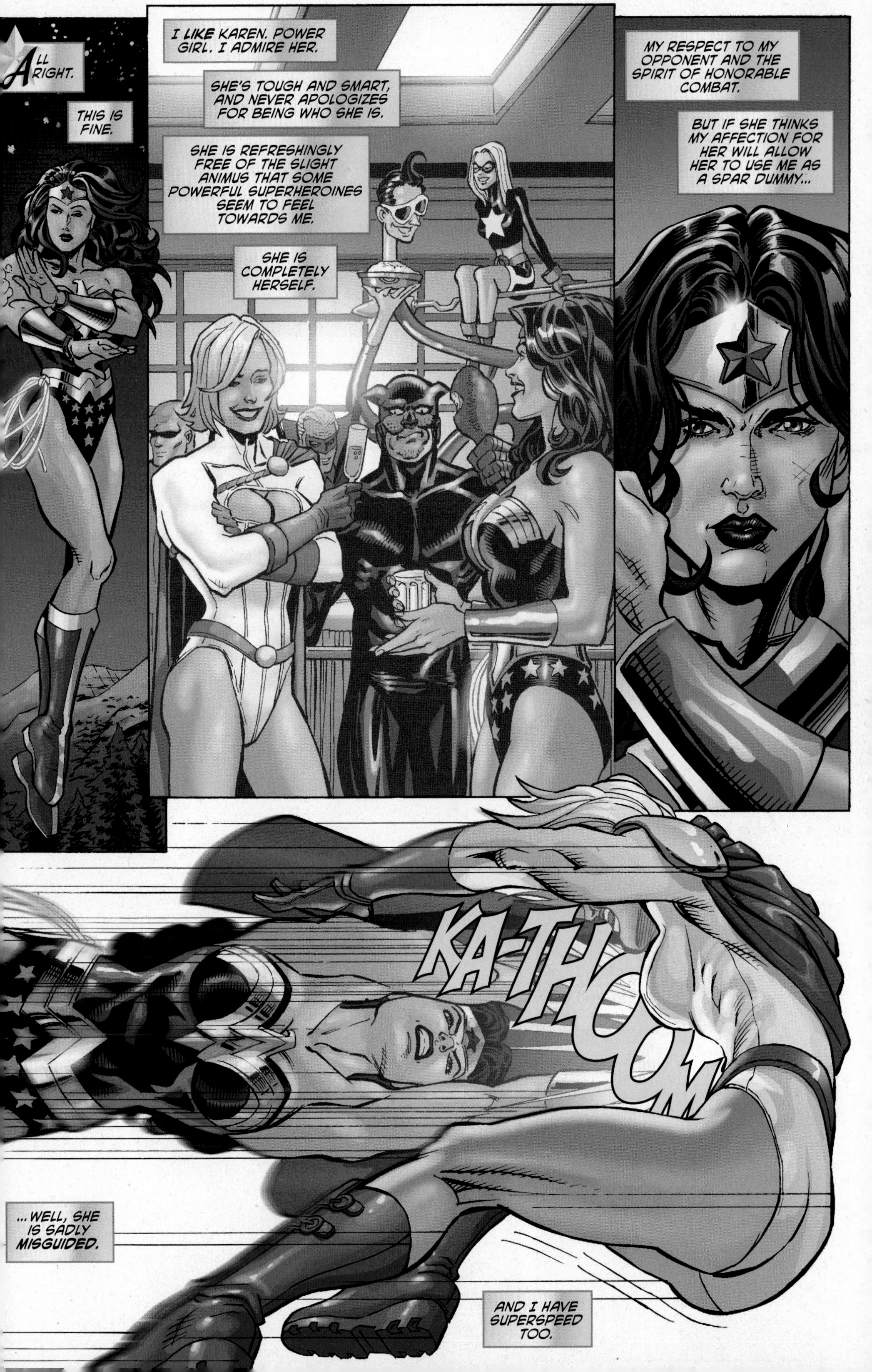
ALL RIGHT.
THIS IS FINE.
I LIKE KAREN. POWER GIRL. I ADMIRE HER.
SHE'S TOUGH AND SMART, AND NEVER APOLOGIZES FOR BEING WHO SHE IS.
SHE IS REFRESHINGLY FREE OF THE SLIGHT ANIMUS THAT SOME POWERFUL SUPERHEROINES SEEM TO FEEL TOWARDS ME.
SHE IS COMPLETELY HERSELF.
MY RESPECT TO MY OPPONENT AND THE SPIRIT OF HONORABLE COMBAT.
BUT IF SHE THINKS MY AFFECTION FOR HER WILL ALLOW HER TO USE ME AS A SPAR DUMMY...
KA-THOOM
...WELL, SHE IS SADLY MISGUIDED.
AND I HAVE SUPERSPEED TOO.

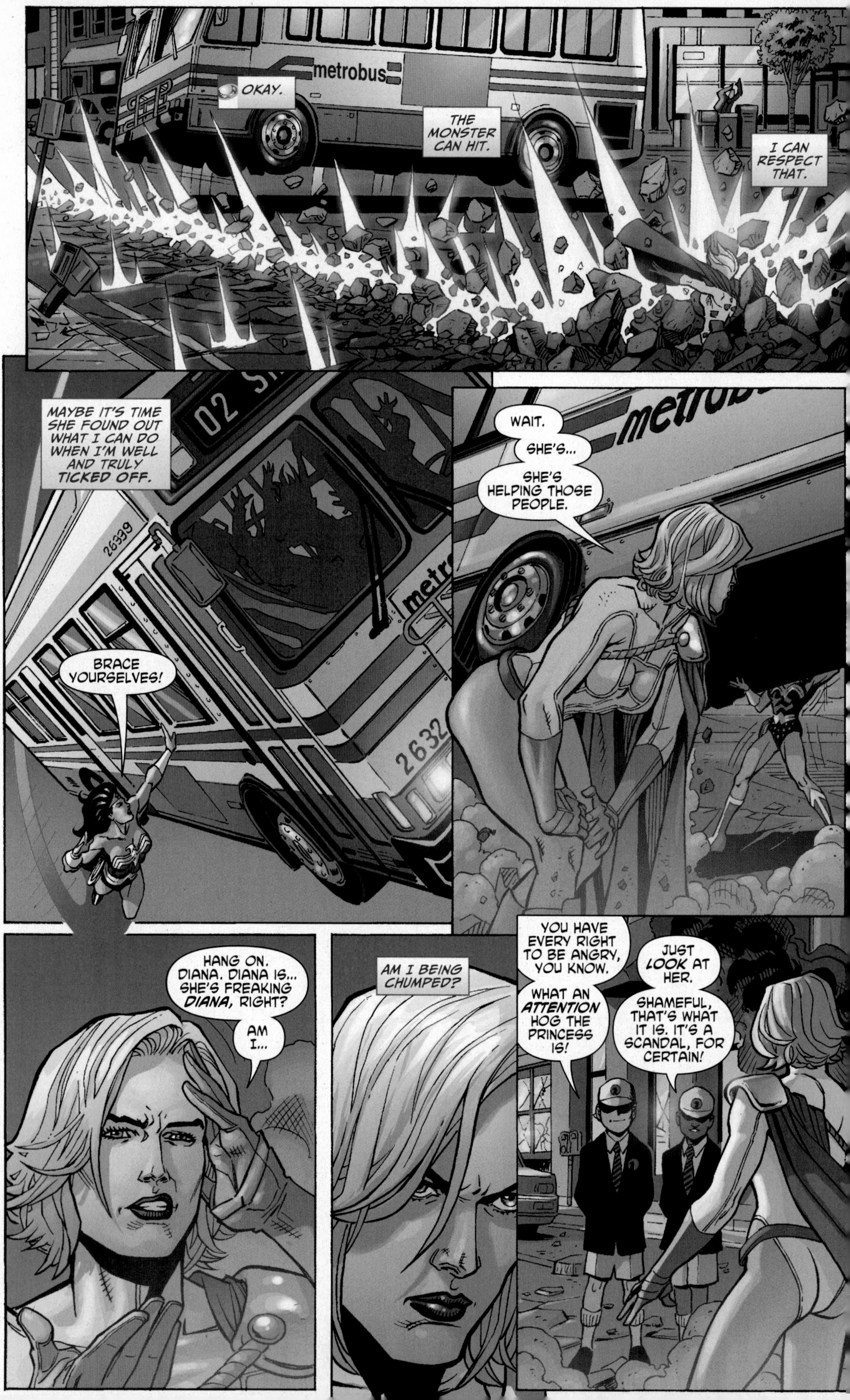
OKAY.
THE MONSTER CAN HIT.
I CAN RESPECT THAT.
MAYBE IT'S TIME SHE FOUND OUT WHAT I CAN DO WHEN I'M WELL AND TRULY TICKED OFF.
BRACE YOURSELVES!
WAIT.
SHE'S...
SHE'S HELPING THOSE PEOPLE.
HANG ON. DIANA. DIANA IS... SHE'S FREAKING DIANA, RIGHT?
AM I...
AM I BEING CHUMPED?
YOU HAVE EVERY RIGHT TO BE ANGRY, YOU KNOW.
WHAT AN ATTENTION HOG THE PRINCESS IS!
JUST LOOK AT HER.
SHAMEFUL, THAT'S WHAT IT IS. IT'S A SCANDAL, FOR CERTAIN!

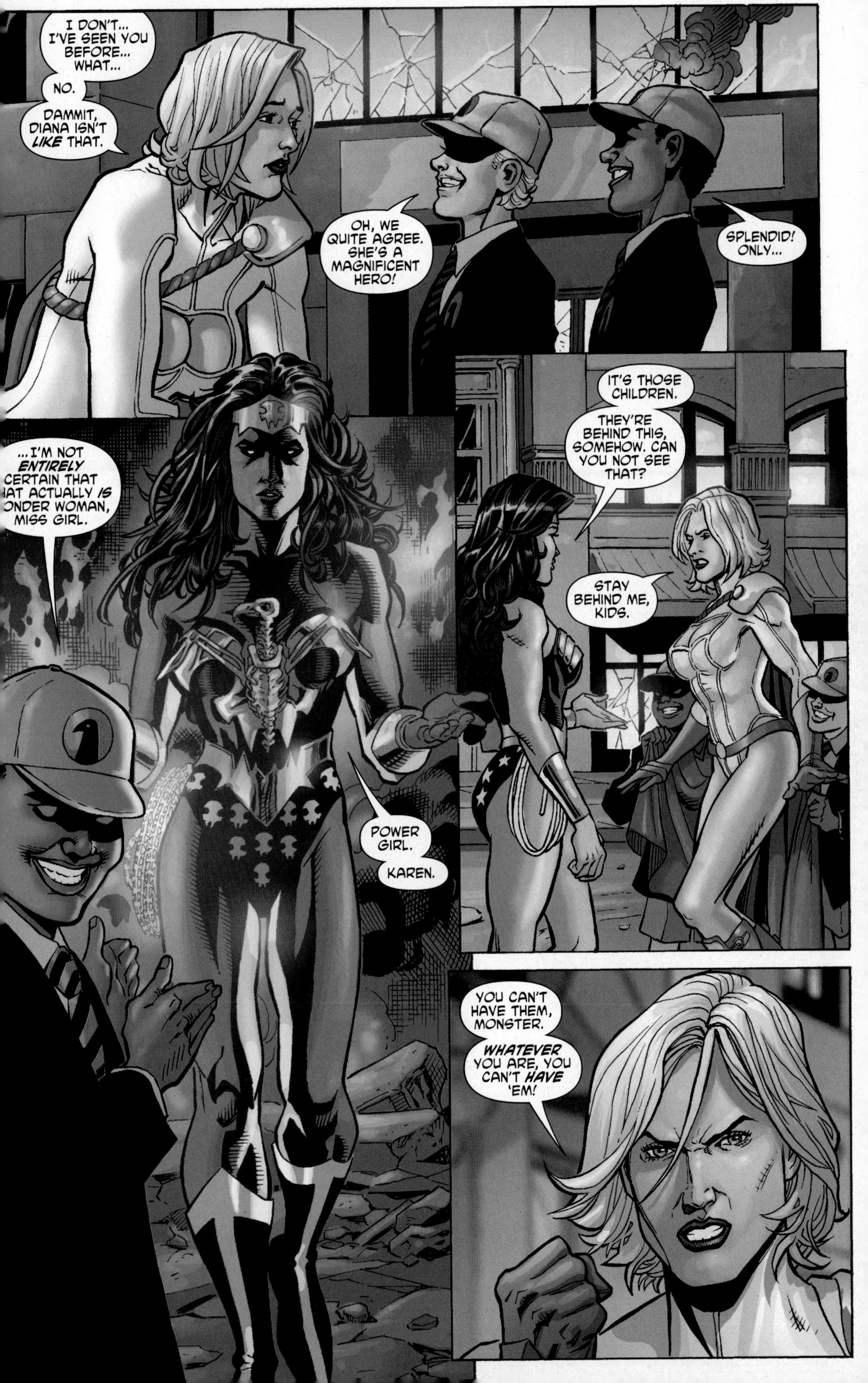
I DON'T... I'VE SEEN YOU BEFORE... WHAT...
NO.
DAMMIT, DIANA ISN'T *LIKE* THAT.
OH, WE QUITE AGREE. SHE'S A MAGNIFICENT HERO!
SPLENDID! ONLY...
...I'M NOT *ENTIRELY* CERTAIN THAT
POWER GIRL.
KAREN.
IT'S THOSE CHILDREN.
THEY'RE BEHIND THIS, SOMEHOW. CAN YOU NOT SEE THAT?
STAY BEHIND ME, KIDS.
YOU CAN'T HAVE THEM, MONSTER.
WHATEVER YOU ARE, YOU CAN'T *HAVE* 'EM!

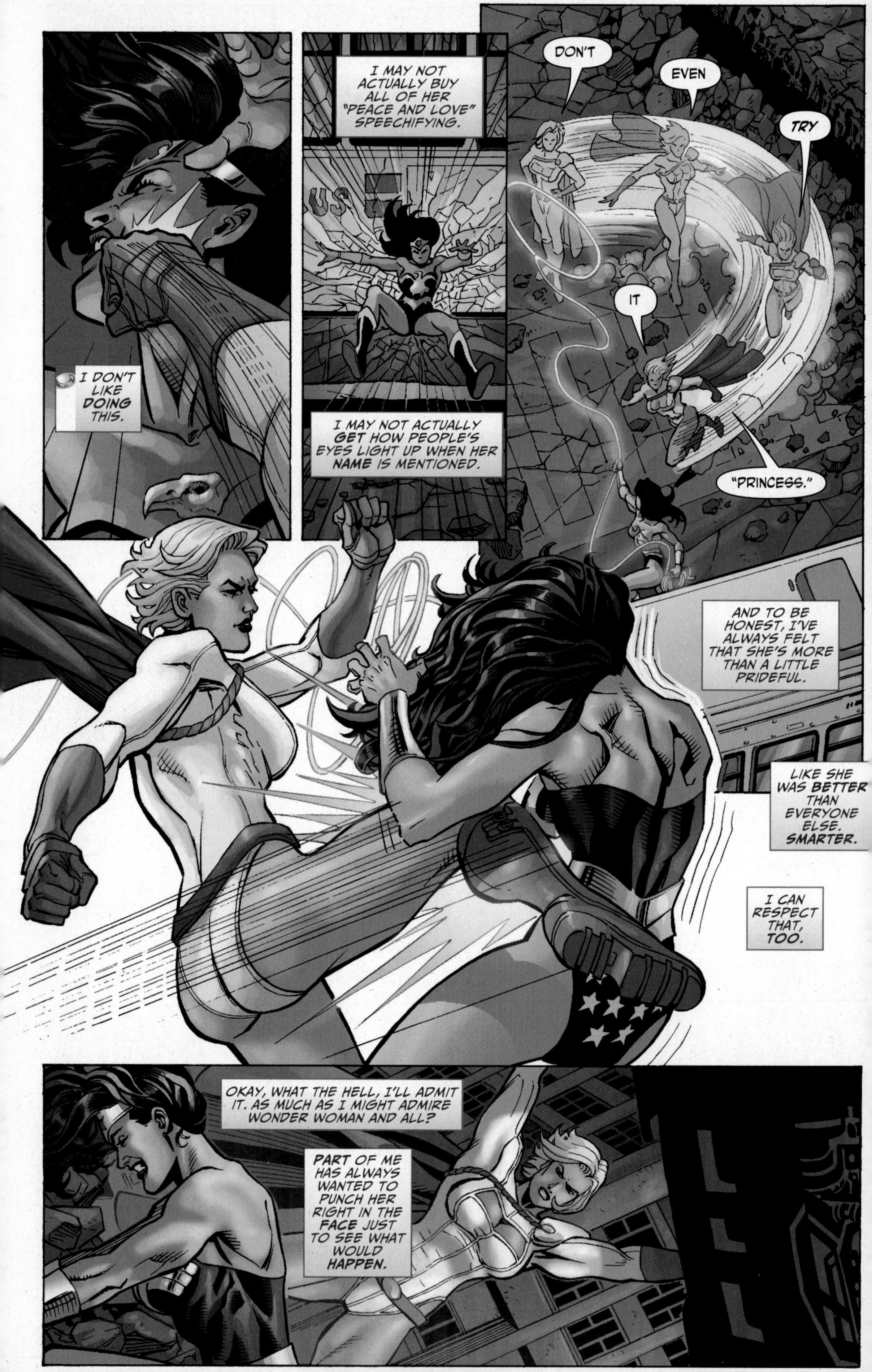

I DON'T LIKE DOING THIS.
I MAY NOT ACTUALLY BUY ALL OF HER "PEACE AND LOVE" SPEECHIFYING.
I MAY NOT ACTUALLY GET HOW PEOPLE'S EYES LIGHT UP WHEN HER NAME IS MENTIONED.
DON'T
EVEN
TRY
IT
"PRINCESS."
AND TO BE HONEST, I'VE ALWAYS FELT THAT SHE'S MORE THAN A LITTLE PRIDEFUL.
LIKE SHE WAS BETTER THAN EVERYONE ELSE. SMARTER.
I CAN RESPECT THAT, TOO.
OKAY, WHAT THE HELL, I'LL ADMIT IT. AS MUCH AS I MIGHT ADMIRE WONDER WOMAN AND ALL?
PART OF ME HAS ALWAYS WANTED TO PUNCH HER RIGHT IN THE FACE JUST TO SEE WHAT WOULD HAPPEN.

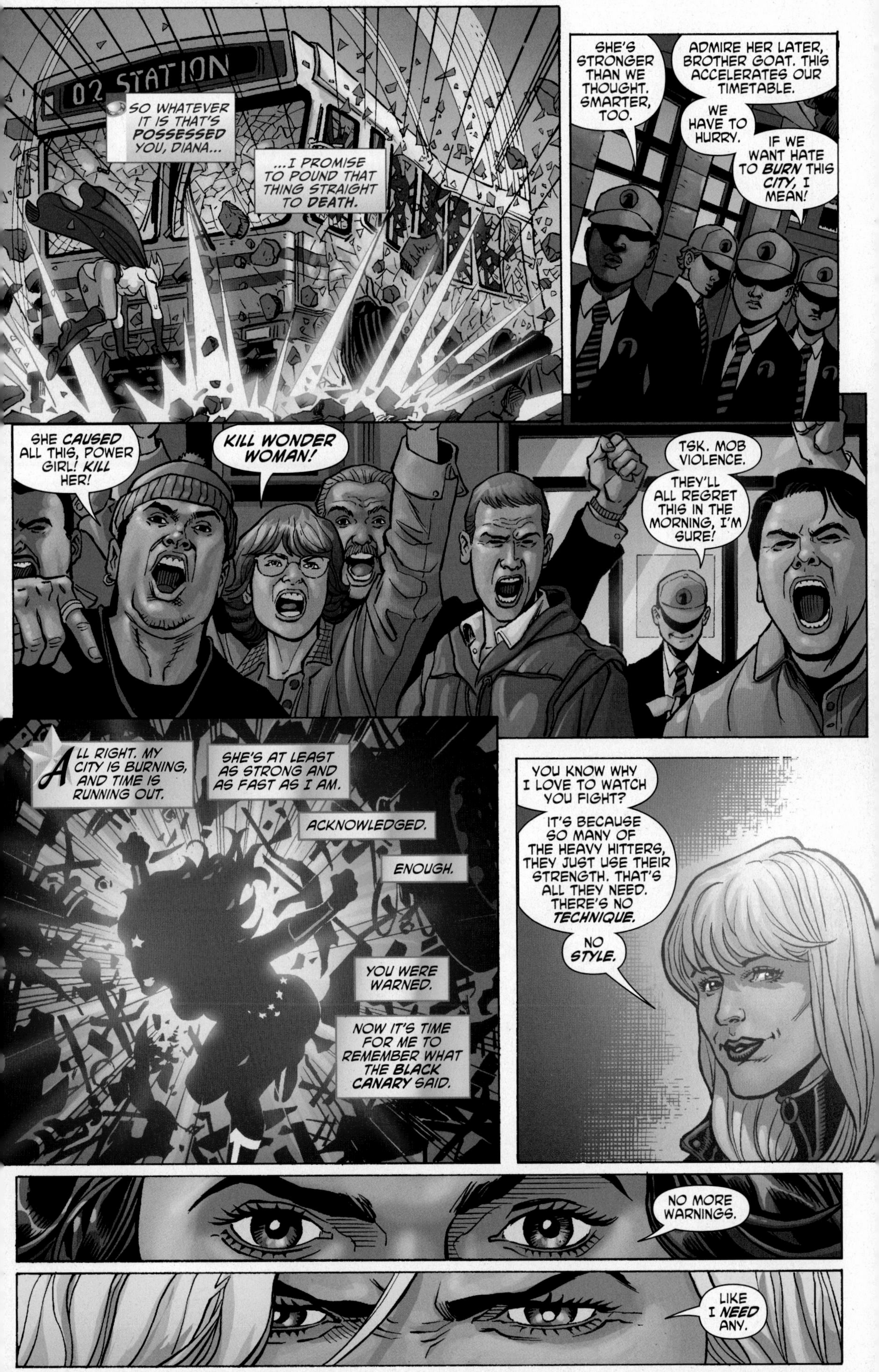
02 STATION
SO WHATEVER IT IS THAT'S POSSESSED YOU, DIANA...
...I PROMISE TO POUND THAT THING STRAIGHT TO DEATH.
SHE'S STRONGER THAN WE THOUGHT. SMARTER, TOO.
ADMIRE HER LATER, BROTHER GOAT. THIS ACCELERATES OUR TIMETABLE.
WE HAVE TO HURRY.
IF WE WANT HATE TO BURN THIS CITY, I MEAN!
SHE CAUSED ALL THIS, POWER GIRL! KILL HER!
KILL WONDER WOMAN!
TSK. MOB VIOLENCE.
THEY'LL ALL REGRET THIS IN THE MORNING, I'M SURE!
ALL RIGHT. MY CITY IS BURNING, AND TIME IS RUNNING OUT.
SHE'S AT LEAST AS STRONG AND AS FAST AS I AM.
ACKNOWLEDGED.
ENOUGH.
YOU WERE WARNED.
NOW IT'S TIME FOR ME TO REMEMBER WHAT THE BLACK CANARY SAID.
YOU KNOW WHY I LOVE TO WATCH YOU FIGHT?
IT'S BECAUSE SO MANY OF THE HEAVY HITTERS, THEY JUST USE THEIR STRENGTH. THAT'S ALL THEY NEED. THERE'S NO TECHNIQUE.
NO STYLE.
NO MORE WARNINGS.
LIKE I NEED ANY.

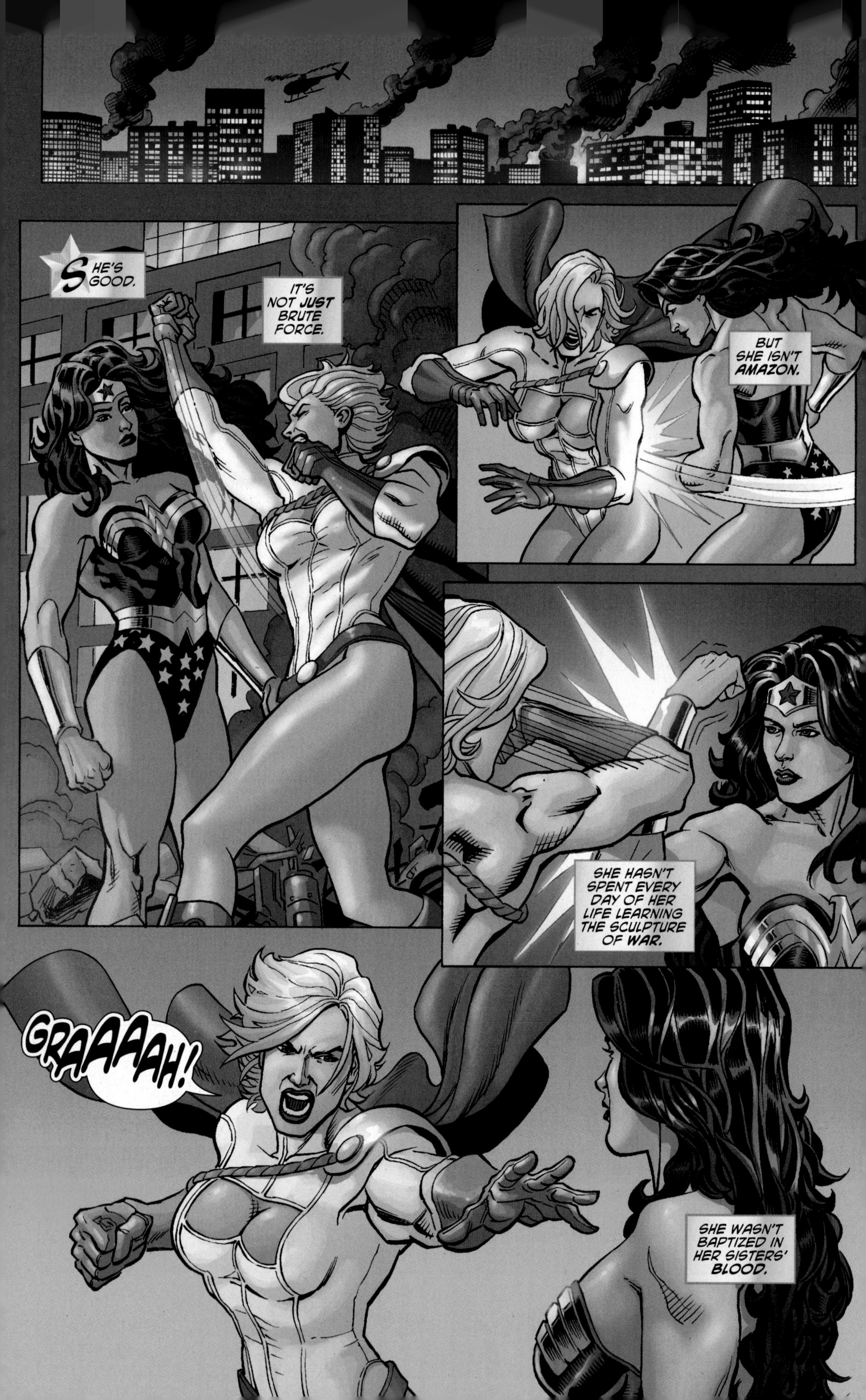
SHE'S GOOD.
IT'S NOT JUST BRUTE FORCE.
BUT SHE ISN'T AMAZON.
SHE HASN'T SPENT EVERY DAY OF HER LIFE LEARNING THE SCULPTURE OF WAR.
GRAAAAAH!
SHE WASN'T BAPTIZED IN HER SISTERS' BLOOD.

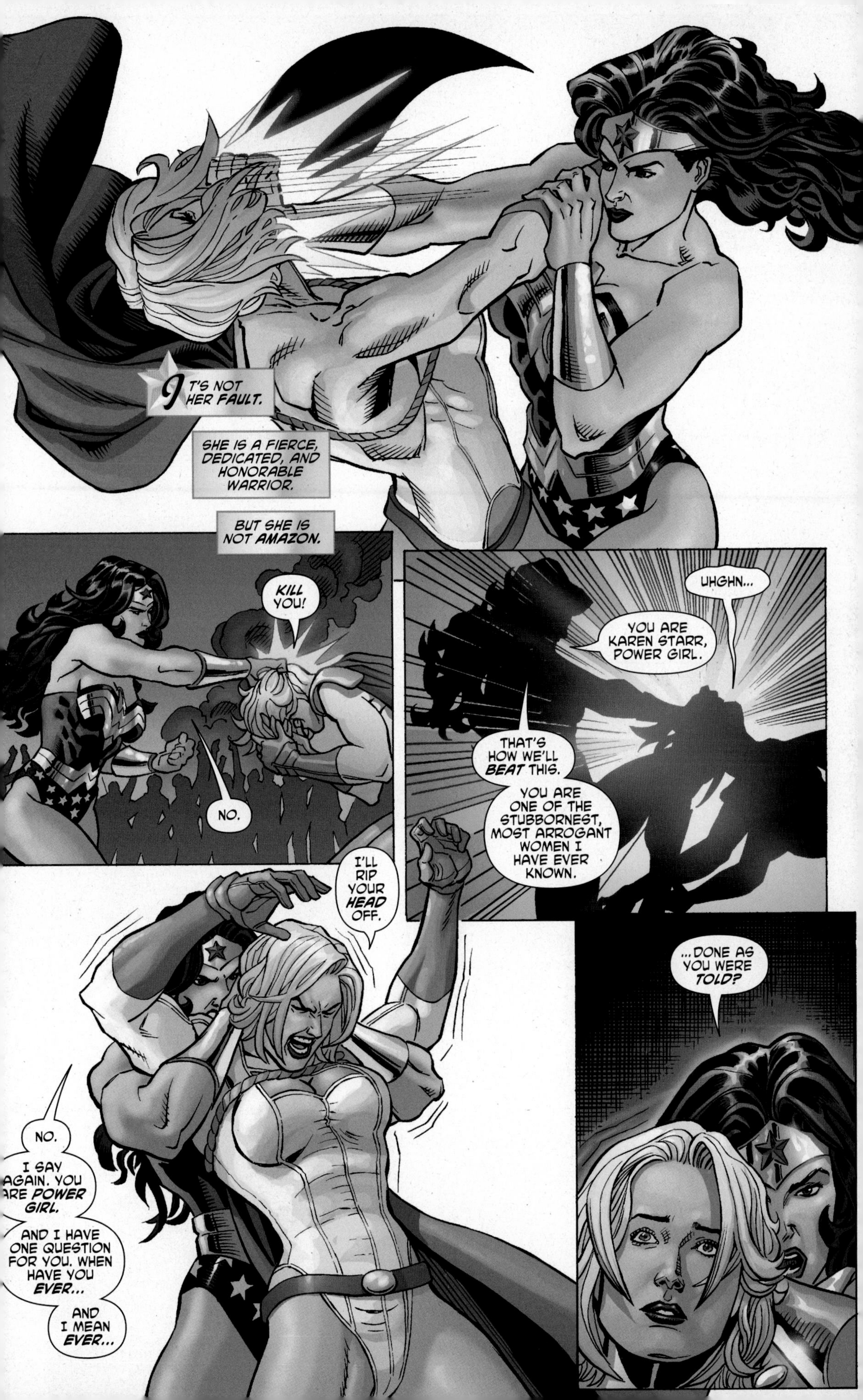
IT'S NOT HER FAULT.
SHE IS A FIERCE, DEDICATED, AND HONORABLE WARRIOR.
BUT SHE IS NOT AMAZON.
KILL YOU!
NO.
UHGHN...
YOU ARE KAREN STARR, POWER GIRL.
THAT'S HOW WE'LL BEAT THIS.
YOU ARE ONE OF THE STUBBORNEST, MOST ARROGANT WOMEN I HAVE EVER KNOWN.
I'LL RIP YOUR HEAD OFF.
NO.
I SAY AGAIN. YOU ARE POWER GIRL.
AND I HAVE ONE QUESTION FOR YOU. WHEN HAVE YOU EVER...
AND I MEAN EVER...
...DONE AS YOU WERE TOLD?

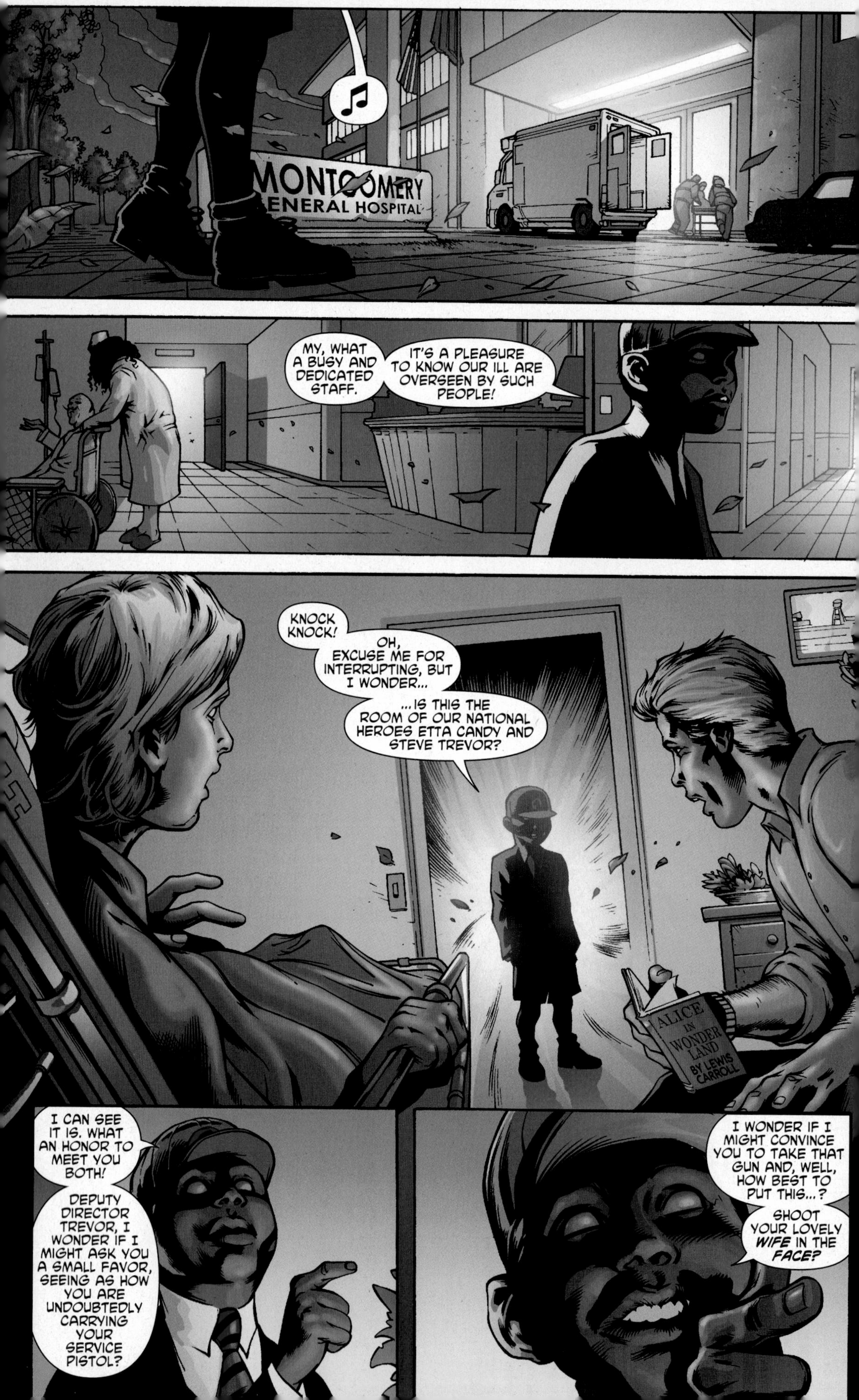
♫
MONTGOMERY GENERAL HOSPITAL
MY, WHAT A BUSY AND DEDICATED STAFF.
IT'S A PLEASURE TO KNOW OUR ILL ARE OVERSEEN BY SUCH PEOPLE!
KNOCK KNOCK!
OH, EXCUSE ME FOR INTERRUPTING, BUT I WONDER...
...IS THIS THE ROOM OF OUR NATIONAL HEROES ETTA CANDY AND STEVE TREVOR?
ALICE IN WONDER LAND BY LEWIS CARROLL
I CAN SEE IT IS. WHAT AN HONOR TO MEET YOU BOTH!
DEPUTY DIRECTOR TREVOR, I WONDER IF I MIGHT ASK YOU A SMALL FAVOR, SEEING AS HOW YOU ARE UNDOUBTEDLY CARRYING YOUR SERVICE PISTOL?
I WONDER IF I MIGHT CONVINCE YOU TO TAKE THAT GUN AND, WELL, HOW BEST TO PUT THIS...?
SHOOT YOUR LOVELY *WIFE* IN THE *FACE?*

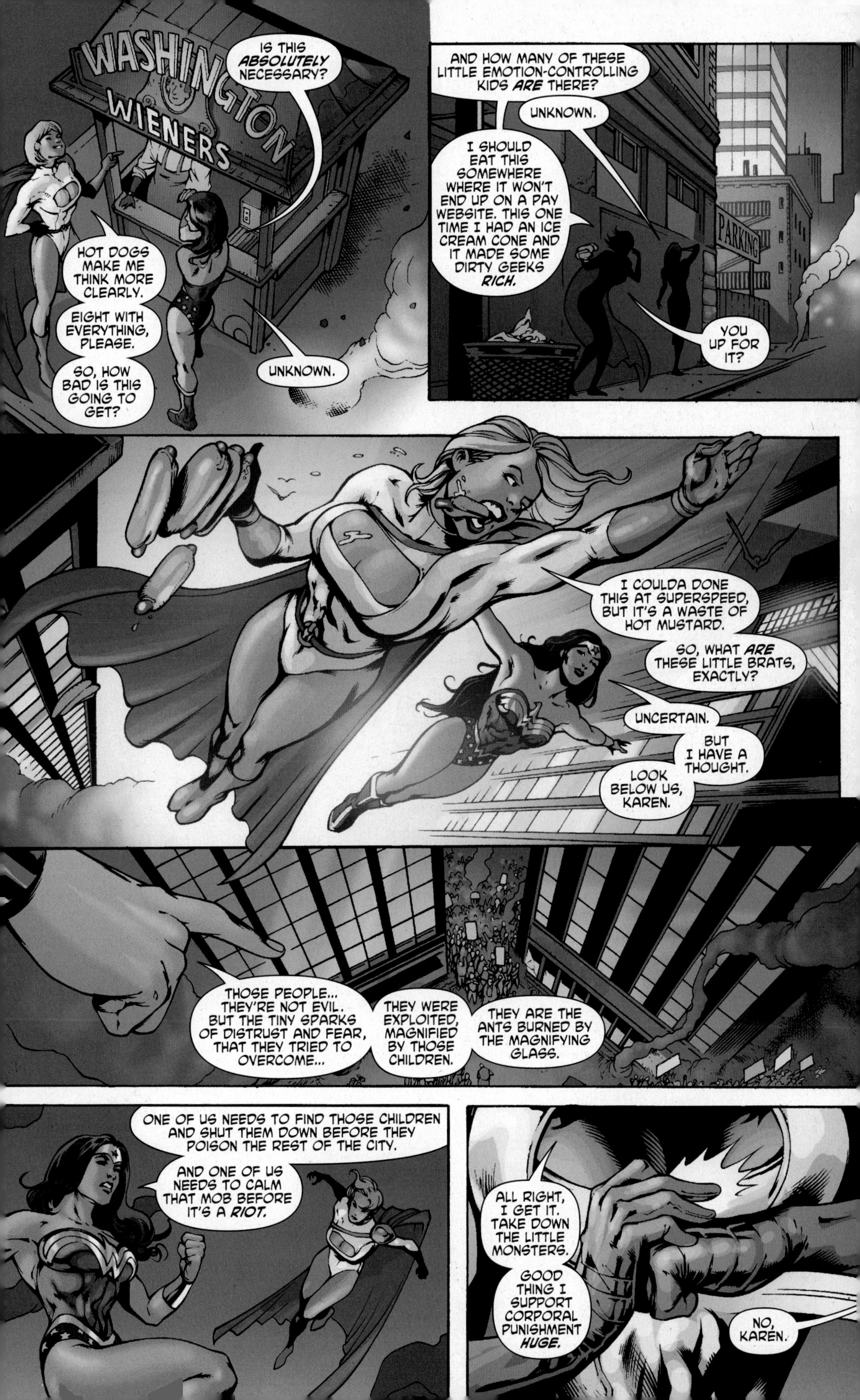
WASHINGTON WIENERS
IS THIS ABSOLUTELY NECESSARY?
HOT DOGS MAKE ME THINK MORE CLEARLY.
EIGHT WITH EVERYTHING, PLEASE.
SO, HOW BAD IS THIS GOING TO GET?
UNKNOWN.
AND HOW MANY OF THESE LITTLE EMOTION-CONTROLLING KIDS ARE THERE?
UNKNOWN.
I SHOULD EAT THIS SOMEWHERE WHERE IT WON'T END UP ON A PAY WEBSITE. THIS ONE TIME I HAD AN ICE CREAM CONE AND IT MADE SOME DIRTY GEEKS RICH.
PARKING
YOU UP FOR IT?
I COULDA DONE THIS AT SUPERSPEED, BUT IT'S A WASTE OF HOT MUSTARD.
SO, WHAT ARE THESE LITTLE BRATS, EXACTLY?
UNCERTAIN.
BUT I HAVE A THOUGHT.
LOOK BELOW US, KAREN.
THOSE PEOPLE... THEY'RE NOT EVIL. BUT THE TINY SPARKS OF DISTRUST AND FEAR, THAT THEY TRIED TO OVERCOME...
THEY WERE EXPLOITED, MAGNIFIED BY THOSE CHILDREN.
THEY ARE THE ANTS BURNED BY THE MAGNIFYING GLASS.
ONE OF US NEEDS TO FIND THOSE CHILDREN AND SHUT THEM DOWN BEFORE THEY POISON THE REST OF THE CITY.
AND ONE OF US NEEDS TO CALM THAT MOB BEFORE IT'S A RIOT.
ALL RIGHT, I GET IT. TAKE DOWN THE LITTLE MONSTERS.
GOOD THING I SUPPORT CORPORAL PUNISHMENT HUGE.
NO, KAREN.

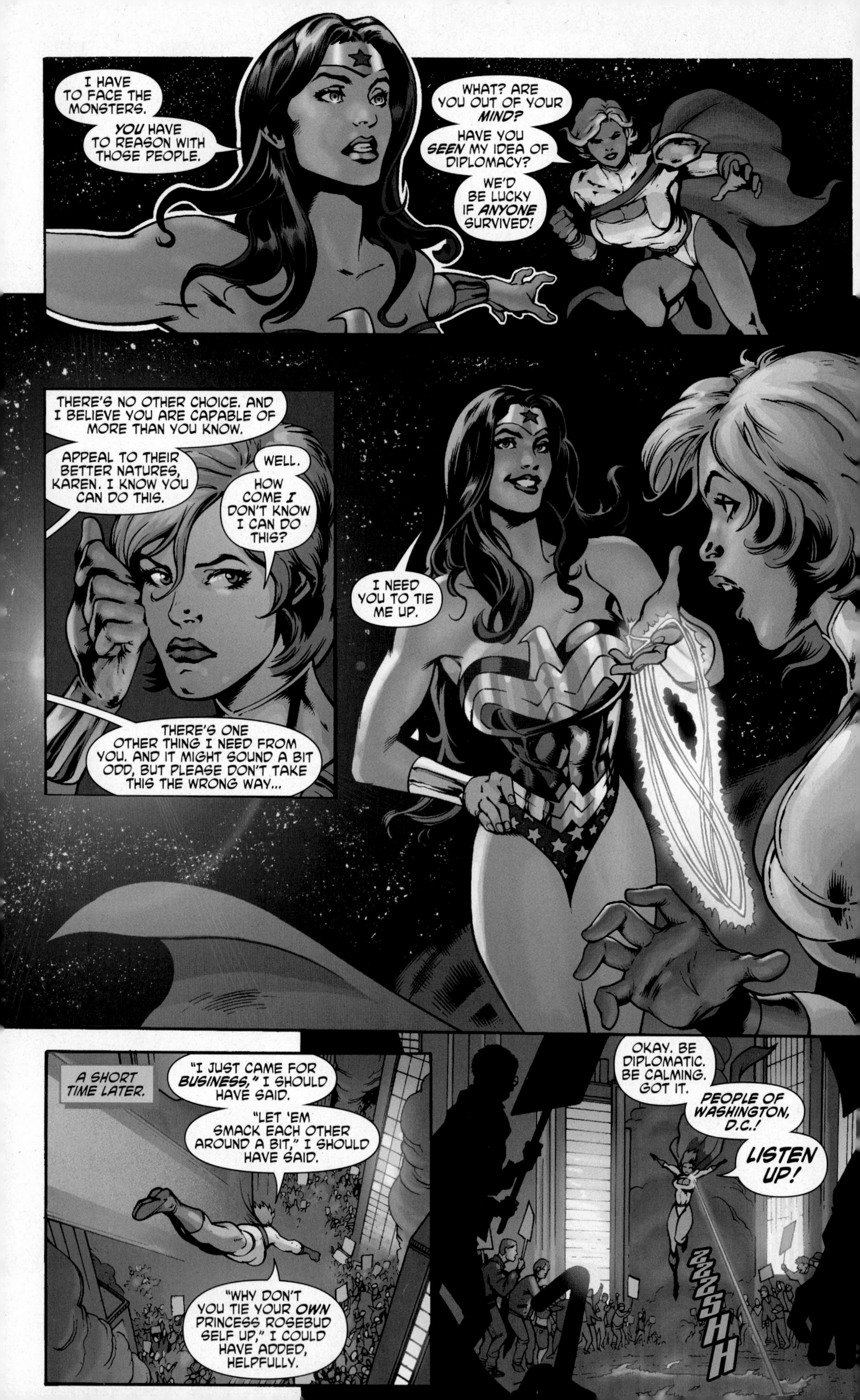
I HAVE TO FACE THE MONSTERS.
YOU HAVE TO REASON WITH THOSE PEOPLE.
WHAT? ARE YOU OUT OF YOUR MIND?
HAVE YOU SEEN MY IDEA OF DIPLOMACY?
WE'D BE LUCKY IF ANYONE SURVIVED!
THERE'S NO OTHER CHOICE. AND I BELIEVE YOU ARE CAPABLE OF MORE THAN YOU KNOW.
APPEAL TO THEIR BETTER NATURES, KAREN. I KNOW YOU CAN DO THIS.
WELL.
HOW COME I DON'T KNOW I CAN DO THIS?
THERE'S ONE OTHER THING I NEED FROM YOU. AND IT MIGHT SOUND A BIT ODD, BUT PLEASE DON'T TAKE THIS THE WRONG WAY...
I NEED YOU TO TIE ME UP.
A SHORT TIME LATER.
"I JUST CAME FOR BUSINESS," I SHOULD HAVE SAID.
"LET 'EM SMACK EACH OTHER AROUND A BIT," I SHOULD HAVE SAID.
"WHY DON'T YOU TIE YOUR OWN PRINCESS ROSEBUD SELF UP," I COULD HAVE ADDED, HELPFULLY.
OKAY. BE DIPLOMATIC. BE CALMING. GOT IT.
PEOPLE OF WASHINGTON, D.C.!
LISTEN UP!
ZZZSHH

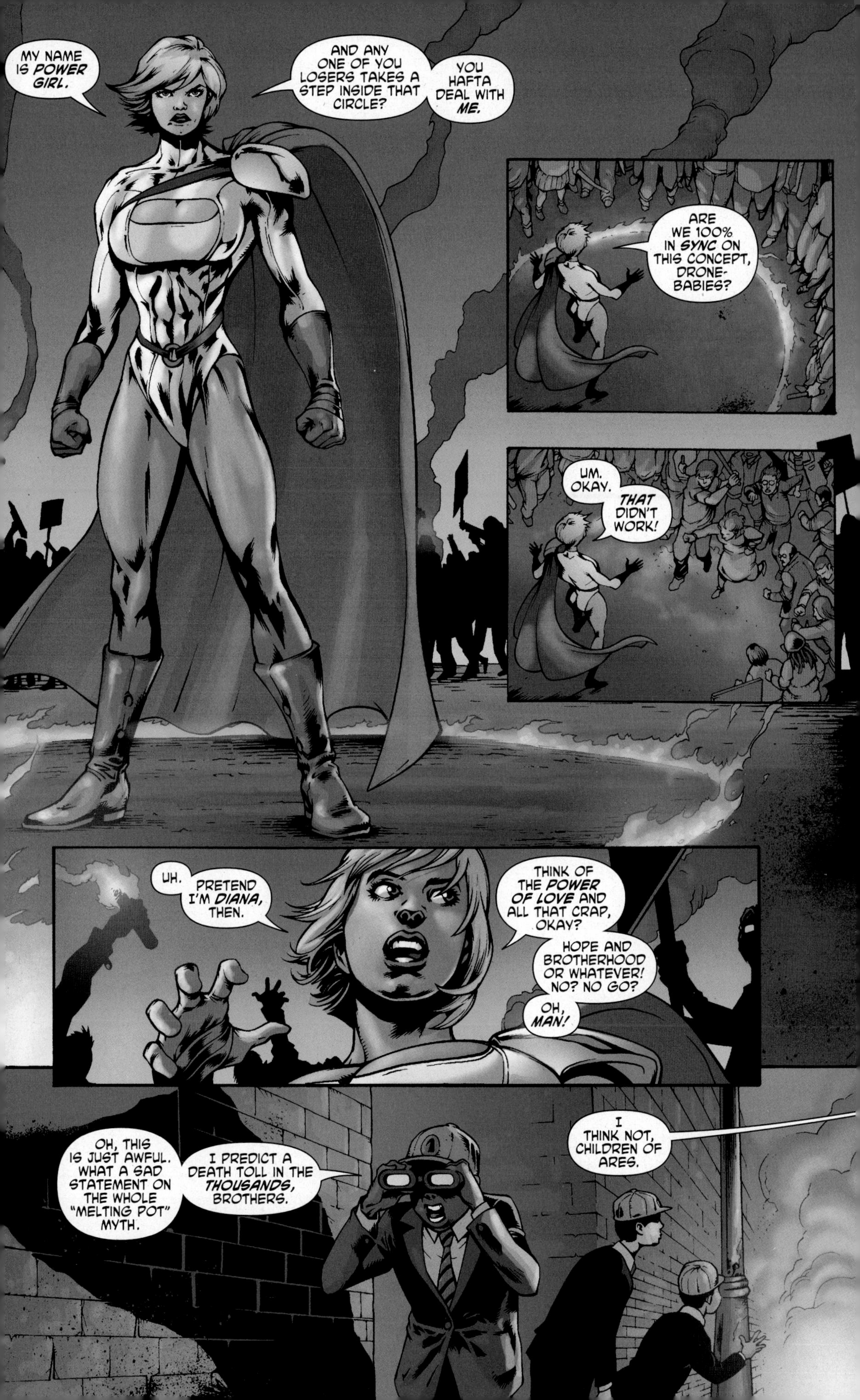
MY NAME IS POWER GIRL.
AND ANY ONE OF YOU LOSERS TAKES A STEP INSIDE THAT CIRCLE?
YOU HAFTA DEAL WITH ME.
ARE WE 100% IN SYNC ON THIS CONCEPT, DRONE-BABIES?
UM. OKAY.
THAT DIDN'T WORK!
UH.
PRETEND I'M DIANA, THEN.
THINK OF THE POWER OF LOVE AND ALL THAT CRAP, OKAY?
HOPE AND BROTHERHOOD OR WHATEVER! NO? NO GO?
OH, MAN!
OH, THIS IS JUST AWFUL. WHAT A SAD STATEMENT ON THE WHOLE "MELTING POT" MYTH.
I PREDICT A DEATH TOLL IN THE THOUSANDS, BROTHERS.
I THINK NOT, CHILDREN OF ARES.

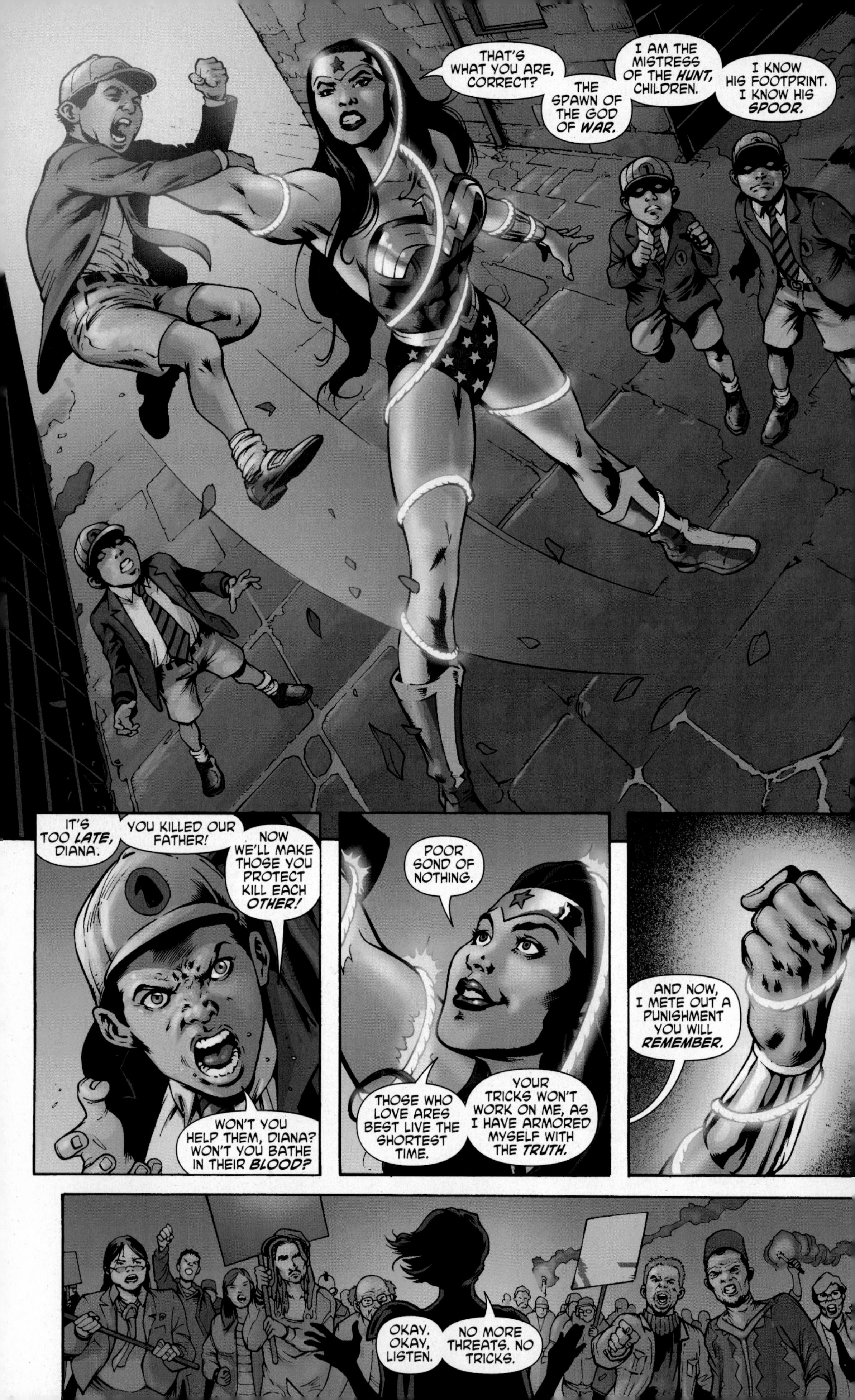
THAT'S WHAT YOU ARE, CORRECT?
THE SPAWN OF THE GOD OF *WAR.*
I AM THE MISTRESS OF THE *HUNT,* CHILDREN.
I KNOW HIS FOOTPRINT. I KNOW HIS *SPOOR.*
IT'S TOO *LATE,* DIANA.
YOU KILLED OUR FATHER!
NOW WE'LL MAKE THOSE YOU PROTECT KILL EACH *OTHER!*
WON'T YOU HELP THEM, DIANA? WON'T YOU BATHE IN THEIR *BLOOD?*
POOR SOND OF NOTHING.
THOSE WHO LOVE ARES BEST LIVE THE SHORTEST TIME.
YOUR TRICKS WON'T WORK ON ME, AS I HAVE ARMORED MYSELF WITH THE *TRUTH.*
AND NOW, I METE OUT A PUNISHMENT YOU WILL *REMEMBER.*
OKAY. OKAY, LISTEN.
NO MORE THREATS. NO TRICKS.

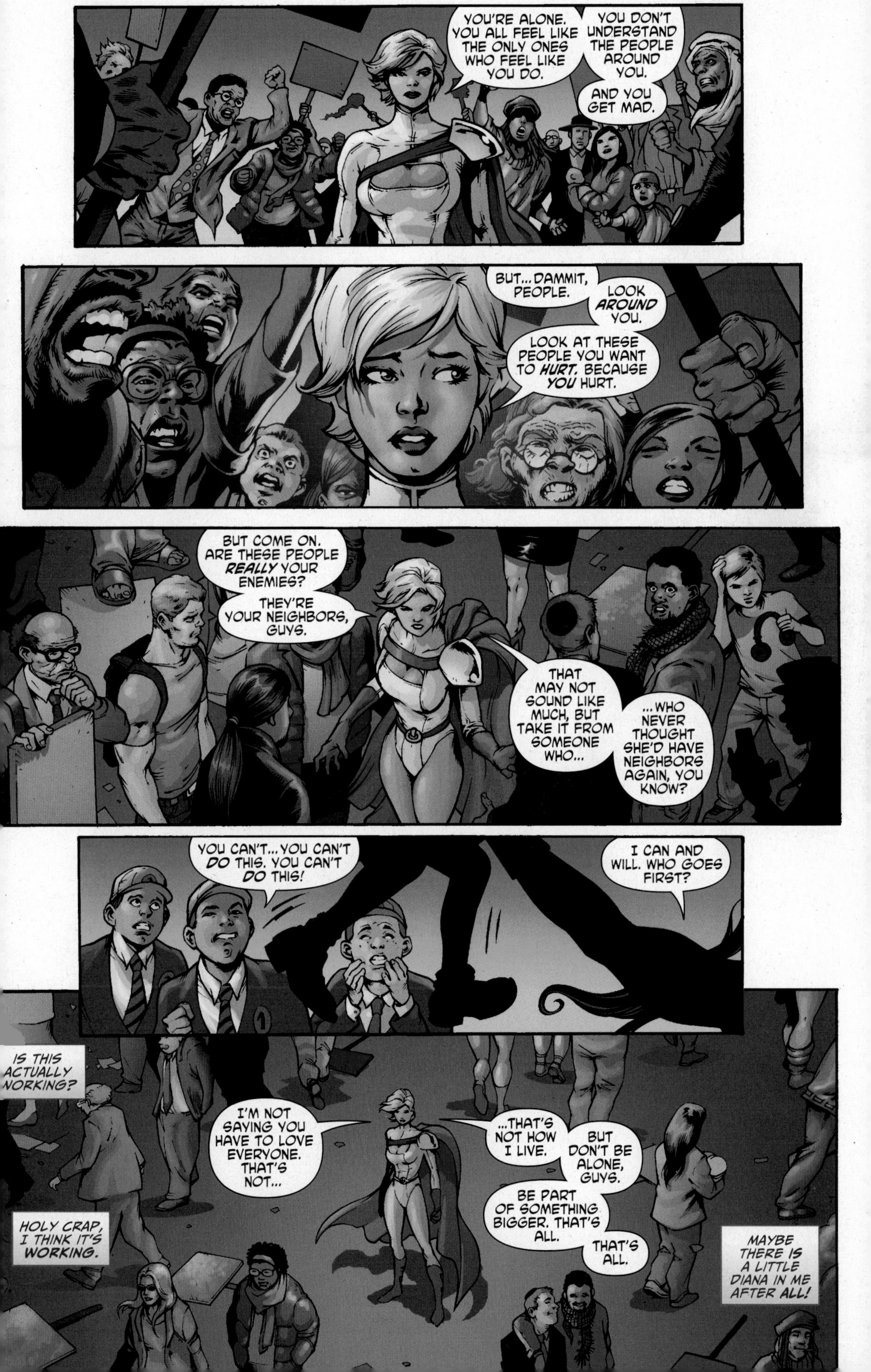

YOU'RE ALONE. YOU ALL FEEL LIKE THE ONLY ONES WHO FEEL LIKE YOU DO.
YOU DON'T UNDERSTAND THE PEOPLE AROUND YOU.
AND YOU GET MAD.
BUT... DAMMIT, PEOPLE.
LOOK AROUND YOU.
LOOK AT THESE PEOPLE YOU WANT TO HURT, BECAUSE YOU HURT.
BUT COME ON. ARE THESE PEOPLE REALLY YOUR ENEMIES?
THEY'RE YOUR NEIGHBORS, GUYS.
THAT MAY NOT SOUND LIKE MUCH, BUT TAKE IT FROM SOMEONE WHO...
...WHO NEVER THOUGHT SHE'D HAVE NEIGHBORS AGAIN, YOU KNOW?
YOU CAN'T... YOU CAN'T DO THIS. YOU CAN'T DO THIS!
I CAN AND WILL. WHO GOES FIRST?
IS THIS ACTUALLY WORKING?
I'M NOT SAYING YOU HAVE TO LOVE EVERYONE. THAT'S NOT...
...THAT'S NOT HOW I LIVE.
BUT DON'T BE ALONE, GUYS.
BE PART OF SOMETHING BIGGER. THAT'S ALL.
THAT'S ALL.
HOLY CRAP, I THINK IT'S WORKING.
MAYBE THERE IS A LITTLE DIANA IN ME AFTER ALL!

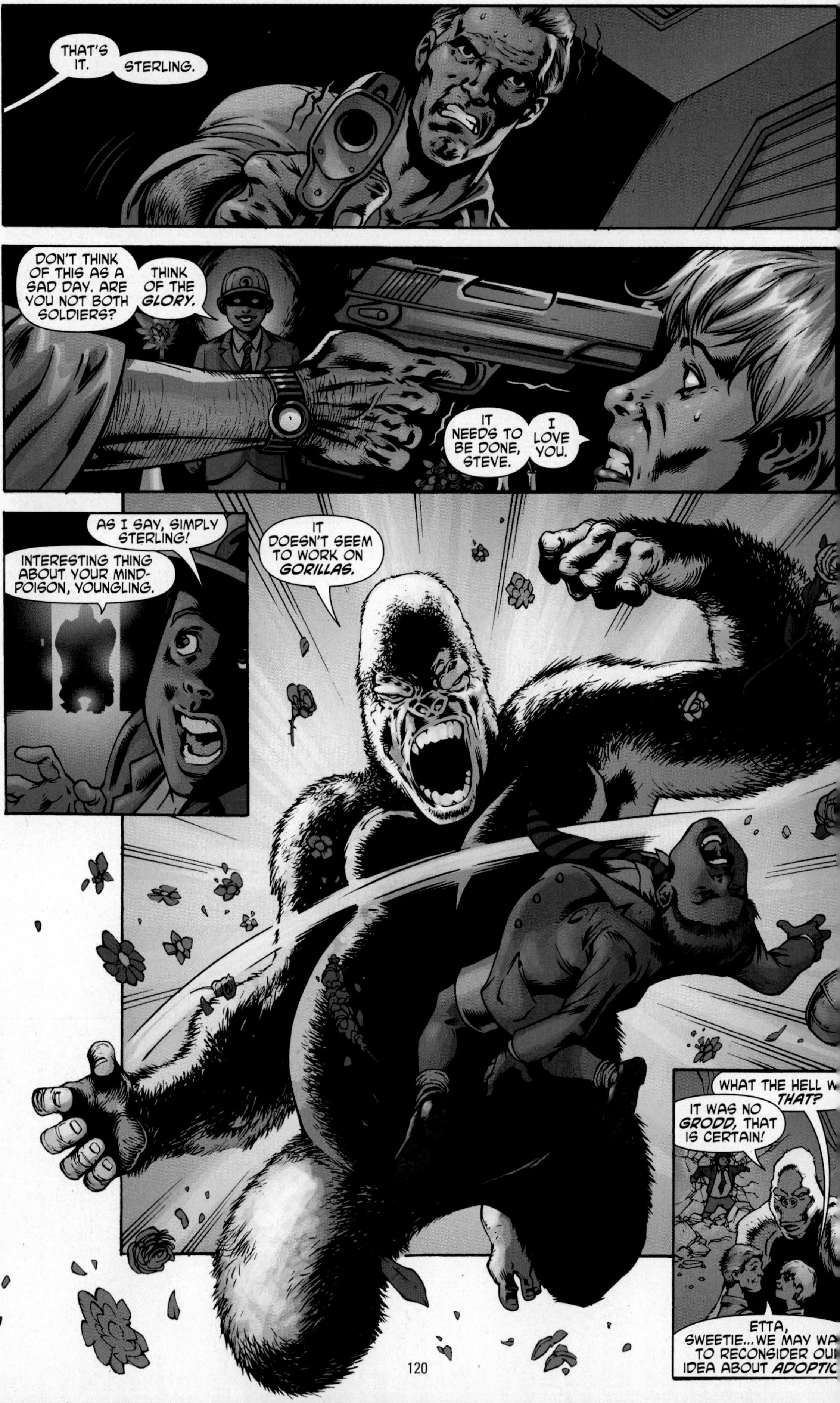

THAT'S IT.
STERLING.
DON'T THINK OF THIS AS A SAD DAY. ARE YOU NOT BOTH SOLDIERS?
THINK OF THE GLORY.
IT NEEDS TO BE DONE, STEVE.
I LOVE YOU.
AS I SAY, SIMPLY STERLING!
INTERESTING THING ABOUT YOUR MIND-POISON, YOUNGLING.
IT DOESN'T SEEM TO WORK ON GORILLAS.
WHAT THE HELL W
THAT?
IT WAS NO GRODD, THAT IS CERTAIN!
ETTA, SWEETIE...WE MAY WA
TO RECONSIDER OU
IDEA ABOUT ADOPTIC

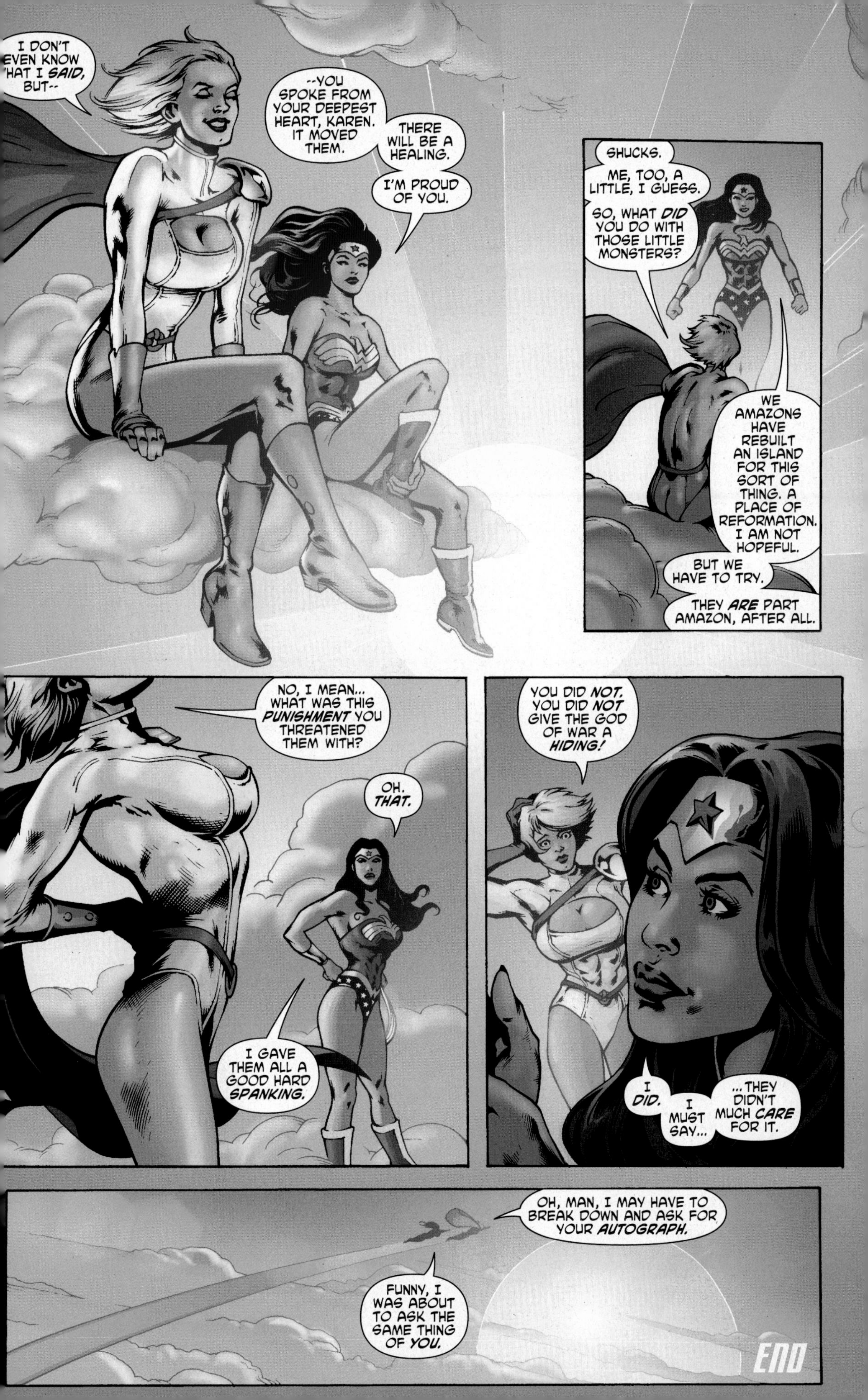
I DON'T EVEN KNOW WHAT I SAID, BUT--
--YOU SPOKE FROM YOUR DEEPEST HEART, KAREN. IT MOVED THEM.
THERE WILL BE A HEALING.
I'M PROUD OF YOU.
SHUCKS.
ME, TOO, A LITTLE, I GUESS.
SO, WHAT DID YOU DO WITH THOSE LITTLE MONSTERS?
WE AMAZONS HAVE REBUILT AN ISLAND FOR THIS SORT OF THING. A PLACE OF REFORMATION. I AM NOT HOPEFUL.
BUT WE HAVE TO TRY.
THEY ARE PART AMAZON, AFTER ALL.
NO, I MEAN... WHAT WAS THIS PUNISHMENT YOU THREATENED THEM WITH?
OH. THAT.
I GAVE THEM ALL A GOOD HARD SPANKING.
YOU DID NOT. YOU DID NOT GIVE THE GOD OF WAR A HIDING!
I DID.
I MUST SAY...
...THEY DIDN'T MUCH CARE FOR IT.
OH, MAN, I MAY HAVE TO BREAK DOWN AND ASK FOR YOUR AUTOGRAPH.
FUNNY, I WAS ABOUT TO ASK THE SAME THING OF YOU.
END

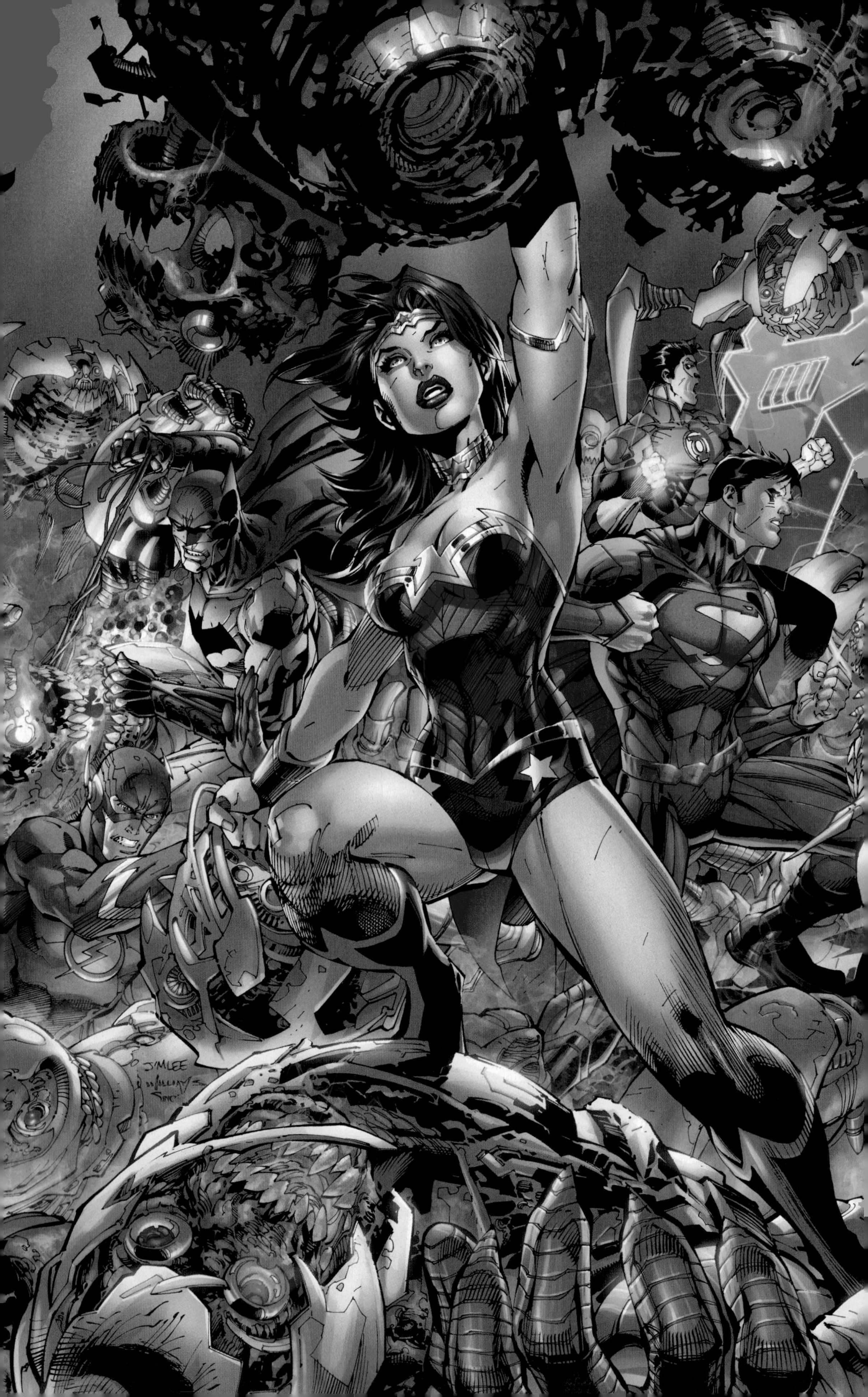

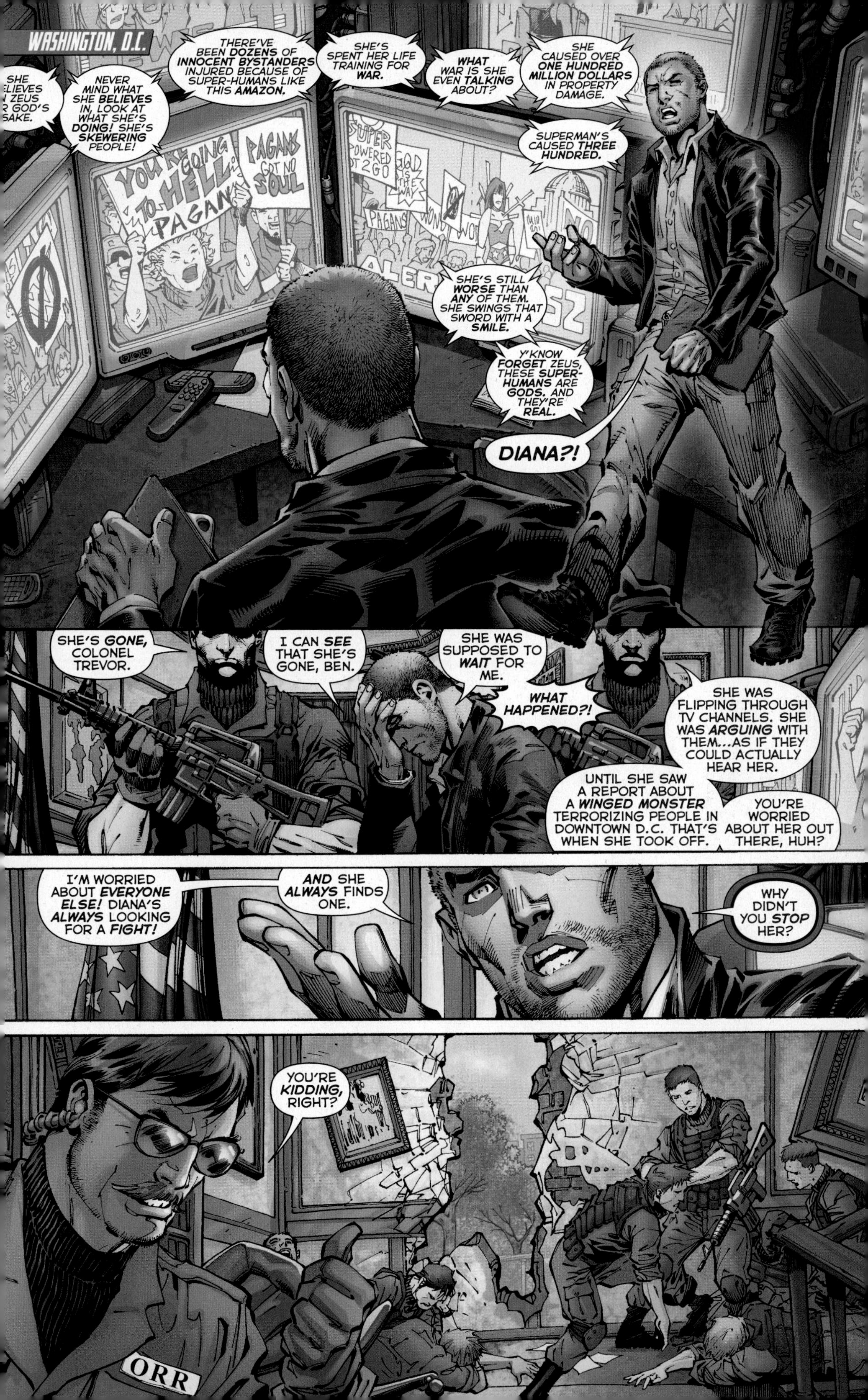
WASHINGTON, D.C.
SHE ELIEVES N ZEUS R GOD'S SAKE.
NEVER MIND WHAT SHE BELIEVES IN, LOOK AT WHAT SHE'S DOING! SHE'S SKEWERING PEOPLE!
THERE'VE BEEN DOZENS OF INNOCENT BYSTANDERS INJURED BECAUSE OF SUPER-HUMANS LIKE THIS AMAZON.
SHE'S SPENT HER LIFE TRAINING FOR WAR.
WHAT WAR IS SHE EVEN TALKING ABOUT?
SHE CAUSED OVER ONE HUNDRED MILLION DOLLARS IN PROPERTY DAMAGE.
SUPERMAN'S CAUSED THREE HUNDRED.
GOING TO HELL PAGAN
PAGANS GOT NO SOUL
SUPER POWERED
GOD IS THE WAY
PAGANS
SHE'S STILL WORSE THAN ANY OF THEM. SHE SWINGS THAT SWORD WITH A SMILE.
Y'KNOW FORGET ZEUS, THESE SUPER-HUMANS ARE GODS. AND THEY'RE REAL.
DIANA?!
SHE'S GONE, COLONEL TREVOR.
I CAN SEE THAT SHE'S GONE, BEN.
SHE WAS SUPPOSED TO WAIT FOR ME.
WHAT HAPPENED?!
SHE WAS FLIPPING THROUGH TV CHANNELS. SHE WAS ARGUING WITH THEM...AS IF THEY COULD ACTUALLY HEAR HER.
UNTIL SHE SAW A REPORT ABOUT A WINGED MONSTER TERRORIZING PEOPLE IN DOWNTOWN D.C. THAT'S WHEN SHE TOOK OFF.
YOU'RE WORRIED ABOUT HER OUT THERE, HUH?
I'M WORRIED ABOUT EVERYONE ELSE! DIANA'S ALWAYS LOOKING FOR A FIGHT!
AND SHE ALWAYS FINDS ONE.
WHY DIDN'T YOU STOP HER?
YOU'RE KIDDING, RIGHT?
ORR

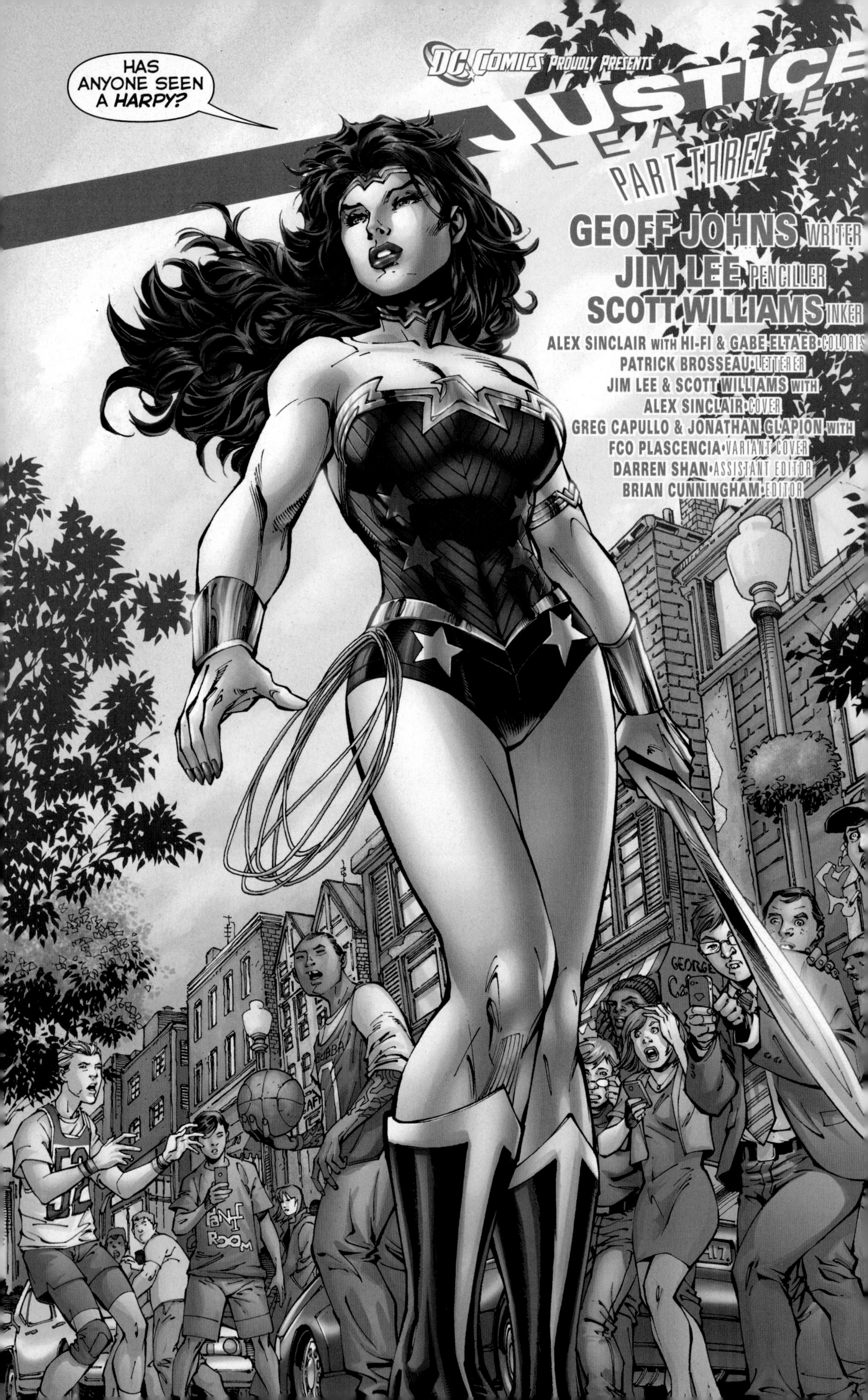
HAS ANYONE SEEN A HARPY?
DC COMICS PROUDLY PRESENTS
JUSTICE LEAGUE
PART THREE
GEOFF JOHNS WRITER
JIM LEE PENCILLER
SCOTT WILLIAMS INKER
ALEX SINCLAIR WITH HI-FI & GABE ELTAEB • COLORIS
PATRICK BROSSEAU • LETTERER
JIM LEE & SCOTT WILLIAMS WITH
ALEX SINCLAIR • COVER
GREG CAPULLO & JONATHAN GLAPION WITH
FCO PLASCENCIA • VARIANT COVER
DARREN SHAN • ASSISTANT EDITOR
BRIAN CUNNINGHAM • EDITOR

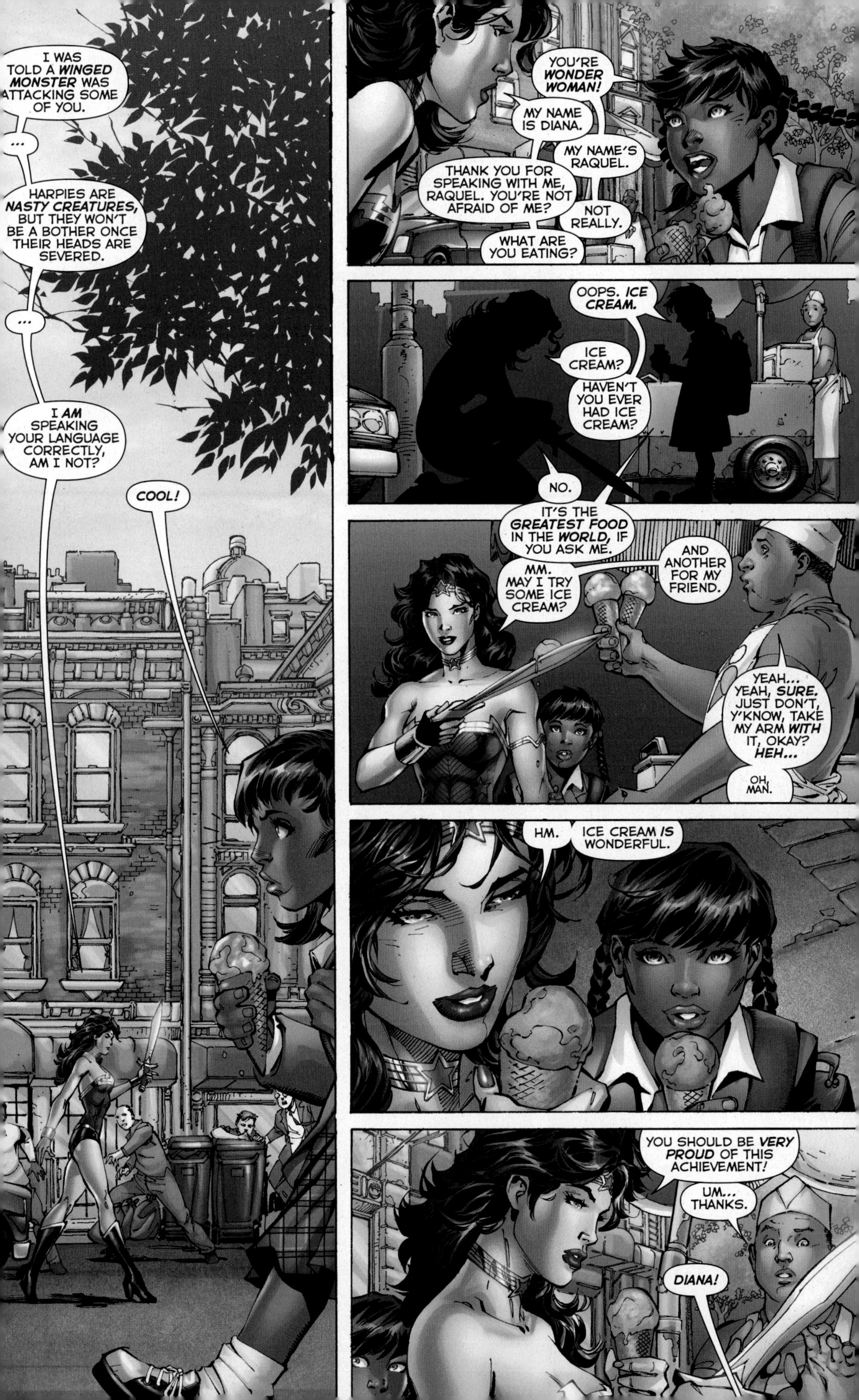
I WAS TOLD A WINGED MONSTER WAS ATTACKING SOME OF YOU.
...
HARPIES ARE NASTY CREATURES, BUT THEY WON'T BE A BOTHER ONCE THEIR HEADS ARE SEVERED.
...
I AM SPEAKING YOUR LANGUAGE CORRECTLY, AM I NOT?
COOL!
YOU'RE WONDER WOMAN!
MY NAME IS DIANA.
MY NAME'S RAQUEL.
THANK YOU FOR SPEAKING WITH ME, RAQUEL. YOU'RE NOT AFRAID OF ME?
NOT REALLY.
WHAT ARE YOU EATING?
OOPS. ICE CREAM.
ICE CREAM?
HAVEN'T YOU EVER HAD ICE CREAM?
NO.
IT'S THE GREATEST FOOD IN THE WORLD, IF YOU ASK ME.
MM. MAY I TRY SOME ICE CREAM?
AND ANOTHER FOR MY FRIEND.
YEAH... YEAH, SURE. JUST DON'T, Y'KNOW, TAKE MY ARM WITH IT, OKAY? HEH...
OH, MAN.
HM.
ICE CREAM IS WONDERFUL.
YOU SHOULD BE VERY PROUD OF THIS ACHIEVEMENT!
UM... THANKS.
DIANA!

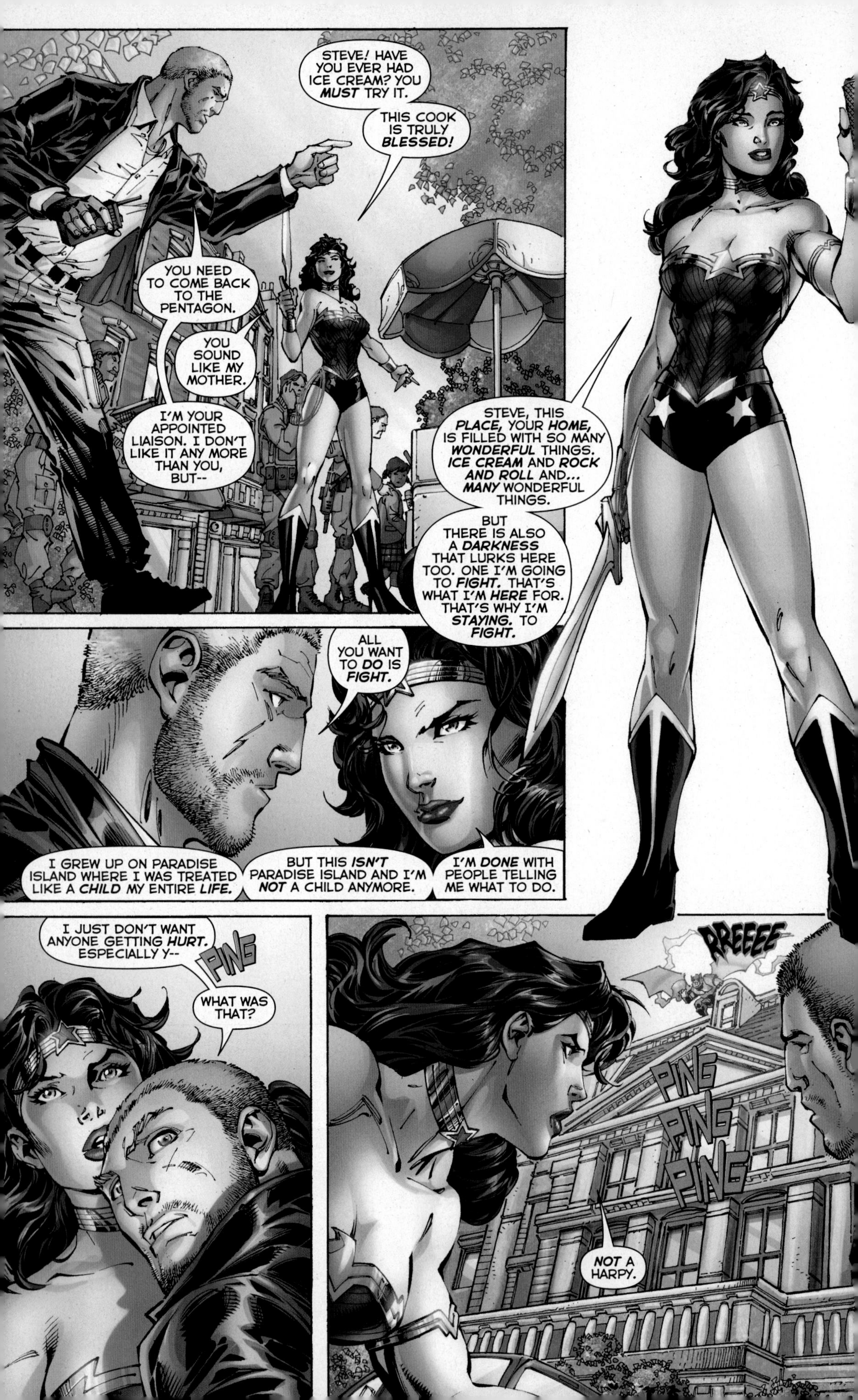
STEVE! HAVE YOU EVER HAD ICE CREAM? YOU MUST TRY IT.
THIS COOK IS TRULY BLESSED!
YOU NEED TO COME BACK TO THE PENTAGON.
YOU SOUND LIKE MY MOTHER.
I'M YOUR APPOINTED LIAISON. I DON'T LIKE IT ANY MORE THAN YOU, BUT--
STEVE, THIS PLACE, YOUR HOME, IS FILLED WITH SO MANY WONDERFUL THINGS. ICE CREAM AND ROCK AND ROLL AND... MANY WONDERFUL THINGS.
BUT THERE IS ALSO A DARKNESS THAT LURKS HERE TOO. ONE I'M GOING TO FIGHT. THAT'S WHAT I'M HERE FOR. THAT'S WHY I'M STAYING. TO FIGHT.
ALL YOU WANT TO DO IS FIGHT.
I GREW UP ON PARADISE ISLAND WHERE I WAS TREATED LIKE A CHILD MY ENTIRE LIFE.
BUT THIS ISN'T PARADISE ISLAND AND I'M NOT A CHILD ANYMORE.
I'M DONE WITH PEOPLE TELLING ME WHAT TO DO.
I JUST DON'T WANT ANYONE GETTING HURT. ESPECIALLY Y--
PING
WHAT WAS THAT?
RREEEE
PING
PING
PING
NOT A HARPY.

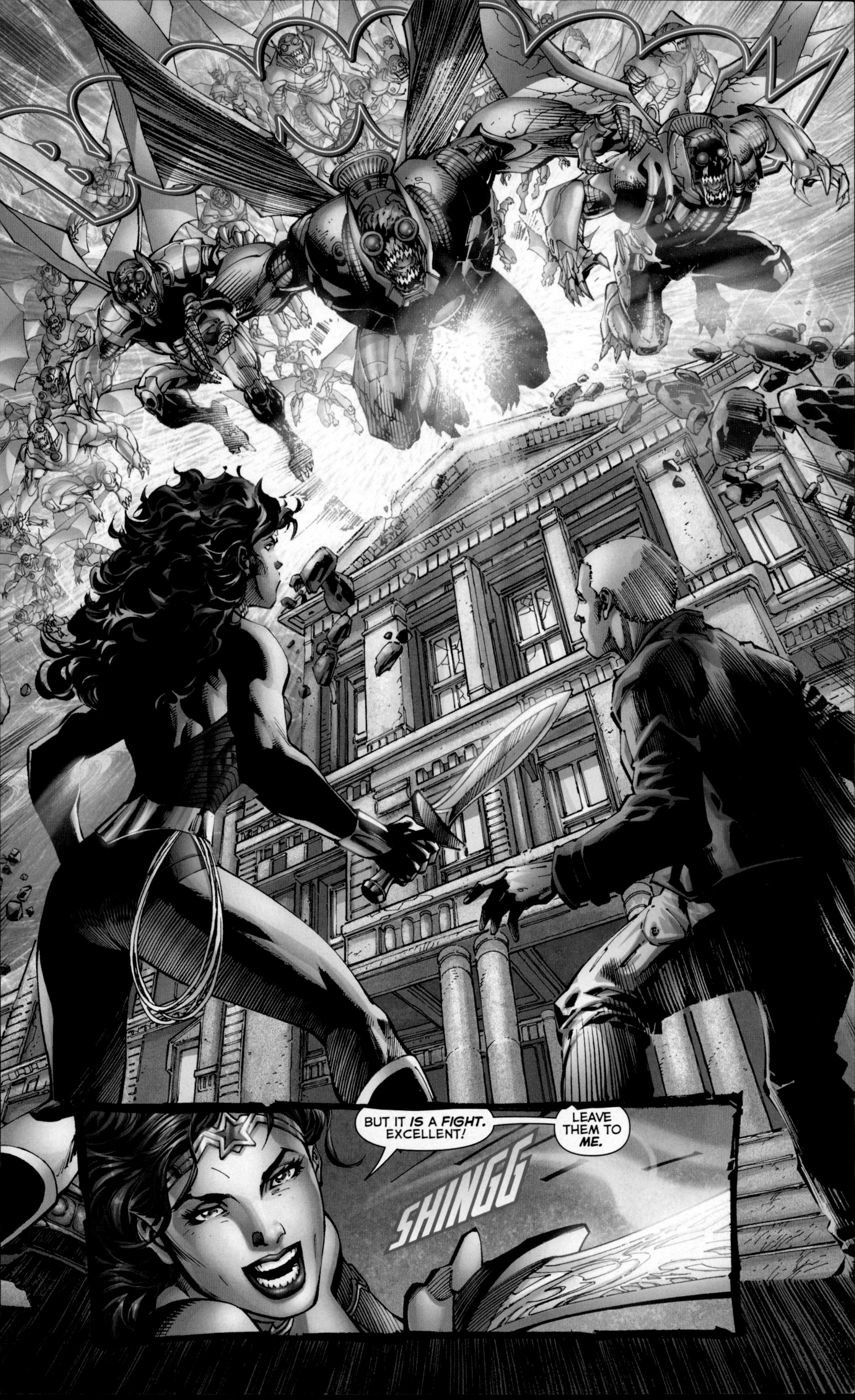
BUT IT IS A FIGHT. EXCELLENT!
LEAVE THEM TO ME.
SHINGG

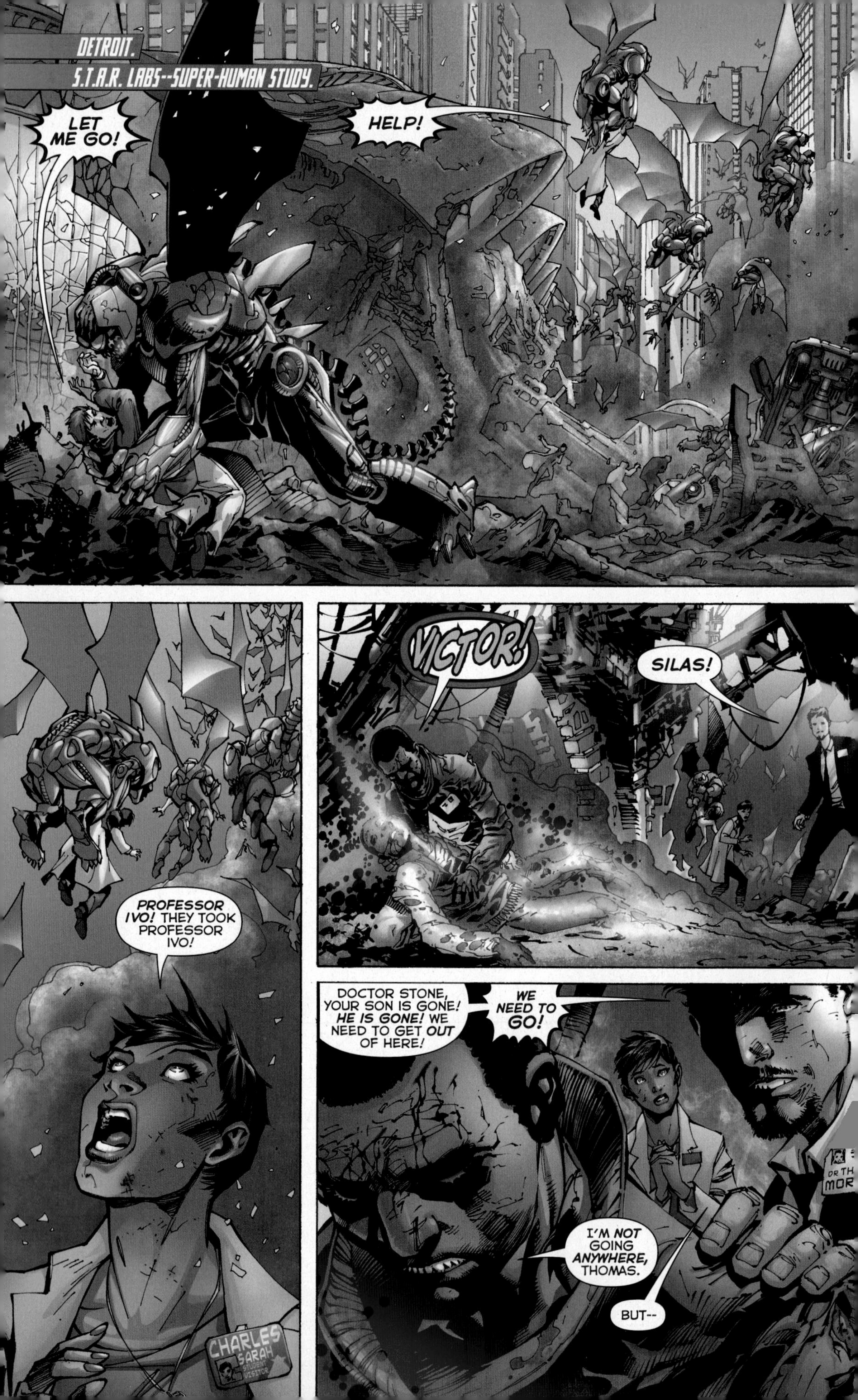
DETROIT.
S.T.A.R. LABS--SUPER-HUMAN STUDY.
LET ME GO!
HELP!
PROFESSOR IVO! THEY TOOK PROFESSOR IVO!
CHARLES SARAH
VICTOR!
SILAS!
DOCTOR STONE, YOUR SON IS GONE! HE IS GONE! WE NEED TO GET OUT OF HERE!
WE NEED TO GO!
I'M NOT GOING ANYWHERE, THOMAS.
BUT--

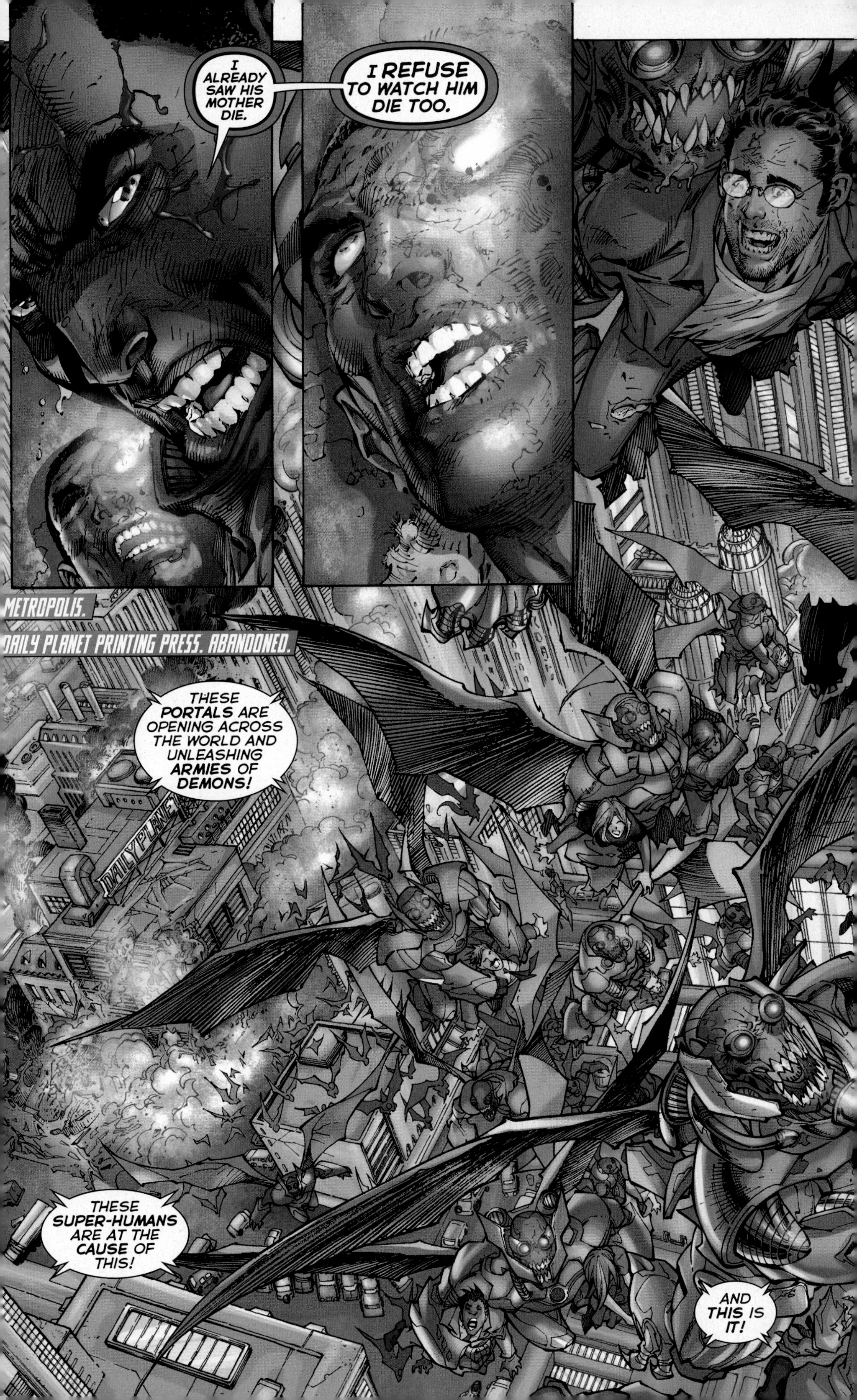
I ALREADY SAW HIS MOTHER DIE.
I REFUSE TO WATCH HIM DIE TOO.
METROPOLIS.
DAILY PLANET PRINTING PRESS. ABANDONED.
THESE PORTALS ARE OPENING ACROSS THE WORLD AND UNLEASHING ARMIES OF DEMONS!
THESE SUPER-HUMANS ARE AT THE CAUSE OF THIS!
AND THIS IS IT!

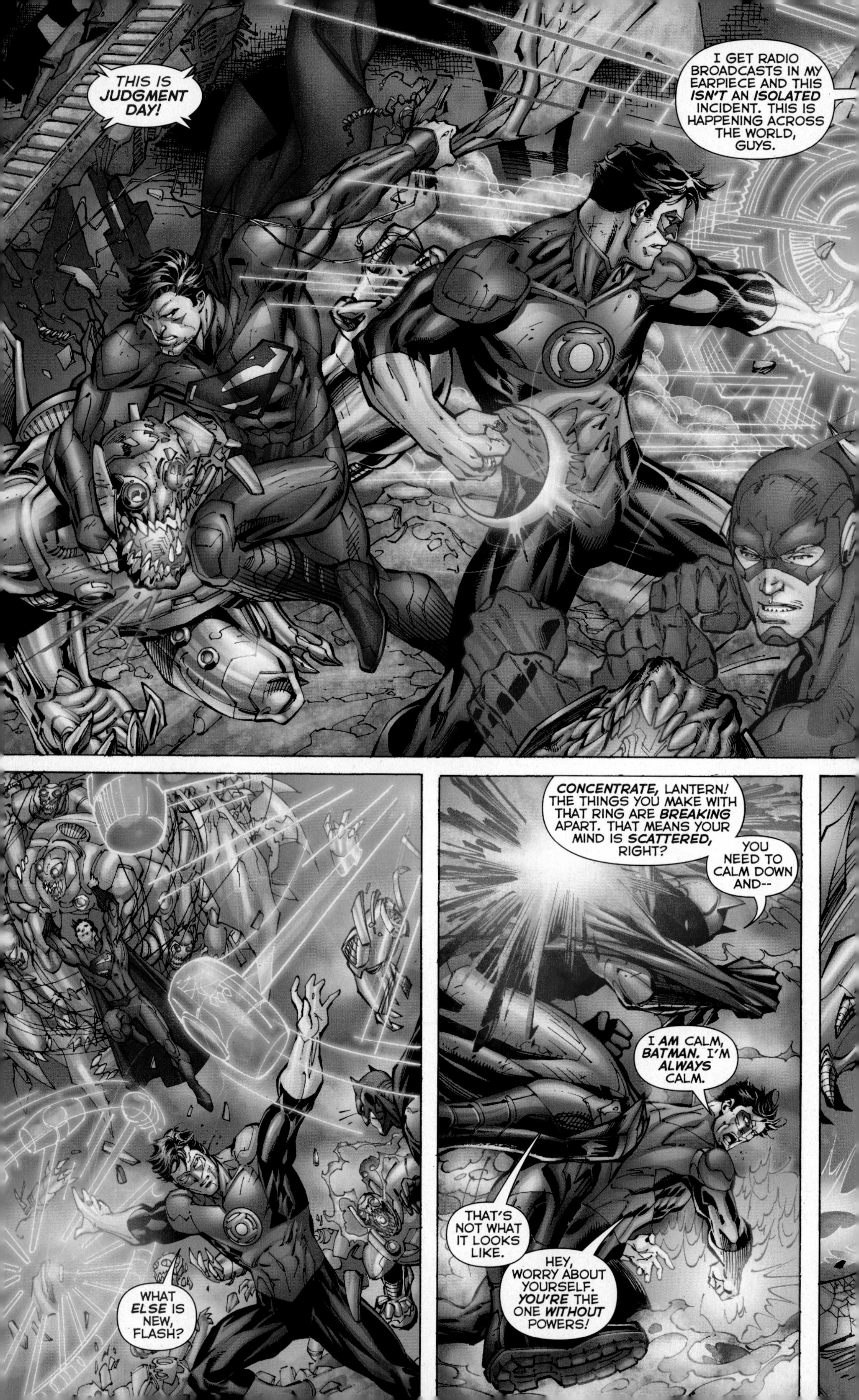

THIS IS JUDGMENT DAY!
I GET RADIO BROADCASTS IN MY EARPIECE AND THIS ISN'T AN ISOLATED INCIDENT. THIS IS HAPPENING ACROSS THE WORLD, GUYS.
WHAT ELSE IS NEW, FLASH?
CONCENTRATE, LANTERN! THE THINGS YOU MAKE WITH THAT RING ARE BREAKING APART. THAT MEANS YOUR MIND IS SCATTERED, RIGHT?
YOU NEED TO CALM DOWN AND--
I AM CALM, BATMAN. I'M ALWAYS CALM.
THAT'S NOT WHAT IT LOOKS LIKE.
HEY, WORRY ABOUT YOURSELF. YOU'RE THE ONE WITHOUT POWERS!

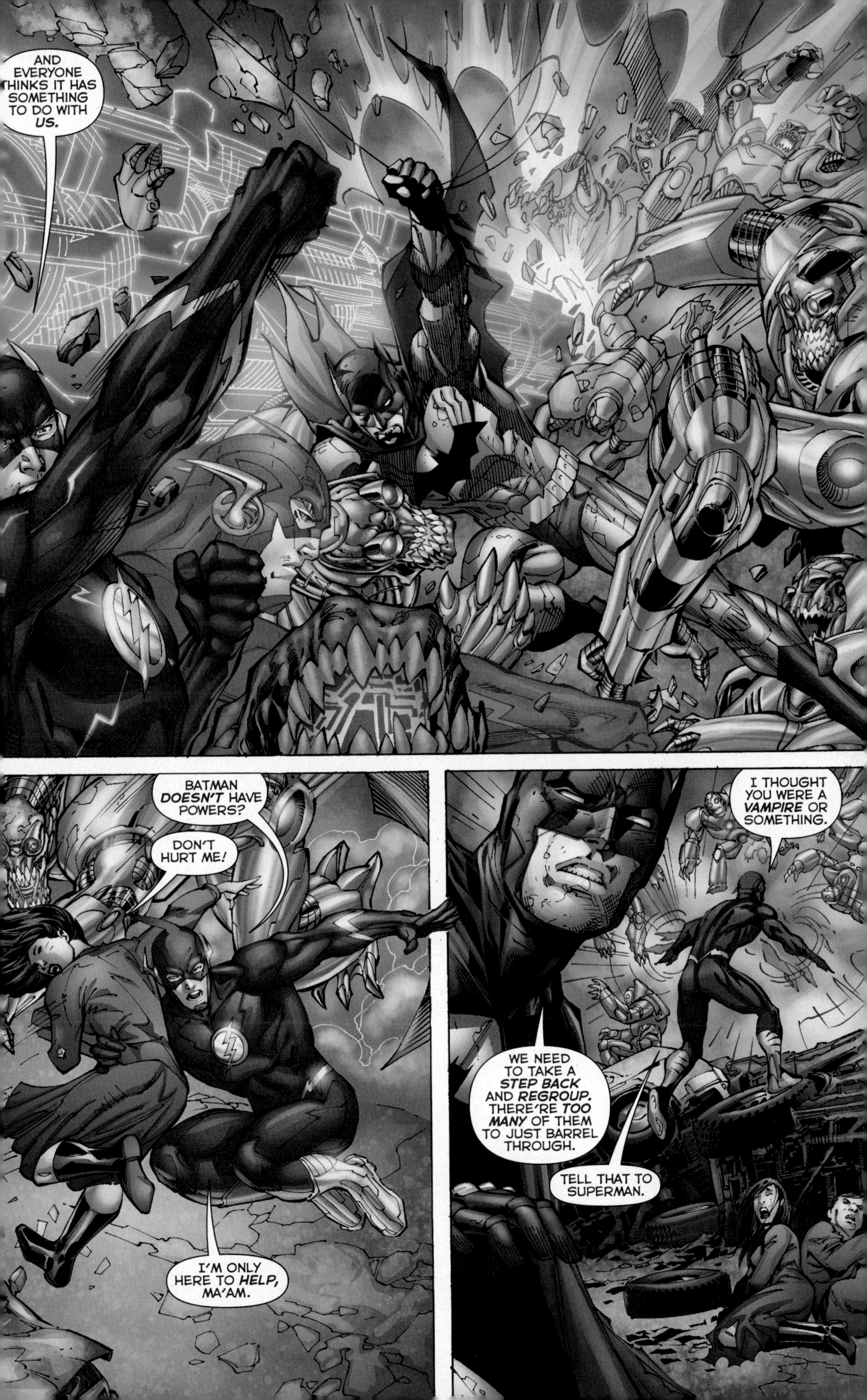
AND EVERYONE THINKS IT HAS SOMETHING TO DO WITH *US.*
BATMAN *DOESN'T* HAVE POWERS?
DON'T HURT ME!
I'M ONLY HERE TO *HELP,* MA'AM.
I THOUGHT YOU WERE A *VAMPIRE* OR SOMETHING.
WE NEED TO TAKE A *STEP BACK* AND *REGROUP.* THERE'RE *TOO MANY* OF THEM TO JUST BARREL THROUGH.
TELL THAT TO SUPERMAN.

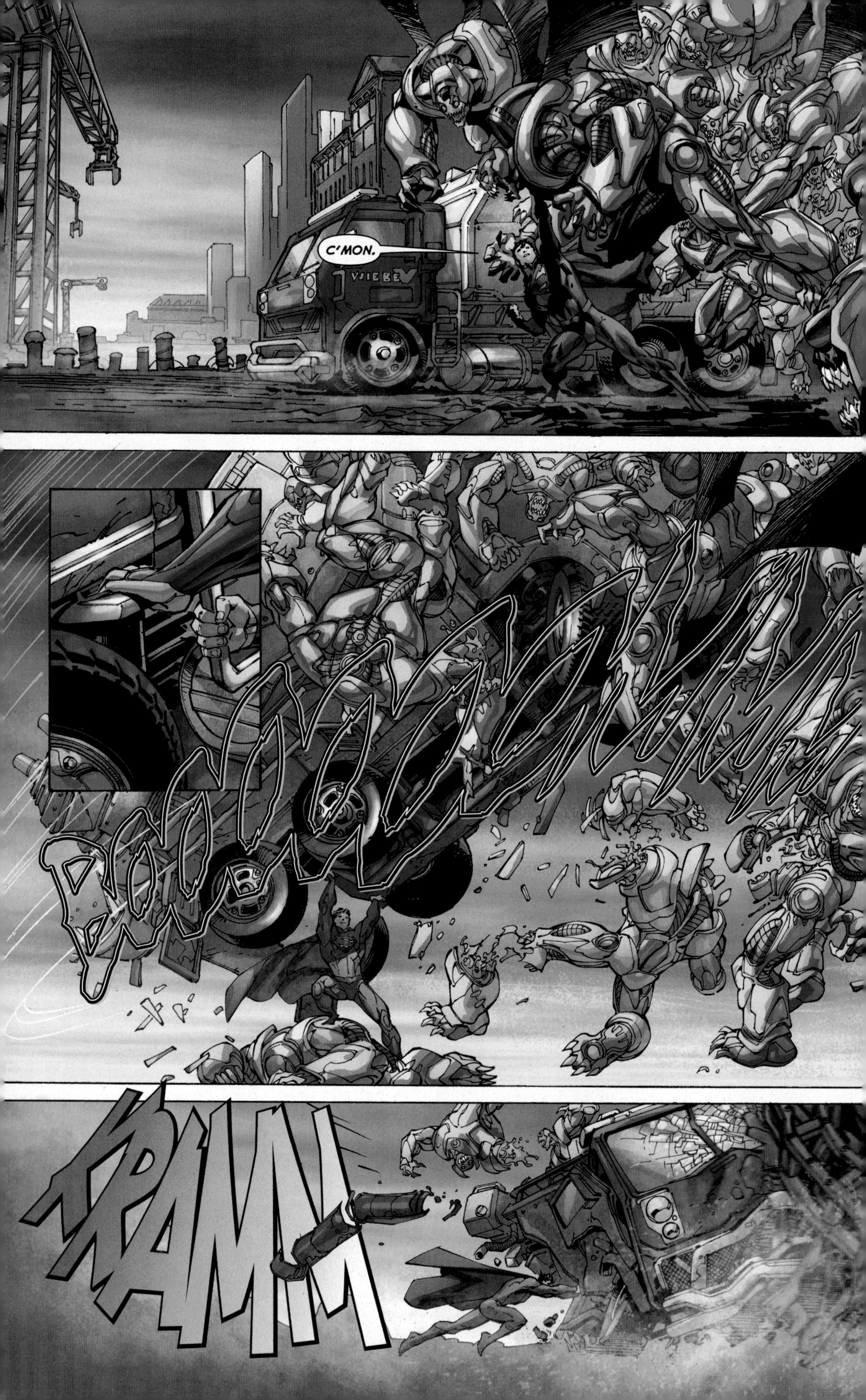
C'MON.
KRAMM

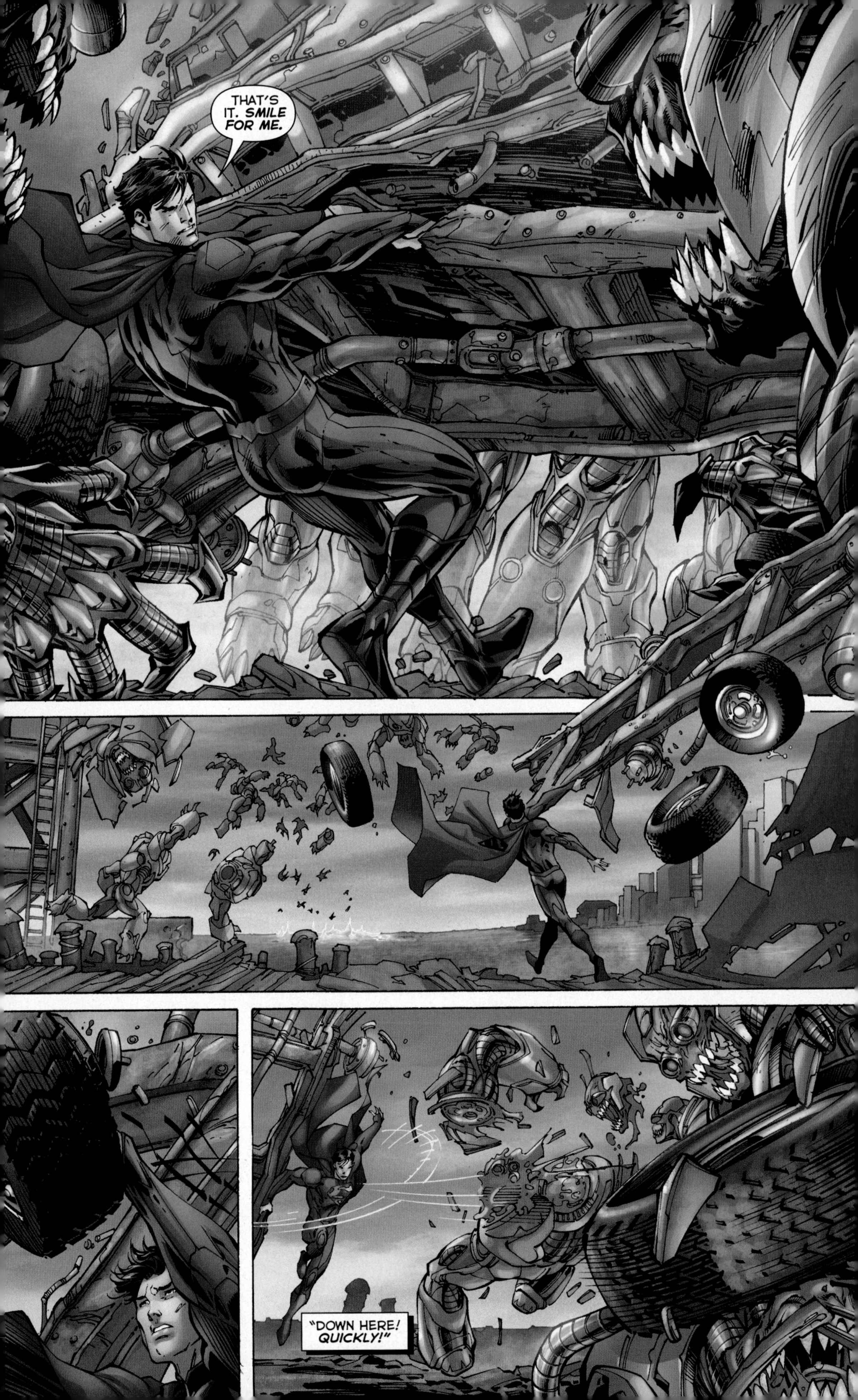
THAT'S IT. *SMILE* FOR ME.
"DOWN HERE! *QUICKLY!*"

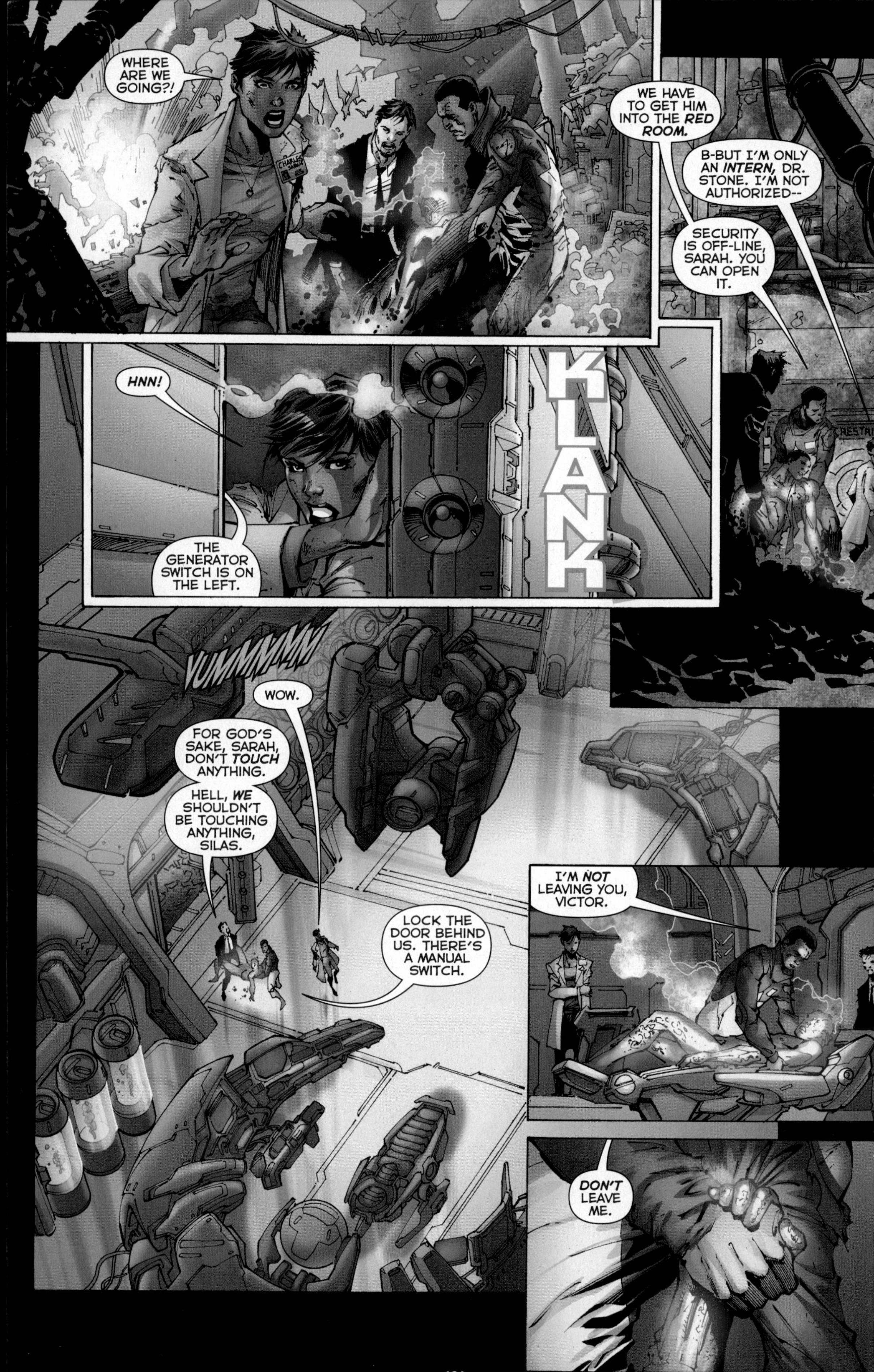
WHERE ARE WE GOING?!
WE HAVE TO GET HIM INTO THE RED ROOM.
B-BUT I'M ONLY AN INTERN, DR. STONE. I'M NOT AUTHORIZED--
SECURITY IS OFF-LINE, SARAH. YOU CAN OPEN IT.
HNN!
THE GENERATOR SWITCH IS ON THE LEFT.
KLANK
VUMMMMM
WOW.
FOR GOD'S SAKE, SARAH, DON'T TOUCH ANYTHING.
HELL, WE SHOULDN'T BE TOUCHING ANYTHING, SILAS.
LOCK THE DOOR BEHIND US. THERE'S A MANUAL SWITCH.
I'M NOT LEAVING YOU, VICTOR.
DON'T LEAVE ME.

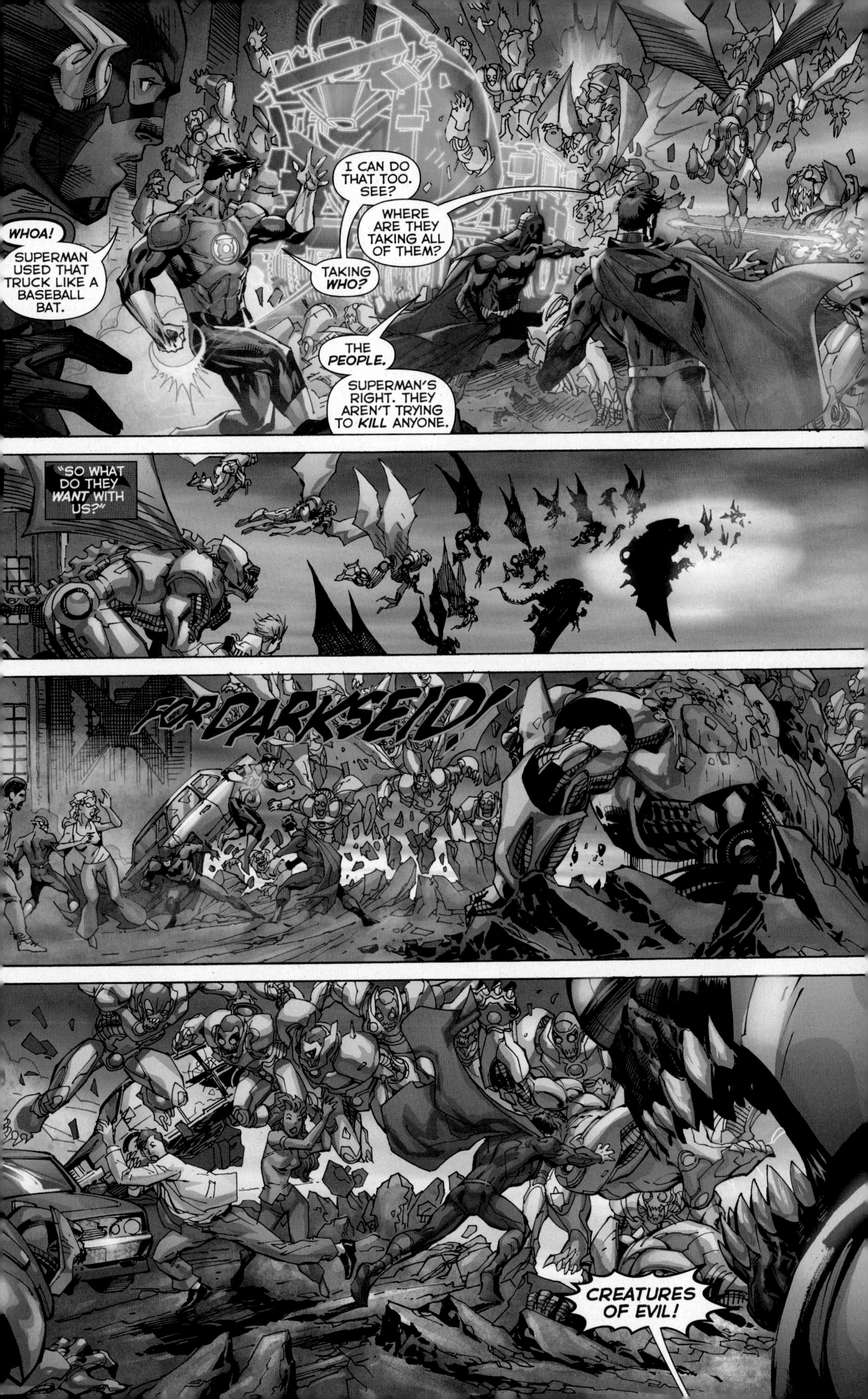

WHOA!
SUPERMAN USED THAT TRUCK LIKE A BASEBALL BAT.
I CAN DO THAT TOO. SEE?
WHERE ARE THEY TAKING ALL OF THEM?
TAKING WHO?
THE PEOPLE.
SUPERMAN'S RIGHT. THEY AREN'T TRYING TO KILL ANYONE.
"SO WHAT DO THEY WANT WITH US?"
FOR DARKSEID!
CREATURES OF EVIL!

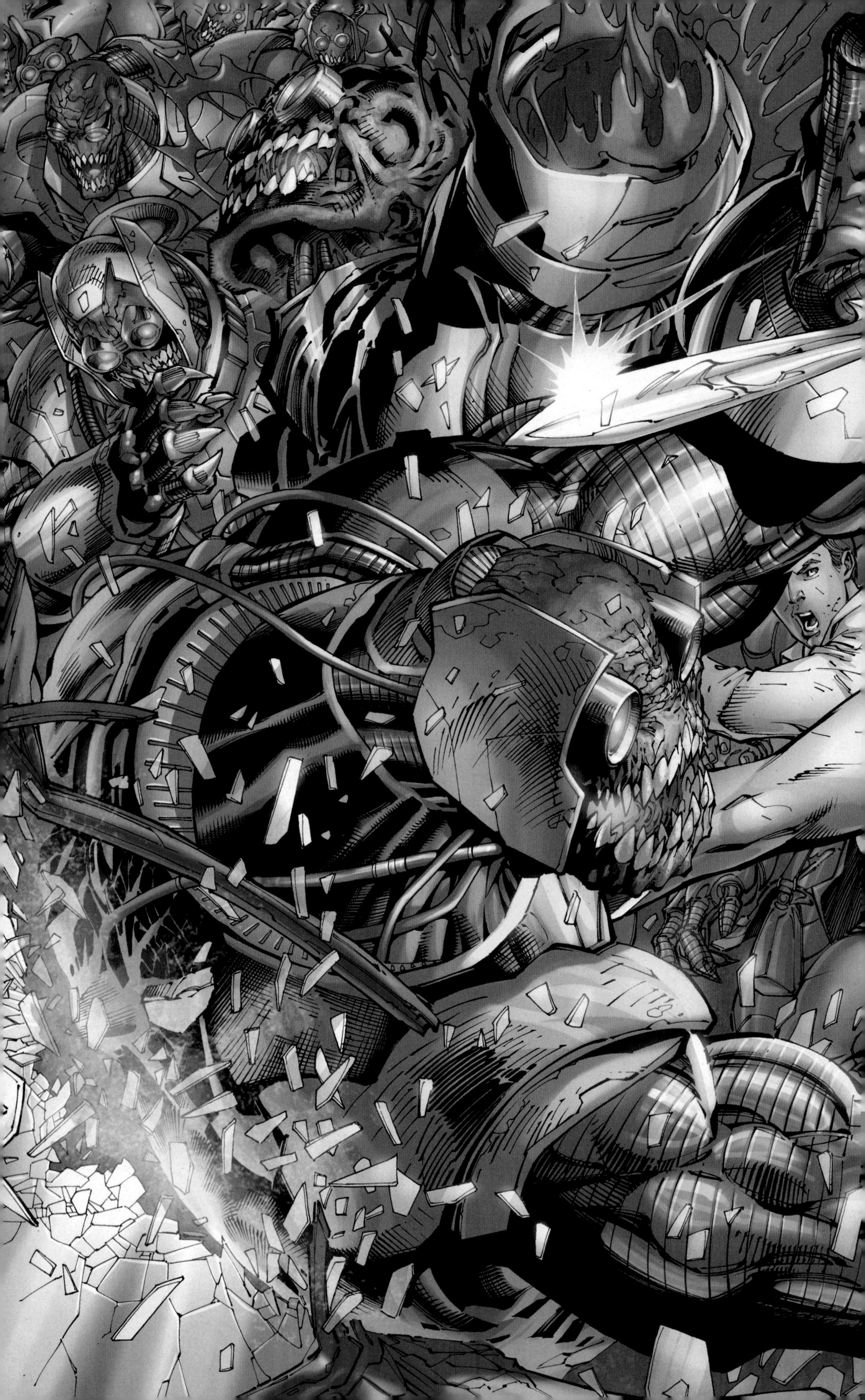

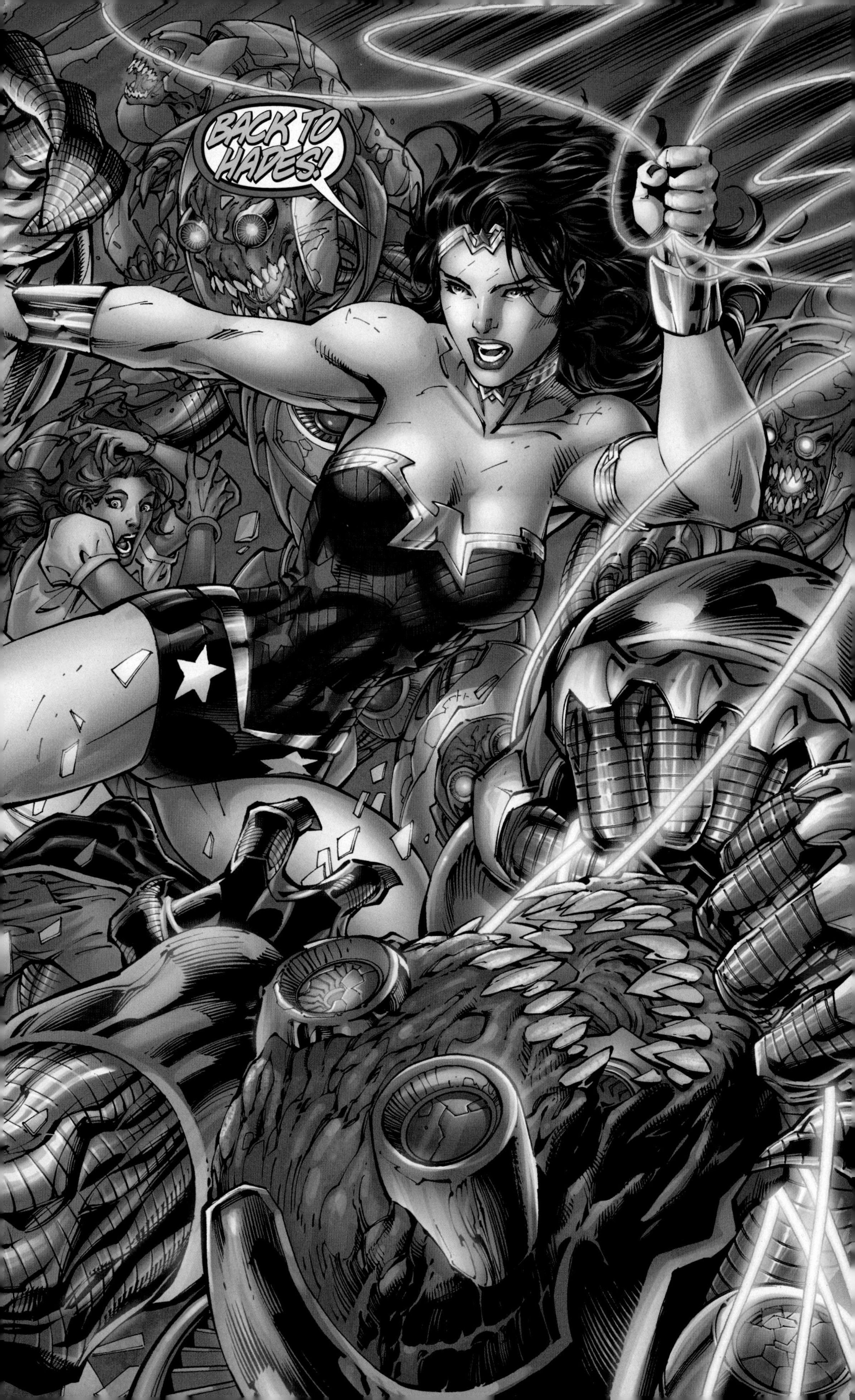
BACK TO HADES!

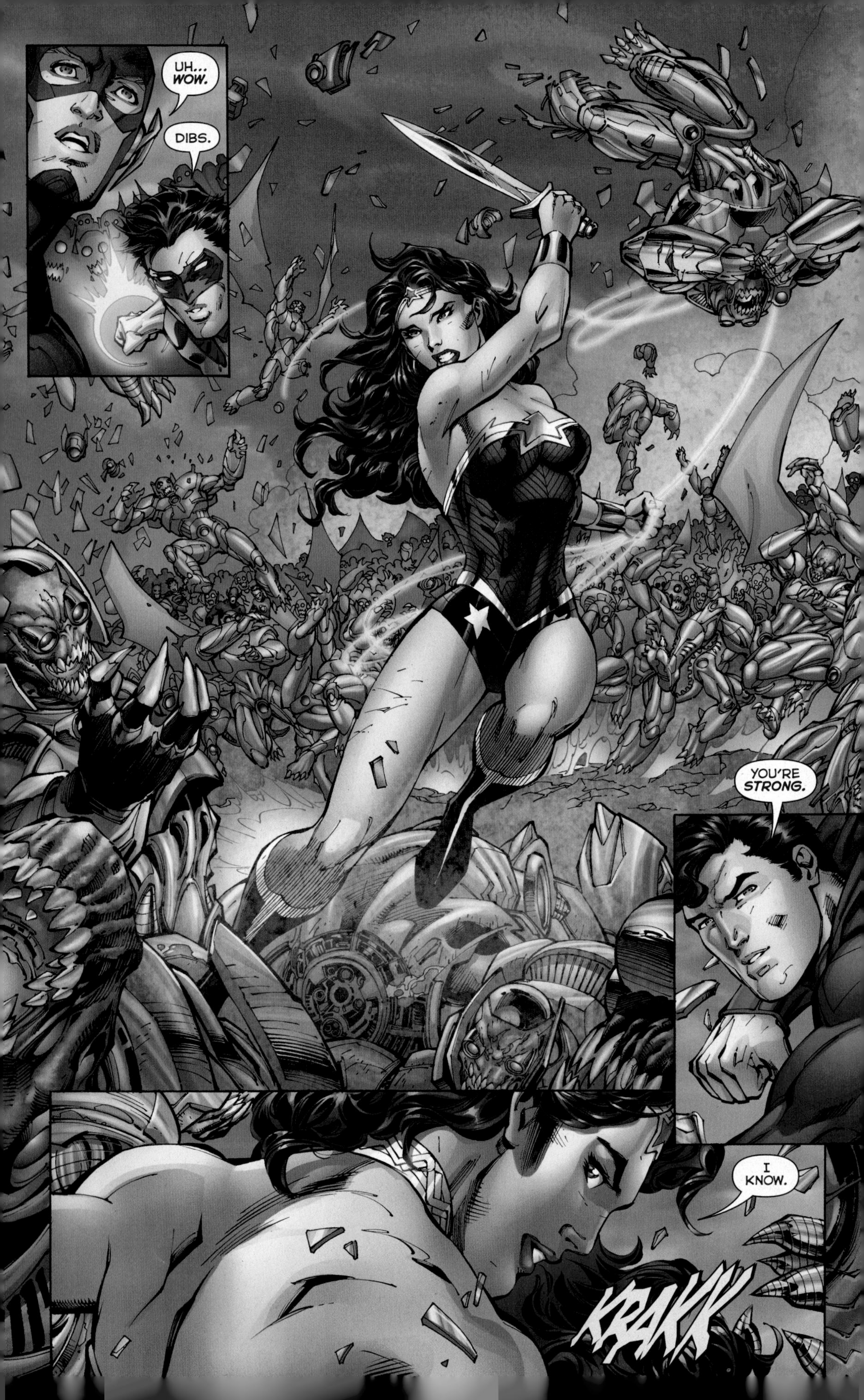
UH... WOW.
DIBS.
YOU'RE STRONG.
I KNOW.
KRAKK

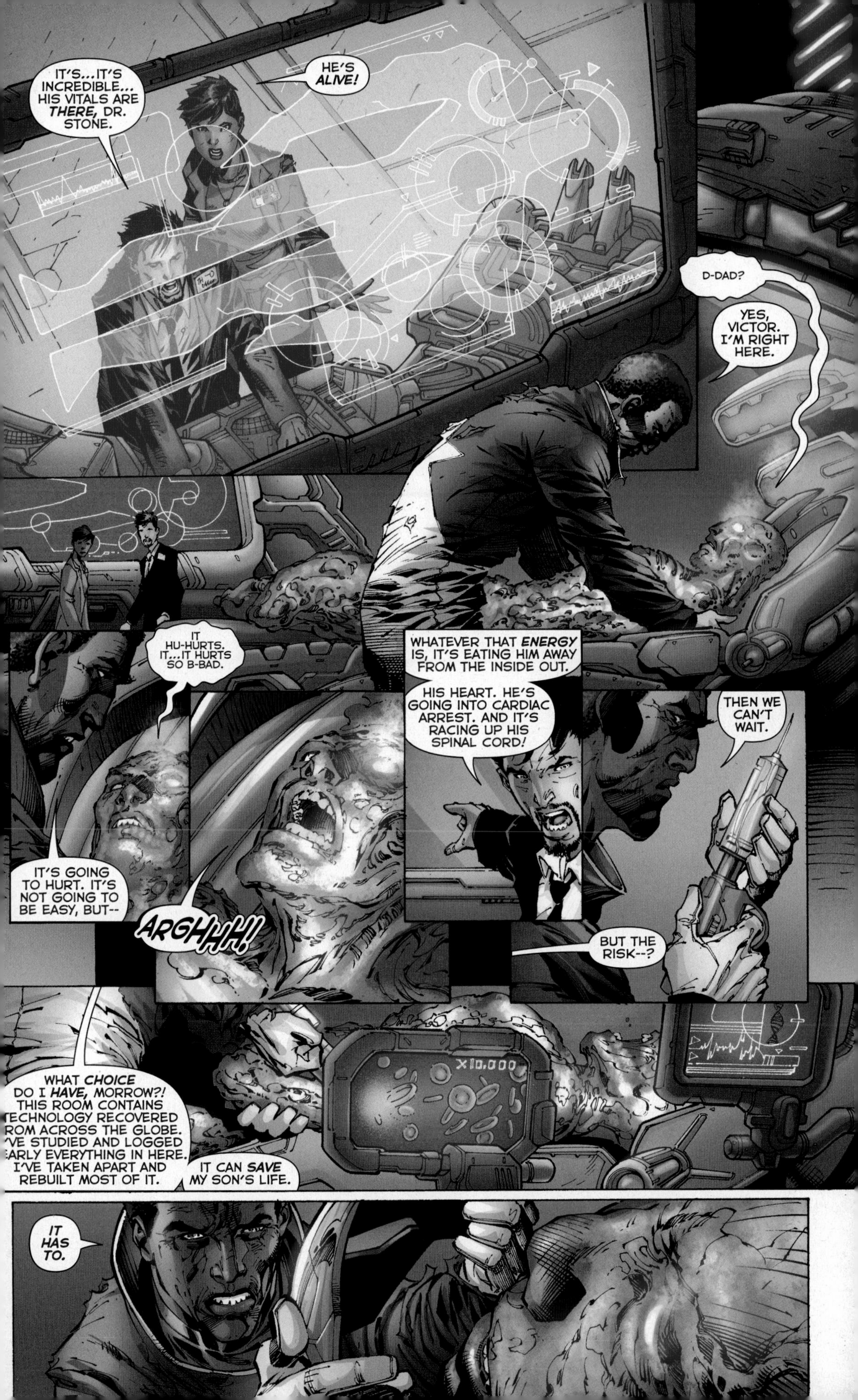
IT'S...IT'S INCREDIBLE... HIS VITALS ARE THERE, DR. STONE.
HE'S ALIVE!
D-DAD?
YES, VICTOR. I'M RIGHT HERE.
IT HU-HURTS. IT...IT HURTS SO B-BAD.
WHATEVER THAT ENERGY IS, IT'S EATING HIM AWAY FROM THE INSIDE OUT.
IT'S GOING TO HURT. IT'S NOT GOING TO BE EASY, BUT--
ARGHHH!
HIS HEART. HE'S GOING INTO CARDIAC ARREST. AND IT'S RACING UP HIS SPINAL CORD!
THEN WE CAN'T WAIT.
BUT THE RISK--?
X10,000
WHAT CHOICE DO I HAVE, MORROW?! THIS ROOM CONTAINS TECHNOLOGY RECOVERED FROM ACROSS THE GLOBE. I'VE STUDIED AND LOGGED NEARLY EVERYTHING IN HERE. I'VE TAKEN APART AND REBUILT MOST OF IT.
IT CAN SAVE MY SON'S LIFE.
IT HAS TO.

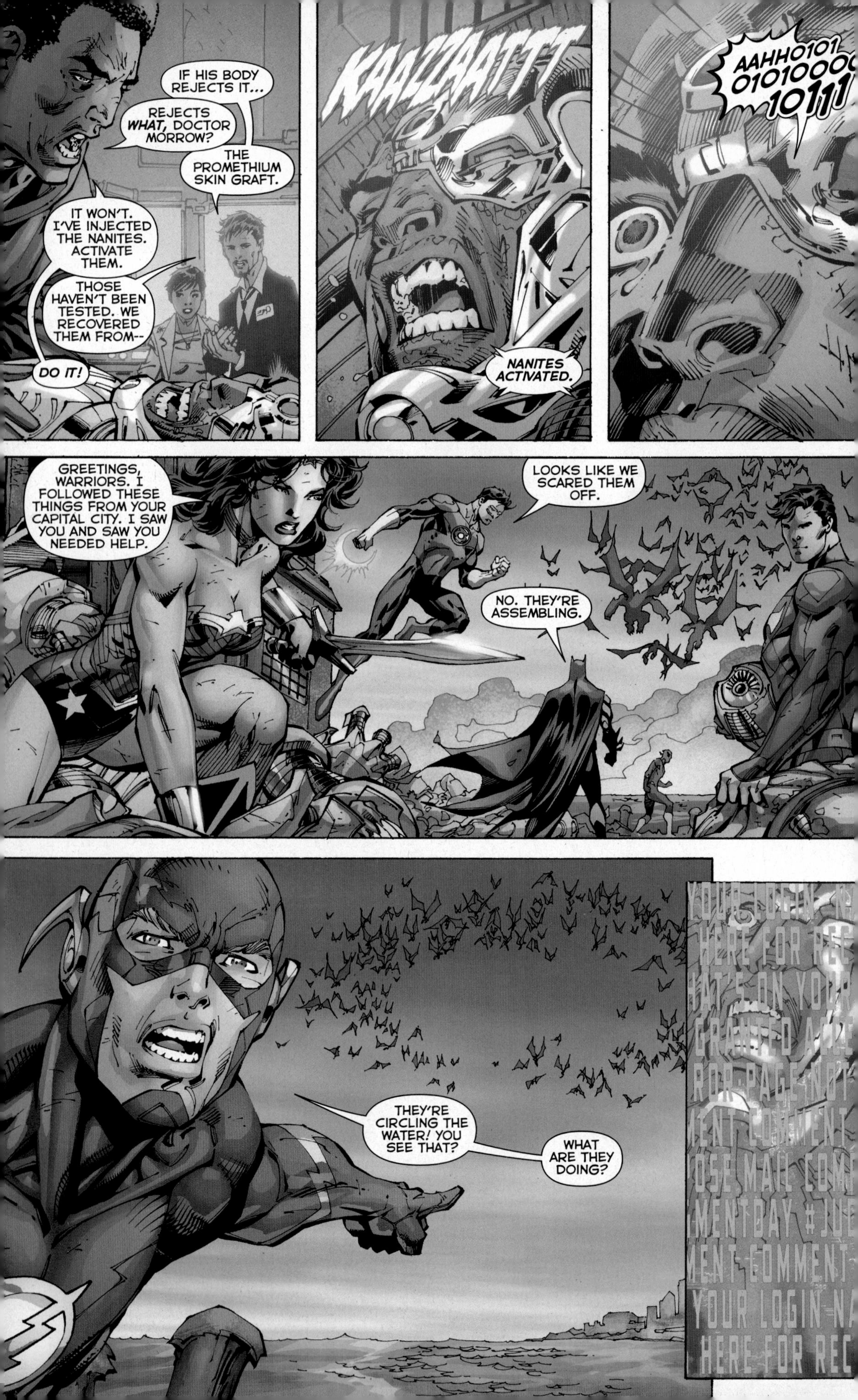
IF HIS BODY REJECTS IT...
REJECTS *WHAT,* DOCTOR MORROW?
THE PROMETHIUM SKIN GRAFT.
IT WON'T. I'VE INJECTED THE NANITES. ACTIVATE THEM.
THOSE HAVEN'T BEEN TESTED. WE RECOVERED THEM FROM--
DO IT!
NANITES ACTIVATED.
AAHH0101
0101000
1011
GREETINGS, WARRIORS. I FOLLOWED THESE THINGS FROM YOUR CAPITAL CITY. I SAW YOU AND SAW YOU NEEDED HELP.
LOOKS LIKE WE SCARED THEM OFF.
NO. THEY'RE ASSEMBLING.
THEY'RE CIRCLING THE WATER! YOU SEE THAT?
WHAT ARE THEY DOING?

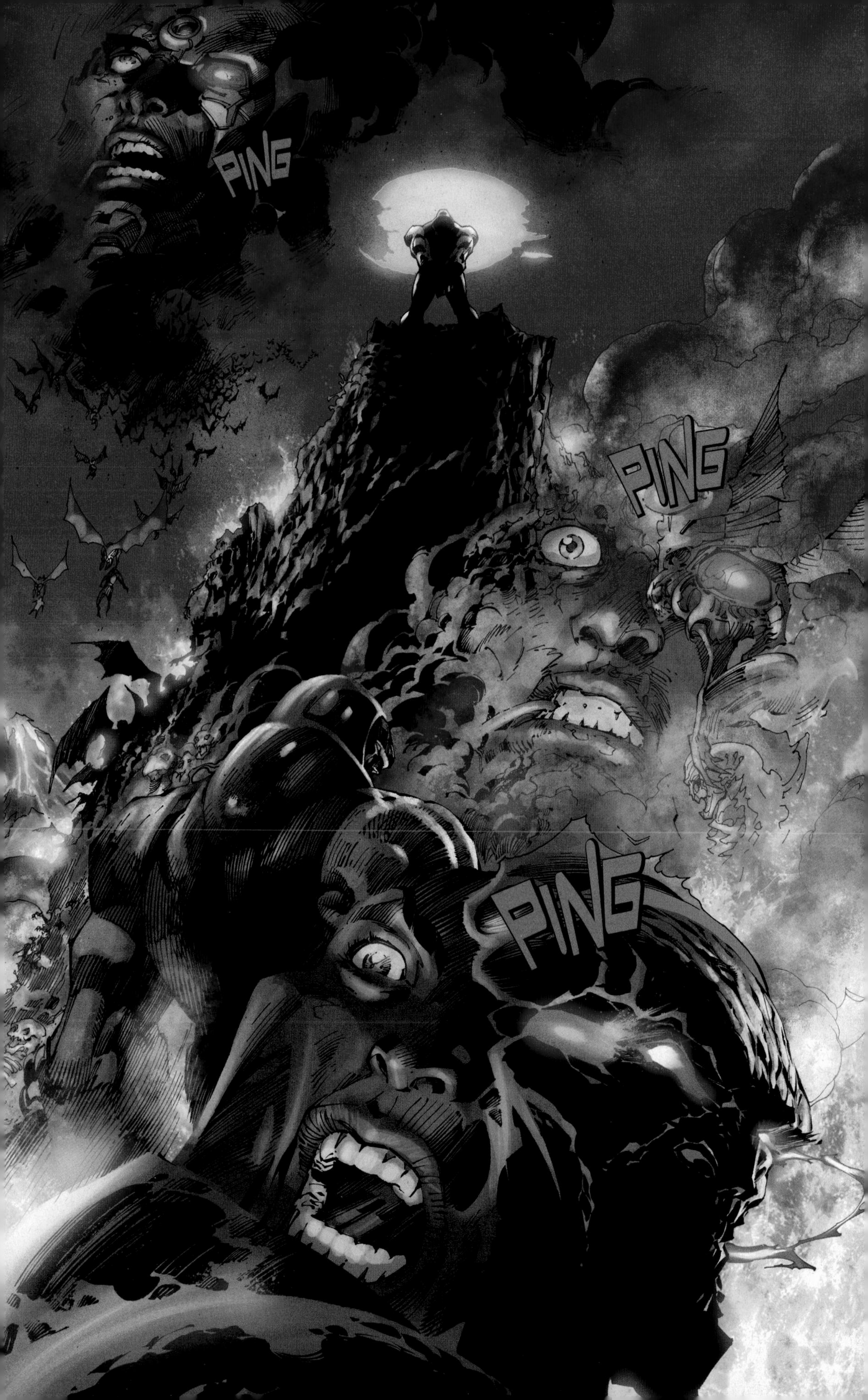
PING
PING
PING

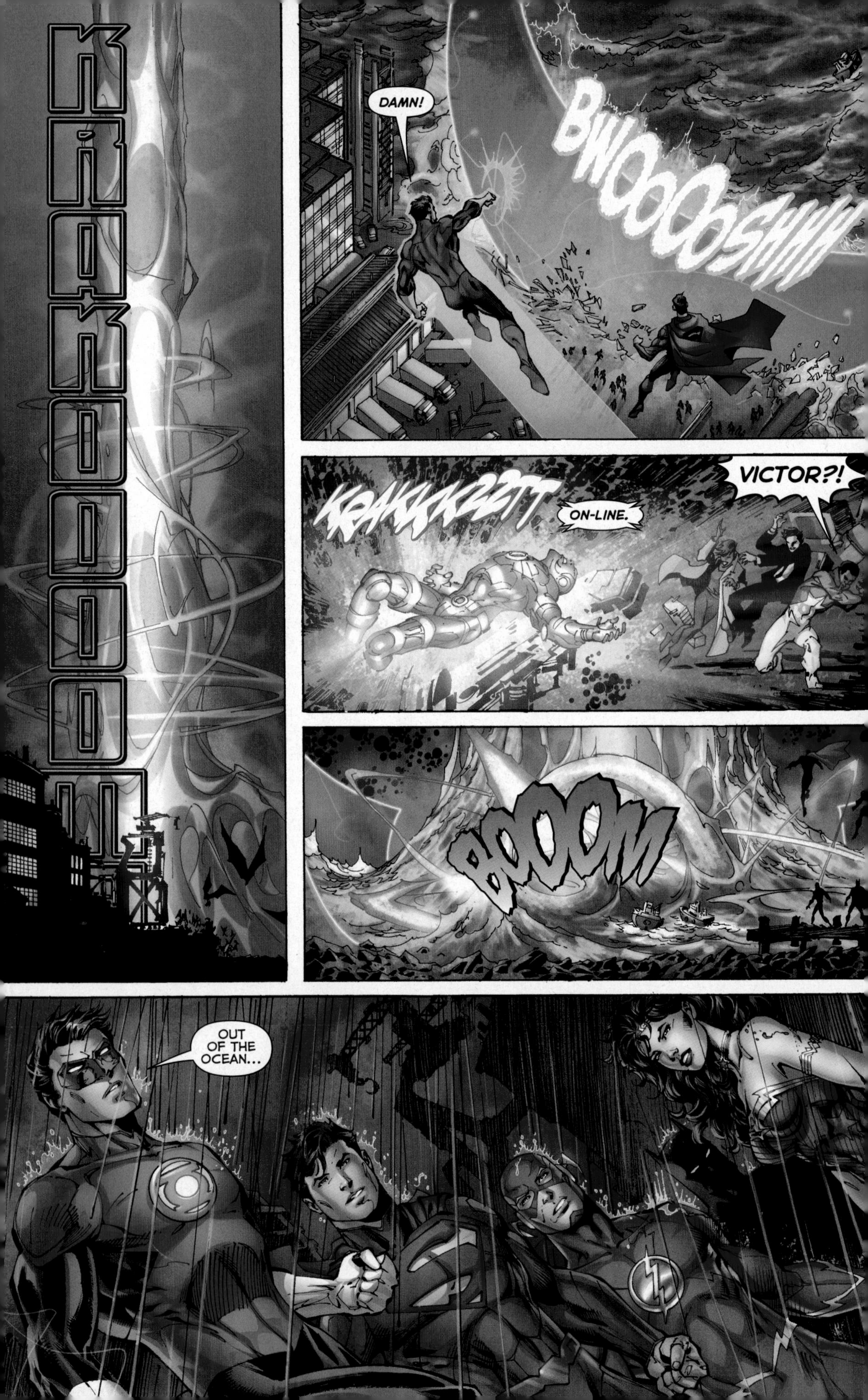
DAMN!
BWOOOOSHHH
ON-LINE.
VICTOR?!
BOOOM
OUT OF THE OCEAN...

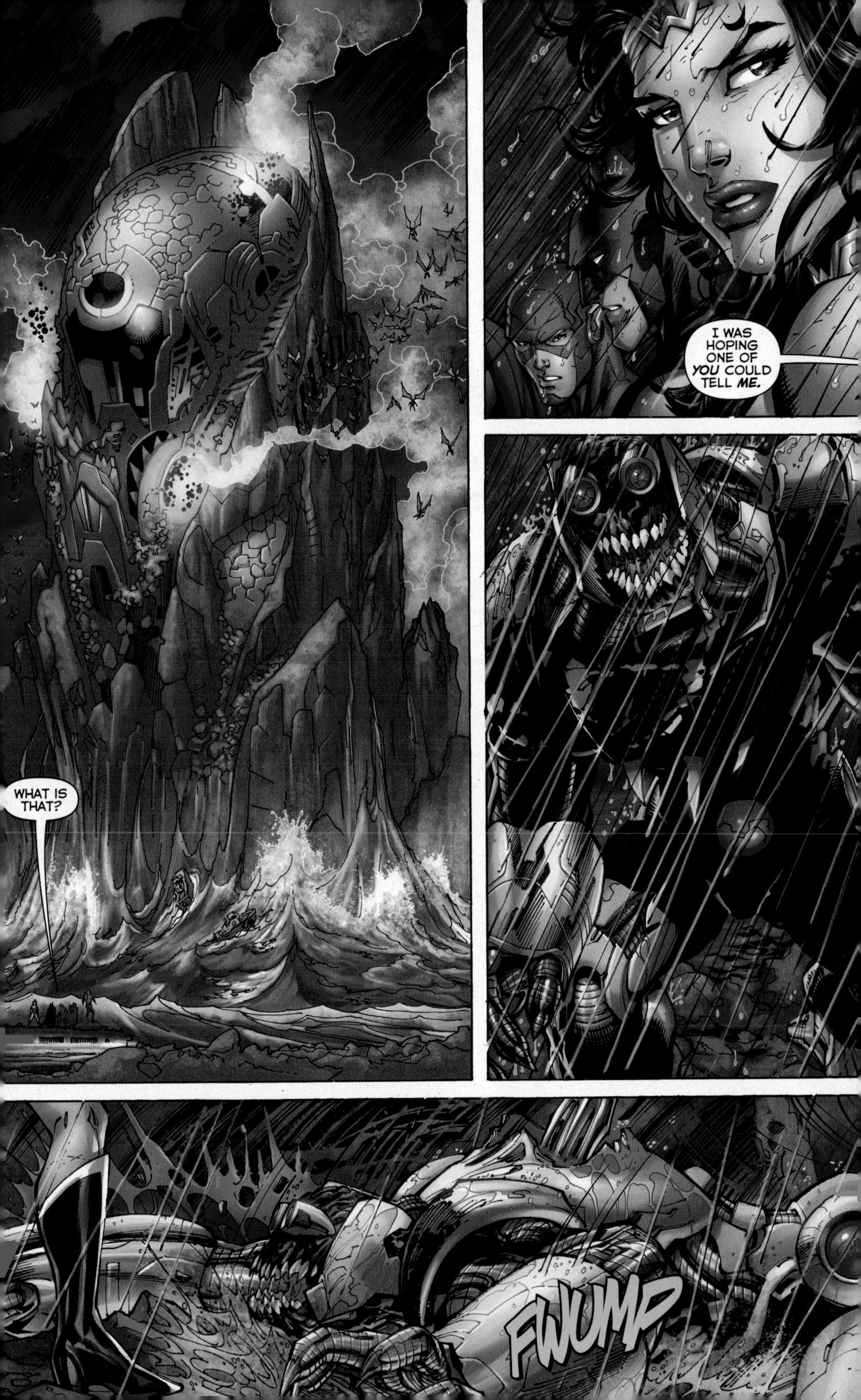
WHAT IS THAT?
I WAS HOPING ONE OF YOU COULD TELL ME.
FWUMP

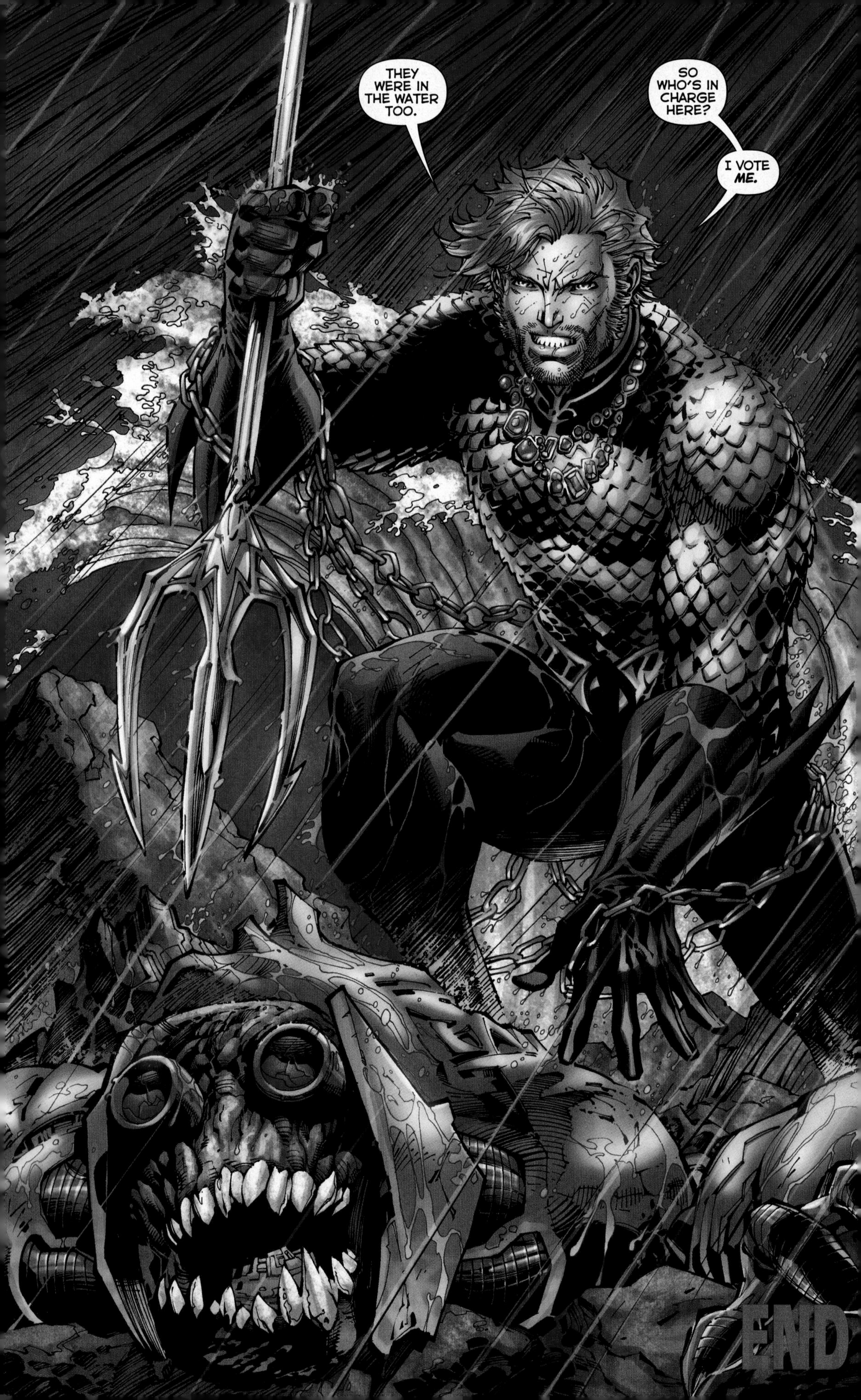
THEY WERE IN THE WATER TOO.
SO WHO'S IN CHARGE HERE?
I VOTE ME.
END

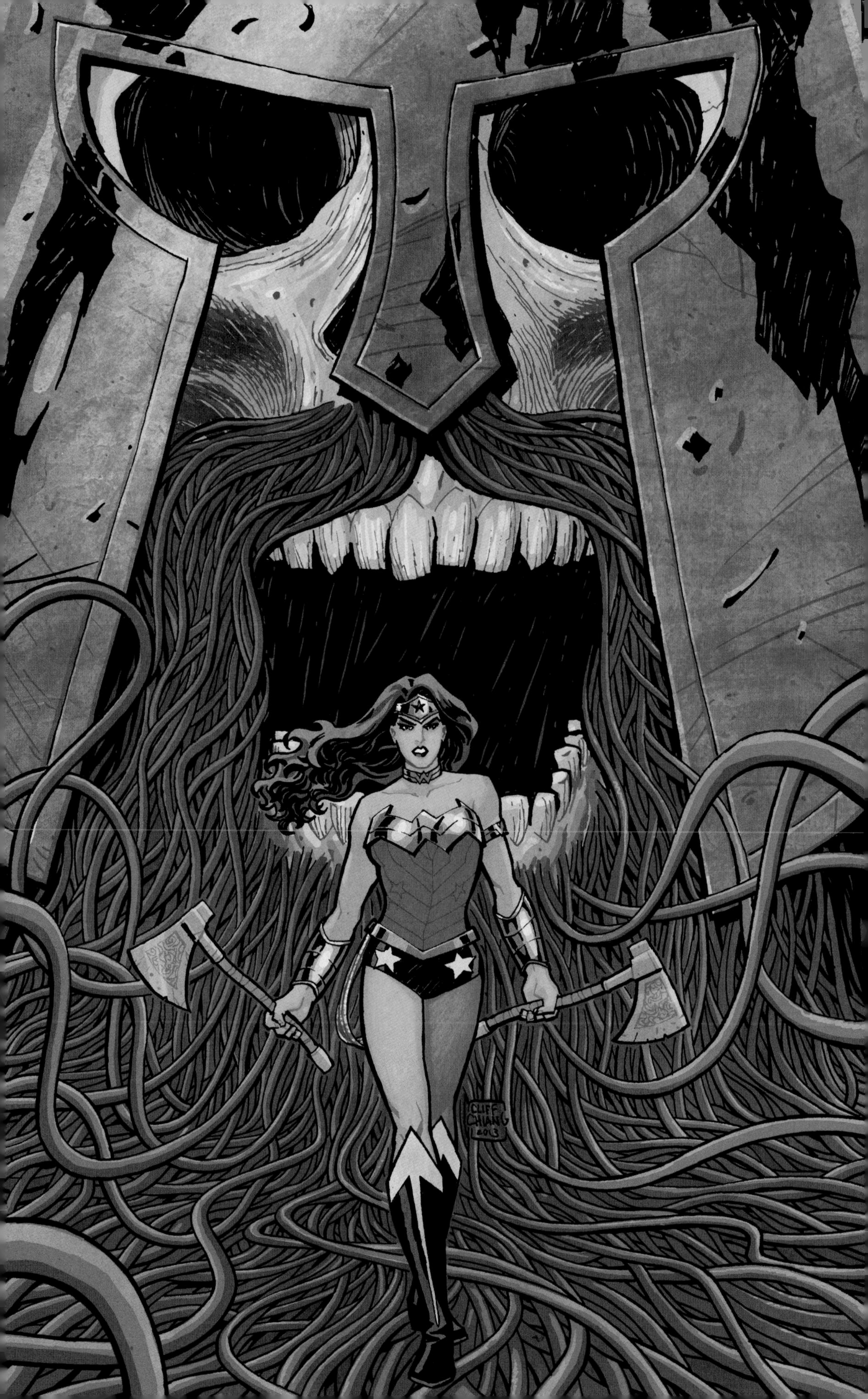
CLIFF CHIANG 2013

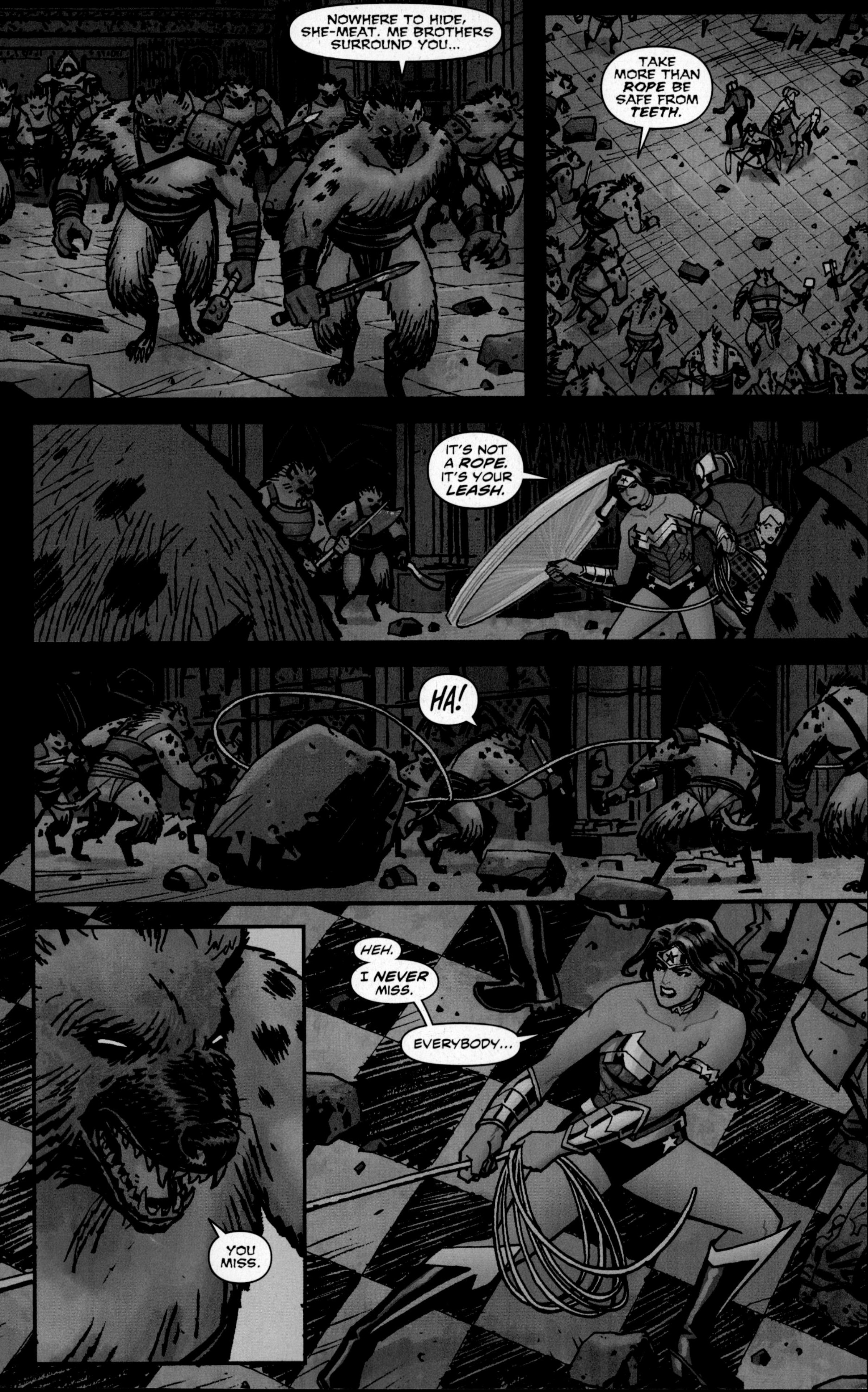
NOWHERE TO HIDE, SHE-MEAT. ME BROTHERS SURROUND YOU...
TAKE MORE THAN ROPE BE SAFE FROM TEETH.
IT'S NOT A ROPE. IT'S YOUR LEASH.
HA!
HEH.
I NEVER MISS.
EVERYBODY...
YOU MISS.

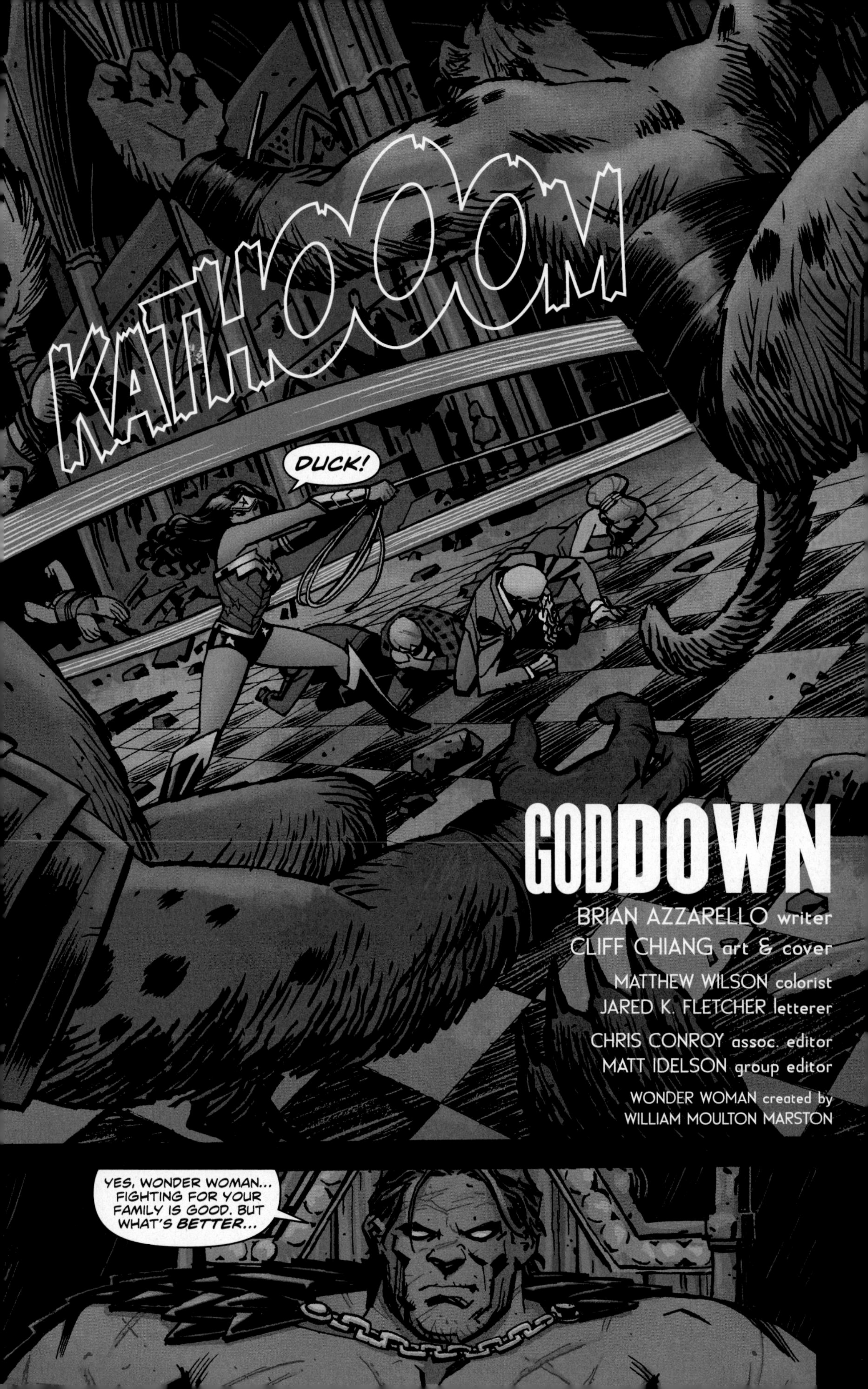
KATHOOOOM
DUCK!
GODDOWN
BRIAN AZZARELLO writer
CLIFF CHIANG art & cover
MATTHEW WILSON colorist
JARED K. FLETCHER letterer
CHRIS CONROY assoc. editor
MATT IDELSON group editor
WONDER WOMAN created by
WILLIAM MOULTON MARSTON
YES, WONDER WOMAN... FIGHTING FOR YOUR FAMILY IS GOOD. BUT WHAT'S BETTER...

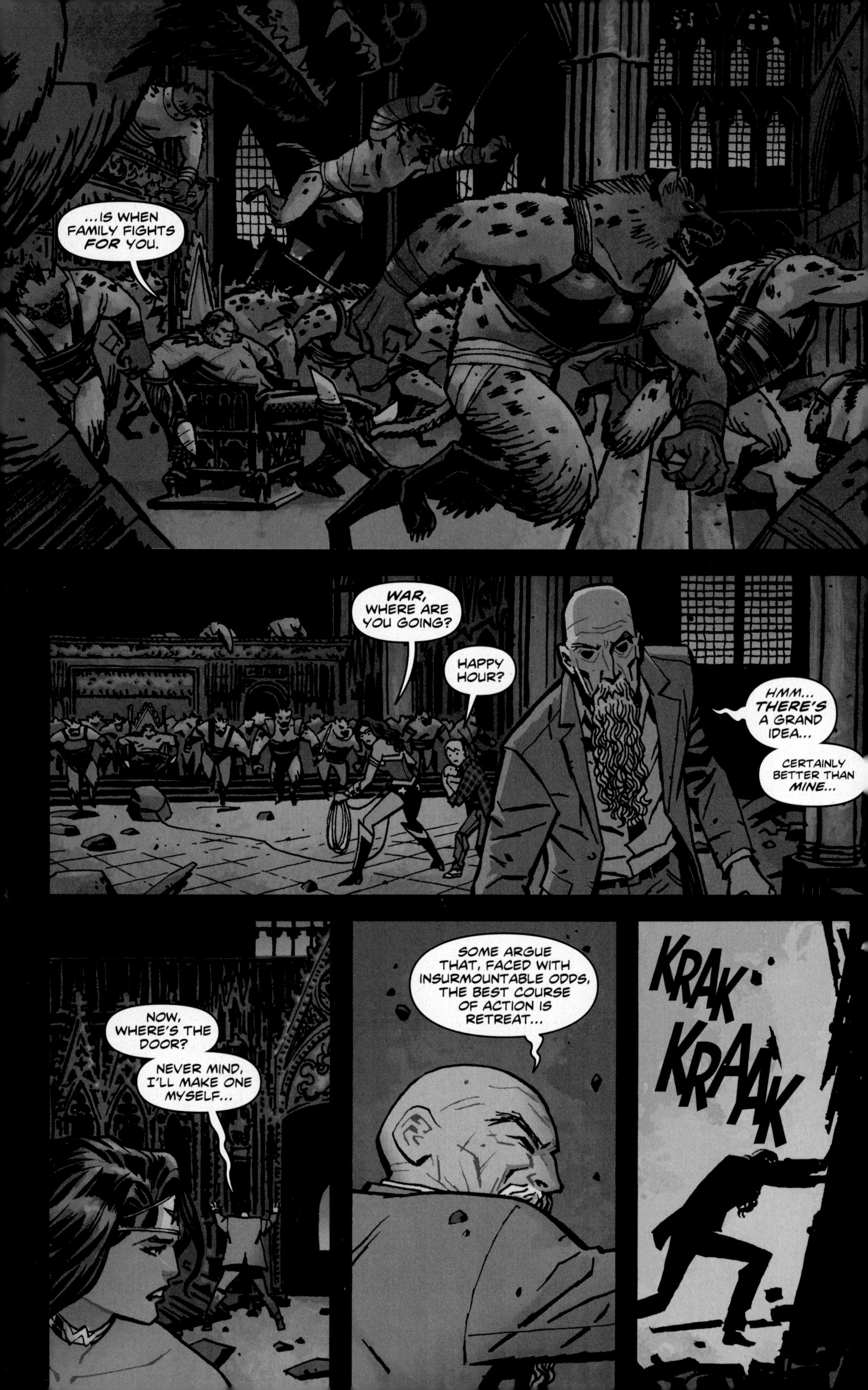
...IS WHEN FAMILY FIGHTS FOR YOU.
WAR, WHERE ARE YOU GOING?
HAPPY HOUR?
HMM... THERE'S A GRAND IDEA...
CERTAINLY BETTER THAN MINE...
NOW, WHERE'S THE DOOR?
NEVER MIND, I'LL MAKE ONE MYSELF...
SOME ARGUE THAT, FACED WITH INSURMOUNTABLE ODDS, THE BEST COURSE OF ACTION IS RETREAT...
KRAK
KRAAAK

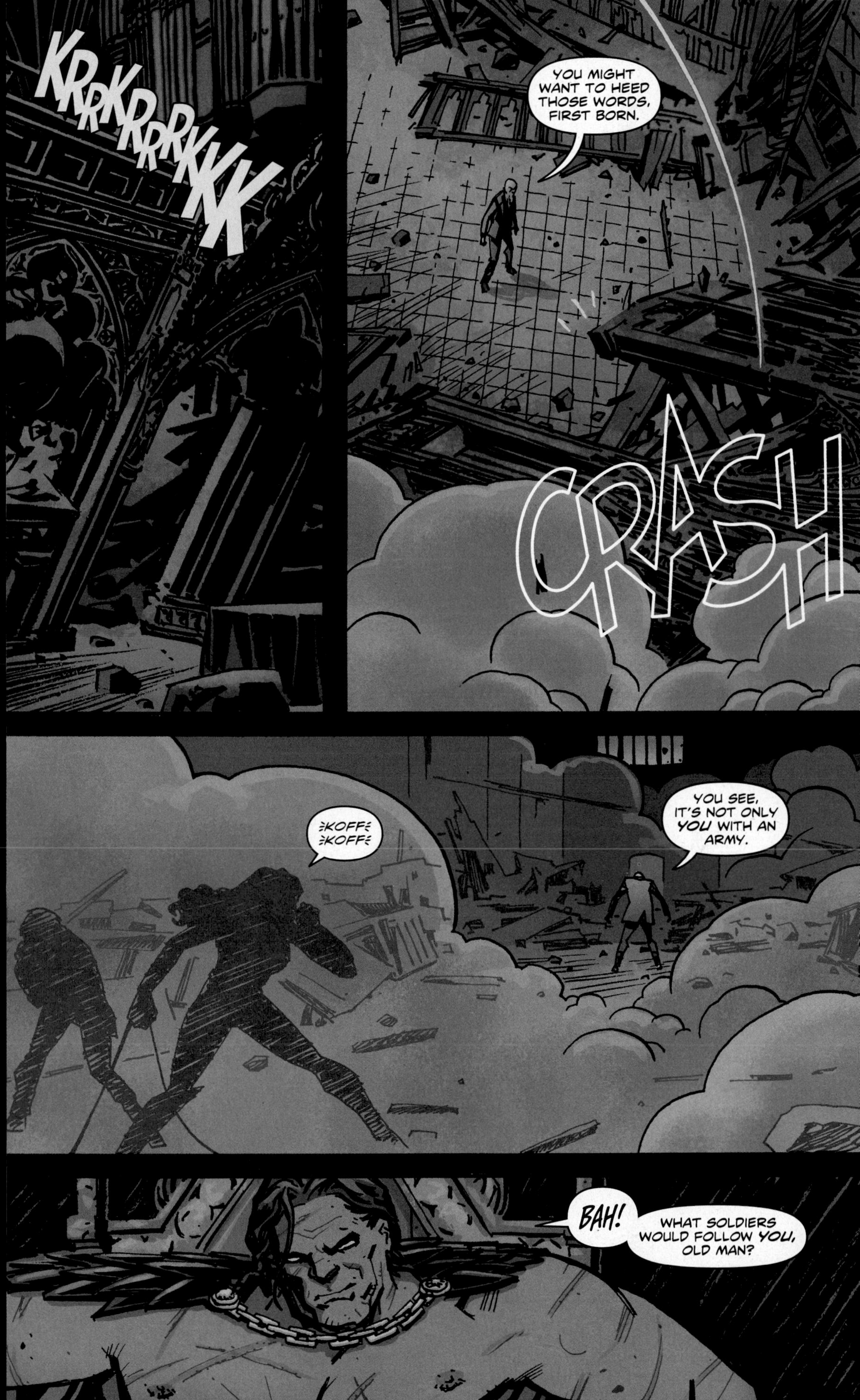
KRRKRRRKKK
YOU MIGHT WANT TO HEED THOSE WORDS, FIRST BORN.
CRASH
KOFF KOFF
YOU SEE, IT'S NOT ONLY YOU WITH AN ARMY.
BAH!
WHAT SOLDIERS WOULD FOLLOW YOU, OLD MAN?

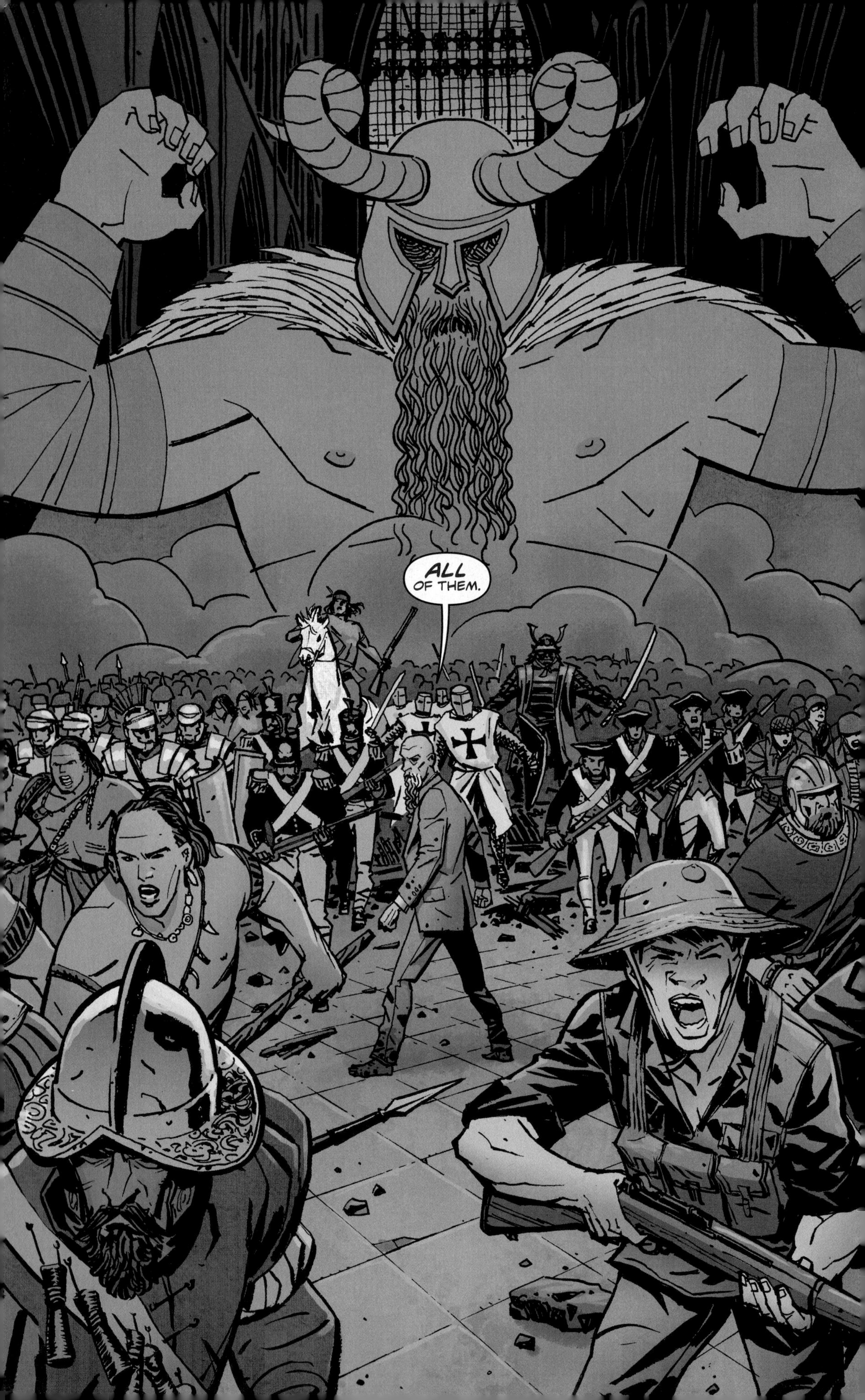
ALL OF THEM.

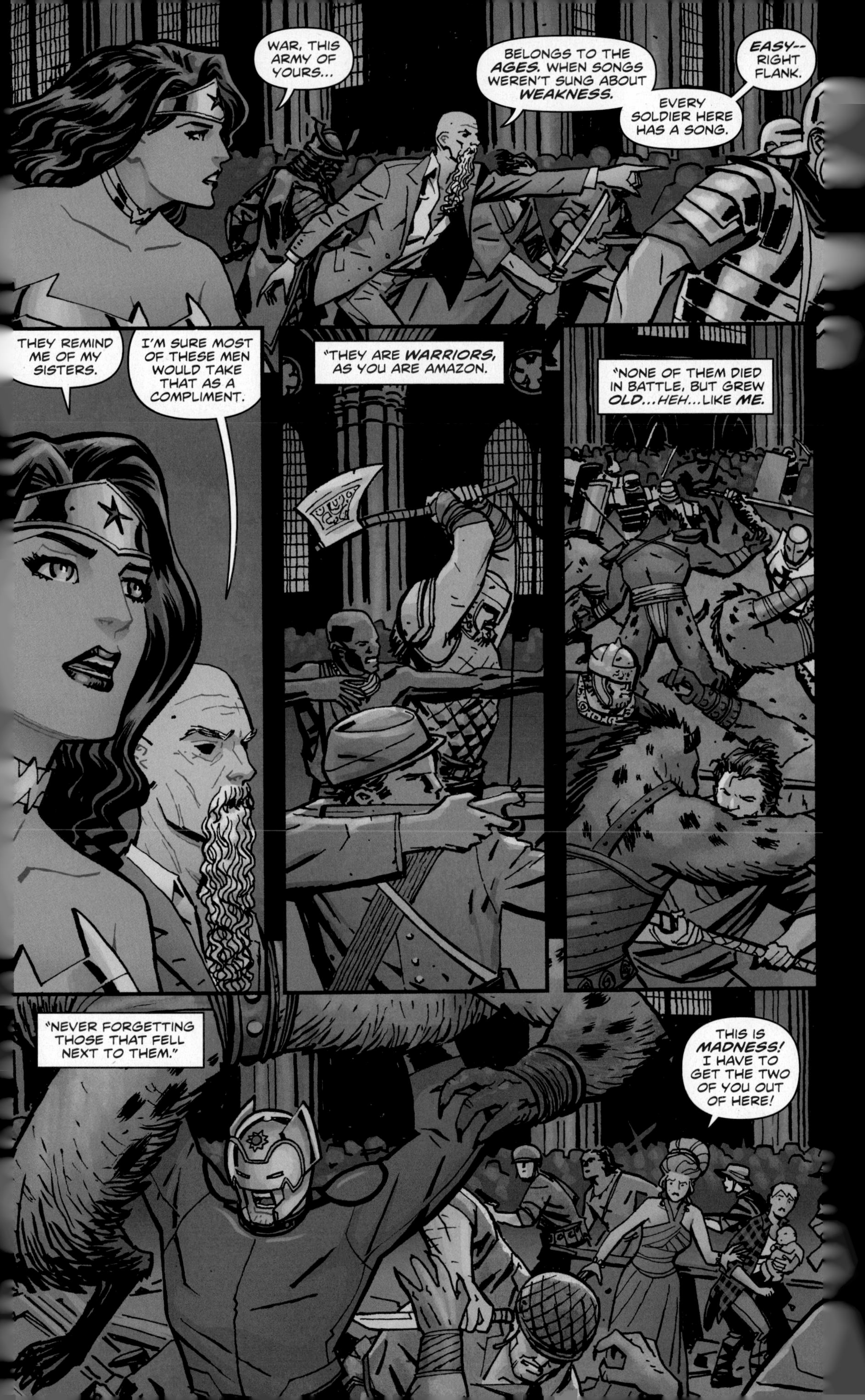
WAR, THIS ARMY OF YOURS...
BELONGS TO THE AGES. WHEN SONGS WEREN'T SUNG ABOUT WEAKNESS.
EVERY SOLDIER HERE HAS A SONG.
EASY-- RIGHT FLANK.
THEY REMIND ME OF MY SISTERS.
I'M SURE MOST OF THESE MEN WOULD TAKE THAT AS A COMPLIMENT.
"THEY ARE WARRIORS, AS YOU ARE AMAZON.
"NONE OF THEM DIED IN BATTLE, BUT GREW OLD...HEH...LIKE ME.
"NEVER FORGETTING THOSE THAT FELL NEXT TO THEM."
THIS IS MADNESS! I HAVE TO GET THE TWO OF YOU OUT OF HERE!

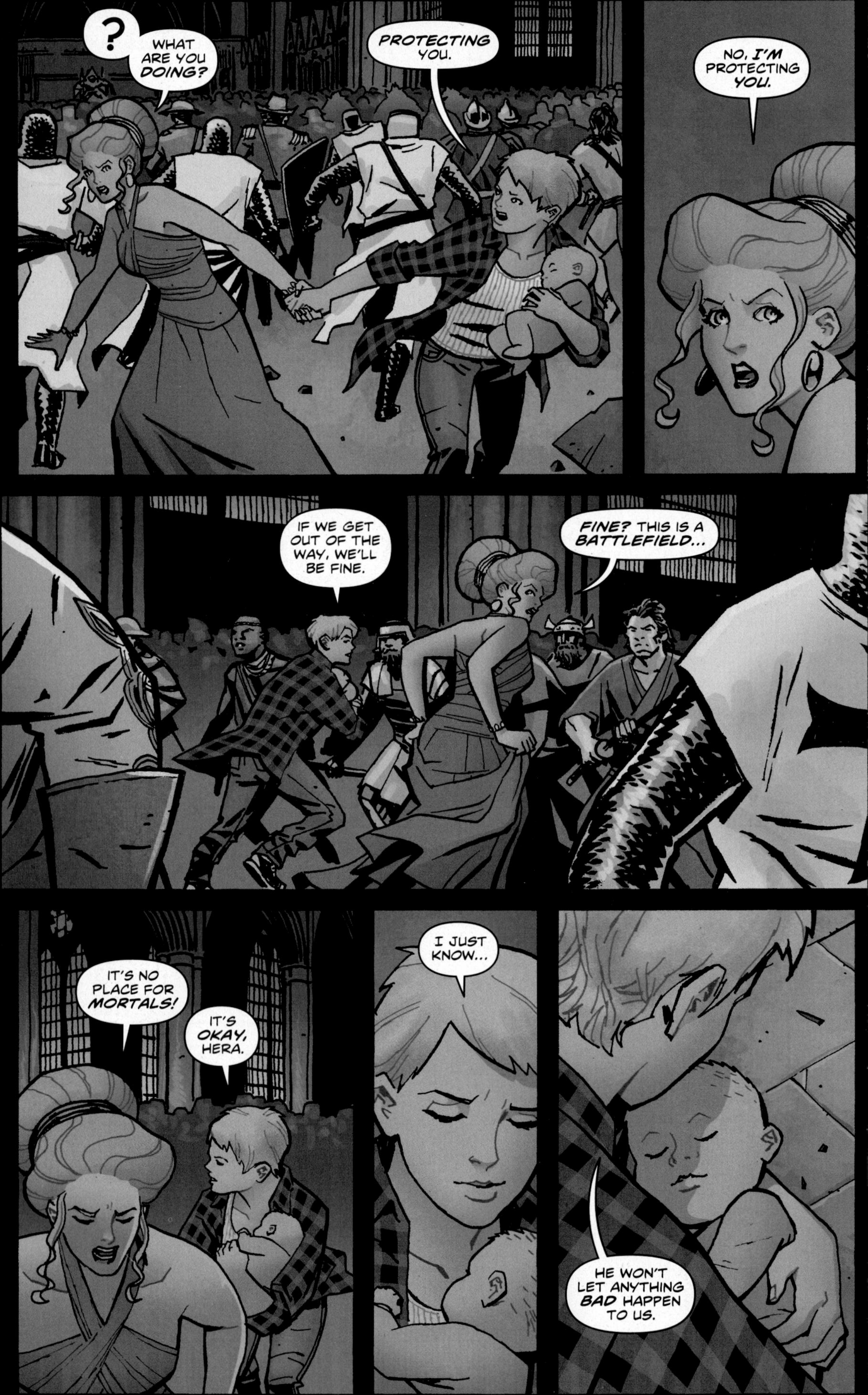
?
WHAT ARE YOU DOING?
PROTECTING YOU.
NO, I'M PROTECTING YOU.
IF WE GET OUT OF THE WAY, WE'LL BE FINE.
FINE? THIS IS A BATTLEFIELD...
IT'S NO PLACE FOR MORTALS!
IT'S OKAY, HERA.
I JUST KNOW...
HE WON'T LET ANYTHING BAD HAPPEN TO US.

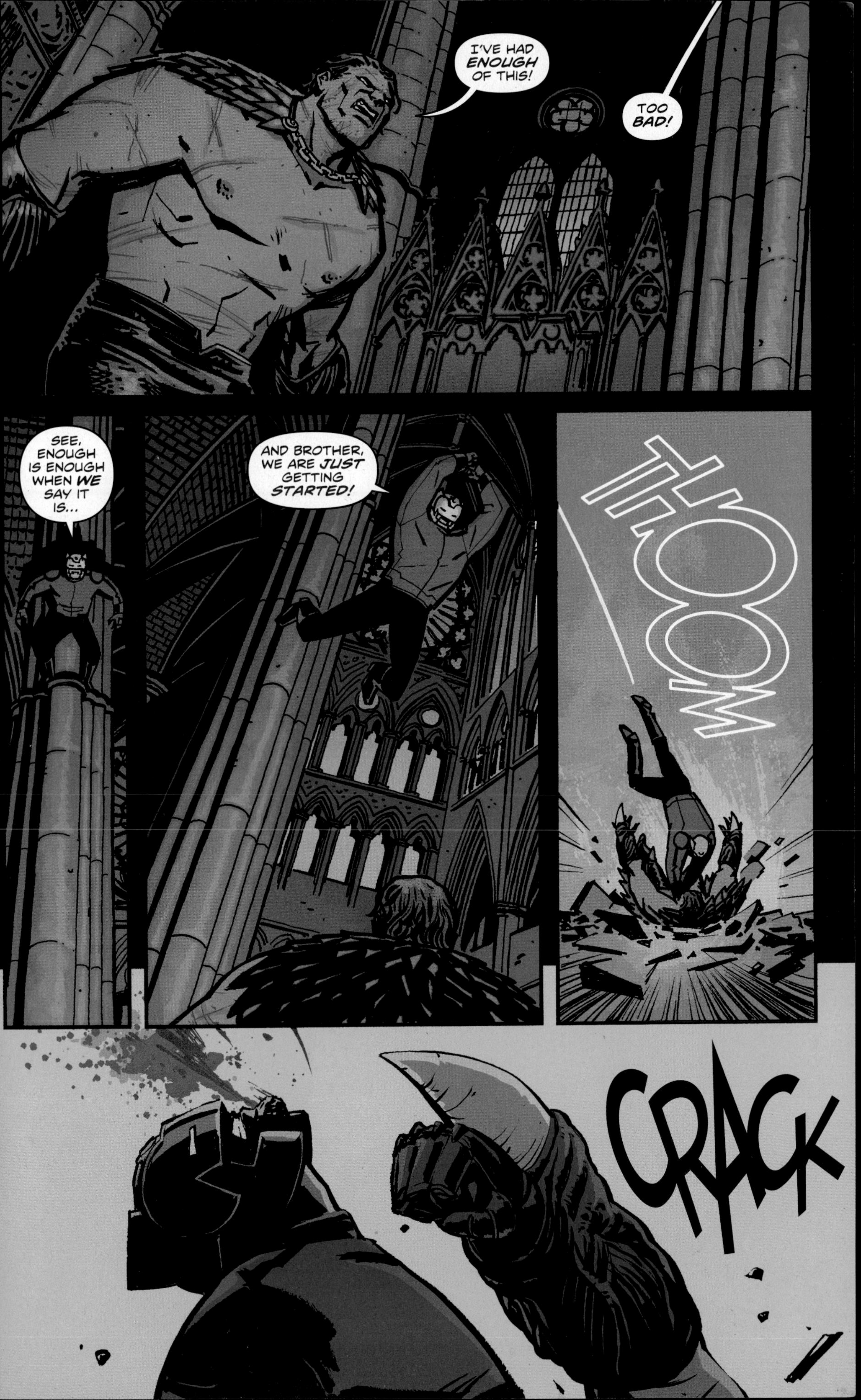
I'VE HAD ENOUGH OF THIS!
TOO BAD!
SEE, ENOUGH IS ENOUGH WHEN WE SAY IT IS...
AND BROTHER, WE ARE JUST GETTING STARTED!
THOOOM
CRACK

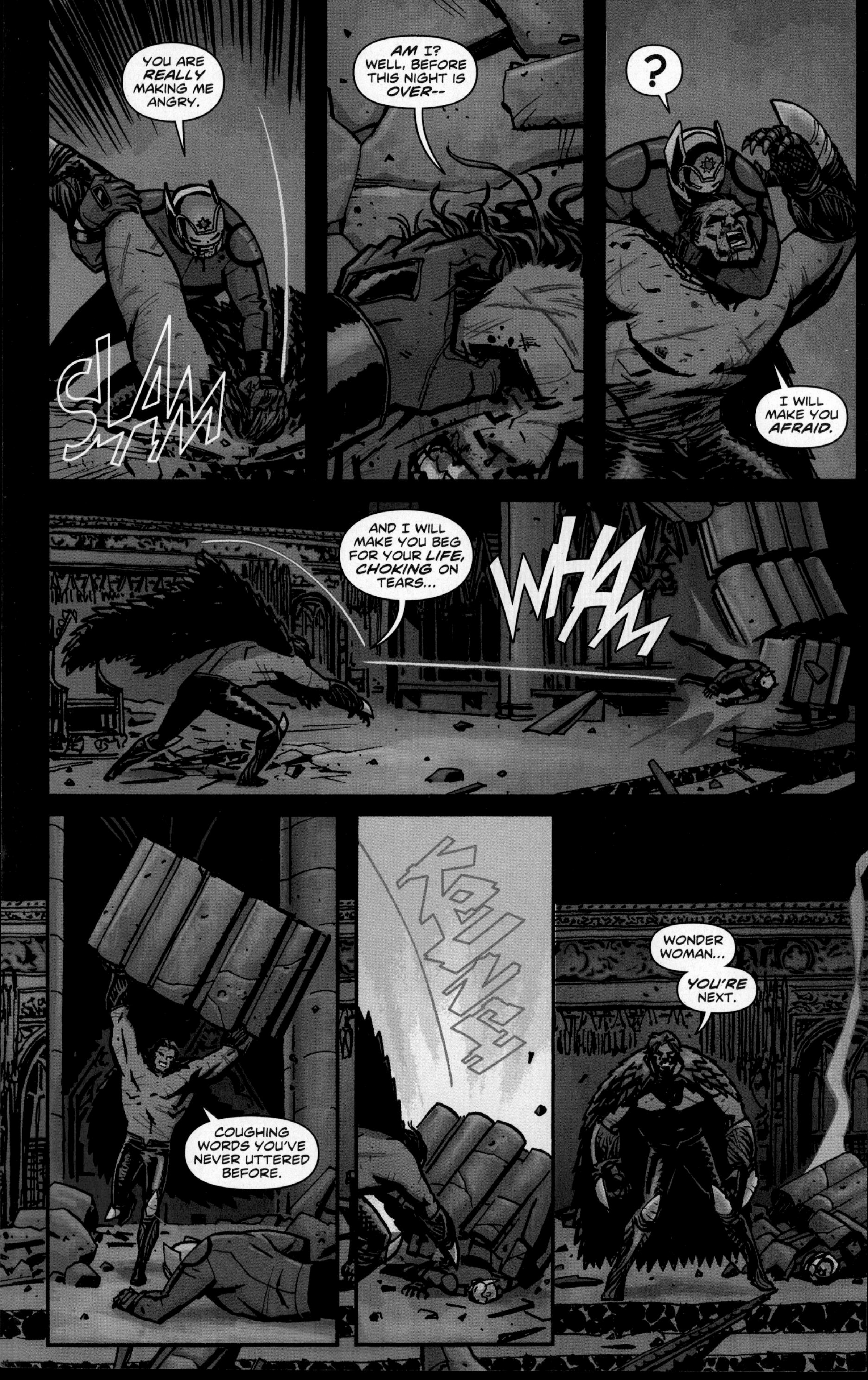
YOU ARE REALLY MAKING ME ANGRY.
SLAM
AM I? WELL, BEFORE THIS NIGHT IS OVER--
?
I WILL MAKE YOU AFRAID.
AND I WILL MAKE YOU BEG FOR YOUR LIFE, CHOKING ON TEARS...
WHAM
COUGHING WORDS YOU'VE NEVER UTTERED BEFORE.
KRUNCH
WONDER WOMAN...
YOU'RE NEXT.

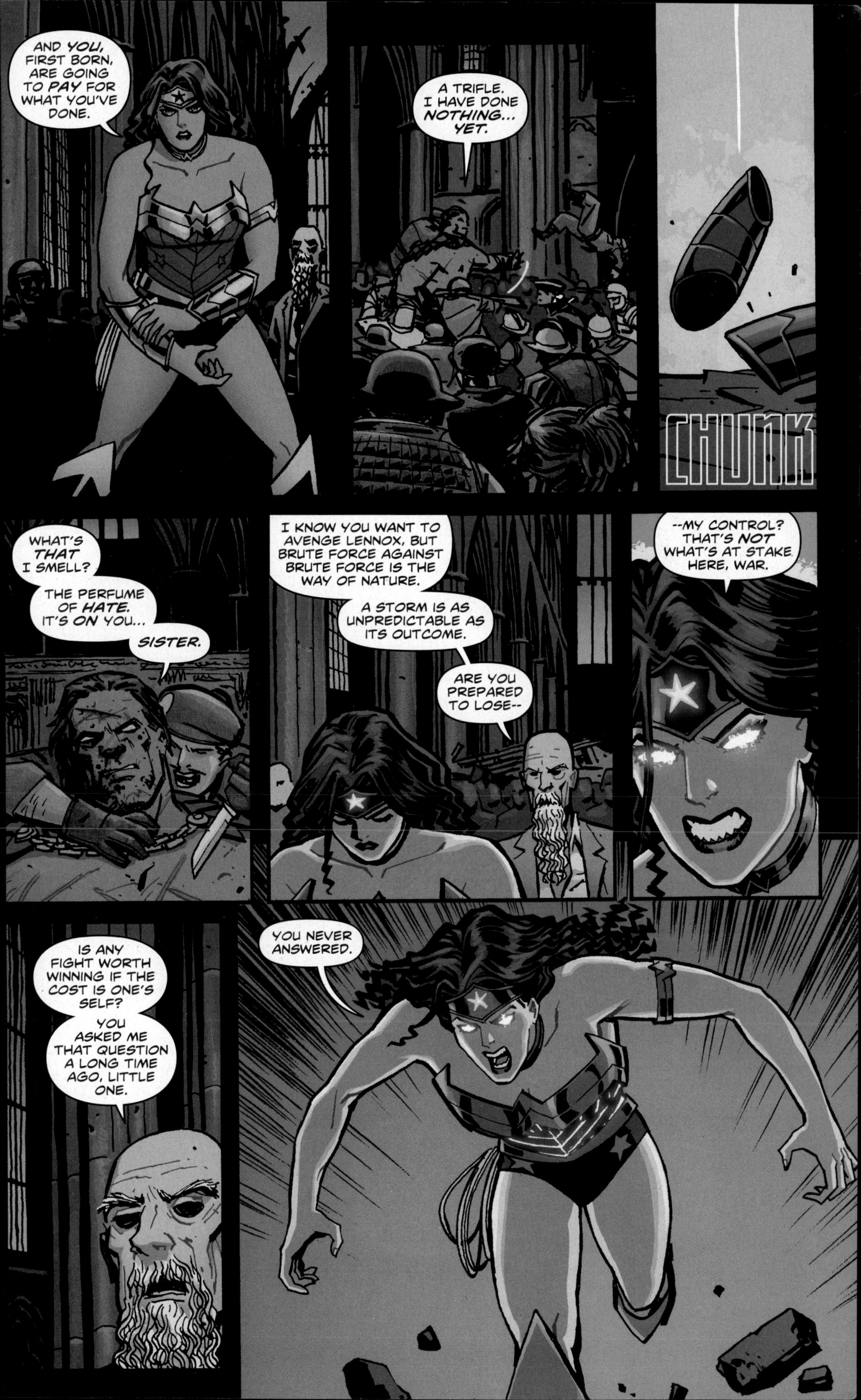
AND YOU, FIRST BORN, ARE GOING TO PAY FOR WHAT YOU'VE DONE.
A TRIFLE. I HAVE DONE NOTHING... YET.
CHUNK
WHAT'S THAT I SMELL?
THE PERFUME OF HATE. IT'S ON YOU...
SISTER.
I KNOW YOU WANT TO AVENGE LENNOX, BUT BRUTE FORCE AGAINST BRUTE FORCE IS THE WAY OF NATURE.
A STORM IS AS UNPREDICTABLE AS ITS OUTCOME.
ARE YOU PREPARED TO LOSE--
--MY CONTROL? THAT'S NOT WHAT'S AT STAKE HERE, WAR.
IS ANY FIGHT WORTH WINNING IF THE COST IS ONE'S SELF?
YOU ASKED ME THAT QUESTION A LONG TIME AGO, LITTLE ONE.
YOU NEVER ANSWERED.

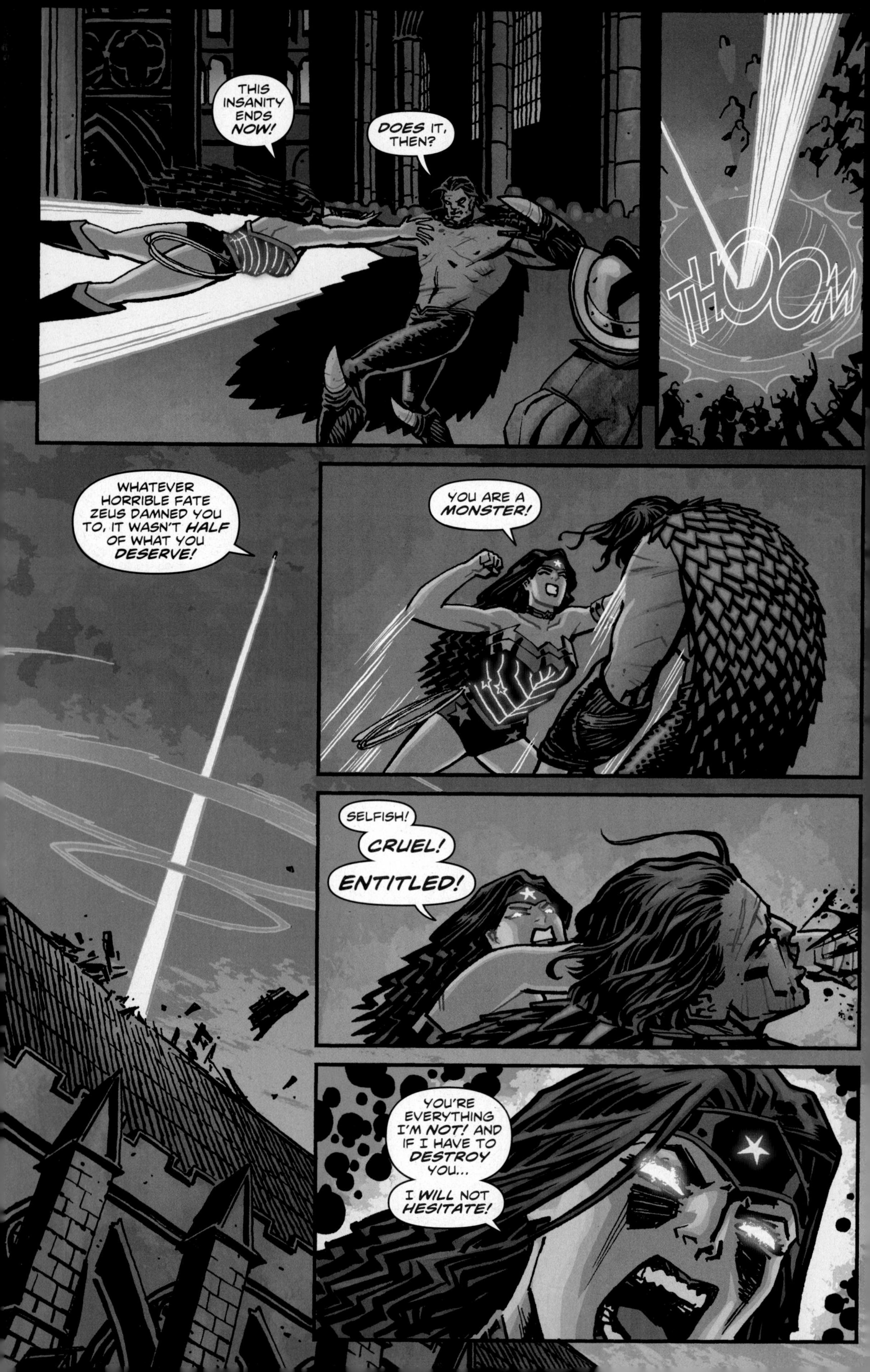
THIS INSANITY ENDS NOW!
DOES IT, THEN?
THOOM
WHATEVER HORRIBLE FATE ZEUS DAMNED YOU TO, IT WASN'T HALF OF WHAT YOU DESERVE!
YOU ARE A MONSTER!
SELFISH!
CRUEL!
ENTITLED!
YOU'RE EVERYTHING I'M NOT! AND IF I HAVE TO DESTROY YOU...
I WILL NOT HESITATE!

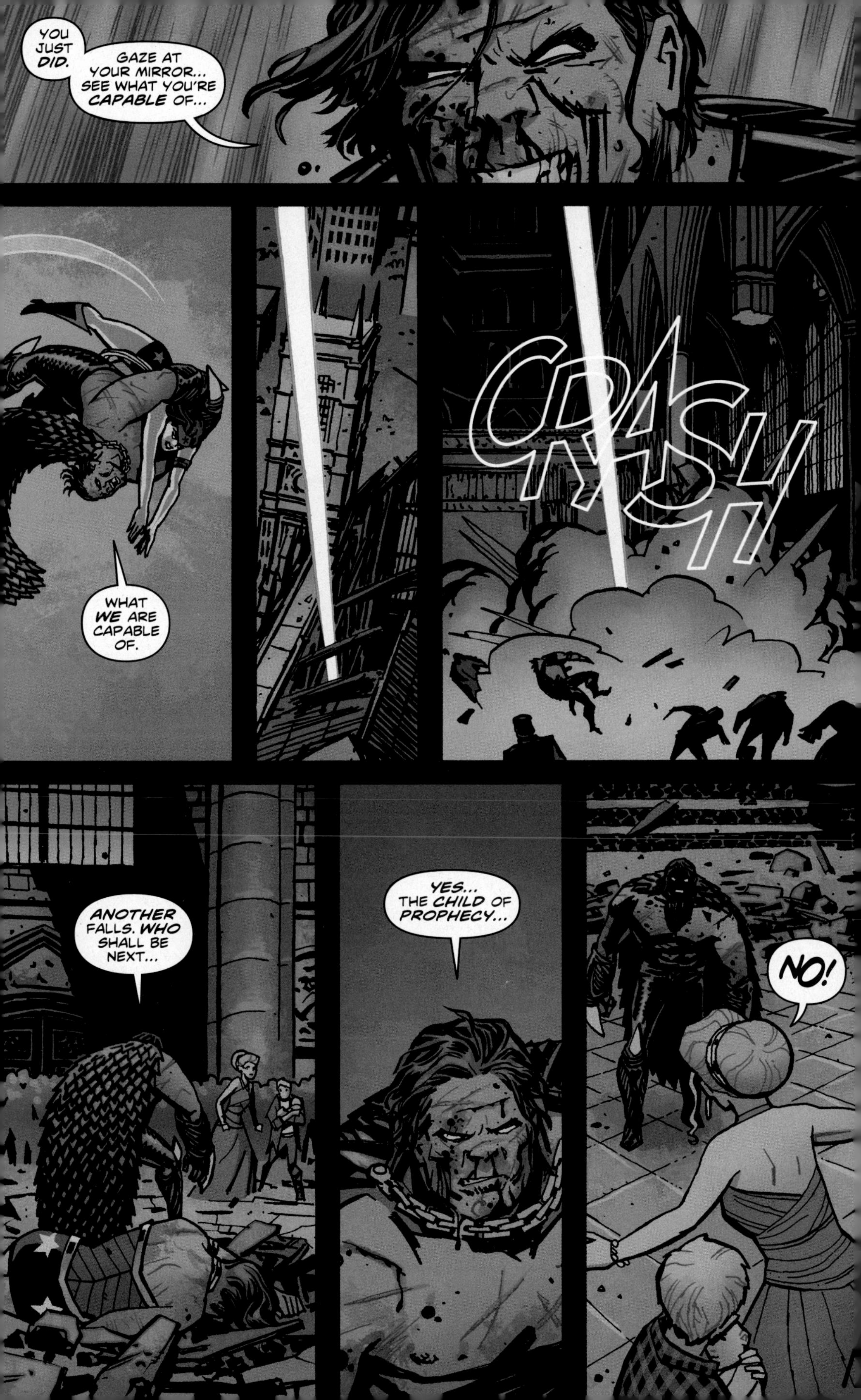
YOU JUST DID.
GAZE AT YOUR MIRROR... SEE WHAT YOU'RE CAPABLE OF...
WHAT WE ARE CAPABLE OF.
CRASH
ANOTHER FALLS. WHO SHALL BE NEXT...
YES... THE CHILD OF PROPHECY...
NO!

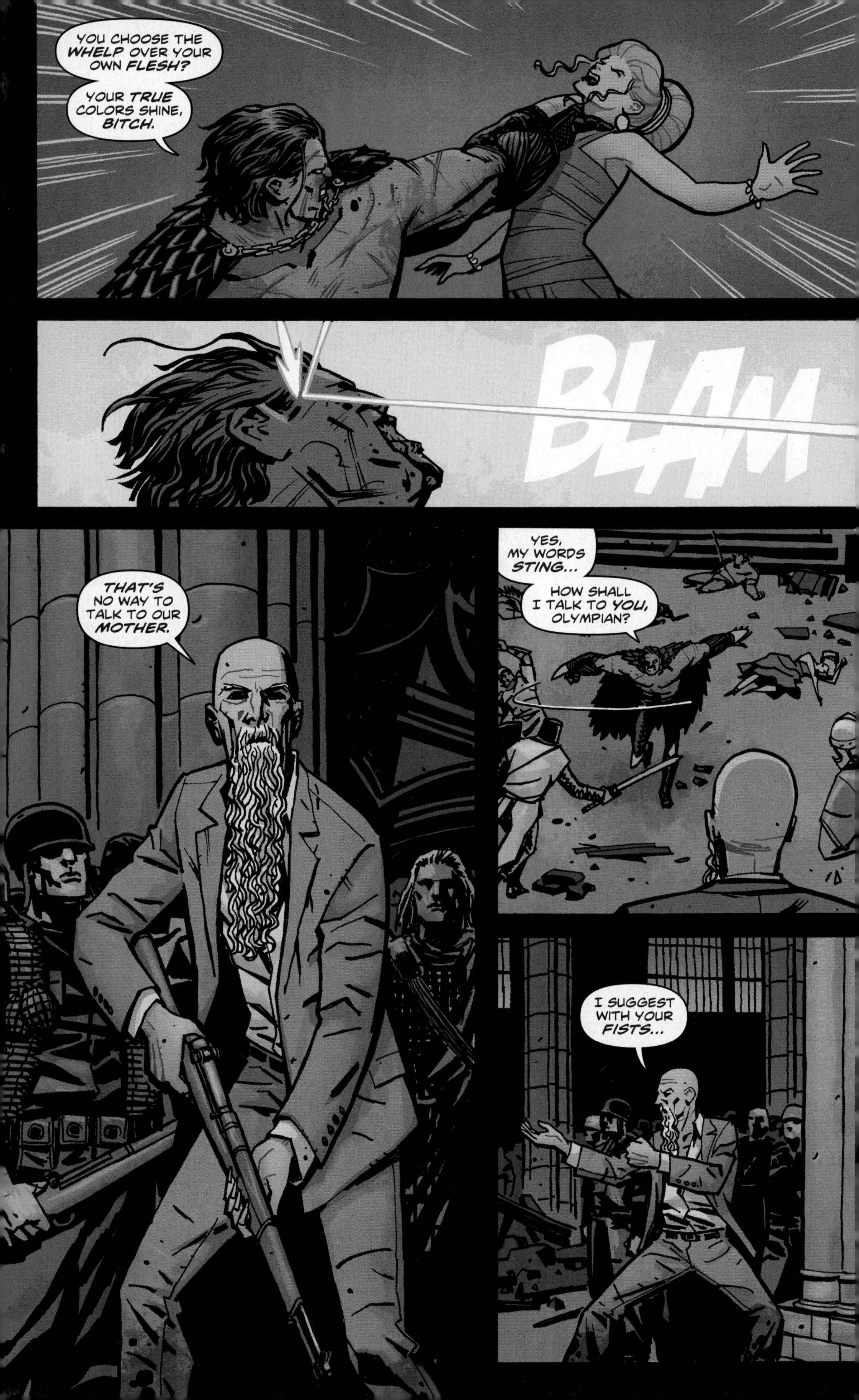
YOU CHOOSE THE WHELP OVER YOUR OWN FLESH?
YOUR TRUE COLORS SHINE, BITCH.
BLAM
THAT'S NO WAY TO TALK TO OUR MOTHER.
YES, MY WORDS STING...
HOW SHALL I TALK TO YOU, OLYMPIAN?
I SUGGEST WITH YOUR FISTS...

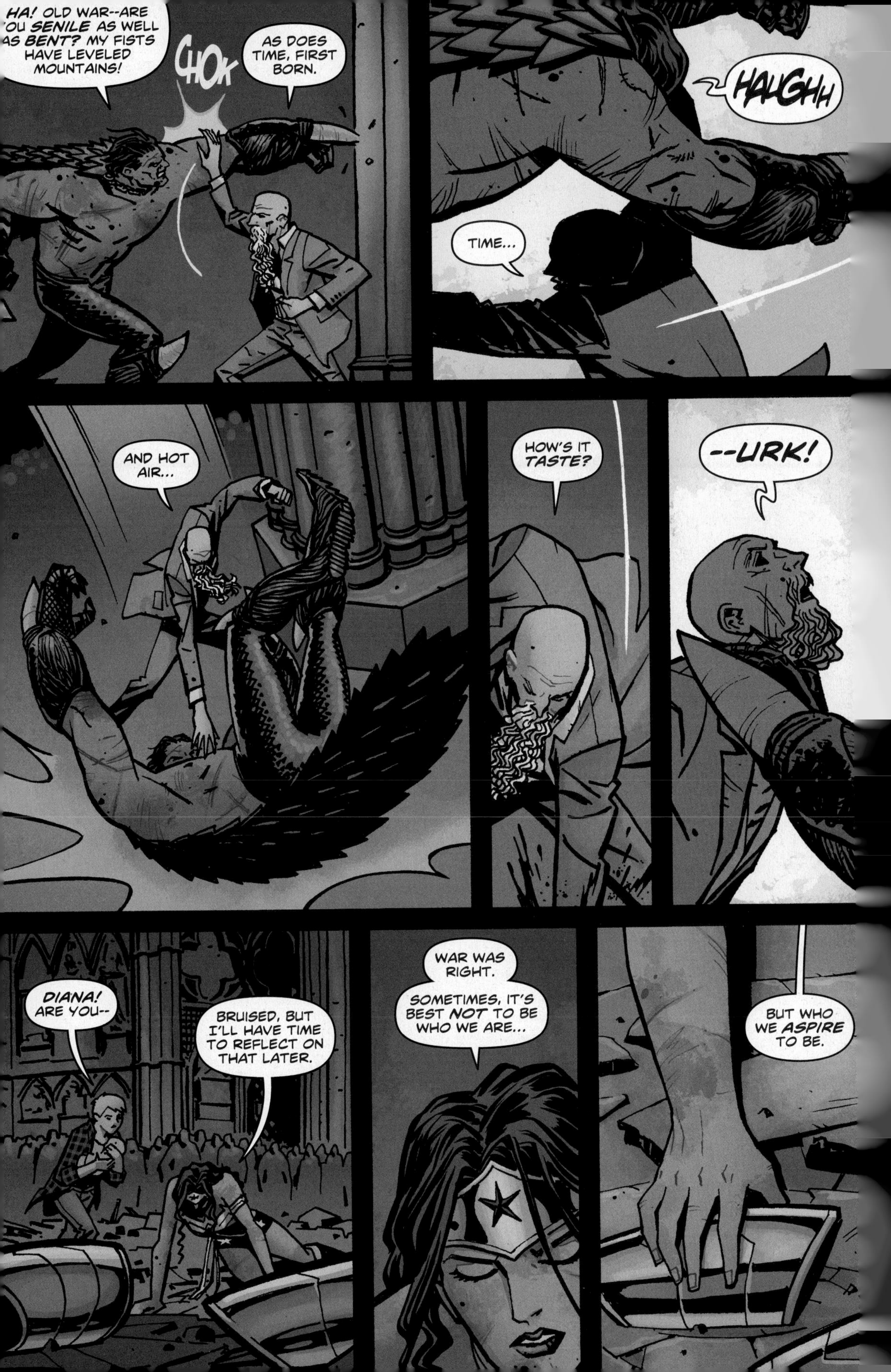

HA! OLD WAR--ARE YOU SENILE AS WELL AS BENT? MY FISTS HAVE LEVELED MOUNTAINS!
CHOK
AS DOES TIME, FIRST BORN.
HAUGHH
TIME...
AND HOT AIR...
HOW'S IT TASTE?
--URK!
DIANA! ARE YOU--
BRUISED, BUT I'LL HAVE TIME TO REFLECT ON THAT LATER.
WAR WAS RIGHT.
SOMETIMES, IT'S BEST NOT TO BE WHO WE ARE...
BUT WHO WE ASPIRE TO BE.

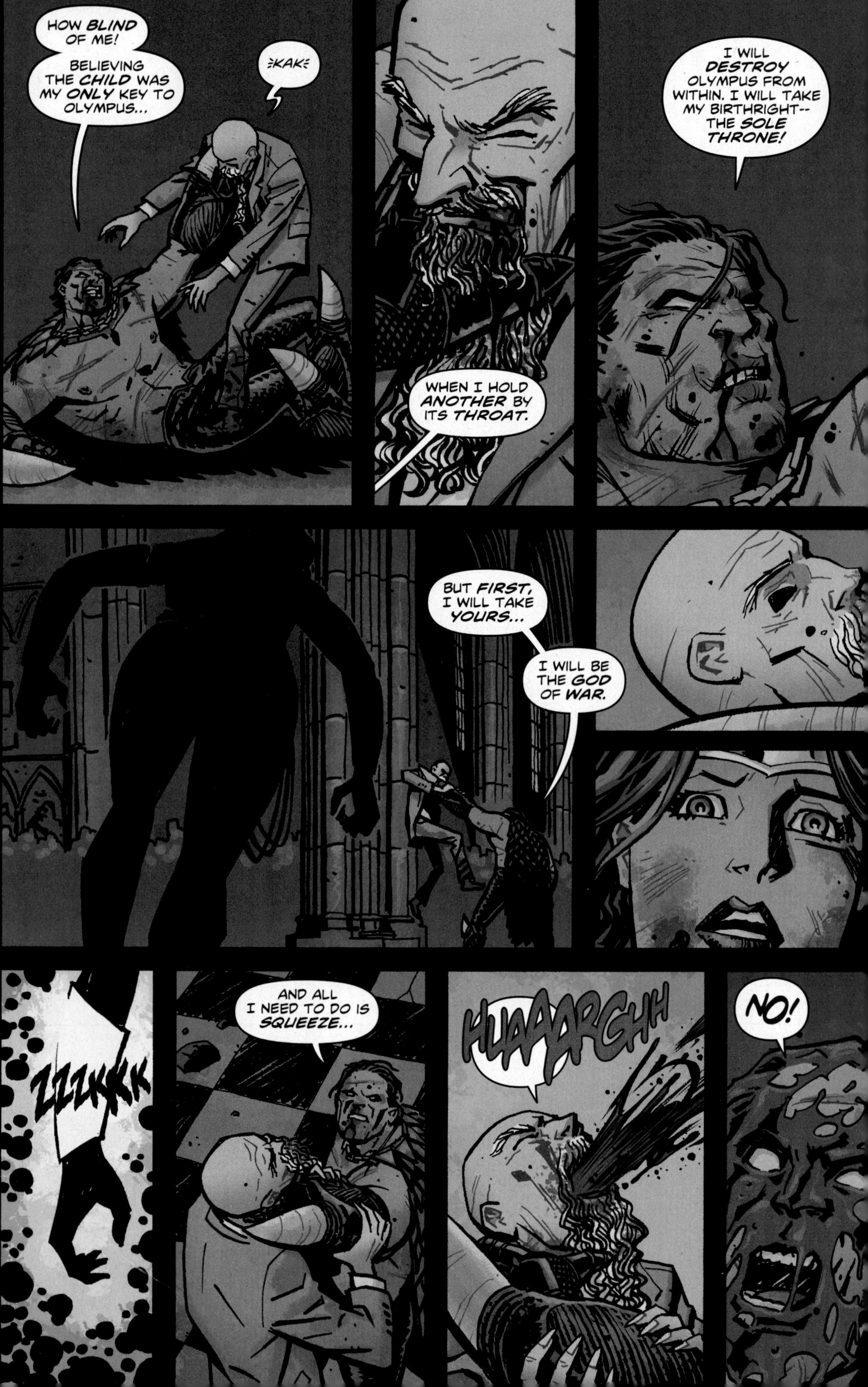
HOW BLIND OF ME!
BELIEVING THE CHILD WAS MY ONLY KEY TO OLYMPUS...
KAK
WHEN I HOLD ANOTHER BY ITS THROAT.
I WILL DESTROY OLYMPUS FROM WITHIN. I WILL TAKE MY BIRTHRIGHT-- THE SOLE THRONE!
BUT FIRST, I WILL TAKE YOURS...
I WILL BE THE GOD OF WAR.
ZZZKKK
AND ALL I NEED TO DO IS SQUEEZE...
KHAAARGHH
NO!

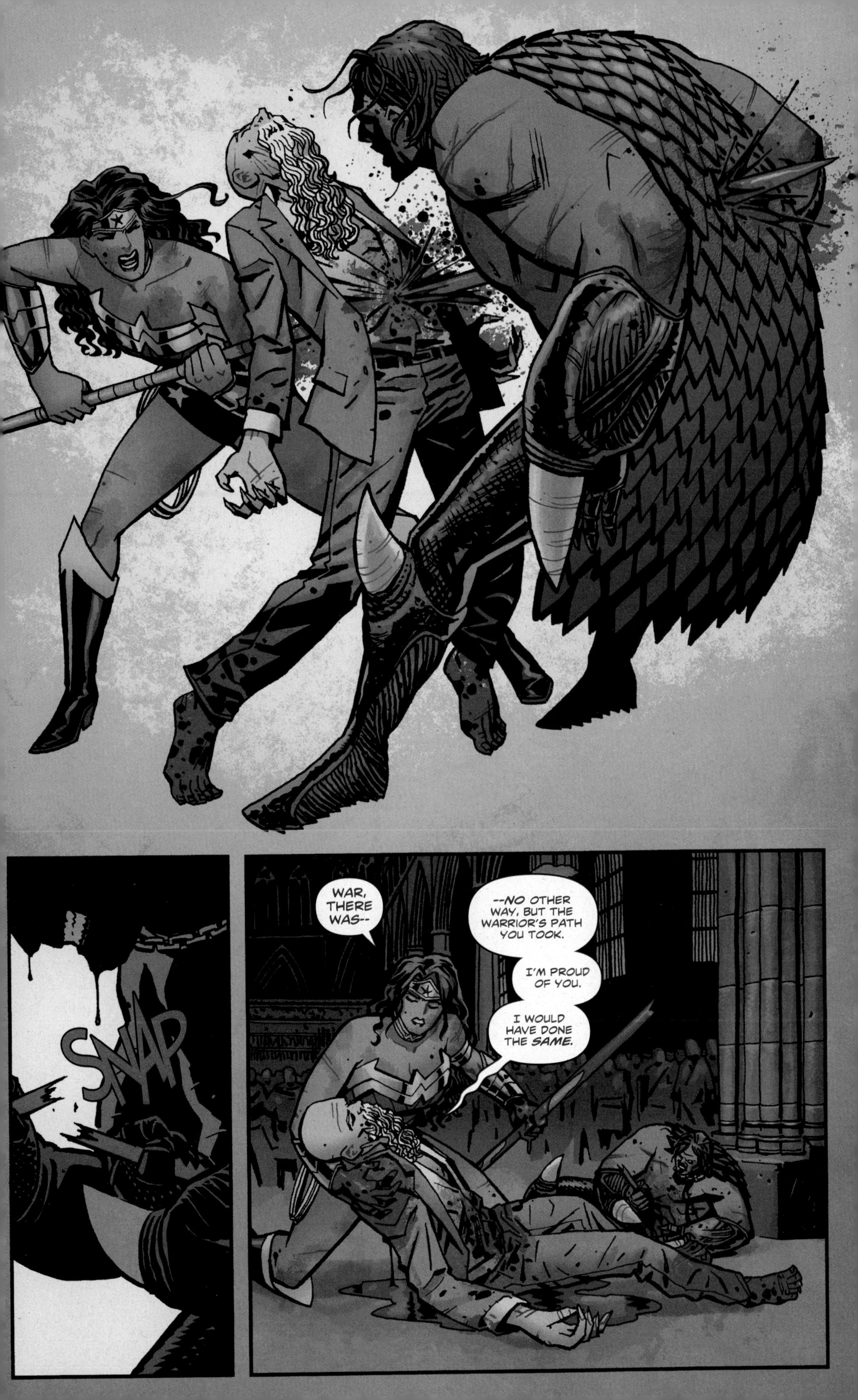
SNAP
WAR, THERE WAS--
--NO OTHER WAY, BUT THE WARRIOR'S PATH YOU TOOK.
I'M PROUD OF YOU.
I WOULD HAVE DONE THE SAME.

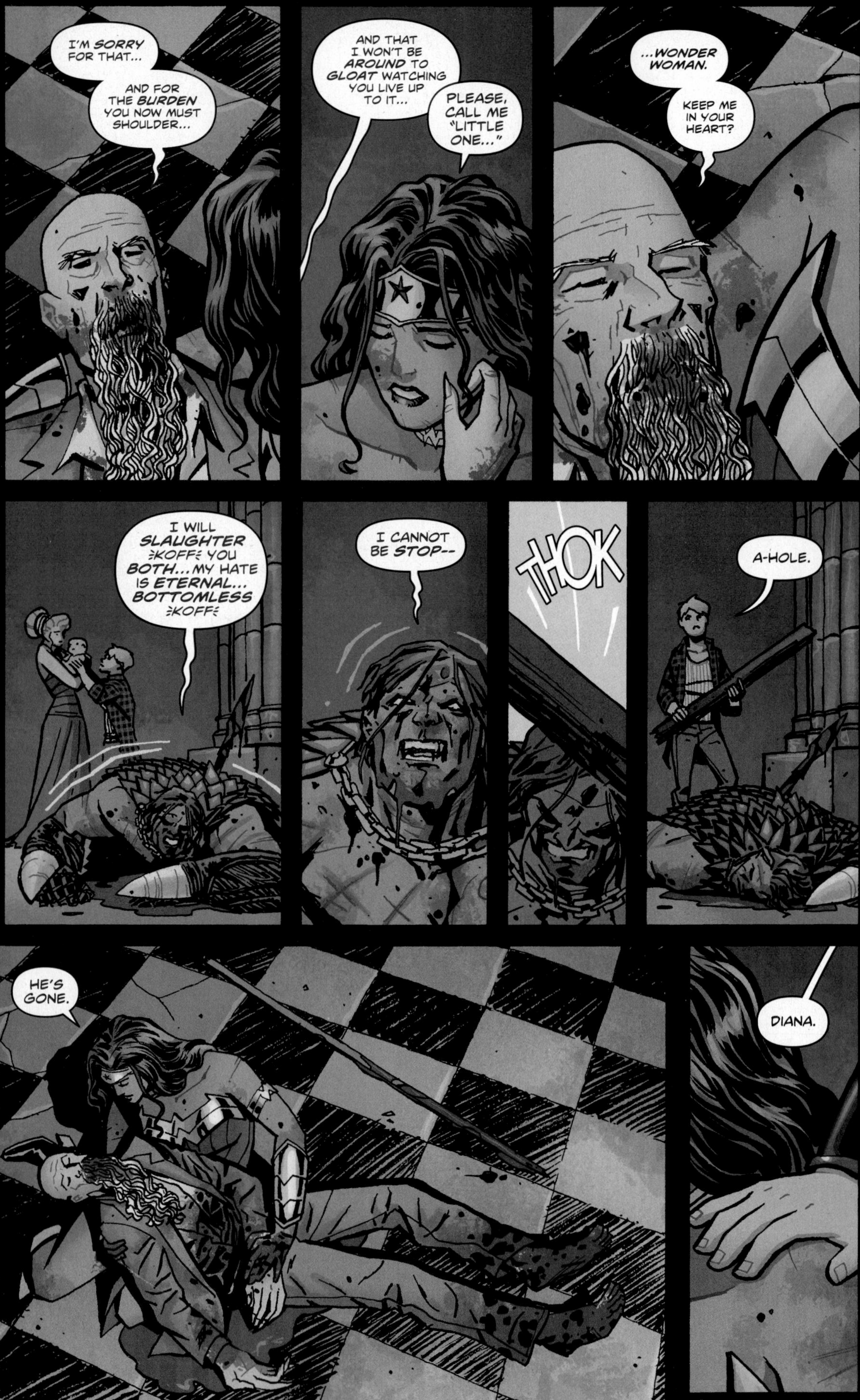
I'M SORRY FOR THAT...
AND FOR THE BURDEN YOU NOW MUST SHOULDER...
AND THAT I WON'T BE AROUND TO GLOAT WATCHING YOU LIVE UP TO IT...
PLEASE, CALL ME "LITTLE ONE..."
...WONDER WOMAN.
KEEP ME IN YOUR HEART?
I WILL SLAUGHTER *KOFF* YOU BOTH... MY HATE IS ETERNAL... BOTTOMLESS *KOFF*
I CANNOT BE STOP--
THOK
A-HOLE.
HE'S GONE.
DIANA.

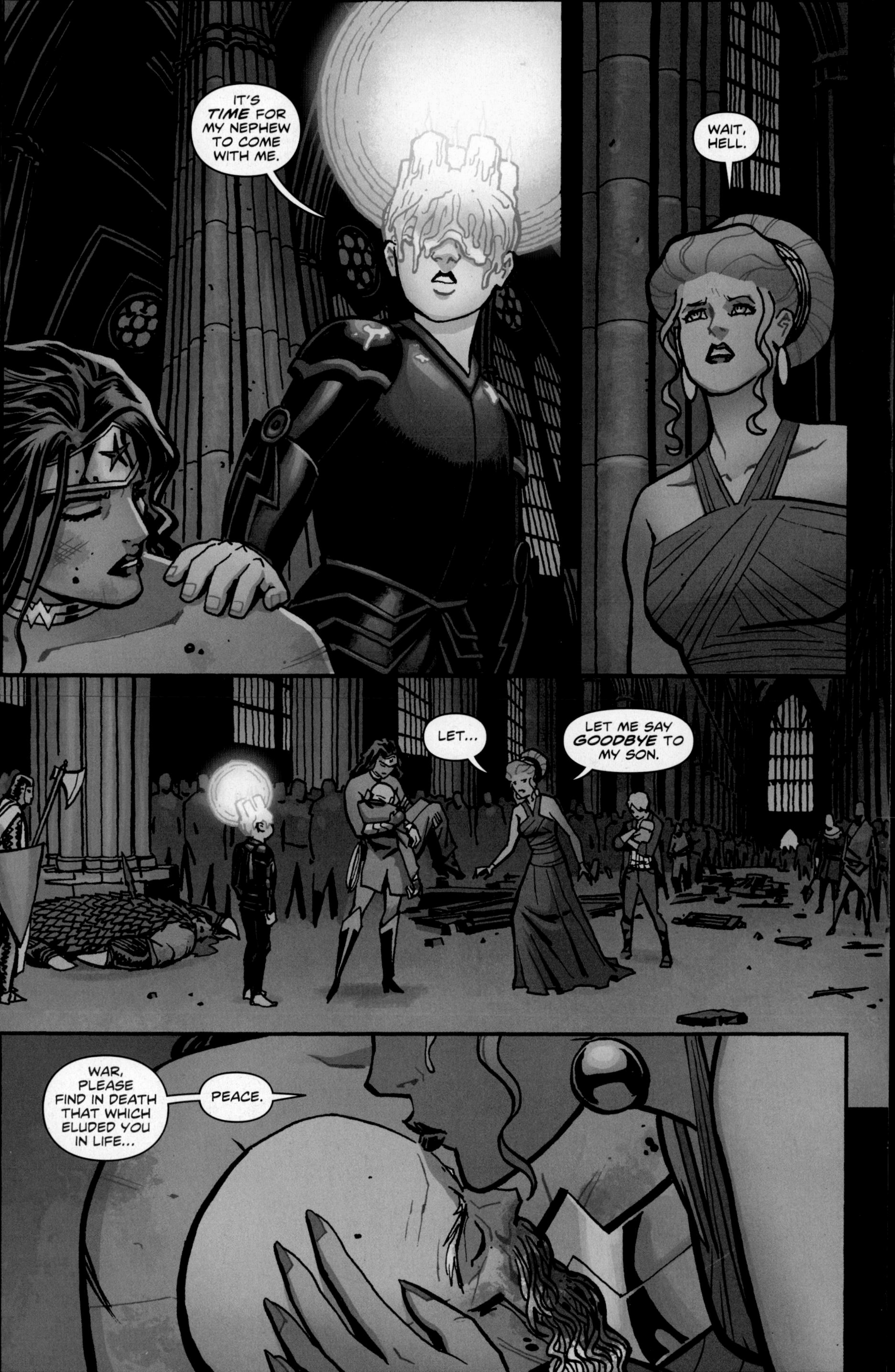
IT'S TIME FOR MY NEPHEW TO COME WITH ME.
WAIT, HELL.
LET...
LET ME SAY GOODBYE TO MY SON.
WAR, PLEASE FIND IN DEATH THAT WHICH ELUDED YOU IN LIFE...
PEACE.

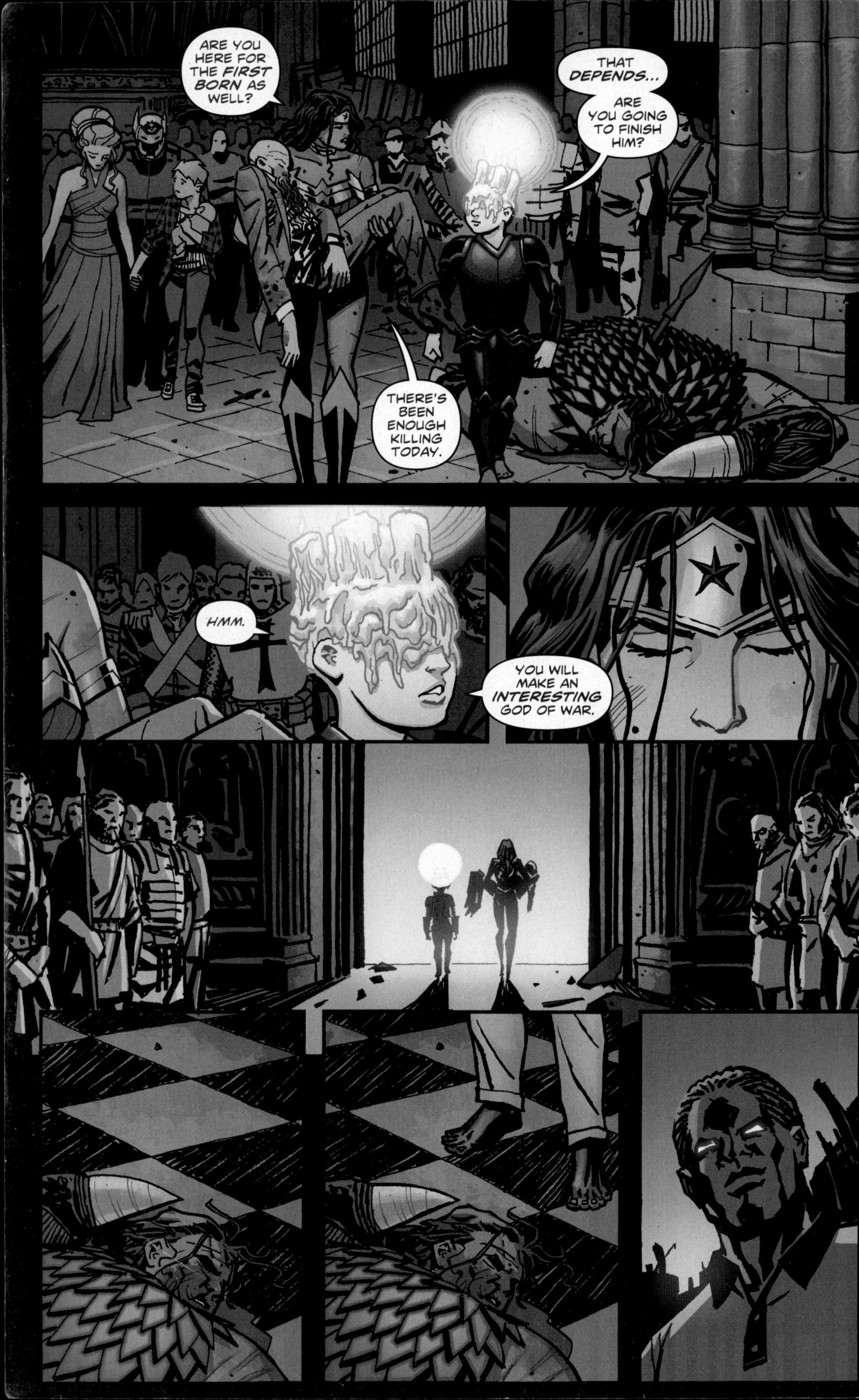
ARE YOU HERE FOR THE FIRST BORN AS WELL?
THAT DEPENDS...
ARE YOU GOING TO FINISH HIM?
THERE'S BEEN ENOUGH KILLING TODAY.
HMM.
YOU WILL MAKE AN INTERESTING GOD OF WAR.

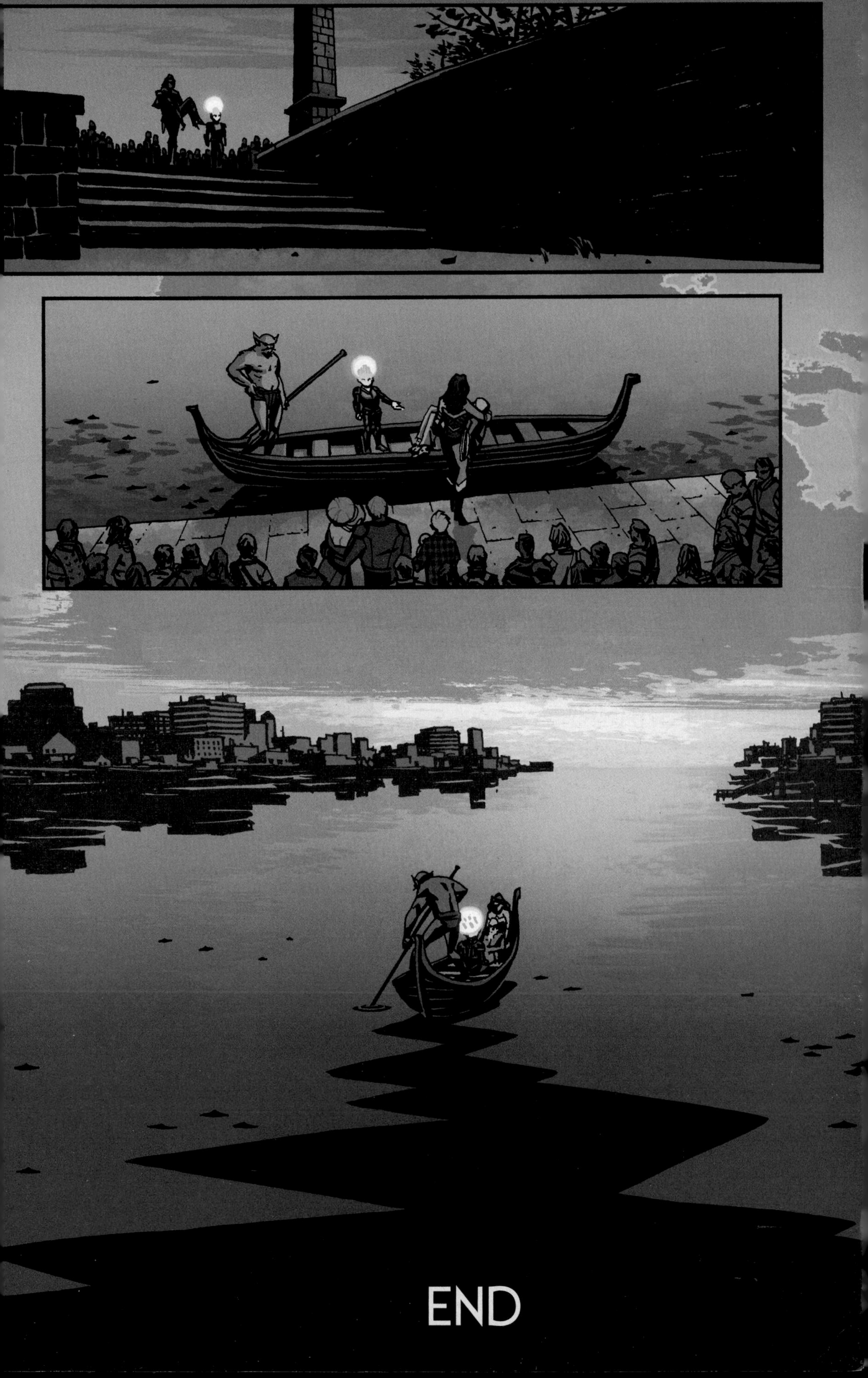
END

"Greg Rucka and company have created a compelling narrative for fans of the Amazing Amazon." **– NERDIST**

"(A) heartfelt and genuine take on Diana's origin." **– NEWSARAMA**

DC UNIVERSE REBIRTH

WONDER WOMAN

VOL. 1: THE LIES
GREG RUCKA
with LIAM SHARP

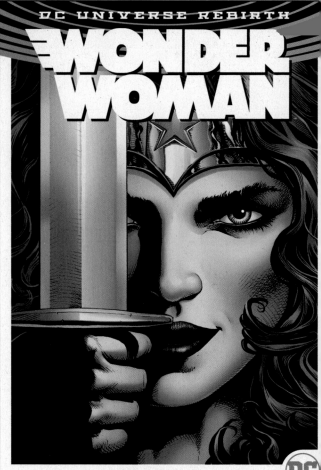

VOL.1 THE LIES
GREG RUCKA * LIAM SHARP * LAURA MARTIN

VOL.1 THE EXTINCTION MACHINES
BRYAN HITCH * TONY S. DANIEL * SANDU FLOREA * TOMEU MOREY

JUSTICE LEAGUE VOL. 1:
THE EXTINCTION MACHINES

VOL.1 REIGN OF THE SUPERMEN
STEVE ORLANDO * BRIAN CHING * MIKE ATIYEH

SUPERGIRL VOL. 1:
REIGN OF THE SUPERMEN

VOL.1 BEYOND BURNSIDE
HOPE LARSON * RAFAEL ALBUQUERQUE

BATGIRL VOL. 1:
BEYOND BURNSIDE

"Some really thrilling artwork that establishes incredible scope and danger."
—IGN

DC UNIVERSE REBIRTH

JUSTICE LEAGUE
VOL. 1: The Extinction Machines

BRYAN HITCH
with TONY S. DANIEL

VOL. 1 THE EXTINCTION MACHINES
BRYAN HITCH • TONY S. DANIEL • SANDU FLOREA • TOMEU MOREY

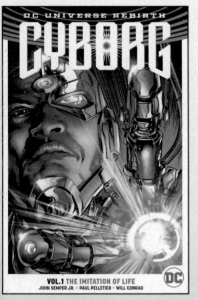

VOL. 1 THE IMITATION OF LIFE
JOHN SEMPER JR. • PAUL PELLETIER • WILL CONRAD

**CYBORG VOL. 1:
THE IMITATION OF LIFE**

VOL. 1 RAGE PLANET
SAM HUMPHRIES • ROBSON ROCHA • ETHAN VAN SCIVER • ED BENES

**GREEN LANTERNS VOL. 1:
RAGE PLANET**

VOL. 1 THE DROWNING
DAN ABNETT • PHILIPPE BRIONES • SCOT EATON • BRAD WALKER

**AQUAMAN VOL. 1:
THE DROWNING**

"Joshua Williamson's writing is on point."
– NERDIST

"Williamson makes [The Flash] as accessible as possible to new readers."
– COMIC BOOK RESOURCES

DC UNIVERSE REBIRTH
THE FLASH
VOL. 1: LIGHTNING STRIKES TWICE
JOSHUA WILLIAMSON
with CARMINE DI GIANDOMENICO and IVAN PLASCENCIA

VOL.1 LIGHTNING STRIKES TWICE
JOSHUA WILLIAMSON • CARMINE DI GIANDOMENICO • IVAN PLASCENCIA

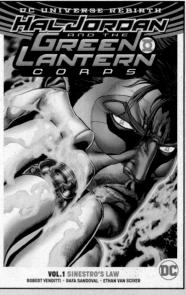

JUSTICE LEAGUE VOL. 1:
THE EXTINCTION MACHINES

TITANS VOL. 1:
THE RETURN OF WALLY WEST

HAL JORDAN AND
THE GREEN LANTERN CORPS VOL. 1:
SINESTRO'S LAW

Get more DC graphic novels wherever comics and books are sold!

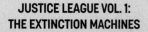